Patterns of
ATTACHMENT

A Psychological Study of the Strange Situation

Mary D. Salter Ainsworth
Mary C. Blehar
Everett Waters
Sally Wall

LEA LAWRENCE ERLBAUM ASSOCIATES, PUBLISHERS
1978   Hillsdale, New Jersey

Lawrence Erlbaum Associates, Inc., Publishers
62 Maria Drive
Hillsdale, New Jersey 07642

Library of Congress Cataloging in Publication Data
Main entry under title:
Patterns of attachment.

1. Infant psychology. 2. Mother and child.
I. Ainsworth, Mary D. Salter. II. Title: Attachment.
BF723.I6P36   155.4'22   78-13303
ISBN 0-89859-461-8

Printed in the United States of America

Contents

Preface

This book is about the attachment of infants to their mother figures. In it we focus on how infant behavior is patterned. We approach this patterning in two main ways. First, we examine the way in which a baby's behavior is patterned when the attachment system is activated at varying levels of intensity through simple manipulations of his environment in a laboratory situation, which we have called the "strange situation." When examining the baby's responses to controlled environmental changes, we observe the way in which his or her attachment behavior interacts with other behavioral systems that are also activated at varying levels of intensity and that may either compete or conflict with attachment behavior or augment the intensity with which attachment behavior is manifested. Second, we identify certain important individual differences in the way in which behavior is patterned— both attachment behavior and behavior antithetical to it—and seek to understand how such differences may have arisen and how different patterns of attachment may influence development.

We undertook writing this book in order to present the information about infant–mother attachment that we had gained through the use of a standard laboratory situation and to compare the manifestations of attachment in that situation with manifestations of attachment observed at home. We also wished to review the findings of other investigations of attachment, especially those that are directly comparable with ours because of their use of our strange-situation procedure, and to compare their findings with ours, including the findings of investigations that studied children older than the 1-year-olds upon which our work focuses and those that are concerned with an infant's attachment to figures other than the mother. We report much empirical detail, which will be of interest to all those who investigate a young child's early interpersonal relations. The empirical detail leads, however, to a discussion of theoretical issues of major significance. Implicit in both the empirical findings and in the theoretical discussions are clues both to the understanding of developmental anomalies and to ways in which such anomalies might be prevented, assuming the feasibility of early intervention in families in which new babies are expected or have recently arrived. Therefore, we believe that this volume will be of interest not only to those concerned with theory and research into early social development, but also to diverse classes of persons concerned with the practical job of providing better infant care and facilitating optimal development in young children.

It seems suitable in this preface to introduce the reader to the strange situation and to describe how we happened to use it and why we judged the findings stemming from its use to be of sufficient significance to focus a book on them. The "strange situation" was the label assigned by Ainsworth and Wittig (1969) to a standardized laboratory procedure in which several episodes, in fixed order, were intended to activate and/or intensify infants' attachment behavior. These episodes were designed to approximate situations that most infants commonly encounter in real life. The adjective "strange" denotes "unfamiliar," rather than "odd" or "peculiar"; it was used because fear of the unfamiliar is commonly referred to as "fear of the strange" (e.g., Hebb, 1946). All of the instigations to attachment behavior used in the strange situation involved unfamiliarity.

The strange situation was originally devised in 1964 for use in conjunction with an intensive longitudinal study of the development of infant–mother attachment throughout the first year of life, a naturalistic study in which infants were observed in their familiar home environments. This study of 26 mother–infant pairs living in the Baltimore area had been preceded by a comparable but less intensive study of 28 dyads living in country villages in Uganda (Ainsworth, 1967). Despite many similarities between the two samples in regard to attachment behavior, three behavioral patterns that had been highlighted in the Ganda study emerged less strikingly in the American study: the use of the mother as a secure base from which to explore; distress in brief, everyday separations from the mother; and fear when encountering a stranger. Perhaps if stronger instigation were provided, the American babies might be induced to behave in much the same ways as had the Ganda infants. In the belief that these behaviors might be evoked more incisively in an unfamiliar situation than in the familiar home environment, the strange situation was devised.

First, let us consider the use by an infant of his mother as a secure base from which to explore the world. One of us (Salter, 1940) had long been interested in the hypothesis, originally formulated by Blatz,[1] that a young child who had gained security in his relationship with his parents was emboldened thereby to strike out to explore the world, willing to risk the insecurity initially implicit in a learning situation because he could rely on his parents to be available, responsive, protective, and reassuring. If his adventure evoked undue anxiety, the child could easily return to "home base," in the expectation that his parents would provide the reassurance he needed. If, on the other hand, his relationship with his parents was insecure, then he might not dare to leave them to explore, not trusting them to remain available to him if he left or to be responsive when he needed them. Lacking trust, he would stick close to his base, fearing to risk the anxiety implicit in exploration and learning. This hypothesis was confirmed in the Ganda study (Ainsworth, 1963, 1967). Infants who were judged to be securely attached to their mothers explored actively while their mothers conversed with the observers, and indeed they might well leave the room or even the house in order to extend their exploratory activities. Yet most of these same infants were acutely distressed and ceased exploration if it were the mother who left them. By contrast, infants who were judged to be anxiously attached tended to remain close to the mother, perhaps clinging to her and exploring little or not at all.

In the course of the longitudinal study of Baltimore infants, however, nearly all babies left their mothers to explore the familiar home environment (Ainsworth, Bell, & Stayton, 1971), whether or not they were judged to be secure in their attachments to their mothers (Stayton & Ainsworth, 1973). Perhaps individual differences could be discriminated in an unfamiliar environment that might hence be expected to provide stronger instigation to attachment behavior.[2] Perhaps those who were anxiously attached to their mothers might be unwilling to explore when placed in an unfamiliar situation, whereas those who were securely attached would explore even a strange situation with the mother present.

Antedating our strange situation was Arsenian's study (1943) of young children in an "insecure" situation and Harlow's (1961) work with rhesus infants in an open-field situation. Both studies showed the effectiveness of the mother or mother surrogate in providing security for exploration. Subse-

---

[1] MDSA first heard William Blatz speak of a child using his parents as a secure base from which to venture forth to learn when she was a student in his course at the University of Toronto in 1934–35. It was not until 30 years later (Blatz, 1966) that he explicitly published his "security theory."

[2] It now seems likely to us that the Ganda infants, being more afraid of strangers than the Baltimore infants were, found even the familiar home environment more stressful because of the presence of the visitor-observers, and that this highlighted individual differences in their use of the mother as a secure base from which to explore.

quently, several studies of infants with and without their mothers in unfamiliar situations have provided clear-cut confirmation of the hypothesis that infants and young children tend to explore an unfamiliar environment in the mother's presence, but slow down or cease exploration in her absence (e.g., Cox & Campbell, 1968; Rheingold, 1969), although infants will indeed leave their mothers *on their own initiative* in order to explore (Rheingold & Eckerman, 1970). The present study not only adds further evidence of these normative tendencies, but also throws light on individual differences in maintaining exploration under conditions that also activate attachment behavior.

Second, distress upon being separated from the mother has long been conceived as an indication that an infant has become attached to her (e.g., Schaffer & Emerson, 1964). Our longitudinal study of Baltimore infants showed, however, that the average baby did not consistently protest his mother's departure in the familiar home environment (Stayton, Ainsworth, & Main, 1973). Indeed some babies, who, by other behavioral criteria, were clearly attached to their mothers, showed very infrequent separation distress. The same finding had been noted in the case of Ganda infants (Ainsworth, 1963, 1967), but nevertheless the latter more frequently protested separation in a familiar environment than did the Baltimore babies. On the other hand, it is well known that, once attached to a mother figure, infants and young children tend strongly to protest being separated against their will and placed in an unfamiliar environment for any substantial length of time (e.g., Bowlby, 1953; Heinicke & Westheimer, 1966; Schaffer & Callender, 1959; Yarrow, 1967). Therefore it was of interest to subject the infants in the longitudinal sample to very brief separation experiences in an unfamiliar environment in order to compare their responses with similar minor separations in the home environment. It was expected that most would be distressed by separation in the strange situation, even though they might be infrequently distressed by little separations at home.

Third, it was of interest to observe infants' responses to a stranger in an unfamiliar environment. Although Spitz (e.g., 1965) maintained that fear of strangers (i.e., 8-month anxiety) was a milestone in normal development and a criterion that an infant had achieved "true object relations," and although Ganda infants (Ainsworth, 1967) had been observed to be conspicuously afraid of strangers toward the end of the first year, the Baltimore babies did not consistently show such fear in the familiar environment of the home. Therefore it was of interest to see whether the context of an unfamiliar environment would heighten their fear of strangers.

The structure of the strange situation followed from these lines of hypothesis and interest. Exploratory behavior was to be observed both in the mother's presence and in her absence. The infant's response to a stranger was likewise to be observed both in the mother's presence and in her absence. His response to his mother's absence was to be seen both when he was alone and when he was left with a stranger. His response to his mother's return after an absence was to be compared with his response to the return of the stranger after an absence. The episodes of the strange situation, which are described in detail in Chapter 2, followed from these considerations.

The 1-year-old, accompanied by his mother, was introduced to an unfamiliar but otherwise unalarming playroom where massive instigation to exploratory behavior was provided by a large array of toys. In the next episode, an adult stranger entered, who was tactful but nevertheless unfamiliar. Then came a brief separation episode in which the mother left the baby with the stranger. Then after an episode of reunion with the mother, there was a second separation in which the baby was first alone in the unfamiliar environment and then again with the stranger, who returned before the mother reentered. Because it was anticipated that experience in each episode would affect behavior in the next episode, the instigation to attachment behavior expected to be the weakest was placed at the beginning and that expected to be strongest toward the end. The expectations that these mild instigations would be cumulative in their effect were fulfilled.

It must be emphasized that the strange situation does not constitute an experiment in the literal meaning of this term. Different groups of subjects were not assigned to different treatments in order to ascertain the relative effect of these treatments on some dependent behavioral variable. Nor was it our intent to assess the relative effects of the different kinds of instigation upon intensity of attachment behavior—an intent that would have demanded control of order effects. On the contrary, the strange situation was designed as a controlled laboratory procedure in which individual differences among infants could be highlighted, precisely because they were exposed to the same situation with the same episodes in the same order.

The findings that have emerged from the use of this procedure have indeed highlighted individual differences in the way infants respond to an accumulation of instigations to attachment behavior. Different patterns of strange-situation behavior, we propose, indicate differences in the way infant–mother attachment has become organized. We have observed the same patterns in four separate samples of 1-year-olds, and other investigators who have used our techniques for the identification of patterns of attachment have confirmed our findings. Just because the procedure provides increasingly strong instigation to attachment behavior through its cumulative nature, one may observe in a relatively short span of time attachment behavior under conditions of activation from relatively weak to very strong. In the familiar home environment, occasions for strong activation of attachment behavior are infrequent, so that it requires many hours of observation to encompass a similar range, especially in the case of a healthy infant reared in a social environment that is sensitively responsive to him.

Nevertheless, in our longitudinal study that provided for approxmiately 72 hours of observation of each infant throughout the first year, it was possible to observe patterns of attachment and, further, to relate these to patterns of maternal behavior. For the sample of infants thus longitudinally observed, it was possible to examine continuities and discontinuities of specific behaviors between the home and laboratory environments; more important, these two sets of data enable one to perceive the patterning or organization of behaviors that reflects continuity of an attachment of a distinctive nature, despite discontinuities in specific behaviors.

Consequently, the findings reported in this volume go far beyond the specific issues that the strange situation was initially designed to investigate. They throw light upon qualitative differences in the nature of the attachment relationship itself, and, in conjunction with longitudinal data provided both by ourselves and by other investigators, they also yield hypotheses of how such qualitiative differences arose and how they exert an influence on subsequent development.

To anticipate a more detailed report of our findings, we can note that the episodes of the strange situation that made the most significant contribution to the identification of patterns of attachment were the reunion episodes—those in which the mother rejoined the baby after having been away for some minutes. This comes as a surprise to some who may have assumed that responses during the separation episodes—the episodes during which the instigation to attachment behavior might be assumed to be strongest—would be most significant. To us it was not surprising. The entire separation literature (cf. Ainsworth, 1962) suggests that the response to reunion after separation may well yield a clearer picture of the state of attachment than did the response to separation itself. After a relatively brief separation—lasting a few days or even a few weeks— it is common to observe a great intensification of attachment behavior upon reunion. The child seeks to be in close bodily contact with his attachment figure and also seeks to maintain close proximity over much longer periods than was previously characteristic of him. It seems that separation has shaken his trust in the mother's accessibility and responsiveness, so that he scarcely dares to let her out of sight lest she disappear again. Furthermore, he may be more ambivalent toward her than previously. It seems that the angry feelings aroused during the separation, when he felt abandoned, are not altogether dissipated upon reunion, but mingle or alternate with his desire for renewed contact, so that he both rejects and seeks to be close to his attachment figure.

Furthermore, a child may respond to separation, especially to a long and depriving separation, with "detachment" behavior, which gives the impression that he is indifferent to the whereabouts and behavior of his attachment figure. In fact, however, detachment seems likely to be a product of intense conflict between attachment behavior activated at high levels of intensity and avoidant behavior evoked by the seeming rejection implicit in the failure of the attachment figure to respond to him during the separation. This detachment behavior, like angry rejecting behavior, is not likely to vanish immediately upon reunion. On the contrary, it may be strengthened by the high-intensity activation of attachment behavior occasioned by reunion. Consequently a child may seem not to recognize his mother or may seem indifferent to her for a period of time after reunion and before intensified attachment behavior overtly reasserts itself.

Although one might expect to find these various reunion behaviors—whether they be intensified attachment behavior, angry resistance, or avoidant detachment—to be less conspicuous and/or less prolonged after the brief separations implicit in our strange situation, nevertheless it seemed reasonable to us to be alert for responses, similar in kind if not in degree, in the reunion episodes. Furthermore, because the strange-situation separations were so brief, it makes sense to suppose that individual differences in reunion behaviors reflect characteristics of the infant's attachment relationship to his mother—characteristics that were consolidated long before the strange situation was first encountered.

The final task of this preface is briefly to outline the structure of this volume. But before proceeding to that task, one further point is most suitably discussed here. The strange situation is admittedly somewhat stressful. Some have suggested that it is unjustifiably stressful. We must disagree. We would not have subjected over 100 infants to an unduly stressful procedure. We designed the situation to approximate the kind of experiences that an infant in our society commonly encounters in real life. All American mothers whom we have encountered do not hesitate to take their babies at least occasionally into unfamiliar environments—for example, to visit an adult friend unfamiliar to the baby or, less commonly, to take him to a day-care center, to a babysitter's home, or to a play group. While they are in this unfamiliar (but not otherwise alarming) environment, the mother may leave her baby for a few minutes—either alone or with a stranger—whether to accompany her hostess to another room, to go to the telephone, or to visit the bathroom. The strange situation was modeled on such common real-life experiences.

None of the mothers in any of our four samples came to the laboratory without having been informed in detail of every step in the procedure, how we expected a range of babies to respond, and why we had designed the episodes in the way that we had. Nearly all mothers that we approached agreed to participate with their babies; only one did so with any apparent misgivings, and she was the one mother in our longitudinal sample who had a full-time job and whose baby had begun to react negatively to her daily departures and returns. We emphasized that any episode could be curtailed if a baby became unduly distressed, but it was we who nearly always initiated a curtailment, while the mother showed no concern.

After the strange situation was over, we always spent substantial time with the mother and baby, giving the mother an opportunity to discuss the baby's reactions if she wished, but in any case offering an occasion for pleasant social interaction. In no case did we observe any continuing distress or any adverse effects attributable to the strange situation, and in the case of our longitudinal sample this was so in a follow-up visit three weeks later. Indeed we were soon convinced that *we* were far more concerned about the anxiety that might have been associated with the brief separation experiences implicit in the strange-situation procedure than were the parents—who had little or no compunction about imposing much longer separations on their babies, often under less than optimum conditions.

Nevertheless we acknowledge that the strange-situation procedure might not approximate common experiences of infants who are reared differently, whether in other societies or by atypical parents in our own society; and we cast no aspersions by our term "atypical," for these may be highly sensitive parents who avoid all unnecessary occasions for separation. It seems entirely likely that Ainsworth's (1967) Ganda infants and Konner's (1972) Bushman babies could not have tolerated the strange situation. Recently Takahashi (personal communication) informed us that the Japanese mothers of her sample would not consent to leaving their babies alone in an unfamiliar situation, although they did not object to leaving them with a stranger. The strange situation surely should not be imposed on a baby whose parents are reluctant to cooperate, especially if they have reason to expect that he would be especially disturbed either by separation or by encountering a stranger. For all but a few infants in our middle-class society, however, we are convinced that there is no uncommon stress implicit in the strange-situation procedure, and we are even more convinced that the scientific yield of the strange-situation procedure has been great indeed.

Now let us introduce the reader to the rest of this volume. Chapter 1 deals with the theoretical background that underlies our research. It is necessary in order to follow our interpretations of the findings. Those who are thoroughly conversant with ethological–evolutionary attachment theory (e.g., Ainsworth, 1969, 1972; Bowlby, 1969, 1973) will perhaps find little new in Chapter 1 and may wish to speed on to later chapters.

Part II deals with method. Chapter 2 introduces the reader to our total sample of 106 infants and presents the strange-situation procedure in the kind of detail necessary if others are to replicate it. Chapter 3 presents the behavioral measures we used in our data reduction. There are three types of assessment: (1) frequency measures of an ordinary kind, which are used chiefly to deal with "discrete" behaviors (specific behaviors considered separately from other behaviors); (2) special scoring of interactive behaviors ("categorical" measures that assume a degree of equivalence among goal-corrected behaviors with a common set-goal, and that thus themselves take behavioral patterning into account); and (3) classification of infants according to the patterns of behavior they displayed. Although the frequency measures are almost self-explanatory, the reader will need to become familiar with the categorical measures and with the classificatory system in order to follow our presentation of findings with understanding and ease.

Part III is concerned with results, both of our own strange-situation research and that of others who have used the strange-situation procedure with little or no modification. Chapter 4 contains a descriptive account of behavior in each episode of the strange situation. This analysis is ethologically inspired. It seemed desirable to provide this detailed account of strange-situation behavior before reducing the data to more manipulable behavioral measures. This account is prerequisite to the analysis of the activation and termination of specific behaviors, of changes in behaviors as the activation of the attachment system becomes more intense, and of the ways in which different attachment behaviors are alternative to each other and hence interchangeable to some extent. Chapter 5 is a normative account of behavioral changes across episodes of the strange situation. This analysis, reported previously for a smaller sample (Ainsworth, Bell, & Stayton, 1971), deals with the variations across episodes of the various behavioral measures. In a sense, it summarizes the detailed episode-by-episode analysis of Chapter 4.

Chapters 6, 7, and 8 deal with individual differences in strange-situation behavior. Chapter 6 is devoted to a multiple discriminant function analysis, which examines the reliability of the classificatory system that is our primary method of identifying patterns of attachment. Among other things, this analysis ascertains the extent to which the specifications for classification actually contribute to discriminating one classificatory group from the others. Chapters 7 and 8 focus on individual differences in our longitudinal sample, comparing strange-situation patterns with behaviors manifested at home during both the first and fourth quarters of the first year. Chapter 7 compares infant behavior at home with behavior in the strange situation. This analysis is highly pertinent to the issue of the stability of both attachment behaviors and patterns of attachment over time and across situations. It is also essential to the interpretation of strange-situation patterns as indicative of qualitative differences in the infant–mother attachment relationship. Chapter 8 examines the relationship of maternal behavior at home to infant behavior in the strange situation—an analysis that throws light upon the influence of individual differences in maternal behavior on individual differences in the quality of the attachment of infant to mother.

Chapters 9 and 10 are review chapters. Chapter 9 deals with the findings of other investigations of the behavior of 1-year-olds in the strange situation, whereas Chapter 10 is concerned with the behavior of children between 2 and 4. These important chapters extend the scope of our research. In most instances the findings reported therein confirm and extend our findings, although some studies, especially some of those dealing with older children, suggest limitations. Other studies yield apparent discrepancies between their findings and ours that seem best explained in terms of the use of different methods of appraisal.

We then return again specifically to a consideration of individual differences. Chapter 11 examines the stability of patterns of attachment and attachment behavior shown when the strange situation is repeated after varying lapses of time. Chapter 12 considers individual differences in patterns of behavior as they are more finely reflected in subgroup differences, over and above the way in which they are reflected in differences among the three main classificatory groups that were the theme of many of the findings reported in Chapters 6 through 11. These subgroups are too small for one to be able to meaningfully assess the statistical significance of the differences among them. Hence the reader who is interested in the general thrust of our argument rather than in possibly suggestive detail may wish to skip on to Part IV.

In Part IV the findings reported in Part III are discussed in the light of both theoretical considerations and other relevant findings reported in the research literature. Chapter 13 focuses on the discussion of the normative findings, which may now be better understood after our consideration of individual differences. Chapter 14 considers individual differences in the light of diverse theoretical paradigms—evolutionary–ethological attachment theory (summarized in Chapter 1) and two paradigms stemming from social-learning theory. Here we attempt to deal with some recent criticisms of attachment research and of the concept of attachment. It seems obvious to us that these criticisms are attributable to divergent paradigms, leading to research asking different questions, and conducted with procedures different from ours. Insofar as it is possible to make a bridge between divergent paradigms, we believe that the findings reported in this volume provide a definitive reply to the kind of criticisms made to date. Finally, Chapter 15 provides an interpretation of the patterns of attachment that have emerged as the most significant set of findings of our research, along with a discussion of some of the ways in which they seem likely to influence early development.

ACKNOWLEDGMENTS

Tied as it has been to our longitudinal research into the development of infant–mother attachment, the body of findings reported in this volume has taken many years to amass, and we are indebted to many who have played significant roles in this endeavor. Our first debt of gratitude is to the Foundations' Fund for Research in Psychiatry, which in 1962–63 awarded the grant, 62-244, that made it possible for this research to be launched. Since then, the research has been supported by USPHS grant RO1 HD 01712 and by grants from the Office of Child Development, the Grant Foundation, and the Spencer Foundation; this support is gratefully acknowledged. The appointment of the first author to the Center for Advanced Studies at the University of Virginia during 1975–77 finally facilitated the preparation of this volume.

Special appreciation goes to Barbara Wittig, who helped devise the strange situation and who carried out many of the original observations of infants both in the strange situation and at home. We also thank George D. Allyn and Robert S. Marvin, who also participated in data collection with the longitudinal sample, Sample 1. We are indebted to Silvia Bell and Mary Main for their independent work in collecting and analyzing data with Samples 2 and 4. Indeed we are deeply grateful to Mary Main both for the special data analysis to which she has given us access for this book and for her theoretical contribution, which has done much to forward our understanding of infants who show an anxious, avoidant pattern of attachment. Among those who played an active part in collecting and scoring Sample 3 data are Donelda Stayton, Larry Schutz, Thomas Pentz, Natalie Hirsch, and Inge Bretherton. Inge deserves special thanks for her excellent analysis of the total sample data in regard to behavior directed toward strangers. We thank the various gracious women who played the unrewarding role of the stranger in the strange situation. We cannot enumerate all those who helped with the analysis of the home-visit data for Sample 1, but we wish to thank them, together with others who helped with the analysis of the strange-situation data—including Elaine Jacobs, Rob Woodson, and Mark Greenberg. We are grateful for the excellent film records that William Hamilton made of the babies in Sample 3, and also for those made by Robert Marvin for some of Sample 1.

We are deeply indebted to the 106 mothers who, with their babies, participated in the strange situation. Most of them were motivated by a desire to support a study that aimed to extend our knowledge of early social development. We trust that their efforts will, in due course, result in some useful guidelines for mothers of young infants to facilitate the establishment of secure and harmonious attachment relationships. As for the 1-year-olds—who will probably not remember—we trust that their adventure in the strange situation and in social interaction afterwards will have been on the whole enjoyable.

Our debt to John Bowlby is great and many faceted. Not only is his formulation of attachment theory focal to the interpretation of our findings, but also his advice and encouragement have been vital throughout the several stages of this long project. In addition, although none of them can be held accountable for the final form of this volume, we were very much helped by John Bowlby, as well as by Robert Hinde and Mary Main, who read all or parts of earlier drafts and made cogent suggestions.

Finally, we wish to express our deep appreciation to those whose independent work with the strange situation has contributed to the literature reviewed in Chapters 9 and 10: Joyce Brookhart, Dante Cicchetti, David Connell, Shirley Feldman, Ellen Hock, Margaret Ingham, Michael Lamb, Alicia Lieberman, Sue Londerville, Eleanor Maccoby, Leah Matas, Saul Rosenberg, Felicissima Serafica, Lisa Tomasini, and Bill Tolan, as well as others acknowledged earlier for their contributions—Silvia Bell, Mary Main, Robert Marvin, and Thomas Pentz. We are indeed grateful for their response to our inquiries, for the unpublished material that many of them provided, and for their care in editing drafts of our review of their work.

MARY D. SALTER AINSWORTH
MARY C. BLEHAR
EVERETT WATERS
SALLY WALL

INTRODUCTION

1 Theoretical Background

INTRODUCTION

Attachment theory was given its first preliminary statement in John Bowlby's 1958 paper entitled "The Nature of a Child's Tie to His Mother." It was fully launched by the first volume of his trilogy on *Attachment and Loss* in 1969, which was followed by a second volume in 1973. The first two reports of research inspired by Bowlby's early formulation were by Ainsworth (1963, 1964) and Schaffer and Emerson (1964). Since then there has been an increasing volume of research relevant to infant–mother attachment, including research into mother–infant interaction and into early social development. There is no doubt that the further formulation of attachment theory, as represented in Bowlby's major works (1969, 1973) was influenced by this research. In the meantime other statements of attachment theory have emerged, some of which (e.g., Ainsworth, 1969, 1972; Sroufe & Waters, 1977) dovetail closely with Bowlby's evolutionary–ethological approach. In contrast, others (e.g., Cairns, 1972; Gewirtz, 1972a, 1972b; Maccoby & Masters, 1970) have attempted to assimilate attachment theory to other earlier paradigms.

ATTACHMENT THEORY AS A NEW PARADIGM

Bowlby's attachment theory stemmed from a convergence of several important trends in the biological and social sciences. An initial psychoanalytic orientation was integrated with the biological discipline of ethology and its

3

insistence on viewing behavior in an evolutionary context; with psychobiology and its focus on neurophysiological, endocrine, and receptor processes that interact with environmental stimuli to activate and terminate the activity of behavioral systems; with control-systems theory, which directs attention to "inner programming" and links behavioral theory to an information-processing model of cognition; and with Piaget's structural approach to the development of cognition. Although this integration was undertaken primarily to understand the origin, function, and development of an infant's early social relations, that part of Bowlby's theory that deals specifically with attachment is embedded in a general theory of behavior that owes much to its several origins.

Attachment theory might be described as "programatic" and openended. It does not purport to be a tight network of propositions on the basis of which hypotheses may be formulated, any one of which, in the event of an adequate but unsuccessful test, could invalidate the theory as a whole. Instead, this is an explanatory theory—a guide to understanding data already at our disposal and a guide to further research. "Validation" is a matter of collecting evidence relevant to "construct validity" (Cronbach & Meehl, 1955), with the implication that the "construct" itself can be elaborated and refined through further research, rather than standing or falling on the basis of one crucial experiment.

Despite its lack of resemblance to a mathematicophysical theory, both the general theory of behavior and attachment theory amount to what Kuhn (1962) termed a paradigm change for developmental psychology—a complete shift of perspective. According to Kuhn, such paradigm changes are at the root of scientific revolutions and account for the major advances in science, even though much constructive endeavor must follow the advancement of a new paradigm before it is fleshed out fully.

Kuhn emphasized the difficulty encountered by adherents of earlier paradigms in assimilating the implications of the new paradigm. Such difficulty is unavoidable, for a new paradigm comes into being in an attempt to account for findings that older paradigms could not deal with adequately. For Bowlby the inexplicable findings pertained to a young child's responses to separation from his mother figure. Although a new paradigm may build on older ones and must also account for the empirical findings that they dealt with adequately, the new paradigm cannot be assimilated to an old paradigm—not without such substantial accommodation that the old paradigm is changed beyond recognition and itself becomes a new paradigm more or less akin to the other new one that could not readily be assimilated. We hold that Bowlby's attachment theory constitutes a new paradigm for research into social development. It is in terms of this paradigm that we interpret our findings—and indeed we view our findings as helping to flesh out the framework of the new paradigm.

Although in Chapters 9, 10, and 14 we also discuss some researches that stemmed from divergent paradigms, we are cognizant of Kuhn's warning that it is difficult to move from one paradigm to another. Ainsworth (1969) attempted an elucidation of the differences between three major paradigms relevant to an infant's relationship with his mother; we shall not repeat this endeavor here. The attachment theory that we shall summarize in this chapter is based on Bowlby's paradigm, with particular emphasis on those aspects that are most relevant to the research with which this volume is concerned.

THE BEHAVIORAL SYSTEM

One of the major features of Bowlby's general theory of behavior is the concept of a behavioral system. To ethologists this "construct" is so fundamental that it scarcely requires explanation. (Nevertheless, see Baerends, 1975, for a detailed discussion of behavioral systems.) Bowlby holds that the human species is equipped with a number of behavioral systems that are species characteristic and that have evolved because their usual consequences have contributed substantially to species survival. Some of these systems are toward the labile end of an environmentally labile vs. environmentally stable continuum. An "environmentally stable" system manifests itself in much the same ways throughout almost all members of the species (or almost all members of one sex) despite wide variations in the environments in which the various populations that compose the species have been reared and in which they now live. The manifestations of a relatively "labile" system vary considerably across the various populations in the species in accordance with environmental variations.

For those who are not conversant with evolutionary theory, it is perhaps useful to explain that "survival," in terms of natural selection means species survival or at least population survival. It implies survival of the individual only to the extent that he or she survives to produce viable offspring and to rear them successfully. Natural selection implies that the genes of the most reproductively successful individuals come to be represented in larger proportion in the "gene pool" than the genes of individuals who do not survive long enough to reproduce, who survive but do not produce as many offspring, whose offspring do not survive to sexual maturity, or whose offspring do not reproduce, and so on. Given the natural-selection process, it is scarcely surprising that among the most environmentally stable behavioral systems characteristic of many species (including the human species) are those concerned with reproduction and with care and protection of the young.

It is generally acknowledged that the relatively long period of infantile helplessness characteristic of humans, together with a relative lack of fixed-action patterns, provides the necessary conditions for flexibility and learning—for adaptation to a very wide range of environmental variation. Nevertheless a long period of immaturity implies a long period of vulnerability during which the child must somehow be protected. Bowlby argues, therefore, that human young must be equipped with a relatively stable behavioral system that operates to promote sufficient proximity to the principal caregiver—the mother figure—that parental protection is facilitated. This system—attachment behavior—supplements a complementary behavioral system in the adult—maternal behavior—that has the same function.

Attachment behavior conceived as a behavioral system is not to be equated with any specific bit of behavior. First, the external, observable behavioral components are not the only components of the system; there are intraorganismic, organizational components as well. These are discussed later. Second, there may be a variety of behaviors that serve the system as action components, and indeed a specific behavioral component may, in the course of development, come to serve more than one behavioral system. Nevertheless several behaviors may be classed together as serving a given behavioral system because they usually have a common outcome. The behaviors thus classed together may be diverse in form. They may be classed together because each is an essential component of a series of behaviors that lead to the outcome, such as nest building among birds, or they may constitute alternative modes of arriving at the outcome, as in the case of attachment behavior. Bowlby refers to the outcome as "predictable," to imply that once the system is activated the outcome in question often occurs, although not invariably. If the outcome did not occur consistently enough and in enough individuals, however, the survival of the species would be at risk.

Predictable Outcome

The predictable outcome of a child's attachment behavior is to bring him into closer proximity with other people, and particularly with that specific individual who is primarily responsible for his care. Bowlby refers to this individual as the "mother figure," and indeed in the human species, as well as in other species, this individual is usually the biological mother. The mother figure is, however, the principal caregiver, whether the natural mother or someone else who plays that role. Some behavioral components of the attachment system are signaling behaviors—such as crying, calling, or smiling—that serve to attract a caregiver to approach the child or to remain in proximity once closeness has been achieved. Other components are more active; thus, once locomotion has been acquired, the child is able to seek proximity to his attachment figure(s) on his own account.

Causation of Activation and Termination of Behavior

Several sets of conditions play a part in the activation of a given behavioral system, both specific and general, and within both the organism and the environment. Bowlby notes that the most specific causal factors are the way in which the behavioral systems are organized within the central nervous system and the presence or absence of certain objects within the environment. From the study of other species, we also know that hormones may have a fairly specific influence on behavior, although our knowledge of hormonal influences on human attachment behavior or reciprocal maternal behavior is sparse indeed. Among the more general factors that play a part in the causation of behavior are the current state of activity of the central nervous system—its state of "arousal"—and the total stimulation impinging on the organism at the time. These five classes of causation act together; no one of them may be sufficient to set a behavioral system into action unless one or more of the other factors are also favorable.

Among the various environmental conditions that may activate attachment behavior in a young child who has already become attached to a specific figure are absence of or distance from that figure, the figure's departing or returning after an absence, rebuff by or lack of responsiveness of that figure or of others, and alarming events of all kinds, including unfamiliar situations and strangers. Among the various internal conditions are illness, hunger, pain, cold, and the like. In addition, whether in early infancy or in later years, it seems apparent that attachment behavior may be activated, sustained, or intensified by other less intense conditions that are as yet not well understood. Thus, for example, an infant when picked up may mold his body to the person who holds him, thus manifesting proximity/contact-maintaining behavior, even though his attachment behavior may not have been activated at any substantial level of intensity before being picked up. Or a somewhat older infant or young child may respond with attachment behavior to a figure—particularly a familiar one—who solicits his response and interaction. Indeed he may seek to initiate such interaction himself, and if the figure is a familiar caregiver or (later) an attachment figure, one could argue that the behaviors involved in the initiation and in the subsequent interaction operate in the service of the attachment system. As for the most specific intraorganismic factor—the organization of behavioral systems within the central nervous system—we shall only say at this juncture that whatever constitutional organization is present at birth becomes substantially modified and elaborated through experience, and that individual differences in experience may be presumed to result in different patterns of organization. Thus, although one may generalize to some extent about the conditions likely to activate attachment behavior, the factor of internal organization is highly specific to the individual and, in addition, specific to his particular stage of development.

The conditions for termination of a behavioral system are conceived by Bowlby as being as complex as the conditions of activation, and as related both to the intensity with which the system had been activated and to the particular behavioral component of the system that was involved. Thus the most effective terminating condition for infant crying is close bodily contact contingent upon being picked up by the mother figure (Bell & Ainsworth, 1972), whereas simple approach behavior in a 1-year-old may be terminated by achieving a degree of proximity without requiring close bodily contact. On the other hand, if the attachment system has been activated at a high level of intensity, close contact may be required for the termination of attachment behavior.

A note on terminology may be helpful to the reader. Bowlby (1969) uses the term "attachment behavior" to refer to both the behavioral system and to the behavioral components thereof—a usage that may occasion confusion among readers unaccustomed to the concept of behavioral systems. We have attempted to use the plural term, "attachment behaviors" to refer to the action components that serve the behavioral system, while reserving the singular term "attachment behavior" or the somewhat clumsy term "attachment behavioral system" to refer to the system.

Biological Function

The biological function of a behavioral system is to be distinguished from the causes of the behavioral system's having been activated. It is an outcome of the behavioral system's having been activated, but whereas there may be more than one predictable outcome, the biological function of the system is defined as that predictable outcome that afforded a certain survival advantage in the "environment of evolutionary adaptedness"—the original environment in which the system first emerged as a more or less environmentally stable system, and to which it may be said to be adapted in the evolutionary sense. Biological programing continues to bias members of the species to behave in the ways that gave survival advantage in this original environment. The biological function of the behavioral system may or may not give special survival advantage in one or another of the various environments in which populations now live, but unless changes in the average expectable environment render the behavioral system a liability, it will be maintained in the repertoire of the species.

Bowlby (1969) proposed that the biological function of the attachment system is protection, and he suggested that it was most specifically protection from predators in the environment of evolutionary adaptedness. Indeed, field studies of other species suggest that infants who get out of proximity to their mothers are very likely to become victims of predation. He argued, however, that even in the present-day environment of Western society a child is much more vulnerable to disaster (for example, to becoming a victim of a traffic accident) if alone rather than accompanied by a responsible adult (Bowlby, 1973). Indeed, he noted that even adults of any society tend to be less vulnerable to mishap if with a companion than when alone. Therefore, he felt comfortable about specifying protection as continuing to be the biological function of attachment behavior and its reciprocal parental behavior.

The implication is that the reciprocal behaviors of child and parent (Hinde, 1976a, 1976b, would term these "complementary" behaviors) are adapted to each other in an evolutionary sense. Thus, a child's attachment behavior is adapted to an environment containing a figure—the mother figure—who is both accessible to him and responsive to his behavioral cues. To the extent that the environment of rearing approximates the environment to which an infant's behaviors are phylogenetically adapted, his social development will follow a normal course. To the extent that the environment of rearing departs from the environment to which his behaviors are adapted, developmental anomalies may occur. Thus, for example, an infant reared for a long period, from early infancy onward, in an institutional environment in which he has so little consistent interaction with any one potential attachment figure that he fails to form an attachment may, when subsequently fostered and thus given an opportunity to attach himself, be unable to attach himself to anyone (e.g., Goldfarb, 1943; Provence & Lipton, 1962.)

The foregoing example raises an important point for attachment theory— namely, that just as an infant is predisposed to exhibit attachment behavior under appropriate circumstances, he is predisposed to form an attachment to a specific figure or figures. The predictable outcome of both the activation of the attachment behavioral system and attachment as a bond is the maintenance of a degree of proximity to the attachment figure(s); and similarly, in each case, the biological function is protection. We discuss attachment as bond and its relation to attachment behavior later in this chapter. Here we merely wish to point out that it is under very unusual circumstances that an infant or young child encounters conditions such that his attachment behavior does not result in the formation of an attachment. Although, as noted above, institution-reared infants may not become attached to anyone, most family-reared infants do become attached, even to unresponsive or punitive mother figures.

Goal-Corrected Behavior

Species-characteristic behavior systems may consist of fixed-action patterns that operate more or less independently of environmental feedback or that may at least have some fixed-action components in the system. Bowlby's general theory of behavior specified, however, that species-characteristic behaviors may also be flexible and goal directed. Here he draws upon control-systems theory. A control system is a machine that may be described as operating purposively. The "goal" is built into the device by the men who program it, or "set" it. Feedback is the essential mechanism through which the machine achieves its goal. There is a mechanism for receiving "input" and one for effecting "output." The results of the output are fed back through the receptor mechanism to affect further output in accordance with the way the device is programed.

The simplest kind of control system is a regulator—for example, a thermostat. The purpose is to maintain the temperature of a room at a level at which the thermostat is set—the specific "set-goal" of the device. (One may change the set-goal by changing the thermostat to another level.) When the receptor mechanism receives information that the room temperature has dropped below the level of the set-goal, it turns on the heating system through its effector mechanism; when information is received that the temperature has reached (or slightly surpassed) the set-goal level, it turns the heating system off. Many of the physiological systems operate homeostatically in essentially the same way as a regulator.

A more complex kind of control system is a servomechanism, such as power steering. In such a system the "setting" is continually changed by the human operator, and the system acts to bring performance into accord with the setting at each change. Another example is the action of the antimissile missile. Here the instructions are built into the machine in the course of its manufacture; its set-goal is the interception of another missile. Its effector system alters the speed and direction of its movement in accordance with feedback from its receptor mechanism, which monitors not only the distance and direction of the other missile but also the way in which the discrepancy between their relative positions changes as a result of their movements relative to each other. The set-goal and action of the missile is like that of the peregrine falcon that "stoops" to intercept another bird in flight. The only substantial difference between the falcon and the antimissile missile is that the missile's program was built into it by its manufacturers, whereas the falcon's biological program results from natural selection. In the case of the falcon this programing provides the equipment that enables continuously changing visual input to guide the movements that control the course and speed of flight, so that the predictable outcome is the achievement of the set-goal—the interception of prey.

"Goal corrected" is the term that Bowlby (1969) suggests as preferable to "goal directed" to describe behavioral systems that are structured in terms of set-goals. He suggests that complex behavioral systems of this sort are characteristic of the human species—systems that may be described as purposive and flexible and yet that have a basis of biological programing. The attachment system provides an interesting example, because it has both the features of a simple regulator and the flexibility of a much more complex control system. The setting of the set-goal—that is, the degree of proximity to an attachment figure specified by the set-goal—differs from time to time depending on circumstances. When the set-goal is set widely, a child may venture a substantial distance from his mother before the set-goal is exceeded, attachment behavior is activated, and the specified degree of proximity restored.

As suggested earlier, however, a variety of different conditions may activate attachment behavior, in addition to exceeding the distance (and time) away from the attachment figure that was specified by the "original" setting of the set-goal. Depending on the intensity with which such conditions may activate the attachment system, the set-goal may abruptly change its setting to specify the required degree of proximity more narrowly. Indeed, when the attachment system is activated to a high degree of intensity, the set-goal may be close bodily contact, and attachment behavior will not be terminated until this new set-goal has been achieved. Furthermore, there is substantial flexibility in the attachment behaviors that may be used for the achievement of the set-goal. The model of the simple regulator is approximated only when the attachment figure is stationary and inactive. The ways in which the attachment figure behaves influence the ways in which the child's repertoire of attachment behaviors is deployed to achieve the current set-goal. Finally, although the "behavioral homeostasis" associated with the simple regulator model has general descriptive value, the attachment behavioral system is organized along much more complex lines. Overemphasis on the simple model has led many to assume that Bowlby's attachment theory defines attachment behavior rigidly and exclusively in terms of seeking literal proximity—a conception that is inadequate even when describing the attachment and attachment behavior of a 1-year-old and that is clearly misleading when attempting to comprehend the behavior of the older child or adult.

Clearly Bowlby conceives of some very complex adult behavior stemming from species-characteristic behavioral systems. An example of this is parental behavior. In this case, however, there seems to be so much flexibility attributable to feedback from environmental conditions that the program followed by the system can only be perceived by stepping back from the details of behaviors in a given situation to look at the consistent pattern of behavior toward a common set-goal that is apparent across a variety of geographical and cultural environments.

Organization of Behavior

The behaviors classed together as serving a given behavioral system may be organized in different ways. The simplest mode of organization is chaining, in which the "output" of each link in the chain provides input to activate the next behavioral link—a mode of organization familiar to us through S–R psychology. Another more complex mode of organization, deemed by

Bowlby to be more characteristic of most human behavior, is a hierarchical form of organization. One form of hierarchical organization is governed by a *plan* (Miller, Galanter, & Pribram, 1960.) In a plan, as Bowlby describes it, the overall structure of the behavior is governed by a set-goal, whereas the individual behavioral components for achieving the set-goal vary according to circumstances.

In the neonate the separate behaviors that may be classed together as attachment behavior because they promote proximity/contact with care-givers form a behavioral system whose components have minimal organiza-tion. Each behavioral component—for example, crying, sucking, smiling—has its distinctive conditions for activation and termination; and indeed, as Bowlby suggested, each might be viewed as a fixed-action pattern. About the middle of the first year of life, however, attachment behavior begins to become goal corrected and to be organized in accordance with plans although these may at first be very primitive.

As an example of a primitive plan of this sort, let us consider the case of the infant, engaged in exploratory play at some distance from his mother, who notices her get up and move away. Her movement may or may not have exceeded the limits of the proximity set-goal operative at the time, but the very fact that she takes the initiative in increasing the distance between them may arouse anxiety about her continuing accessibility, may narrow the limits of the set-goal, and may activate attachment behavior at a higher level of intensity. In such a case the baby may follow his mother with more urgency, seeking to establish closer proximity with her than before; he may signal to her by crying or calling, which may induce her to stop and wait for him or reverse direction and approach him; or he may do both. Even though this situation may evoke behavior no more complex than this, the baby may be viewed as having a primitive plan—namely, to get into closer proximity to his mother, and as having alternative behaviors available to him in terms of which he can implement his plan, choosing the one that best seems to suit his evaluation of the situation. Thus even a very simple plan has a set-goal and a choice of alternative behaviors, or perhaps a sequence of behaviors in terms of which the plan may be implemented and the set-goal achieved.

The Role of Cognitive Processes and Learning

It is clear that the organization of behavior in accordance with a plan involves cognitive processes and that these are far beyond the ability of the neonate. Only after considerable cognitive development has taken place does an infant become capable of plans. Although attachment theory cannot be identified as primarily a cognitive theory, Bowlby clearly conceives of the development of attachment as intertwined with cognitive development. Later in this chapter we mention some of the cognitive acquisitions that precede or coincide with important shifts in the course of the development of attachment. Here, however, we wish to make special mention of Bowlby's (1969) concepts of "working models" and "cognitive maps," which consist of inner representations of the attachment figure(s), the self, and the environment. Although it is obvious that such representational models become increasingly complex with experience, it is clearly necessary that some kind of simple representations of this sort be constructed before there may be hierarchical organization of behavior according to plans.

It is inconceivable that the way in which behavior systems characteristic of the human species operate would not be changed to a degree commensurate with the elaboration of representational models, and also with the further development of communication, especially the acquisition of language. Bowlby plainly indicates that this must be the case with the attachment system. Critics of attachment theory do not seem to have grasped the implications of either goal-corrected attachment behavior or hierarchical organization according to plans; on the contrary they seem to have paid attention only to the simple regulatory or homeostatic model, which Bowlby did discuss in detail in conjunction with presenting the concept of set-goal. Under certain circumstances and within a certain early age range, this model does indeed capture the main features of the regulation of attachment behavior. Bowlby would agree with his critics that literal proximity specified in feet and yards is a very inadequate way of delineating the set-goal of the attachment system in the case of the older child or adult. Even for an infant this model yields an oversimplified picture.

Bowlby (1973) emphasizes the importance of the infant's confidence in his mother's accessibility and responsiveness. If in the course of his experience in interaction with his mother he has built up expectations that she is generally accessible to him and responsive to his signals and communications, this provides an important "modifier" to his proximity set-goal under ordinary circumstances. If his experience has led him to distrust her accessibility or responsiveness, his set-goal for proximity may well be set more narrowly. In either case, circumstances—her behavior or the situation in general—may make her seem less accessible or responsive than usual, with effects on the literal distance implicit in a proximity set-goal. (Carr, Dabbs, and Carr, 1975, have demonstrated this point by comparing the effects of the mother's facing or facing away from the child.) Simple expectations regarding the mother's accessibility and responsiveness, as they differ with circumstance, are incorporated into the representational model a child constructs of his mother figure.

As the representational model of his attachment figure becomes consolidated and elaborated in the course of experience, the child becomes able to sustain his relationship with that figure over increasingly longer periods of absence and without significant distress—provided that the separations are agreed to willingly and the reasons for them understood. Under such circumstances the older child or adult may employ distant modes of interaction to reaffirm the accessibility and responsiveness of the attachment figure. Telephone calls, letters, or tapes may help to ameliorate absence; photographs and keepsakes help to bolster the symbolic representation of the absent figure. (Robertson and Robertson, 1971, reported deliberate use of such symbolic modes in supporting the ability to withstand separation of children even in the second and third years of life.) Our language usage offers testimony that proximity/contact is often conceived at the representational level. We talk about "feeling close" to some one, "keeping in touch," and "keeping in contact."

Nevertheless, inner representations cannot entirely supplant literal proximity and contact, nor can they provide more than minimal comfort in the case of inexplicable and/or permanent loss of an attachment figure—neither for a young child nor for a mature adult. When people are attached to another, they want to be with their loved one. They may be content for a while to be apart in the pursuit of other interests and activities, but the attachment is not worthy of the name if they do not want to spend a substantial amount of time with their attachment figures—that is to say, in proximity and interaction with them. Indeed, even an older child or adult will sometimes want to be in close bodily contact with a loved one, and certainly this will be the case when attachment behavior is intensely activated—say, by disaster, intense anxiety, or severe illness.

Interplay Among Behavioral Systems

Let us return to a consideration of attachment behavior as one of several behavioral systems that may be activated at a greater or lesser degree of intensity in any given situation. What happens when two or more systems are activated simultaneously? If one is very much more intensely activated than the others, that system determines the resulting overt behavior, and neither the observer nor the "behaver" may discern any conflict. If two systems are activated at more nearly equal levels of intensity, the more strongly activated may nevertheless determine the behavioral outcome, and the less intensely activated system may be represented only in terms of behavioral fragments, or perhaps identified in terms of the behavior that swings into action when the dominant system is terminated. An example is the behavior of a bird at a window feeding tray when a person comes to the window to observe the bird. In such a situation there is likely to be conflict for the bird between tendencies to feed and to flee. If feeding behavior is activated more strongly than flight, the bird will remain, but it may well manifest its conflict by interspersing feeding behavior with incipient "take-off" movements, which ethologists term "intention movements." These movements are overt manifestations of the activation of the flight system, even though the bird continues to feed intermittently without actually flying away. If, on the other hand, the flight system is activated more strongly than the feeding system, the bird will fly away, but the fact that the feeding system is still at a significant level of activation will be shown if, as often happens, he soon returns to the feeding tray. And if the human observer is tactful enough to withdraw somewhat, it is likely that the flight system's level of activation will be reduced to the extent that the level of activation of feeding behavior becomes relatively stronger and the bird will remain to feed. This kind of conflict with similar behavioral solutions may be seen in the responses of 1-year-olds to the stranger in the strange situation, and is reported and discussed in later chapters.

When the two competing behavioral systems are more nearly equal in level of activation, it is likely that both will be represented in overt behavior in one way or another. One way in which both might be represented is in alternate behaviors. Thus the bird, in our previous example, might alternate between flights away from the feeding tray and returns to peck a few grains before flying away again. Or in our strange situation, a 1-year-old child, conflicted between friendly approach to a pleasant but unfamiliar adult and a tendency to avoid her because she *is* unfamiliar, may approach the stranger but then immediately withdraw (usually returning to the mother), only to pause for a moment and then approach the stranger again, perhaps repeating this sequence several times.

Another way in which both competing systems may express themselves in overt behavior is in some kind of combination. Coy behavior represents such a combination. A person—child or adult—both attracted to another person and wary of him/her, may simultaneously smile and look away, the smile serving an affiliative or sociable system and the look away serving a wary/fearful system. Sometimes a behavior, not activated intensely enough to override another behavioral system that blocks its expression, may be redirected toward a goal object other than toward the one that elicited it. Thus a person whose aggressive/angry behavior is activated by the actions of another of whom he is also afraid or fears to offend may "redirect" aggressive behavior toward a third person or toward an inanimate object—an outcome referred to by psychoanalysts as "displacement."

Even when there is no substantial degree of conflict between systems—that is, when one system is activated so strongly as to clearly override another— our understanding of the organization of behavior is greatly enhanced if we view the operation of one behavior system in the context of other systems. Thus, to comprehend how 1-year-olds manifest attachment behavior in the strange situation, we must trace through, episode by episode, the interplay among attachment behavior, wary/fearful behavior, exploratory behavior, and in some episodes, sociable (or affiliative) behavior directed toward the stranger. The training that most of us have received does not make it easy to conceptualize the interplay of as many as four complex systems, let alone to take into account the complex conditions that determine the level of activation of each of them. Bischof (1975) provides a control-systems model that illustrates the interplay among the four systems that are of most concern to us in strange-situation research. Bischof would be the first to agree that even his complex model represents an oversimplification of the complexities of real-life behavior. Nevertheless, we believe it to be a fine contribution toward an understanding of how intraorganismic and environmental conditions operate to determine which of four behavior systems will be activated most intensely and thus will control behavioral output. The model is not complex enough, however, to handle the manifestations of conflict behavior described earlier in this section.

Behaviors May Serve More Than One System

In each species there may be a few specific behaviors that are unique to one and only one behavioral system. Examples of this are difficult to find in the human species. Looking, for example, may serve a wide variety of behavioral systems, perhaps from earliest infancy onward. One looks at a novel object, and this serves the exploratory system. One seeks eye contact with an attachment figure, or at least monitors his/her whereabouts with an occasional glance. One glares at an antagonist toward whom one feels animosity. One may give a good, long look at a novel object, person, or situation that arouses wariness/fear, before either putting it at a distance, or "cutting off" the stimulus by looking away, or deciding that the object is more interesting than frightening and approaching it. Approach behavior itself may serve more than one system, as Tracy, Lamb, and Ainsworth (1976) have argued. Locomotor approach can serve the attachment system when the individual seeks proximity to an attachment figure. It can also serve exploration, food seeking, affiliation with figures other than an attachment figure, play, anger/aggression, and probably other systems as well. Furthermore, behaviors that in an early stage of development were especially linked with one behavioral system may at later stages occur, if only in fragmentary form, to serve either the same system or other systems. Thus, for example, behaviors displayed by an infant toward his mother may occur also in the adult as part of courtship/mating behavior. Thus in some species of birds, begging for food may be an integral feature of courtship—and human equivalents are not difficult to identify.

Bowlby (1969), in his chapter on "Beginnings," enumerated various forms of behavior that "mediate attachment"—that is to say, specific behaviors that promote proximity, contact, and interaction with other persons and thus play a significant role in the development of attachment to one or a few such persons. We may identify these as "attachment behaviors," because they clearly serve the attachment-behavior system, or as "precursor attachment behaviors" as Ainsworth (1972) did, because they are part of the equipment of the neonate and/or very young infant before he has become attached to anyone. There is nothing in attachment theory to imply that these behaviors serve the attachment system exclusively, even in early infancy. In his next chapter Bowlby listed a number of behaviors suggested by Ainsworth (1967) to be differentially displayed by an infant during his first year toward a particular figure toward whom he is, or is becoming, attached. Bowlby implied that these were useful indicators of the process of focusing on a specific figure. Some of them may also prove useful as criteria for describing an infant as having become attached to a particular figure. It was not intended by Bowlby and Ainsworth to imply: (1) that behaviors displayed differentially during an early phase of development necessarily continue throughout childhood and into adulthood to be displayed differentially to attachment figures; (2) that this list constitutes an adequate roster of behaviors that serve the attachment system during the second year of life and later; or (3) that these behaviors serve the attachment system exclusively. Indeed, as the organization of the attachment system becomes elaborated in the course of development, and as more and more forms of behavior become employed as alternative means of implementing the plans pertinent to interaction with attachment figures, it seems less and less useful to attempt an enumeration of attachment behaviors. Increasingly, the organization and patterning of behaviors become the focus of interest.

ATTACHMENT AND ATTACHMENT BEHAVIORS

Here we are concerned with the distinction between *attachment* as a bond, tie, or enduring relationship between a young child and his mother and *attachment behaviors* through which such a bond first becomes formed and that later serve to mediate the relationship. In developing attachment theory, Bowlby (1969) devoted much attention to attachment behavior as a behavior system, in the course of which he also discussed the specific behaviors that serve that system in infancy and early childhood. He devoted relatively little attention to an exposition of the relation between such behaviors and attachment as a bond. Indeed, we can assume that he considered it self-evident that the way in which the attachment-behavioral system became internally organized in relationship to a specific figure itself constituted the bond or attachment to that figure. Some readers, however, working within the framework of other paradigms, failed to grasp the organizational implications of the concept of a behavioral system, and concluded that attachment and overt attachment behavior were identical. Such a conclusion led to a variety of theoretical misconceptions: for example, that attachment has disappeared if attachment behavior, including separation distress, is no longer overtly manifested; that the intensity with which a child shows attachment behavior in a given situation may be taken as an index of the strength of his attachment; or that attachment consists in nothing more than the contingencies of the interaction between a child and his mother.

We have attempted to deal with the distinction between attachment and attachment behavior elsewhere (e.g., Ainsworth, 1969, 1972), and we return to this issue later in this volume, after presenting our findings. Here, however, we should like to remind the reader that Bowlby's attachment theory came about through his efforts to account for the response of a young child to a major separation from his mother and to reunion with her afterwards (Bowlby, 1969, preface). Therefore, it seems appropriate here to review a few of the phenomena that it make it necessary to assume the existence of a bond between a child and his mother that, once formed, continues despite separation, independent of either overt manifestations of attachment behavior or the contingencies implicit in ongoing mother–child interaction. First, it is necessary to distinguish between brief separations of minutes (or even hours) that take place in the familiar home environment and about which a child will have formed a system of expectations and an involuntary separation lasting for days, weeks, or months, during which a child may be cared for by unfamiliar persons in an unfamiliar environment. It is the latter that we have termed "major" or "definitive" separations, to distinguish them from brief "everyday" separations in a familiar environment.

A child's initial response to a major separation—either at the moment of parting or later when his expectations of a prompt reunion are violated—is to greatly intensify attachment behavior, protesting the separation and trying by all means at his disposal to regain proximity/contact with his attachment figure. This protest is usually more than momentary, but how long it lasts and how intense it is depend on a variety of circumstances. As separation continues, however, the child's attachment behavior becomes either muted or more intermittently manifested, and eventually it may drop out altogether. If one were guided entirely by his overt behavior, one would say that he is no longer attached; but that the bond endures, despite absence of attachment behavior directed toward the absent figure, is vividly demonstrated in most children when reunited with the attachment figure. Whether with or without some delay, attachment behavior is activated at a high level of intensity— much higher than that characteristic of the child before separation. Were attachment identical with attachment behavior, one would be forced to conclude that separation first strengthens the bond, then weakens it, and finally destroys it. If one holds that the bond has altogether disappeared, it then becomes impossible to account for the fact that it reconstitutes itself so quickly after reunion. It seems to us more reasonable to view the bond as enduring despite the vicissitudes of attachment behavior.

If during separation from his mother a child is fortunate enough to be cared for by a substitute figure who plays a thorough maternal role, separation distress may be greatly alleviated, and the child may come to direct attachment behavior toward the substitute figure. Nevertheless such sensitive foster care does not diminish a child's attachment to his own mother figure; on the contrary it facilitates rather than hampers the prompt reestablishment of normal relations with her upon reunion (Robertson & Robertson, 1971).

To be sure, there may be some delay in the reemergence of attachment behavior after a long period of separation, especially if separation was experienced in a depriving environment without adequate substitute mothering—and this delay is associated with the length and extent of disappearance of overt attachment behavior during the separation itself. Upon reunion the child may seem not to recognize his mother, or he may reject her advances, or he may seem merely to be uninterested in proximity to or contact with her. It is noteworthy that such behavior is not displayed to the father or to other familiar figures. Robertson and Bowlby (1952) identified such a response as "detachment" and attributed it to repression. The implication was that the bond—the attachment—had not disappeared but was still somehow internally represented, even though attachment behavior was absent. In support of the view that attachment as bond had not been lost are the many observations of children whose "detachment" suddenly gives way to intense attachment behavior—following the mother wherever she goes, showing distress when she is out of sight for a moment, and wanting close bodily contact much more frequently and intensely than was characteristic of them in the preseparation period. Given the sudden and dramatic shift between detached behavior and very intense attachment behavior, it is difficult to attribute the change to a process of relearning.

Whereas responses to separation and reunion especially highlight the distinction between attachment and attachment behavior, there are other more ordinary sources of evidence. The presence or absence of overt attachment behavior and the intensity with which it is manifested clearly depend on situational factors. For example, a child is more likely to manifest attachment behavior when he is hungry, tired, or ill than when he is fresh, fed, and in good health. It is difficult to conceive that his bond to his mother varies in strength from day to day or from moment to moment, even though the intensity of activation of attachment behavior so varies.

EMOTION AND AFFECT IN ATTACHMENT THEORY

In his general control-systems theory of behavior, Bowlby (1969) identified affect and emotion as "appraising processes." Sensory input, whether conveying information about the state of the organism or about conditions in the environment, must be appraised or interpreted in order to be useful. Feelings (i.e., both affect and emotion) serve as appraising processes although not all appraising processes are felt (i.e., conscious). In the course of appraisal, input is compared to internal "set-points," and certain behaviors are selected in preference to others as a consequence of this comparison. In this sense, feelings—whether "positive" or "negative," pleasant or unpleasant —are focal in the control of behavior.

It was not until his 1973 volume, however, that Bowlby expanded on the role of feelings, giving particular attention to security, fear, anxiety, and anger. Let us briefly consider some important features of his argument. In the course of evolution each species develops a bias to respond with fear to certain "natural clues to an increased risk of danger." It is of survival advantage for the individual to respond with avoidance, flight, or some other comparable form of behavior to situations that signal an increased risk of danger, without having had to learn through experience how to assess such risk. Among such natural clues to danger for the human species, he listed strangeness (unfamiliarity), sudden change of stimulation, rapid approach, height, and being alone. He particularly emphasized the tendency to respond especially strongly to compound situations in which two or more natural clues are simultaneously present. Although other clues to danger may be learned as derivatives of natural clues, through observation of the behavior of others or in more sophisticated risk-assessing processes, and although through experience a person's fear may be reduced when natural clues to danger occur in now-familiar situations in which no risk has been encountered, these natural clues to danger nevertheless tend to continue to be appraised in terms of fear. Even a sophisticated adult is likely to experience fear in a compound situation, such as being alone in an unfamiliar environment in which illumination is suddenly reduced and strange noises are heard.

Fear behavior and attachment behavior are often activated at the same time by the same set of circumstances. When a young child is alarmed by one of the clues to increased risk of danger, whether natural or learned, he tends to seek increased proximity to an attachment figure. Should the attachment figure be inaccessible to him, either through absence or through an expectation of unresponsiveness built up through experience, he faces an especially frightening compound situation. Both components of such a situation are frightening, and the term *fear* may be applied to the appraisal of both. Bowlby presents a military analogy. The safety of an army in the field depends both on its defense against attack and on maintaining a line of communications with its base. Should the field commander judge that retreat is the best tactic, it is essential that the base be available to him, that he not be cut off from it, and that the commander in charge of the base be trusted to maintain the base and the support implicit in it. By analogy, the young child may be afraid of the threat implicit in the clues to danger he perceives in a situation, but he may also be afraid if he doubts the accessibility of his "base"—his attachment figure. Bowlby suggests that "alarm" be used for the former class of fear and "anxiety" for latter. This brings us squarely face to face with the issue of separation anxiety.

Bowlby emphasizes how crucial it is in a potentially fear-arousing situation to be with a trusted companion, for with such a companion fear of all kinds of situation diminishes, whereas when alone fear is magnified. Attachment figures are one's most trusted companions. We all fear separation from attachment figures, but "separation" cannot be defined simply as a matter of absence of such a figure. What is crucial is the availability of the figure. It is when a figure is perceived as having become inaccessible and unresponsive, that separation distress (grief) occurs, and the anticipation of the possible occurrence of such a situation arouses anxiety.

Whereas a young infant is more likely to cry when he is alone than when he is in proximity or contact with his mother and his crying is most likely to be terminated promptly if his mother picks him up (Bell & Ainsworth, 1972), an older infant is likely to begin to form expectations and to experience anxiety relevant to his mother's departure and / or absence. Thus, at some time in the second half of his first year, he begins to experience anxiety when his mother leaves the room, and may manifest this by crying or, after locomotion develops, by attempting to follow her.

Infants differ, however, in the consistency with which they exhibit distress in brief, everyday separations. It seems to us reasonable to suppose that there are concomitant differences in expectations. An infant who has experienced his mother as fairly consistently accessible to him and as responsive to his signals and communications may well expect her to continue to be an accessible and responsive person despite the fact that she has departed; and if she is absent for but a short time, his expectations are not violated. (This, of course, presupposes that the infant in question has developed a concept of his mother as a "permanent object" as Piaget (1937) used the term, but also that he has developed a "working model" of his mother as available to him in Bowlby's sense of these terms.) On the other hand, an infant whose experience in interaction with his mother has not given him reason to expect her to be accessible to him when out of sight or responsive to his signals is more likely to experience anxiety even in little everyday separation, as Stayton and Ainsworth (1973) have shown. Such an infant may be identified as anxiously attached to his mother, and Bowlby (1973) elaborates the theme of anxious attachment, both in terms of the kinds of experience that may contribute to it, not only in infancy but also in later years, and in terms of the ways in which anxious attachment may affect later behavior.

The opposite of feeling afraid (whether alarmed or anxious) is feeling secure—or, according to the Oxford Dictionary, feeling "untroubled by fear or apprehension." When an infant or young child is with an attachment figure, he is likely to be untroubled by fear or apprehension, unless he is troubled by his expectations that he/she may become inaccessible at any moment and/or fail to be responsive to his needs and wishes. Thus the mere physical presence of an attachment figure is not necessarily enough to promote a feeling of security, although it very frequently seems to do so. One could expect that the older the child and the better articulated his representational model of the attachment figure, the less likely that the mere physical presence of the figure would be enough to provide a secure or untroubled state; whereas in the case of an infant whose expectations and representational models are still in an early formative stage, it is perhaps not surprising that he appears to be secure in his mother's presence, until her actions or some other aspect of the situation activate his anxieties.

Just as when an infant feels afraid, his attachment behavior is likely to be activated (as well as fear behavior), likewise when he feels secure, his attachment behavior may be at a low level of activation. This accounts for the phenomenon that we have termed "using the mother as a secure base from which to explore." When the attachment behavioral system is activated at low intensity, the situation is open for the exploratory system to be activated at a higher level by novel features of the environment. It seems of obvious survival advantage in evolutionary terms for a species with as long and as vulnerable a period of infancy as that characteristic of humans to have developed an interlocking between the attachment system, whose function is protection, and exploratory (and also affiliative) behavior, which promotes learning to know and to deal with features of the environment (including persons other than attachment figures.) This interlocking permits a situation in which an infant or young child is prompted by intriguing objects to move away from his "secure base" to explore them, and yet tends to prevent him from straying too far away or from remaining away for too long a time; and the reciprocal maternal-behavioral system provides a fail-safe mechanism, for "retrieving" behavior will occur if the child does in fact go too far or stay away too long. The interlocking between systems of this sort has led some to propose that the biological function of attachment behavior is (or should include) providing an opportunity for learning. Bowlby (1969) obviously gives first place to the protective function and indeed might well have said explicitly that the biological function of exploratory behavior is learning about the environment, whereas the protective function of attachment behavior and reciprocal maternal behavior makes this possible. Obviously the functions of both systems are of crucial importance.

After this divergence from the theme of feelings as appraisal processes, let us return to anger. Bowlby (1973) reminded his readers about the literature on responses to separation that makes it clear that anger is engendered by separation or a threat of separation, and that this anger is particularly likely to be manifested at the time of reunion. The separation literature to which he referred, however, dealt with "major" or "definitive" separations in which a child was separated from attachment figures for a period of days, weeks, or months and was usually also removed to an unfamiliar environment. Perhaps separations of but a few minutes, whether in a familiar or unfamiliar environment, do not so consistently arouse angry feelings as do major separation experiences. Attachment-relevant anger is activated under conditions other than separation, however. If attachment behavior is activated at high intensity but not terminated by an appropriate response by the attachment figure, anger is very likely to ensue—whether the reasons for the nontermination are the absence of the figure (as in the case of separation) or its chronic tendency to be unresponsive.

This brief discussion of the affective implications of attachment has dealt with some of the most obvious aspects of affective involvement, but is far from complete. Both Bowlby (1969, 1973) and Ainsworth (e.g., 1972) have emphasized the notion that attachments imply strong affect—not only security, anxiety, fear, and anger, but also love, grief, jealousy and indeed the whole spectrum of emotions and feelings.

THE DEVELOPMENT OF
CHILD-MOTHER ATTACHMENT

Because this volume is not primarily devoted to the development of a child's attachment to his mother figure, here we merely summarize what has been published in more detail elsewhere about the course of such development (Ainsworth, 1967, 1972; Bowlby, 1969). In 1972 we distinguished four phases of development of child-mother attachment; these correspond to Bowlby's four phases, but with somewhat different titles. Three of these occur in the first year of life: (1) the initial preattachment phase; (2) the phase of attachment-in-the-making; and (3) the phase of clear-cut attachment. The 1-year-olds, to whom most of this volume is devoted, may be assumed to have reached Phase 3, and hence this phase will be considered more fully than either of the two earlier phases. A final phase was initially identified by Bowlby (1969) as: (4) the phase of goal-corrected partnership, which, he suggested, did not begin until about the end of the third year of life, or perhaps later. It is therefore only the 4-year-olds, and possibly some of the 3-year-olds discussed in Chapter 10, who are likely to have reached this final phase of development.

1. *The Initial Preattachment Phase.* Bowlby (1969) called this the phase of "orientation and signals without discrimination of figure." It begins at birth and continues for a few weeks. From the beginning the baby is more "tuned in" to stimuli within certain ranges than to others, and it seems likely that the stimuli to which he is most responsive come from people. At first, however, he does not discriminate one person from another, and hence responds to his mother figure (i.e., his principal caregiver) in much the same way as he responds to other persons.

The infant can orient toward anyone who comes into close enough proximity, directing his gaze toward that person and tracking the latter's movements with his eyes. He is equipped with a repertoire of signaling behaviors—for example, crying, which is present from birth onwards, and smiling and noncrying vocalizations, which soon emerge. These signals serve to induce other people to approach him and perhaps to pick him up, thus promoting proximity and contact; hence they are classed as attachment behaviors. In addition, the infant is equipped with a few behaviors through which he himself can actively seek or maintain closer contact—for example, rooting, sucking, grasping, and postural adjustment when held. (Rooting and sucking obviously serve the food-seeking system as well as the attachment system, and indeed in bottle-fed babies, they tend to become splintered apart from the attachment system.) When the baby is not in actual contact with a caregiver, however, he can rely only on his signaling behaviors to promote proximity/contact—a state of affairs that persists throughout this phase and the next one.

As mentioned earlier, Bowlby (1969) suggested that the original behavioral equipment of the neonate consists of fixed-action patterns and that these become organized together and linked to environmental stimulus situations in accordance with processes of learning that have become well known through S–R psychology. At the same time it is easy to consider the neonate's fixed-action patterns as equivalent to Piaget's (1936) reflex schemata and to account for their modification in Piagetian terms. In either case the infant, even during this first phase of development, begins to build up expectations (anticipations), although at first, as Piaget held, these are inextricably tied to his own sensorimotor schemata and do not extend to using one environmental clue as a basis for anticipating another environmental event.

Phase 1 may be said to come to an end when the baby is capable of discriminating among people and, in particular, of discriminating his mother figure from others. Because discrimination is learned much earlier through some modalities than through others, it is difficult to judge when Phase 1 has ended and Phase 2 begun. There is evidence that the mother can be discriminated very early through olfactory or somasthetic cues, whereas visual discrimination is relatively late in developing. Nevertheless, it is convenient to consider Phase 1 as continuing until the baby can fairly consistently discriminate his mother by means of visual cues, which tends to occur between 8 and 12 weeks of age.

2. *The Phase of Attachment-in-the-Making.* Bowlby termed this the phase of "orientation and signals directed towards one (or more) discriminated figure(s)." During this phase the baby not only can clearly discriminate unfamiliar from familiar figures, but also becomes able to discriminate between one familiar figure and another. He shows discrimination in the way he directs his various proximity-promoting (attachment) behaviors toward different figures, and these figures may also differ in how readily they can terminate an attachment behavior, such as crying. During this phase the baby's repertoire of active attachment behaviors becomes expanded—for example, with the emergence of coordinated reaching. This phase of development roughly coincides with Piaget's (1936) second and third stages of sensorimotor development, but here we shall not attempt to link cognitive development with the development of attachment, except to point out that the development of discrimination may be thought to involve Piaget's processes of recognitory assimilation—or, for that matter, discrimination learning.

If simple preference of one figure over others is the criterion of attachment, then one could identify a baby as attached to a preferred figure in Phase 2. We prefer, however, to characterize a baby as incapable of attachment until Phase 3, during which he can take active initiative in seeking the proximity of an attachment figure.

3. *The Phase of Clear-cut Attachment.* Bowlby identified this as the phase of "maintenance of proximity to a discriminated figure by means of locomotion as well as signals." As Bowlby's label implies, the baby in this phase is very much more active than before in seeking and achieving proximity and contact with his discriminated (and preferred) figures on his own account, rather than relying as he did before on signaling behavior to bring them into proximity. Chief among his newly acquired behaviors is locomotion. Obviously locomotion can also serve other behavioral systems. But when a baby approaches a preferred figure, whether following a departing figure, greeting a returning figure, or merely seeking to be in closer proximity, we may infer that locomotion is serving the attachment system. A number of other active behaviors emerge that can be put into the service of the attachment-behavior system, including "active contact behaviors," such as clambering up, embracing, burying the face in the body of the attachment figure, "scrambling" over the figure in an intimate exploration of face and body, and so on. Signaling behaviors continue to be emitted and may on occasion be intentional communications. Indeed language begins to develop during Phase 3.

Although the Phase-3 child is more active in seeking proximity/contact, clearly he does so only intermittently. He is active also in exploring his environment, manipulating the objects he discovers, and learning about their properties. The Phase-3 child is by no means focused constantly on his attachment figures, even though they may provide the secure background from which he moves out to familiarize himself with his world.

Bowlby (1969), using his control-systems model, pointed out that an infant's behavior first becomes organized on a goal-corrected basis in Phase 3, and then gradually becomes hierarchically organized in terms of overall plans. To the extent that attachment behavior is so organized, certain of the attachment behaviors are to a greater or lesser extent interchangeable. In a given episode of activation, the set-goal of the attachment system may be set for a certain degree of proximity, but there may be a variety of alternative behaviors through which a child may attempt to approximate that set-goal. Thus the specificity of each form of attachment behavior becomes increasingly less important, whereas the set-goal and overall plan for accomplishing it grow increasingly significant. Furthermore, the characteristic way in which a child has learned to organize his behavior with reference to a specific attachment figure is of clearly greater importance than the intensity or frequency with which he manifests each of the behavioral components of the attachment system. It is our conviction that the onset of goal-corrected attachment behavior is an acceptable criterion of the onset of attachment. In offering this criterion, however, we do not mean to imply that attachment, once present ceases to develop; on the contrary there is much further development of attachment during Phase 3 and beyond. We shall not here go into descriptive detail about Phase-3 attachment behavior, for both Bowlby (1969) and we in this chapter have tended to cite our illustrative material from Phase-3 behavior.

Phase 3 commonly begins at some time during the second half of the first year, perhaps as early as 6 months in some cases, but more usually somewhat later. Its onset may be conceived as coincident with the onset of Piaget's Stage 4 of sensorimotor development. The emergence of goal-corrected behavior may be conceived as coincident with the onset of the ability to distinguish between means and ends; and certainly hierarchical organization of behavior according to plans depends on means–ends distinctions and on achieving the ability for "true intention." The notion of alternative means of achieving a set-goal that is implicit in plans has its parallel in Piaget's concept of schemata becoming "mobile." Furthermore, the achievement of at least a Stage-4 level of development of the concept of persons as having permanence—that is, as existing when not actually present to perception—seems to us (as well as to Schaffer & Emerson, 1964, and to Bowlby, 1969) a necessary condition for a child's becoming attached to specific discriminated figures. In other words, our view of attachment implies a conception of the attachment figure as existing even when absent, as persistent in time and space, and as moving more or less predictably in a time–space continuum.

Despite the obvious connection between the concept of person permanence and separation distress, we are not convinced that the onset of crying when the mother leaves the room implies the acquisition of even a Piagetian Stage 4 concept of person permanence. Both Ainsworth (1967), in her study of Ganda babies, and Stayton, Ainsworth, and Main (1973), reporting on our longitudinal study of a sample of American babies, reported that crying when mother leaves the room occurs as early as 15 weeks. (In the latter study we were careful to eliminate episodes in which the baby was left alone or in which he had been just put down after having been held, because these were conditions likely to evoke crying from birth onwards.) We are inclined to believe that these very early instances of crying when mother leaves are an extension of the phenomenon, mentioned by Wolff (1969), of distress when a figure moves out of the infant's visual field—an extension because in this case it is a discriminated figure disappearing at a substantial distance from the infant, implying both an extension of the visual field and the ability to visually discriminate among figures at a distance. There is no indication merely from the distress that the baby yet conceives of his mother as having existence after having disappeared from the visual field. For this, one would require, as Piaget suggested, search for the vanished person.

Nevertheless, even though instances of separation distress may occur before Phase 3 of the development of attachment (and before Stage 4 of the account by Piaget, 1936, of sensorimotor development), there is much evidence that separation distress is particularly likely to occur in Phase 3, even though it is clearly not inevitable in very brief separations either at home (Stayton, Ainsworth, & Main, 1973) or in the strange situation—as the findings reported in later chapters demonstrate. To us it is suggestive that it occurs fairly commonly at about the same time that locomotion and goal-corrected behavior first emerge. One could argue that a baby does not need to be attached to a specific figure or to organize his behavior on a goal-corrected basis until locomotion makes it possible to move away from his mother figure to explore the world. In any event it is a happy circumstance that these developmental acquisitions coincide—and as for crying and attempts to follow a mother who is disappearing or who has already disappeared, these acquisitions also have a survival function for the active, mobile child.

We have already mentioned expectations (anticipations) as beginning to be formed as early as Phase 1. It is clear that by the time an infant reaches Phase 3, these expectations become even more important. By this time, as Piaget (1936) points out, the child can begin to use one environmental event as a cue that another environmental event will follow. This implies that he can begin to anticipate his mother's actions, insofar as these have a reasonable degree of consistency. Bowlby (1969) suggested that a baby in Phase 3, whose behavior has become goal corrected, is capable of taking into account in the plans through which he organizes his attachment behavior his expectations of how his mother is likely to act. That is to say he is capable of adjusting his plans to his mother's expected behavior.

Phase 3 is conceived as continuing through the second and third years of life and thus obviously continues beyond the limits of Piaget's Stage 4, spanning the rest of the sensorimotor period and comprehending at least the first portion of his preoperational period. This being so, it follows that attachment becomes increasingly a matter of inner representation of attachment figures and of the self in relation to them.

Bowlby emphasized that, although an infant's attachment behavior and a mother's reciprocal behavior are preadapted to each other in an evolutionary sense, the behavior of each partner is often dominated by other "antithetical" behavior systems. When an infant's attachment behavior is activated, his mother may well be occupied with some activity antithetical to "maternal' behavior. Although the Phase-3 infant becomes increasingly capable of adjusting his plan for achieving the desired degree of proximity/contact with his mother in accordance with her current activity as interpreted in the light of the representational model of her that he has built up, there are limits to the success that his efforts are likely to meet, unless his mother abandons her plans in order to accommodate herself to his plan. The Phase-3 child is conceived as too "egocentric," in Piaget's (1924) sense, to be able to divine what his mother's current plan might be and to act to change it so that it is in greater harmony with his own.

4. *The Phase of a Goal-Corrected Partnership.* To Bowlby (1969) the fundamental feature of the fourth and final phase of the development of child–mother attachment is the lessening of egocentricity to the point that the child is capable of seeing things from his mother's point of view, and thus of being able to infer what feelings and motives, set-goals and plans might influence her behavior. To be sure, this increased understanding of his mother figure is far from perfect at first and develops only gradually. To the extent that a child has developed his representational model of his mother to include inferences of this sort, he is then able to more skillfully induce her to accommodate her plans to his, or at least to achieve some kind of mutually acceptable compromise. Bowlby suggested that when this point of development has been reached, mother and child develop a much more complex relationship, which he terms a "partnership." That he termed it a "goal-corrected" partnership underlines the flexible, hierarchical organization of the child's attachment behavior and of his mother's reciprocal behavior that is implicit in the concept of "plans." He surely did not mean to imply that goal-corrected behavior did not emerge until Phase 4, for he is explicit in pointing out that such behavior is characteristic of Phase 3 and serves to differentiate it from Phase-2 behavior.

Furthermore, as we have already implied, because of the development of communication and of the symbolic representations implicit in working models of self and of attachment figures, the kinds of interactions between a child and his attachment figures undergo much change. And as we have also previously implied, the forms of behavior through which the attachment system is mediated become much more varied, although they still feature, under certain circumstances, overt proximity/contact seeking.

Despite the increasing sophistication of the processes mediating a child's attachment to his mother and others, and despite the fact that developmental changes continue, Bowlby did not conceive of such changes as involving processes different enough from those operating in Phase 4 to specify further phases of development. On the contrary, the processes implicit in Phase 4 were conceived as characteristic of mature attachments. Although Bowlby (1969, 1973) was specifically concerned with the attachment of a child to his mother figure, he conceived of attachments to other figures as approximating the same model—and he clearly stated that attachments continue throughout the entire life span. Attachment to parent figures may become attentuated as adulthood approaches and may become supplemented and to some extent supplanted by other attachments; but few if any adults cease to be influenced by their early attachments, or indeed cease at some level of awareness to be attached to their early attachment figures.

II METHOD

2 Procedures

SUBJECTS

The subjects come from white, middle-class, Baltimore-area families, who were originally contacted through pediatricians in private pratice. They were observed in the strange situation at approximately 1 year of age. The total N of 106 infants is comprised of four samples that were observed in the course of four separate projects. (See Table 1.)

Sample 1

Sample 1 was observed in the course of a longitudinal study of the development of infant–mother attachment throughout the first year. Twenty-six infants were visited at home at intervals of 3 weeks from 3 to 54 weeks of age. In lieu of or to supplement the second-to -last visit at 51 weeks, the babies were brought into the laboratory for the strange situation. Three subjects were dropped from the strange-situation sample, the first because he was 64 weeks of age by the time the strange situation was devised, the other two because they were ill when brought to the strange situation.

Sample 2

Sample 2 was observed in the course of short-term longitudinal research into the development of the concept of the object as related to infant–mother attachment (Bell, 1970). Thirty-three babies were given cognitive tests at home three times between the ages of 8½ and 11 months, and 1 week after the

TABLE 1
Description of the Four Samples

Sample	N	Boys	Girls	Median Age in Weeks/Days	Range of Age in Weeks/Days	Origin
1.	23	14	9	51/0	50/1 to 57/6	Ainsworth longitudinal study
2.	33	21	12	49/0	48/6 to 50/6	Bell (1970)
3.	23	12	11	50/0	49/3 to 50/5	Test–retest study
4.	27	13	14	52/2	49/6 to 57/6	Main (1973)

third testing session they were observed in the strange situation in the laboratory.

Sample 3

Sample 3 was especially assembled for a study of the effect on strange-situation behavior of repetition of the procedure with an interval of 2 weeks between the first and second session. Twenty-four babies were observed, but one was discarded from the sample because, after he had cried throughout the entire first session, it was discovered that he was terrified of an electric fan in the experimental room, and, indeed, of all noise-producing appliances. Because this was a specific fear, and not merely fear of the strange, his record was considered atypical and was discarded.

Sample 4

Main (1973), in a short-term longitudinal study on the relation between infant–mother attachment and later exploration, play, and cognitive function, used Sample 3 (first session) and added to it 27 infants who constitute Sample 4.

The infants of Samples 1 and 2 were observed at home before the strange-situation procedure was experienced, whereas those of Samples 3 and 4 were not, except for one home visit that served also to explain the procedure to the mother and to gain her informed consent. For each sample, however, the strange situation was the occasion for the first visit to the laboratory. It may be noted in Table 1 that the four samples differ somewhat in median and range of age. For all major analyses of data, differences among the four samples were tested for significance.

THE STRANGE-SITUATION PROCEDURE

The strange situation consists of eight episodes presented in a standard order for all subjects, with those expected to be least stressful occurring first. After a brief introductory episode, the baby was observed with his mother in the unfamiliar, but not otherwise threatening, environment of the experimental room, to see how readily he would move farther away from her to explore a novel assembly of toys. While the mother was still present, a stranger entered and made a very gradual approach to the baby. Only after this did the mother leave, because it was anticipated that separation from her would constitute a greater stress than the presence of a stranger and/or of an unfamiliar environment per se. After a few minutes the mother returned and the stranger slipped out. The mother was instructed to interest her baby in the toys again, in the hope of restoring his exploratory behavior to the baseline level characteristic of when he was previously alone with his mother. Then followed a second separation, and this time the baby was left alone in the unfamiliar environment. As some check on whether any increased distress was a response to being alone rather than to have been separated a second time, and also to ascertain whether separation was more distressing than the presence of a stranger, the stranger returned before the mother finally returned.

There are undoubtedly other sequences of episodes that would be interesting to study, and there may be others that would have been equally or more effective in evoking the responses for which the situation was designed. But as it turned out, the sequence just summarized was very powerful both in eliciting the expected behaviors and in highlighting individual differences. The sequence of episodes is described in more detail as we proceed.

The Physical Situation

Two adjacent rooms were employed for the experimental room and the observation room, connected by two one-way-vision mirror windows. The experimental room was furnished, not bare, but was so arranged that there was a 9-by-9 foot square of clear floor space. For the first 13 subjects of the Sample 1, the floor was covered by a braided rug, but for the last 10 subjects and for all subsequent samples, the mastic tile floor was bare but marked off into 16 squares to facilitate recording of location and locomotion. For Samples 1 and 2, the furnishings approximated those of a university office, with desk, chair, and a bookcase at one side of the room. Bright postcards were tacked around the periphery of the mirror windows. In the period between Samples 2 and 3, the office furniture was moved out and replaced by metal storage cabinets. The postcards had been removed, but colorful posters were tacked to three walls of the room.

Film records were made of the last 10 subjects of Sample 1, as well as of the babies of Sample 3. For the purpose of filming, a glass-covered photography port was put in the wall opposite the observation windows, and sun-gun lights were introduced high in the room. To obscure the noise of the camera, as well as to counter the heat from the bright lights, an electric fan was placed on the bookcase (later on top of the cabinets).

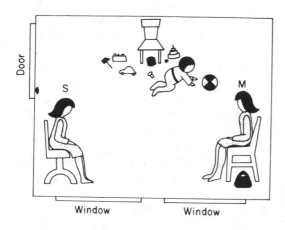

FIG. 1. Sketch of the physical arrangements of the strange situation. (Adapted from Bretherton & Ainsworth, 1974.)

At one end of the experimental room (see Figure 1) was a child's chair heaped with and surrounded by toys. Near the other end of the room in square 16 was a chair for the mother, and on the opposite side in square 13 was a chair for the stranger. The baby was put down on the line between squares 14 and 15, facing the toys, and left free to move where he wished.

This much attention has been paid to a description of the physical arrangement of the experimental room because even minor variations seemed to affect babies' behavior. For example, the desk and bookcases attracted more exploratory interest in Samples 1 and 2 than did the cabinets in Samples 3 and 4. More important, it seems likely that the position of the door on the stranger's side of the room may have affected the likelihood of a baby's approaching it when the stranger was present. Furthermore, the arrangement of the room in orientation to the observation windows obviously affected what sequences of behavior and facial expression the observers were able to see most clearly. They had a good view of a baby's face as he approached either the mother's or stranger's chair, a profile view (at best) of a baby oriented to the door or to a person entering, but only a back view when the baby was approaching the child's chair and the heap of toys.

Either one or two observers (more frequently and preferably two) dictated a play-by-play account into Stenorettes of what the baby did, and as much as possible also of what the adult(s) did. The Stenorette microphones also picked up the sound of a buzzer that marked off 15-second time intervals. The observers wore earphones that both enabled them to hear what went on in the experimental room and prevented them from hearing each other's dictation. An intercom system also made sounds from the experimental room audible in the observation room. This system was not reversed to give instructions to the adults in the experimental room, lest a disembodied voice alarm the infants. Predetermined signals were given by knocks on the wall. On the few occasions when special intervention was necessary, someone went to the door of the experimental room to deliver the message directly.

Personnel

The usual number of personnel included two observers (O1 and O2), a stranger (S), and an experimenter (E). It was E's task to time the episodes and to give cues to the mother and stranger that determined their entrances and exits. Whenever possible a fifth person received the mother and baby upon their arrival, reviewed the instructions (of which the mother had a copy and that had previously been discussed with her at a home visit), and introduced them to the experimental room; otherwise either O2 or E did this. The irreducible minimum of personnel (used in Sample 2) was one observer and a second person to act as both E and S.

A necessary complication of the procedure is that separation episodes were curtailed if a baby became so distressed that he clearly would continue to cry throughout an episode of standard duration. Although it is obviously undesirable to allow a baby to become unduly distressed, an effort was made not to curtail episodes unnecessarily, for some babies may protest briefly and then settle down either to play or to search for the mother, or both. Sometimes it is also desirable to prolong an episode. Thus, for example, the first reunion episode was sometimes prolonged so that a baby could fully recover from distress occasioned by the first separation and settle down again to play. Furthermore, should a baby make contact with his mother just before a signal is due for her to leave, the episode may be somewhat prolonged so that the mother's departure does not constitute a direct rebuff to the baby. The responsibility for deciding when episodes should be curtailed or prolonged was usually delegated to E, if he were experienced enough, so as not to distract O from his primary task of observing.

Toys

The original set of toys used for Samples 1 and 2 were selected at a local toy shop and supplemented by other attractive objects, such as bangles, a shiny pie plate, and a long red tube. (See lists in Table 2.) For the two sessions that Sample 3 was to undergo, the original set of toys was divided in half, and each half was supplemented by new toys, mostly Creative Playthings, so that there was an entirely different array of toys in Session 2. Although it was likely that some of the toys were duplications of toys a baby had at home, it was assumed that the total array of toys would be novel enough to activate exploration.

Because so many of the toys were noise-makers, and because so many babies played banging games, it proved not feasible to tape the vocalizations of mother and baby in the experimental room. The observers could distinguish crying from noncrying vocalizations better at first-hand than from the tape. Thus the chief information that was lost by not making taped records was the precise content of some of the adults' speech, which the observers found difficult to include exactly while dictating an account of all the action.

TABLE 2
Toys Used by Different Strange-Situation Samples

Samples 1&2	Sample 4 and First Session of Sample 3	Second Session of Sample 3
Large red ball	Chime ball	Large red ball
Chime ball	Racing-car pull toy	Plastic butterfly ball
Plastic butterfly ball	Toy telephone	Musical clown
Racing-car pull toy	Raggedy Andy doll	Plastic milk bottle
Toy telephone	Plastic shapes & sticks	containing small objects
Musical clown	Hammer-shaped rattle	Long red tube
Raggedy Andy doll	Silver bangles	Peg bus
Plastic shapes & sticks	Foil pie plate	Shape box
Hammer-shaped rattle	Thumper drum	Mirror
Plastic milk bottle	Clutch ball	Baby doll
containing small objects	Baby shapes	Toy iron
Silver bangles	Wooden chicken	Wooden grasshopper
Foil pie plate	Hammer-peg toy	Wooden hand "mixer"
Long red tube		

Episodes of the Strange Situation

The episodes of the strange situation are delineated in the following general instructions to the personnel—the observers, stranger, and experimenter. (Separate instructions were given to the mother in advance of her arrival at the laboratory, and are shown in Appendix I.) A summary of the episodes is given in Table 3.

Episode 1: Mother, Baby, and Experimenter. This is a very brief, introductory episode. M and B are introduced to the experimental room. M is shown where to put the baby down and where she is to sit after having put him down. M has been instructed to carry the baby into the room. Meanwhile the O notes the B's response to the new situation from the safety of M's arms. E leaves as soon as he has completed his instructions.[1]

Episode 2: Mother and Baby. M puts B down midway between S's and M's chairs (on the line between squares 14 and 15), facing the toys. She then goes to her chair and reads (or pretends to read) a magazine. It is expected that B will explore the room and manipulate the objects in it, especially the toys. M has been instructed not to initiate an intervention, although if B obviously wants a response from her, she is to respond in whatever way she considers appropriate.

---

[1]Here and elsewhere in these instructions, M stands for mother, B for baby, E for experimenter, O for observer, and S for stranger.

TABLE 3
Summary of Episodes of the Strange Situation

Number of Episode	Persons Present	Duration	Brief Description of Action
1	Mother, baby, & observer	30 secs.	Observer introduces mother and baby to experimental room, then leaves.
2	Mother & baby	3 min.	Mother is nonparticipant while baby explores; if necessary, play is stimulated after 2 minutes.
3	Stranger, mother, & baby	3 min.	Stranger enters. First minute: Stranger silent. Second minute: Stranger converses with mother. Third minute: Stranger approaches baby. After 3 minutes mother leaves unobtrusively.
4	Stranger & baby	3 min. or less[a]	First separation episode. Stranger's behavior is geared to that of baby.
5	Mother & baby	3 min. or more[b]	First reunion episode. Mother greets and/or comforts baby, then tries to settle him again in play. Mother then leaves, saying "bye-bye."
6	Baby alone	3 min. or less[a]	Second separation episode.
7	Stranger & baby	3 min. or less[a]	Continuation of second separation. Stranger enters and gears her behavior to that of baby.
8	Mother & baby	3 min.	Second reunion episode. Mother enters, greets baby, then picks him up. Meanwhile stranger leaves unobtrusively.

[a]Episode is curtailed if the baby is unduly distressed.
[b]Episode is prolonged if more time is required for the baby to become re-involved in play.

For 2 minutes M will direct B's attention neither to the toys nor to other objects in the room. If, after 2 minutes, B has not begun to explore the toys, a signal is given to M (a knock on the wall) for her to take him to the toys and to try to stimulate his interest in them. One minute is allowed for this stimulated exploration. Meanwhile E times the episode, beginning when M puts B down. He signals M when 2 minutes are up if, in his judgment, B needs stimulation. When 3 minutes are nearly up, he cues S to go to the experimental room.

The focus of the observation is on the amount and nature of B's exploration of the strange-situation—locomotor, manipulatory, and visual—and on the amount and nature of his orientation to M.

Episode 3: Stranger, Mother, and Baby.   S (who has never met B before) enters and says to M: "Hello! I'm the stranger." She immediately seats herself in S's chair and remains silent for 1 minute. She may watch B, but should not stare at him if B seems apprehensive of her. At the end of 1 minute, E knocks on the wall to signal S to begin a conversation with M. M, meanwhile, has been instructed not to begin talking until S initiates interaction with B. At the end of another minute, S is signaled to initiate interaction with B. At the end of 3 minutes, E knocks to signal the end of the episode. At this signal M leaves the room unobtrusively, leaving her handbag behind on her chair and choosing a moment to leave when B seems occupied either with S or with the toys.

The focus of the observation is on how much and what kind of attention B pays to S, in comparison with the attention he pays to M or to exploration, and on how B accepts S's advances.

Episode 4: Stranger and Baby.   E begins to time the episode as soon as M leaves the room. M, meanwhile, comes to the observation room. As soon as M has gone, S begins to reduce interaction with B, so that B has a chance to notice that M has gone, if, indeed he had not already noticed. If B resumes exploring, S retreats to her chair and sits quietly as M did previously, although she is to respond to any advances B may make. We are primarily interested in the amount of exploring B will undertake in contrast with the amount he did when he was alone with M.

If, however, B cries, S will intervene, trying to distract B with a toy; if this fails to calm him, S will attempt to comfort B by picking him up if he permits and/or by talking to him. If S is successful in comforting B, she then puts him down and again attempts to engage his interest in the toys.

Three minutes are allowed for this episode, although it may be curtailed should B become highly distressed and unresponsive to S's efforts to distract or comfort him. Just before 3 minutes are up (or sooner if the episode is to be curtailed), E cues M to return to the experimental room.

We are interested in the amount and nature of B's exploration in contrast with earlier episodes. We are also interested in B's response to M's departure—crying, search behavior, and any acute distress. B's response to the stranger is also of importance, including his response to being picked up and put down, and any clinging that he does.

Episode 5: Mother and Baby.   M approaches the closed door and speaks outside, loudly enough that B can hear her voice. She pauses a moment, opens the door, and pauses again, to allow B to mobilize a response to her if he is going to. M is instructed to make the baby comfortable, finally settling him on the floor, and interesting him in the toys. Meanwhile S leaves unobtrusively. After 3 minutes, or when it is judged that B is settled enough to be ready for the next episode, M is signaled to leave. She picks a moment (if possible) when

B seems cheerfully occupied with the toys, gets up, puts her handbag on her chair, and goes to the door. At the door she pauses and says "bye-bye" to B and leaves the room, closing the door securely behind her.

In general in this episode we are interested in observing B's response to M after her absence and their interaction after her return.

Episode 6: Baby Alone.   E begins timing when M leaves. Three minutes are allowed for B to explore the room while he is alone. If he cries when M departs, he is given a chance to recover in the hope that he may do some exploring, but if he becomes acutely distressed the episode is curtailed.

We are interested, of course, both in B's exploratory play (if any) when he is left alone in an unfamiliar situation and in his reaction to his mother's departure—crying, search behavior, grumbling vocalizations, tension movements, and so on.

Episode 7: Stranger and Baby.   Just before the end of the 3 minutes (or upon a decision to curtail Episode 6), E cues S to return. S approaches the closed door and speaks outside, loudly enough that B can hear her voice. She pauses a moment, opens the door, and pauses again, to allow B to mobilize a response if he is going to do so. E begins timing Episode 7 as soon as S enters.

If B is crying, S will first attempt to soothe him, picking him up if he will permit it. When and if he calms, she will put him down and attempt to engage him in play. If he gets interested in the toys and begins to play, S will gradually retreat to her chair. If B is not distressed at the time S enters, she invites him to come to her. If B does not come, she approaches B and attempts to initiate play. If he becomes interested in the toys and begins to play with them himself, S will gradually retreat to her chair. In either case, if B signals that he wants interaction or contact with S, she will respond to his wishes, and in general she is to gear her behavior to B's behavior.

In this episode we are interested primarily in B's response to S—how readily he is soothed by her, whether he seeks or accepts contact, whether he will interact with her in play—and in how this response compares with B's response to M in the reunion episodes. Also we are interested to see whether the pull of the toys is strong enough that B permits S to become nonparticipant.

Episode 8: Mother and Baby.[2]   Just before the end of 3 minutes (or upon a decision to curtail Episode 7), E cues M to return. M opens the door and

---

[2]For the first 13 subjects of Sample 1, Episode 8 was terminated as soon as the initial reunion behavior was observed, perhaps after only 1 minute had elapsed. It soon became apparent, however, that this second reunion episode was important in its own right, and thenceforward observation was continued for a standard 3 minutes for subsequent subjects and samples. The brief duration of Episode 8 for the majority of Sample 1, however, made it impossible to use, in this episode for this sample, all of the measures that were used in the rest of the episodes.

pauses a moment before greeting B, giving him an opportunity to respond spontaneously. She then talks to the baby and finally picks him up. Meanwhile S leaves.

The Stranger and Her Behavior

Each of our four samples had a different stranger, and Sample 3 had a different stranger in Session 2 from Session 1. On occasion, substitutes were necessary, so that there were 10 strangers in all. All strangers were female.

The role of stranger is a difficult one. On the one hand, she is expected to refrain from undue intervention in order to permit the baby to play, search for his mother, or even display distress spontaneously. On the other hand, she is instructed in Episode 3 to approach the baby and to attract his attention away from the mother and to the toys, and in the separation episodes to distract or comfort the baby if he is distressed. All strangers to some extent geared their behavior to that of the baby, but they had individual styles in approaching the baby, in interacting with him in play, and in attempting to comfort him if he was distressed. A baby's cries were distressing to all strangers, and consequently it was especially difficult to control, through instruction, just how they should behave in separation episodes.[3] Should these differences in stranger behavior affect substantial differences in infant behavior, this should be reflected in intersample differences in the relevant episodes.

The Mother and Her Behavior

Each mother was instructed in advance about the purpose and procedures of the strange situation and about the role she was to play. This instruction almost invariably took place in the course of a home visit. The mother was then given a mimeographed set of instructions. (See Appendix I.) When she arrived at the laboratory, the instructions were again discussed, if she felt uncertain of them, and she was provided with a small card that summarized the episodes and the cues for which she was to be alert. Adequate advance briefing is considered important, so that the mother does not feel anxious or uncertain about her role in the situation.

The instructions were intended to control the mother's behavior, especially in the preseparation episodes, in which it was desired to see what the baby would do spontaneously and without undue intervention from his mother. It was impossible, however to prevent all individual differences in maternal

---

[3]Initially, for the first 13 cases of Sample 1, there were somewhat more complex instructions for the stranger in Episode 7 (see Ainsworth & Wittig, 1969). But so many infants were distressed in Episode 6 and continued to be distressed in Episode 7 that we shifted to the aforementioned instructions, which corresponded to the way in which the stranger had actually behaved in Episode 7 in respect to the first 13 infants.

behavior from manifesting themselves. Indeed, little effort to control maternal behavior was exerted by the instructions covering the reunion episodes. It was recognized that maternal behavior would be much affected by individual differences in infant behavior, that it would be difficult to provide for such contingencies in the instructions, and that in any event mothers would tend to behave in their own characteristic ways in reunion.

There were two ways in which our instructions to the mother made the situation more artificial than we would have liked for a few infant–mother pairs, although this outcome seems unavoidable if there is to be any attempt at standardization. Some mothers reported feeling unduly constrained in the preseparation episodes. To them it seemed unnatural to put the baby down to play without first introducing him to the toys by playing with him briefly, and indeed their infants tended to look puzzled when the mother sat down in a nonparticipant role. For such infants the strange situation was perhaps stranger than for others. Second, the instructions for Episode 5 specified chiefly that the mother was to reinterest the baby in the toys. It was our distinct impression that some mothers would have spent more time in comforting and reassuring their infants had it not been for this instruction.

Despite the fact that individual differences in maternal behavior were somewhat smoothed out by our instructions, the strange situation yields a surprisingly large amount of information about the mother's role in interaction although it was not intended to do so and although this report does not analyze maternal behavior. On the other hand, differences in maternal behavior, especially in the reunion episodes, required that measures of attachment be based on a scoring system that took into account the contingencies of maternal behavior.

Finally, we must emphasize that no apologies are offered for these difficulties. A tight control of maternal behavior is impossible and indeed undesirable. The compromise represented in our procedures turned out to have effected a reasonable degree of standardization of the situation, while allowing most mothers to behave naturally and fairly comfortably.

Training of Observers

The observers, except for the first two,[4] were trained by apprenticeship. They first watched a number of subjects in the strange situation and listened to experienced observers dictate their narrative reports of the action. Then, in turn, each was permitted to act as O2 and later to check their narrative reports against those of O1. Meanwhile, the prospective observers familiarized themselves with the instructions for coding strange-situation behavior, so that they could appreciate the distinctions that need to be made in regard to the behaviors to be reported.

---

[4]Mary Ainsworth and Barbara Wittig.

In general, observers were instructed to report in as much detail as possible what the baby did and what interaction he had with the mother and with the stranger. Specifically, they were instructed to report the following:

—all locomotion, tracing the baby's progress by noting the identifying numbers of the squares entered;

—the baby's posture and body orientation and changes therein;

—the toys and other objects he reached for, touched, or manipulated; the nature of his manipulation; and whether he put a toy down, dropped it, or threw it;

—any touching or rubbing of his own body or clothing;

—what he looked at, whether at the mother, stranger, toys, door, or other features of the physical environment; whether he glanced, watched, or stared; and whether he pointedly refused to look, or looked away;

—smiles and at what or whom the baby looked when he smiled;

—vocalizations and at what or at whom the baby looked when he vocalized;

—crying of all kinds and degrees, whether unhappy noises, cryface, fussing, clear-cut crying, or screaming, and when crying ceased;

—oral behavior, including putting objects (or fingers or thumb) into the mouth, or sucking or chewing them;

—in addition to looking, vocalizing, and smiling, any interaction with either mother or stranger across a distance, such as pointing to toys, showing toys, or offering toys;

—any locomotor approach behavior to mother or stranger, whether it was speedy or slow or interrupted, whether it was spontaneous or invited by the adult, whether it was partial or ended in close proximity or actual physical contact;

—any avoidance behavior, either of mother or stranger, especially upon the entrance or approach of either figure, including moving away, turning away, or looking away;

—if an adult and baby came into physical contact, who initiated the contact; whether the baby merely touched the adult or clambered up or held on; and whether the adult merely steadied the baby or picked him up;

—if the baby was picked up, did he cling, sink in, or hold on, or did he resist contact by pushing away, hitting, kicking, stiffening, or squirming to get down;

—if he was put down, who initiated the put-down, and did the baby protest it or actively resist release;

—initial response to the entrances of the mother or stranger were especially noted—whether the baby smiled, vocalized, cried, reached, leaned, or approached, or whether he ignored or avoided the person; similarly responses to the approach of either mother or stranger were especially noted;

—any angry or resistant behavior in any context, whether it is pushing away, throwing away, or dropping toys offered by an adult, or resistance when physical contact is offered, or tantrums;

—during separation episodes, whether the baby looked at, approached, banged on, or tried to open the door, and whether he looked at, approached, or touched his mother's empty chair or her handbag.

Finally, the observers were advised to dictate as quickly as possible and to keep talking even when little new was occurring. Advice to "talk like a sports-caster" seemed helpful to apprentice observers.

Number of Observers and Their Reliability

The observers differed from one sample to another. (See Table 4.) For Sample 2 there was only one observer. For the other samples there were always two observers, paired in a variety of combinations. For Sample 3 there were particularly many observers, both because there were two sessions of the strange situation and because emphasis was placed on training graduate students in the strange-situation procedure. Those who were to be observers of the second session for any given infant, however, were not even present at the first session.

A reliability check was undertaken with the four subjects observed jointly by Observers A and D. For this purpose their separately dictated accounts were coded separately for four frequency measures: locomotor exploration, exploratory manipulation, visual exploration, and crying. Product-moment coefficients of .99 were found for each of the exploratory behaviors, and one of .98 for crying. Further tests of interobserver agreement were not made, because (except for Sample 2, which had only one observer) our practice was to base all measures on the consolidated reports of the two observers.

Transcriptions

The final transcription of the dictated accounts brought together the accounts of two observers. Each account was divided into separate paragraphs, one for each 15-second time interval, with the paragraphs for the two observers side

TABLE 4
Observers for the Four Samples

Sample	Number of Observers	Identity of Observers
1	4	A, B, C, D
2	1	D
3	10	A, E, F, G, H, I, J, K, L, M
4	6	F, G, H, I, N, O

by side to facilitate comparison. The only problem in preparing the transcriptions was to ascertain when one episode ended and the next began. The following rules were adopted. Episode 5 began with the entrance of the mother and ended when she went out the door. Episode 7 began with the entrance of the stranger and ended with the entrance of the mother.

Film Records

A series of still photographs were taken of the first 13 infants in Sample 1, shot through the one-way mirrors. Cinematic records were made of the last 10 infants in Sample 1 and all of Sample 3 through a plate-glass photography port. It was impossible, however, to avoid breaks in continuity, for even with a camera equipped with an electric drive mechanism and with a cumbersome chamber holding a 400-foot reel of film, only 10 minutes of a 20-minute situation could be filmed. Furthermore, except when the infant and adult were near to each other, the camera could not pick up the behavior of both participants in an interaction. For these reasons the continuously dictated accounts of the observers were more useful than the film records for research purposes, although the latter are useful for illustrative purposes.

Videotape equipment was not available, but even had it been, dictated accounts would still have been used as a supplement to the videotape records in order to record sequences of interaction that the videotape could not pick up.

3 Measures and Methods of Assessment

INTRODUCTION

In the analysis of data, three kinds of measures were used: (1) incidence of specific behaviors (or combinations of behaviors) in specific episodes, indicated by the percentage of infants who manifested each; (2) frequency measures; and (3) special scores for dimensions of interactive behavior. These measures were useful in describing normative trends across episodes. They proved less useful in representing individual differences in strange-situation behavior than another method of assessment—(4) classification of infants according to the patterning of their behaviors. The classificatory system that reflects the organization of behavior in relationship to the mother may be seen in Chapters 6, 7, 8, 9, and 11 to yield robust, stable, and psychologically significant assessment of individual differences.

PERCENTAGE MEASURES OF BEHAVIOR

An important feature of the data analysis is to ascertain the percentage of babies in the total sample who show each specific behavior in each episode of the strange situation, or specific combinations of behaviors. It would be redundant here to list all the behaviors and behavioral combinations that were examined, for these are implicit in the discussion of findings. In general, the definitions of behaviors are implicit in the definitions included in the Appendices, but where any doubt might arise, the definitions are given in the context of the report of findings.

FREQUENCY MEASURES

Two types of frequency measure were used. One was preferred for behaviors that were discrete and of brief duration; the other for behaviors of extended duration or for those that consisted of a continuous sequence of coordinated separate behaviors. The first type was a simple frequency count of number of times the behavior was emitted in a given episode (or, in the case of Episode 3, in each of three subepisodes). This type of measure was used for smiles and vocalizations. The second type of frequency measure was based on the 15-second time intervals into which the narrative records were divided. For each behavior or class of behavior measured thus, the score was the sum of the time intervals in any given episode in which the behavior occurred, whether it occured continuously, intermittently, or momentarily. The standard length of an episode was 3 minutes, and therefore the highest obtainable frequency score was 12. If an episode were either longer or shorter than 3 minutes, the frequency scores were prorated to make them equivalent to those obtained from a 3-minute episode.

It is obvious that the measure of frequency per 15-second interval is a substitute for precise measure of duration, which was not possible to obtain with our method of recording. (See Omark & Marvin, 1978). The degree of error introduced by the use of this substitute was deemed tolerable, however, for behaviors like crying and exploration. In the separation episodes once crying had begun it tended to continue, and exploratory behavior once it had stopped tended not to recur. In the reunion episodes once crying had stopped it tended not to recur. In all episodes exploratory behavior tended to operate over continuous blocks of time rather than to be emitted in sporadic "bursts" like smiles and vocalizations.

As a preliminary step to obtaining the frequency measures, the behavior shown by an infant in each 15-second time interval in each episode was coded according to a coding system described fully in Appendix II. The specific kinds of behavior coded were as follows: locomotion, body movement, body posture, hand movements, visual regard, adult contact behavior, infant contact behavior, crying, vocalization, oral behavior, and smiling. The coding yields a condensed sequential description of the behavior of an infant in each episode of the strange situation. It also lends itself to ready tabulation of the absolute frequency of behaviors. The original coding system was more complex than the one now in use; it attempted to deal in more detail with the behaviors shown by the infant in interaction with others. It emerged, however, that simple frequency measures were inadequate to deal with the complexities of interactive behavior. Nevertheless, some vestiges of the coding of such behavior remain for descriptive purposes and to aid in the use of the coding sheet as a convenient index to the narrative protocol.

Detailed instructions for tabulation of the frequency coding are also given in Appendix II. The tabulation yielded the following measures for each episode of the strange situation.

Exploratory Locomotion. This refers to locomotion that is clearly in service of getting to the toys or some other aspect of the physical environment in order to explore it, or that seems undertaken for the mere sake of the activity itself. It differs from the measures of locomotion and mobility used by others (e.g., Cox & Campbell, 1968; Maccoby & Feldman, 1972) in that it excludes locomotion with social, interactive, or distress implications, such as approaching a person, following, searching for the mother during the separation episodes, moving away from a person to avoid her, or moving about while highly distressed. For this analysis, as well as for the other two measures of exploration, we used the frequency per 15-second interval. In the case of episodes curtailed because of crying, it was assumed that no further exploratory behavior—whether locomotor, manipulative, or visual—would have occurred had the episode lasted the full 3 minutes.

Exploratory Manipulation. This refers, similarly, to hand movements that are clearly exploratory, and is intended to exclude hand movements that are used in social interaction or in physical contact, or those that are expressive gestures, whether with communicative intent or not. The coding system attempts to distinguish between fine and gross manipulation. With 1-year-olds, however, this distinction was found to be difficult and seemingly of little significance. Therefore, the measure used in our analysis is the total measure of exploratory manipulation.

Visual Exploration. Like the other exploratory measures, visual exploration refers to exploration of the toys or other aspects of the physical environment. It excludes looking at persons or looking at objects that in the separation environment may be considered to be of interest because they are associated with the mother rather than for their own intrinsic interest—for example, the door through which the mother departed, the chair in which she previously sat, or the handbag that she left behind her.

Visual Orientation. There are three scores representing visual orientation: looking at the mother, looking at the stranger, and looking at the toys or at some other aspect of the physical environment. The third score is identical with the visual-exploration score. Within any episode or when comparing one episode with another, it is possible to ascertain what proportion of the baby's visual attention goes to the physical environment in contrast to persons, and to the mother in contrast with the stranger.

For this analysis we used the frequency-per-15-second-interval measure, because looking at aspects of the physical environment tends, like other forms of exploratory behavior, to be of extended duration, even though looks at persons—especially looks at the mother—tend, like smiles and vocalizations, to be momentary and sporadic. In the episode most important for comparison of orientation to mother versus stranger—Episode 3—Bretherton and Ainsworth (1974) used absolute frequency of looks. This latter measure also introduced some distortion, because looks at the stranger were often stares and of longer duration than the glances at the mother. Nevertheless both measures of frequency yielded essentially the same findings when comparison of the two target figures was the issue.

Crying. A distinction has been made between "real crying"—which includes screaming and fussing as well as crying, and includes intermittent and isolated cries as well as continuous crying—and "minimal crying," in which there is a cryface without vocalization or unhappy vocalization, or protest without a cryface. This distinction has descriptive utility, but in our analyses we have used a total crying score, including both. Babies who cry minimally in regard to intensity also cry relatively infrequently in the strange situation, so that little or no information is lost by using the total crying score. Here our measure was frequency-per-15-second interval. In the case of episodes that were curtailed because of crying, it was assumed that the baby would have continued to cry had the episode lasted for the full 3 minutes.

Smiling. Although most interactive behaviors could not be dealt with meaningfully in terms of frequency measures, smiling has been included among them, as indeed are looking (visual orientation), vocalization, and crying. There are three measures of smiling: smiles clearly directed toward the mother, smiles clearly directed toward the stranger, and total number of smiles including those not clearly directed toward any person. These three measures were expressed as the absolute number of smiles.

Vocalization. It is more difficult to ascertain whether a vocalization is directed toward a person than to judge whether a smile is so directed. Nevertheless, the frequency of vocalization was handled in the same way as the frequency of smiling—the number of vocalizations clearly directed to the mother, the number clearly directed toward the stranger, and the total number of vocalizations including those not clearly directed toward any person. These were expressed as the absolute number of vocalizations.

Oral Behavior. It is assumed that, in a 1-year-old, oral behavior in a situation such as the strange situation is unlikely to be either nutritive or exploratory. It is assumed to be "autoerotic," tension reducing, or, in ethological terminology, a "displacement" activity that occurs in a situation in which two or more incompatible behavioral systems are simultaneously activated (Bowlby, 1969). Therefore, it is of interest to compare one episode with another in regard to frequency of oral behavior. To be sure, sucking and chewing are not the only kinds of autoerotic or displacement activities that occurred, but they were the only ones that occurred commonly enough to be represented in our frequency measures. This class of behavior was scored in terms of frequency per 15-second interval.

Intercoder Agreement in Regard to Frequency Measures

Throughout this study our major efforts toward reliability have been: (1) to have all measures based on coding undertaken by at least two coders working independently, with any discrepancies resolved in conference; and (2) on training of personnel. Under these circumstances, conventional assessments of intercoder agreement provide a very conservative estimate of the reliability of the measures actually used in the statistical treatment of the data. The coding of frequency measures is very straightforward. When discrepancies between coders arise, they are almost invariably due to carelessness on the part of one coder or the other and are easily corrected by checking back to the protocols themselves. Nevertheless, because Bell in her 1970 study (which yielded Sample 2) had to work alone, a check was made of the agreement between her coding and that of a then-more-experienced coder (MDSA). Eight cases were selected at random for the reliability check. Product-moment reliability coefficients for four frequency measures obtained by these two independent coders were as follows: exploratory locomotion, .99; exploratory manipulation, .93; visual exploration, .98; and crying, .99. Connell (1974) and Rosenberg (1975) independently coded the frequency measures for 23 subjects, counting as a "match" scores that were not more than one whole number apart for an entire episode. A reliability of .950 was obtained (459 matches/483 scores).

SCORING OF INTERACTIVE BEHAVIOR

Although the frequency measures and the percentage measures play a role in the analysis of data, they are not adequate to represent certain of the more significant infant behaviors, especially those involved in interpersonal interaction. To be sure, the frequency measures include measures of various behaviors commonly assumed to be attachment behaviors—smiling, vocalization, and looking. These measures, whether considered separately or together, do not provide an adequate assessment of infant attachment behavior directed toward the mother, to say nothing of sociable behavior directed toward the stranger. The "percentage measures" of behavior are of descriptive value when dealing with normative trends across the various episodes of the strange situation, and these can and do deal with combinations of behaviors. Percentage measures do not, however, lend themselves to the kind of quantification that is useful when one wishes to assess the interrelationships between behavioral measures (as, for example, in multivariate analyses) or the interrelationships between strange-situation behavior and either infant behavior or maternal behavior at home.

One of the major difficulties in relying upon frequency assessments of behaviors implicated in interpersonal interaction is that (perhaps especially in the last quarter of the first year, or after a baby's behavior has become goal-corrected—to rely on the concept of Bowlby, 1969) behaviors that are superficially quite different may have a certain degree of interchangeability. If this is the case, then assessments based on specific behaviors separately considered may well fail to reflect the true state of affairs.

Furthermore, in any naturalistic situation and even in our laboratory situation, in which the behavior of the adults (mother and stranger) was only partially controlled through instructions, the behavior shown by an infant toward another person can scarcely be assessed without considering the context provided by that person's behavior. Such considerations wreak havoc with comparisons across individuals or across situations, unless one can find some way of taking into account the contingencies of interchangeability of behavior and of reciprocal behavior (or lack of it) in the partners in the interpersonal transactions in question.

These difficulties were particularly apparent in the reunion episodes of the strange situation in which the meager instructions to the mother permitted much latitude in behavior and in which interchangeability of behaviors was particularly conspicuous in the case of the infant. Furthermore, the need to overcome the difficulties and to make accurate assessment of infant "interactive" behavior in the reunion episodes was increased by our emerging conviction that it was precisely the reunion episodes that afforded the most discriminating occasion for assessment.

Let us examine some considerations. It seems significant, for example, to note whether a baby approaches his mother when she returns, and whether he does so immediately or only after a delay—or whether he does so only after an invitation from her or fails to do so despite such an invitation. It is of interest whether he merely seeks increased proximity, or whether he seems to want close physical contact. If the latter, he may clamber up on his own initiative, or he may merely reach as a signal to elicit his mother's help in gaining contact. On the other hand, he may not approach at all, but merely redouble his cries when his mother enters, obviously wanting her—and indeed, in most such cases, the mother goes quickly to the distressed baby and picks him up without delay.

Ainsworth and Wittig (1969), reporting on the first 13 cases of Sample 1, did not attempt to devise measures of interactive behavior that might take into account the various combinations of infant and maternal behaviors. Rather they chiefly relied upon percentage measures. So did Bretherton and Ainsworth (1974), who focused on infant behavior toward the stranger. Ainsworth and Bell (1970), however, based their report of interpersonal behavior on a then-new set of measures that we report here.

The first step toward analysing individual differences in strange-situation behavior was to devise a classification of infants into groups showing similarities in the ways in which their behavior was organized. In the earliest attempt at classification (Ainsworth & Wittig, 1969), first attention was given to the presence or absence of distress in the separation episodes; but subsequently the reunion episodes were perceived to be more significant. In the course of refining the classificatory system (first reported by Ainsworth, Bell and Stayton, 1971, and described later in this chapter) it was possible to identify four dimensions of behavior that seemed crucial in distinguishing the various classificatory groups and subgroups.

These four dimensions were: proximity- and contact-seeking behavior, contact-maintaining behavior, avoidance, and resistance. Although behavior to the mother was of especial interest, the same dimensions were implicit in behavior toward the stranger. The scoring system therefore comprehended both and was therefore applicable to all episodes save Episode 1, which was merely introductory, and Episode 6, when the baby was alone.

For each of these four behavioral variables, the protocols of 56 infants (Samples 1 and 2) were examined, and "behavioral items" were extracted from them. A behavioral item consisted of all the behavior in an episode that each child showed relevant to each of the behavioral variables, as that behavior was directed to the mother or, in a separate record, to the stranger. Each behavioral item was typed on a slip of paper, ready to be sorted. Each variable was then dealt with separately, without regard for the episode in which it was shown or for whether it was directed toward mother or stranger.

First, for proximity and contact seeking, for example, the behavioral items were sorted into seven piles, each representing a point on the proximity- and contact-seeking dimension. The dimension was defined in terms of the degree of initiative and active effort implicit in the specific proximity- or contact-promoting behavior displayed. Point 7 included those behavioral items in which the baby had shown most active initiative in seeking proximity to an adult—approaching without delay and without needing to be invited, and approaching fully to make contact, clambering up on the adult without needing to elicit her cooperation. Point 1 included all items in which there seemed to be no overt effort to gain proximity and no behavior that seemed to be a clear-cut signal inviting the adult's approach. Point 2 included behavioral episodes in which a baby made an "intention movement" toward a person—a slight and incomplete approach. Points 6, 5, 4, and 3 represented various degrees of active initiative as contrasted with mere signalling.

The considerations entering into the disposition of a behavioral item to one point or another included: (1) the degree of activity and initiative of the behavior; (2) promptness of the behavior; (3) frequency of the behavior; and (4) duration of the behavior. Thus, for example, active approaching was considered a stronger proximity-promoting behavior than either reaching or a directed cry signal. An immediate approach was considered stronger than a delayed approach. Several approaches, other things being equal, were considered stronger than one approach. Or, to turn to contact-maintaining behavior, it was considered stronger if contact lasted 2 minutes than if it lasted for 1 minute, or for only 30 seconds.

Furthermore, the sorting had to consider the behavior of the adult. Thus, for example, some mothers picked the baby up, whereas others did not; and those that did might do so either immediately or only after a delay. A baby whose mother was promptly responsive to his desire for contact could scarcely be given the highest score, which was reserved for infants who achieved contact entirely on their own initiative; on the other hand, though, his active initiative in eliciting maternal behavior had to be given due weight. Similarly, in regard to contact-maintaining behavior, highest scores were given to infants who persistently resisted attempts of the mother to put them down. But if the mother held the baby for a long period and attempted to put him down only after he was fully soothed and reassured, then he had little opportunity to resist release. In such instances it was assumed that the baby somehow signaled to his mother his desire for continuing contact while she held him, perhaps by clinging or by "sinking in", and thus if the contact was indeed maintained for a prolonged period, the baby was given a high score despite his lack of opportunity to resist release.

The seven-point scales resulting from this sorting procedure are shown in Appendix III. The behaviors that define each point of each scale are drawn from the actual behaviors shown by the infants of Samples 1 and 2. It was clearly impossible to comprehend in the scale every degree and combination of behavior that might be met empirically in subsequent data collection. Therefore, when scoring the behaviors of Samples 3 and 4, the scorer might not find a precise match for the behavior of a given child in the behavioral definitions of the scale points, and would have to find the best match that he could or assign an interpolated score.

The initial system for scoring interactive behavior included a fifth behavior variable that has not heretofore been mentioned. Although search for the mother in the separation episodes had not entered into the classificatory system as a differentiating variable, it lent itself to scoring by the method described above. A sixth variable—distance interaction—was added to the scoring system much later. This variable did in fact enter into the classificatory system as distinguishing between subgroups, but had not been dealt with initially.

Although the instructions for scoring these six behavioral variables are presented fully in Appendix III, here we give a brief indication of what is covered by each.

Proximity and Contact Seeking.   As previously stated, this variable refers to the degree of active initiative a baby shows in seeking physical contact with or proximity to another person.

Contact Maintaining.   This refers to the degree of active initiative a baby exerts in order to maintain physical contact with a person, once such contact is achieved. The highest scores are given to infants who repeatedly resist release and who, as a consequence, succeed in maintaining physical contact throughout most of the episode in question. Resisting release implies intensified clinging when the adult attempts to put the baby down (or merely to shift his position), or turning back immediately to clamber up again when put down. Mere protest, without active effort to maintain contact, is scored lower.

Resistance.   The highest scores are given to babies who persistently manifest intense angry and/or resistant behavior to an adult. The resistance is shown by pushing away from, striking out at, or squirming to get down from an adult who has offered contact, or by pushing away, throwing away, or otherwise rejecting toys through which an adult attempts to mediate interaction. The highest scores imply an obviously angry emotional tone, although in lower scores the resistant behavior may be seemingly without negative affect. Resistant behavior is not incompatible with proximity seeking or contact maintaining. An angry, resistant infant may nevertheless strongly seek to gain and to maintain contact, although such a combination suggests ambivalence.

Avoidance.   As reported by Ainsworth and Bell (1970), some babies actively avoid proximity and interaction with their mothers in the reunion episodes, in which a common response is to seek closer proximity or contact. Highest scores are given to infants who persistently ignore their mothers, continuing to play without acknowledging mother's return despite her effort to invite the baby's approach. Somewhat lower scores are given to infants who mingle greeting responses with moving away, turning away, or looking away. Appendix III presents parallel scales for mother and for stranger, although it is not meant to imply thereby that the behavior has the same dynamics for these two figures.

Search.   When a baby is separated from his mother, two major classes of attachment behavior may be activated—crying and search. Crying constitutes a proximity-promoting signal—one that instructions to the mothers tended to make ineffective, except insofar as the episode would be curtailed if the infant seemed intensely distressed. Crying behavior was assessed in terms of the frequency measures described in an earlier section. Searching for the mother did not lend itself to a frequency measure, however. Search behavior is defined as behavior in which the baby, through means other than crying, attempts to regain proximity to his mother. The strange-situation procedure prevents a baby from succeeding in his search; so the most active behavior that an infant can manifest is going to the closed door (through which his mother left) without delay, attempting to open it, and furthermore remaining oriented toward the door throughout most of the rest of the separation episode. Some babies, who were scored lower, show a toned-down version of this behavior by merely looking at the door either persistently or frequently. Others manifest search behavior by approaching (or merely looking at) the place associated with the mother—her chair.

Distance Interaction.   Some babies who are clearly attached to their mothers do not show heightened proximity or contact seeking in the reunion episodes, but rather show heightened interest in interacting with the mother across a distance—smiling or "talking" to her, pointing to things of interest, showing her toys, or offering them to her across a distance. In 1-year-olds this kind of reaction is substantially less frequent than either proximity seeking or avoidance or resistance, whereas in 2-, 3-, and 4-year-olds it occurs more often (Blehar, 1974; Maccoby & Feldman, 1972; Marvin, 1972). Nevertheless, even in this study of 1-year-olds it seemed desirable to include among our scores of interactive behaviors a measure of infant initiative in distance interaction.

Interscorer Agreement for Measures of Interactive Behavior

The scoring of interactive behaviors is obviously more complex than the routine tabulations involved in coding the frequency measures, and requires more judgment on the part of the scorer. This being so, it was necessary to demonstrate that a satisfactory degree of interscorer agreement could be achieved. Several formal assessments of interscorer agreement are reported here.

First, 14 protocols were selected from among those of Sample 1 to provide a full range of the behaviors in question. The degree of agreement between two independent scorers for behaviors directed to the mother, assessed by reliability (rho) coefficients, was as follows: proximity- and contact-seeking behavior, .93; contact maintaining, .97; resistance, .96; avoidance, .93; and search, .94.

Second, interscorer agreement for the two sessions of the 24 subjects of Sample 3 was found for six pairs of graduate-student judges in the course of their training in strange-situation procedure. Each pair dealt with six protocols—somewhat too few to represent an adequate range of scores in all variables. Agreement was assessed for behavior both to the mother and to the stranger in each relevant episode separately. The median coefficients of agreement for five variables were as follows: Proximity and contact seeking, .90; contact maintaining, .85; resistance, .88; avoidance, .75; and search, .87.

Third, Main (1973) reports the agreement for two independent scorers of two behaviors directed to the mother for Sample 4: resistance, .94 and avoidance, .93.

Finally, Connell (1974) and Rosenberg (1975) independently scored the interactive measures for 23 subjects, using a statistic consisting of the proportion of matches (i.e., less than one whole number) for four of the scales (excluding search) for behavior directed at mother and stranger in all relevant episodes considered separately. The overall index of interscorer agreement was .876.

The measure of distance interaction was devised later than the other scales and was assessed separately for interscorer agreement. Protocols for the total sample of 106 infants were scored by one research assistant, but in the course of training and checking the scoring of that assistant, one of us (MCB) independently scored 92 protocols. The correlation between the two sets of scores was .85.

In conclusion, a satisfactory degree of interscorer agreement can be achieved for these scales. It may be noted, however, that training and experience is required before a high level of interscorer agreement can be achieved. In our opinion such training is particularly important for the scoring of avoidant behavior. In the case of Sample 3, which was scored by students in training, the degree of reliability of the scores is better than the coefficients of interscorer agreement would indicate, because the final scores used were settled in conference, with any interscorer discrepancies resolved.

CLASSIFICATION OF INFANTS IN TERMS OF THEIR STRANGE-SITUATION BEHAVIOR

As implied earlier, classification of infants in terms of the patterning of their behavior in the strange situation preceded the identification of the dimensions in terms of which their interactions with the mother and with the stranger could be described. Indeed, classification was the first procedure that we used to help us make sense of the enormously complex variety of behaviors manifested by 1-year-olds in interaction with their mothers in the strange situation.

Contemporary psychologists tend to be biased against classificatory procedures, deeming them not only subjective and hence unreliable but also dedicated to a belief in a more or less rigid typological concept of the way in which human behavior is organized, with implications of discontinuity in the various quantitative dimensions that may be implicit in the description of types or categories. It is not in this spirit that we offer a classificatory system. On the contrary we view it as a first step toward grasping the organization of complex behavioral data. We agree with Hinde (1974) that one must first describe and classify when one sets out to study natural phenomena:

> Description and classification may not seem very difficult tasks, but their neglect hampered many aspects of psychology for half a century. ... This descriptive phase, essential in the development of every science, was bypassed by those experimental psychologists who attempted to model their strategies on classical physics. These workers overlooked the fact that classical physics was a special case in that its subject matter—falling apples, the apparent bending of sticks in water, floating logs—were everyday events, so that the descriptive phase was part of common experience, and not especially a job for the scientists. Of course, the way people behave is also part of everyday experience, but to describe behavior precisely is much more difficult than appears at first sight [p. 5].

Although Hinde was directing his comments toward the classification of behavior—for example, classifying behaviors into systems in terms of their common outcome—his comments also seem relevant to classification of individuals in accordance with the different patterns of behavior they manifest in comparable situations. He goes on to caution us, however, that there are limitations to classificatory systems. If pressed far enough, they do not work. The categories are tools, not "absolutes."

Two ways in which a classification of patterns of behavior can be a useful tool are: (1) to identify the chief behavioral dimensions in terms of which the groups so classified differ; and (2) to raise the issue of how such disparate patterns of behavior happened to develop. The identification of dimensions of difference between classificatory groups may lead to a quantification of such dimensions and hence to a more precise description of individual differences in terms of new variables not previously considered relevant. This was indeed the case in the present study, for the primary step of classification led to the development of the measures described in the preceding section.

As for the second issue, one's immediate response to a perception of patterning of behavior is to entertain the notion that there is some good reason that the component behaviors should be interrelated in this way— perhaps because they tend to serve the same function or have a common cause or interacting sets of causal influences. When faced with a species-characteristic patterning, the answer may be that this is the nature of the beast—which merely pushes the questions of why and how into a search to understand phylogenetic development, or the processes of evolution. When faced with a perception of patterns of individual variations, one can also attribute them to basic genetic differences between individuals. Because classificatory systems—usually termed typologies—have indeed appealed to ingrained genetic predispositions as explanation for patterning, it has become all too common to believe that this is characteristic of all. Another approach, which also should be explored, is to examine the developmental histories of the individuals in question for common antecedent experiences that may be hypothesized to have an influence in the development of similar patterns in one group of individuals that distinguish them from other groups of individuals who have other patterns. This is the way we have chosen to approach the issue of patterning. (The reader is referred to Chapters 7 and 8, in which differences in maternal and infant behavior at home during the first year are related to differences in strange-situation behavior patterns at the end of that year.)

Because the qualitative distinctions implicit in our classificatory system yielded significant quantitative dimensions, it might be asked why classification is not supplanted, instead of being merely supplemented, by quantitative measures. There are three reasons why we have chosen to retain classification. The first, and perhaps most important, is that the definitions of classificatory groups retain the picture of patterns of behavior, which tend to become lost in—or at least difficult to retrieve from—the quantification process. (This becomes evident in Chapter 6, which deals with the discriminant-function analysis of the three main classificatory groups.)

Second, we would be foolish to believe that the dimensions that we have so far subjected to quantification take into account all the behaviors that are important components of the patterning of individual differences in strange-situation behavior not only in this sample but also in other samples drawn from other populations. Although there may be themes common to a wide variety of samples, our sample of 106 1-year-olds cannot exhaust all possible variations on the common themes. A classificatory system can remain flexible, with the possibility of refining classificatory criteria in the light of further knowledge or, indeed, the possibility of elaboration in order to accommodate new patterns into new groups or subgroups. To abandon the classificatory system in favor of our present set of component behavioral scores (or in favor of the discriminant weights, which is discussed in Chapter 6) would freeze our knowledge in its present state.

Third, let us return to the issue of understanding why and how the patternings arose. We believe that the patternings described and differentiated within a classificatory system keep this issue to the forefront rather than burying it in a welter of refined statistics. It is perhaps a reflection of our own modest level of expertise that we so believe, but it seems that a preoccupation with measurement may lead one to forget that this is a tool and not an end in itself. Because the classificatory system was a useful tool in achieving a beginning of understanding, we wish to retain it in the belief that it will continue to be a useful tool in future research, supplemented but not supplanted by quantitative efforts. Ainsworth and Wittig (1969) made the first, relatively crude classification of 1-year-olds' strange-situation behavior. When examining individual patterns of the first 13 infants of Sample 1, they found the presence or absence of separation distress to be the most conspicuous way in which differences might be ordered. They used it, therefore, in classifying infants into three loose groups. Not wishing to assign descriptive labels at this point, they called the groups A, B, and C. Group-A infants showed minimal disturbance in the separation episodes, whereas Group-B infants were distressed by separation. Even in this first attempt at classification, one dimension (i.e., crying in the separation episodes) proved insufficient, for Group-C babies were distinguished from Group B, even though they, too, were distressed by separation, in terms of the "maladaptive" nature of their behavior.

After 10 more infants had been added to Sample 1, it seemed wise to undertake a more careful and systematic classification. Working with the protocols of the total sample of 23 infants, we began by grouping infants whose behavior in all episodes was alike in as many respects as possible. This purely empirical exercise yielded seven clusters of infants. Similarities between the clusters were then sought, resulting in three main groups of infants, which we again designated as Groups A, B, and C. The seven clusters were retained as subgroups—two in each of Group A and Group C, and three in Group B.

The most conspicuous feature of the new Group A was avoidance of the mother in the reunion episodes, although many other behavioral features were common to the infants so classified, including minimal crying in the separation episodes. Only one of the infants classified by Ainsworth and Wittig (1969) in Group A was retained in the new Group A, together with five of the new subsample. The four infants originally classed in Group C were retained in the new Group C, and none of the new subsample were so classified. Instead of the loose designation of "maladaptive," it was now perceived that Group-C infants shared, in addition to strong interest in proximity to and contact with the mother in the reunion episodes, a tendency to manifest angry resistance to the mother upon reunion. The new Group B consisted of 13 infants, including three previously classified by Ainsworth and Wittig in Group A, five previously classified in Group B, and five of the new subsample. Although not all of the new Group-B infants were distressed in the separation episodes, they shared a manifest interest in gaining proximity to and contact (or at least interaction) with their mothers in the reunion episodes, without evidence of antithetical behaviors, such as avoidance or resistance. The criteria for classification were then prepared in detail, on the basis of the behavioral similarities (and differences) that had led to the original sorting into subgroups and groups.

Before giving these criteria, however, two further steps must be reported. When Bell (1970) had observed her 33 subjects in the strange situation (Sample 2) she applied this new classificatory system to them. It proved applicable in all cases, except that she specified a further subgroup of Group B (Subgroup B₄) in order to accommodate three of her sample. The same classificatory system was later used without change for the classification of infants in Samples 3 and 4. All but one of the 50 additional infants were accommodated in existing subgroups—and she was eventually classified in Group A, without being assigned to a subgroup. It may be noted that in the criteria for classification that follow, the emphasis has shifted from behavior in the separation episodes to behavior relevant to the mother in the reunion episodes—not because of preconceived theoretical convictions but because behavior in the reunion episodes contributed the most convincing evidence of clustering behaviors, in contrast to a continuous distribution along one or even two major dimensions.

Criteria for Classification

Group A:

—Conspicuous avoidance of proximity to or interaction with the mother in the reunion episodes. Either the baby ignores his mother on her return, greeting her casually if at all, or, if there is approach and/or a less casual greeting, the baby tends to mingle his welcome with avoidance responses— turning away, moving past, averting the gaze, and the like.

—Little or no tendency to seek proximity to or interaction or contact with the mother, even in the reunion episodes.

—If picked up, little or no tendency to cling or to resist being released.

—On the other hand, little or no tendency toward active resistance to contact or interaction with the mother, except for probable squirming to get down if indeed the baby is picked up.

—Tendency to treat the stranger much as the mother is treated, although perhaps with less avoidance.

—Either the baby is not distressed during separation, or the distress seems to be due to being left alone rather than to his mother's absence. For most, distress does not occur when the stranger is present, and any distress upon being left alone tends to be alleviated when the stranger returns.

Subgroup A₁

Conspicuous avoidance of the mother in the reunion episodes, which is likely to consist of ignoring her altogether, although there may be some pointed looking away, turning away, or moving away.

If there is a greeting when the mother enters, it tends to be a mere look or smile.

Either the baby does not approach his mother upon reunion, or the approach is "abortive" with the baby going past his mother, or it tends to occur only after much coaxing.

If picked up, the baby shows little or no contact-maintaining behavior. He tends not to cuddle in; he looks away; and he may squirm to get down.

Subgroup A₂

The baby shows a mixed response to his mother on reunion, with some tendency to greet and to approach, intermingled with a marked tendency to turn or move away from her, move past her, avert the gaze from her, or ignore her. Thus there may be moderate proximity seeking, combined with strong proximity avoiding.

If he is picked up, the baby may cling momentarily; if he is put down, he may protest or resist momentarily; but there is also a tendency to squirm to be put down, to turn the face away when being held, and other signs of mixed feelings.

Group B:

—The baby wants either proximity and contact with his mother or interaction with her, and he actively seeks it, especially in the reunion episodes.

—If he achieves contact, he seeks to maintain it, and either resists release or at least protests if he is put down.

—The baby responds to his mother's return in the reunion episodes with more than a casual greeting—either with a smile or a cry or a tendency to approach.

—Little or no tendency to resist contact or interaction with his mother.

—Little or no tendency to avoid his mother in the reunion episodes.

—He may or may not be friendly with the stranger, but he is clearly more interested in interaction and/or contact with his mother than with the stranger.

—He may or may not be distressed during the separation episodes, but if he is distressed this is clearly related to his mother's absence and not merely to being alone. He may be somewhat comforted by the stranger, but it is clear that he wants his mother.

Subgroup B₁

The baby greets his mother, smiling upon her return, and shows strong initiative in interaction with her across a distance, although he does not especially seek proximity to or physical contact with her.

If picked up, he does not especially seek to maintain contact.

He may mingle some avoiding behavior (turning away or looking away) with interactive behavior, but he shows little or no resistant behavior and, in general, seems not to have feelings as mixed as an A_2 baby.

He is likely to show little or no distress in the separation episodes.

Subgroup B_2

The baby greets his mother upon reunion, tends to approach her, and seems to want contact with her, but to a lesser extent than a B_3 baby. Some B_2 babies seek proximity in the preseparation episodes, but not again until Episode 8, and then perhaps only after some delay.

The B_2 baby may show some proximity avoiding, especially in Episode 5, but this gives way to proximity seeking in Episode 8, thus distinguishing him from the A_2 baby.

Although he accepts contact if he is picked up, he does not cling especially, and does not conspicuously resist release.

On the other hand, he shows little or no resistance to contact or interaction, and in general shows less sign of mixed feelings than A_2 babies.

He tends to show little distress during the separation episodes.

He resembles a B_1 infant, except that he is more likely to seek proximity to his mother.

Subgroup B_3

The baby actively seeks physical contact with his mother, and when he gains it he is conspicuous for attempting to maintain it, actively resisting her attempts to release him. Most B_3 babies show their strongest proximity-seeking and contact-maintaining behavior in Episode 8, but some do so in Episode 5 and are so distressed in the second separation episode that they cannot mobilize active proximity seeking and resort to signaling. Occasionally, a baby who seems especially secure in his relationship with his mother will be content with mere interaction with and proximity to her, without seeking to be held.

At the same time, the B_3 baby may be distinguished from other groups and subgroups by the fact that he shows little or no sign of either avoiding or resisting proximity to or contact or interaction with his mother.

He may or may not be distressed in the separation episodes, but if he shows little distresss, he is clearly more active in seeking contact and in resisting release than B_1 or B_2 babies.

Although his attachment behavior is heightened in the reunion episodes, he does not seem wholly preoccupied with his mother in the preseparation episodes.

Subgroup B₄

The baby wants contact, especially in the reunion episodes, and seeks it by approaching, clinging, and resisting release; he is, however, somewhat less active and competent in these behaviors than most B₃ babies, especially in Episode 8.

He seems wholly preoccupied with his mother throughout the strange situation. He gives the impression of feeling anxious throughout, with much crying. In the second separation, particularly, he seems entirely distressed.

He may show other signs of disturbance, such as inappropriate, stereotyped, repetitive gestures or motions.

He may show some resistance to his mother, and indeed he may avoid her by drawing back from her or averting his face when held by her. Because he also shows strong contact-seeking behavior, the impression is of some ambivalence, although not as much as is shown by Group-C infants.

Group C

—The baby displays conspicuous contact- and interaction-resisting behavior, perhaps especially in Episode 8.

—He also shows moderate-to-strong seeking of proximity and contact and seeking to maintain contact once gained, so that he gives the impression of being ambivalent to his mother.

—He shows little or no tendency to ignore his mother in the reunion episodes, or to turn or move away from her, or to avert his gaze.

—He may display generally "maladaptive" behavior in the strange situation. Either he tends to be more angry than infants in other groups, or he may be conspicuously passive.

Subgroup C₁

Proximity seeking and contact maintaining are strong in the reunion episodes, and are also more likely to occur in the preseparation episodes than in the case of Group-B infants.

Resistant behavior is particularly conspicuous. The mixture of seeking and yet resisting contact and interaction has an unmistakably angry quality and indeed an angry tone may characterize behavior even in the preseparation episodes.

Angry, resistant behavior is likely to be shown toward the stranger as well as toward the mother.

The baby is very likely to be extremely distressed during the separation episodes.

Subgroup C₂

Perhaps the most conspicuous characteristic of C₂ infants is their passivity. Their exploratory behavior is limited throughout the strange situation, and their interactive behaviors are relatively lacking in active initiative.

Nevertheless in the reunion episodes they obviously want proximity to and contact with their mothers, even though they tend to use signaling behavior rather than active approach, and protest against being put down rather than actively resist release.

Resistant behavior tends to be strong, particularly in Episode 8, but in general the C_2 baby is not as conspicuously angry as the C_1 baby.

Interjudge Agreement in Classification

The classificatory system was established on the basis of the strange-situation behaviors exhibited by the 23 subjects of the main project. As a result of applying the classificatory system to her 33 subjects, Silvia Bell proposed the addition of another subgroup to Group B—the B_4 subgroup. After the classificatory system had been expanded to accommodate this proposal, one of us (MDSA) classified all Bell's subjects, without any knowledge of these subjects beyond the strange-situation protocols themselves. In regard to 31 infants there was virtually total interjudge agreement. One of the disagreements was indeed minor; one judge placed the baby in Subgroup B_1 and the other in Subgroup B_2. The other disagreement was more substantial, although obviously the protocol in question was difficult to classify. One judge placed the infant in Group A, whereas the other did not classify him at all.

A second test of interjudge agreement was undertaken for Sample 3 in conjunction with the test of interscorer agreement discussed earlier, in which students were trained in the use of the strange-situation procedure. For this assessment we consider only Session 1. The judges were divided into two teams, one of four and the other of three students. The members of each team were independently to classify 12 of the 24 subjects and then meet in conference to resolve any discrepancies and to decide on a final classification. If we take the conference classification as the criterion, there was 96% agreement with the criterion for the seven subjects finally placed in Group A, 92% agreement for the 15 finally placed in Group B, and 75% agreement for the two placed in Group C.

As might be expected, classification into subgroups was accomplished with somewhat less agreement. There was 100% agreement with the criterion for the two infants placed in Subgroup A_1, and 76% agreement for the five placed in Subgroup A_2. Most of the discrepancies between judges involved classifying as A_1 infants finally placed in A_2; the rest involved classifying them as B_1. One infant was finally placed in Subgroup B_1 with 100% agreement, four in B_2 with 79% agreement, nine in B_3 with 87% agreement, and one in B_4 with only 50% agreement. Most of these discrepancies were between B_2 and

B_3. One baby was finally placed in C_1 with 100% agreement, and one in C_2 with only 50% agreement. The discrepancies here were nearly all between C_2 and B_4.

These findings suggest that the classificatory system can be used with highly satisfactory reliability by experienced judges and with somewhat less agreement among less experienced judges. We suggest that training is necessary before a high degree of reliability of classification can be achieved. The final classification of Sample 3, achieved after the resolution of discrepancies in conference, is undoubtedly a closer match to the criteria for classification than the foregoing discussion of interjudge agreement would suggest.

The smallest group, Group C, presented the most difficulty to the judges, not only in Sample 3 but also in other samples. If a baby's behavior precisely matches the specifications of one of the subgroups, there is likely to be a high degree of interjudge agreement, even though the judges have not previously been acquainted with that pattern of behavior. But the classificatory specifications in many cases can be only guidelines; and under these circumstances judges build on the experience they have gained with previous cases, as though they had to see several infants in each classificatory group (and subgroup) before they "get the feel" for the range of variation covered by each. However—as in the case of Group C and Subgroup B_4 in Sample 3—if there are too few cases that match the specifications even approximately, then difficulties and disagreements are especially likely to arise.

III

RESULTS

The results are presented in nine chapters. the first two constitute a normative account of the behavior of 1-year-olds in the strange situation. Chapter 4 provides a description of the ways in which the 106 infants in our total sample typically responded in each episode of the strange situation. Chapter 5 gives a broad picture of behavior across episodes, presented in terms of our major frequency and social-interaction measures.

The next three chapters deal with individual differences. Chapter 6 first reports the distribution of infants into the three main classificatory groups and then presents the results of a multiple discriminant function analysis, which checks whether the three groups do indeed differ significantly from one another and investigates the nature of their differences. Chapter 7 compares individual differences in infants' strange-situation behavior with individual differences in their behavior at home in both the first and fourth quarters of the first year. The findings indicate that the quality of an infant's interaction with his mother, as assessed in the strange situation, reflects certain long-standing features of his behavior toward her. Chapter 8, which compares infant strange-situation behavior with maternal behavior at home, suggests that the mother's contribution to the interaction between them also relates significantly to the quality of the infants attachment to her.

The next two chapters review the findings of other investigators who have used our strange-situation procedure with little or no change in the nature, length, or order of the episodes. Chapter 9 reviews studies of 1-year-olds in the strange situation, whereas Chapter 10 reviews studies of children between 2 and 4 years of age. Not only do the results of these investigations tend to confirm and/or extend the findings reported here, but our present findings help to clarify the issues and points of controversy raised by some of these other investigations. Because one of these issues is stability of strange-situation behavior over time, it seemed suitable to present Chapter 11, which reports on the effects of repeating the strange situation after a time interval.

Finally, Chapter 12 considers the matter of classification into subgroups, as well as into the three major classificatory groups. We consider it necessary to include this chapter, for it seems important to throw what light we can on an integral part of our classificatory procedure, although it is of less interest to the general reader than the other chapters.

4 Descriptive Account of Behavior in Each Episode

INTRODUCTION

Here we present a descriptive account of how the 1-year-olds in our sample dealt with the vicissitudes of the strange situation. This description gives some indication of the ways in which the average baby responded to the sequence of episodes with which he was faced, and serves as an introduction to the normative trends of each of the behavioral measures presented in the next chapter. The description also suggests the nature and scope of individual differences. It remains for other chapters to show how individual differences in the various measures are related to each other and to behavior in the home environment.

EPISODE 1

Because Episode 1 was a very brief introductory episode in which the baby was carried into the experimental room by his mother, little can be said about it. Most infants looked around the room with apparent interest and without seeming alarmed. Indeed, 7% strained from their mothers' arms toward the toys as though they were eager to get to them. Even while still in their mothers' arms, however, 11% showed distress upon encountering the unfamiliar environment, giving a cry or a fuss.

EPISODE 2

Most infants accepted being put down by their mothers in the unfamiliar situation at the very beginning of Episode 2. Only 9% briefly resisted release either by clinging or by vocal protest. Twenty-eight percent moved toward the toys immediately, and 78% had begun to approach them within 1 minute. Only two babies moved to explore other aspects of the room first. Of the remainder who delayed, a few (13%) went to the mother, but the rest remained sitting, looking at the toys and perhaps occasionally at the mother. Only 2% of the sample first approached the toys during the second minute of the episode. The 20% who had not spontaneously approached the toys during the first 2 minutes were encouraged to do so by their mothers or were actually carried to the toys. With this encouragement all but one infant at least touched a toy.

Ninety-four percent[1] engaged in active manipulative behavior during Episode 2. Eighty-nine percent showed locomotion in the course of approaching, pursuing, or otherwise attending to a toy or some other feature of the physical environment. All exhibited at least visual exploratory behavior.

Nevertheless, some infants (12%) cried at some time during Episode 2, although this tended to be brief fussing. There were a few, therefore, who found the strange situation mildly disturbing, even before the stranger and separations from the mother were introduced. Fifteen babies (14%) approached the mother, including five of those who fussed; and 14 of them actually made contact with her on their own initiative. Of those who approached the mother and made contact, the mean latency to achieve contact was 55 seconds.

In Episode 2, 53% of the total sample smiled at the mother, although on the average they did so only once during the episode. Eighty percent vocalized at some time during the episode, although only 47% vocalized directly to their mothers, and on the average did so only once. All of the infants looked at their mothers at least once during the episode, and most could be described either as keeping visual tabs on their mothers by occasional glances or, perhaps, as seeking reassurance through these glances.

Thus, it is clear that for the great majority of these 1-year-olds the unfamiliar situation activated exploratory rather than attachment behavior, and this exploration tended to be sustained throughout most of the episode. Only a small minority displayed either alarm or proximity seeking in this least stressful of all episodes. Most kept visual tabs on their mothers or smiled and vocalized to her across a distance, but on the whole they paid much more attention to the toys than to their mothers.

EPISODE 3

In Episode 3 our chief interest was to observe how a baby responds to a stranger in the presence of his mother. Behavior toward the stranger certainly dominated this episode.

---

[1]The percentages of infants who exhibited locomotor, manipulative, and visual exploration, and also crying, in each episode are shown in Appendix IV, Tables 30 and 31.

All forms of exploratory behavior decreased precipitously. Only 51% of the sample engaged in exploratory locomotion. Ninety-two percent continued to manipulate toys, but the amount of such behavior diminished substantially. Nearly all babies continued visual exploration, but they spent more time looking at the stranger than at the toys. All babies looked at the stranger when she entered, and 58% stared at her for periods lasting from 5 to 45 seconds.

Bretherton and Ainsworth (1974) have reported in detail the infants' responses to the stranger and have compared it with their behavior toward the mother in Episode 3; their findings are all summarized here. Very few (4%) cried or fussed when the stranger first entered, although as many as 23% evinced some distress at some time during the total episode. Some fussed or cried as a delayed response to the stranger's entrance, and 8% cried when the stranger actually approached them in the third minute of the episode.

On the other hand, 18% of the sample greeted the stranger's entrance with a smile, and 58% smiled at her at least once in Episode 3—significantly more than the number (37%) who smiled at the mother, and even slightly more (53%) than those who had smiled at the mother in Episode 2. When the stranger actually approached in the third minute of Episode 3, only 12% of the babies smiled, however.

Although smiling increased in Episode 3, vocalization decreased. Whereas 80% of the sample vocalized at some time in Episode 2, only 56% did so in Episode 3. Only 19% directed vocalizations toward their mothers in this episode, in contrast with the 47% who did so in Episode 2. Twenty-five percent directed vocalizations toward the stranger.

Very few infants (9%) showed any tendency to approach the stranger during the first 2 minutes of Episode 3 while the stranger sat in her chair, and only 3% actually approached and touched her. This is a striking contrast to the babies' responses to the toys in Episode 2, when 80% approached and touched the toys within the first two minutes. Apparently the stranger, while evoking some sociable[2] behavior (smiling) across a distance, does not evoke approach, whether the latter be considered sociable or exploratory.

We follow Bretherton and Ainsworth's (1974) interpretation of these findings—namely, that the stranger tends to activate in nearly all infants wary behavior that conflicts with the friendly behavior that tends to be evoked by an unfamiliar person who behaves pleasantly and tactfully.

Wariness and its conflict with a sociable tendency is shown in several ways in addition to actual crying. One way is gaze aversion. When the stranger first entered, 30% of the babies averted their gaze from the stranger after looking at

---

[2]Bretherton and Ainsworth (1974) used the term "affiliative" to refer to friendly or sociable behavior directed toward the stranger. Because this term has been used by others to refer to behavior directed by offspring to parent—as indeed its Latin root would suggest—we now prefer to use the terms "sociable" or "friendly."

her—that is, they looked away but did not do so in order to look at something else, whether the mother, or a toy; they looked at the floor or off into space. Twenty-one percent similarly averted their gaze when the stranger later approached them in the third minute of the episode. Sometimes the gaze aversion gave the impression of coyness—a sidewise cocking or ducking of the head, often accompanied by a smile. More frequently a baby either interrupted prolonged staring by briefly averting his gaze or looked away after a brief glance at the stranger, only to follow this with another hurried look. Another manifestation of wariness was moving away from the stranger. Almost invariably such avoidance implied seeking to be closer to the mother. Before considering approach to the mother, however, let us give further attention to looking behavior.

The stranger, rather than the mother, seemed the focus of the babies' visual attention. During the first minute, when the stranger was sitting quietly in her chair, the babies looked at her more frequently ($\overline{X} = 4.2$) than at the mother ($\overline{X} = 1.7$). While the mother and stranger conversed during the second minute, they still looked more frequently at the stranger ($\overline{X} = 3.2$ in comparison with $\overline{X} = 2.0$). During the third minute, when the stranger approached and tried to engage the baby in play, nearly all the looks went to the stranger ($\overline{X} = 3.8$ in comparison with ($\overline{X} = 1.2$). All these differences are highly significant (Bretherton & Ainsworth, 1974). Nevertheless all but 4% of the sample glanced at the mother at least once, and most of them seemed to be alert to their mothers' whereabouts. Despite the mothers' attempts to leave unobtrusively at the end of the episode while the stranger was engaging the baby in play, 65% of the sample clearly noticed her departure, although not all looked up before she had left.

During Episode 3 more babies (31%) approached the mother than in Episode 2 (14%), and 13% more attracted the mother into closer proximity through signaling behavior. Nearly half the sample (44%) were thus successful in getting into close proximity with the mother, and 30% actually achieved physical contact with her. These approaches implied a retreat to the mother from the stranger, as though for reassurance, for the babies continued to scrutinize the stranger after gaining proximity or contact with the mother. Only 8%, however, stayed in continuous proximity to the mother throughout most of Episode 3.

Ten infants spontaneously approached the stranger during the first 2 minutes of Episode 3, five fully and five partially; nine of these retreated to the mother after their excursion toward the stranger. In all, 19 infants approached the stranger at some time during the whole episode. Of these, 17 also approached the mother. Thus only two babies who were bold enough to approach the stranger did not also at some time retreat to the mother. Retreat to the mother therefore does not seem necessarily to imply extreme fear of the stranger but, often enough, merely wariness. The alternation between approach to the stranger and retreat to the mother objectifies the conflict between sociable behavior to the stranger, on one hand, and both wary behavior evoked by the stranger and attachment behavior directed toward the mother, on the other hand.

During the last minute of Episode 3, the stranger approached the baby and attempted to engage him in interaction by offering him a toy. Eighty-five infants (80%) were near the toys rather than near the mother at this point. Most of them remained where they were, eight approached the stranger, and nine withdrew from her—all but one of these retreating to the mother. Of the 20% who happened to be close to the mother when the stranger approached, all either continued to hold on to her or actually initiated contact with her at this point. Nevertheless, the stranger induced all but two of the babies who were or got into contact with the mother at the time of her approach to let go of the mother by the end of Episode 3.

The stranger's offer of a toy met with varied reactions, which seem to reflect various degrees of wariness. Only five of the babies actively rejected the toy; 21% mildly snubbed it by turning their attention to another toy; 11% made intention movements toward it; 16% reached for it but did not take it; 9% touched it gingerly and then withdrew the hand. One baby would not even look at the stranger's toy. Nevertheless, 56 (53%) eventually accepted the toy; of these, 29 played with it briefly, and seven were enticed into interactive play. Thus, despite a high incidence of mildly wary behavior, half the sample could be induced by a friendly stranger to come or to remain close enough to accept the toy she offered and, thus, in a sense, to accept her; for it seemed that the babies considered the stranger's toy to be somehow an extension of her.

If accepting close proximity to the stranger and taking a toy from her represents a tipping of the balance from wary to sociable behavior to a greater extent than accepting the stranger at a distance, this raises a question about the role of smiling in response to a stranger. Smiling was infrequent when the stranger was close, but fairly common when she was at a distance. This suggests that smiling is not incompatible with wary behavior; and when in a context activating wariness, rather than inviting proximity, it seems to be placatory—a way of acknowledging the stranger while appraising her.

EPISODE 4

As mentioned earlier, a majority of the babies noticed the mother's unobtrusive departure at the end of Episode 3, and all the rest seemed sooner or later to realize that she had gone. Separation protest, however, was by no means invariably activated by the baby's realization of the mother's departure. Only 20% of the sample cried immediately after the mother left, and no more than 49% cried at any time during this episode. Of those who cried, the mean latency to cry was 64 seconds. Infants who were highly distressed were in the minority. For only 19% of the sample did the episode have to be curtailed, and for only 10% did this need to be done before 2 minutes had elapsed.

However, crying was not the only indication that a baby missed his mother. Exploratory behavior declined substantially. Only 37% of the sample exhibited any exploratory locomotion, and only 18% moved about as much as they had in Episode 2. Exploratory manipulation was shown by most infants in this episode (81%), but only 36% maintained at least their level in Episode 2. Only visual exploration held up, manifested by 95% of the sample.

Another indication that a baby misses his mother is his search for her. Strong search behavior was not conspicuous in this episode, however. Only 10% followed the mother to the door when she left; only 21% went to the door at any time during the episode; and only 8% touched the door, banged on it, or tried to open it. Thirteen percent both followed and cried; 8% followed but did not cry; 37% cried but did not follow. (We have wondered whether the fact that the stranger's chair, and often the stranger, were closer to the door than the baby may have prevented some from going to the door in this episode.) Thirty percent of the sample, however, showed no sign of disturbance at the mother's absence; they continued to explore actively and neither cried nor went to the door.

Weaker forms of search were more common than following to the door. Twelve percent approached the mother's chair. The commonest form of search behavior was looking at the door (63%) or looking toward the mother's chair and/or handbag (45%). Only 29% showed no form of search behavior.

The behavior of the stranger during Episode 4 was contingent upon the behavior of the baby. Usually the stranger continued her efforts to engage the baby in play for at least a few seconds after the mother had left. Although she had been instructed to withdraw to her chair if the baby was playing satisfactorily, she prolonged her efforts to play with him if he showed signs of becoming upset. If he seemed about to cry after she had withdrawn, she usually resumed her efforts to play with him in the hope of distracting him. The stranger offered a toy to 95 of the 106 infants in the sample. Twenty-eight of the infants to whom such an offer was made accepted the toy immediately, even though some only touched it momentarily before resuming crying. Twenty-six of the infants accepted the stranger's toy after some delay. Only eight actually pushed the toy away, seeming to reject the stranger in rejecting her toy.

As implied earlier, the stranger frequently offered interaction in an attempt to avert crying and not merely as a distraction after crying had emerged. Consequently a substantial minority of infants (33%) played well with the stranger for most of Episode 4—somewhat more than had engaged in interactive play with her during the last minute of Episode 3. Other positive responses to the stranger were not uncommon. These included smiling (42%) and vocalizing (23%). Fewer babies smiled or vocalized to the stranger, however, than in Episode 3 when the mother was present. On the other hand, few babies actively avoided the stranger. Only 17% turned away from her—substantially fewer than had done either in Episode 3.

If a crying baby could not be distracted from his distress by attempts to reengage him in play, the stranger was very likely to pick him up in an effort to console him. In Episode 4 only 30 (28%) were picked up, all because they were crying. Of these, 10 had shown some desire for contact by reaching or leaning toward the stranger. Nevertheless the stranger was usually unsuccessful in soothing the baby completely by picking him up. Only five responded positively to being picked up, by decreasing or stopping crying, or by clinging or holding on to the stranger. Over twice as many responded negatively to the pick-up by stiffening, squirming, trying to get down, or by increasing the intensity of crying. Of the 30 who were picked up, 14 showed mixed responses to the stranger, appearing to find some comfort by clinging or sinking in; but they also cried harder, resisted the stranger, or turned away from her.

Of the 25 who responded negatively or with mixed positive and negative behavior to being picked up by the stranger, 23 cried as hard as or harder than before, six became stiff or rigid in the stranger's arms, and nine squirmed or struggled to get down, leaned back or away from the stranger, or kicked. Another four pushed away from either the stranger or the toy she was offering, and four resisted the stranger's attempts to pick them up.

As might be expected from the high incidence of negative or mixed responses to being held, the stranger who had picked up a distressed infant tended somewhat more frequently (in 17 of 30 instances) to put him down rather than to continue holding him. Of those whom she attempted to put down, six protested by crying, but only one actively clung in an effort to maintain contact. Of these six who protested, two had responded totally positively to contact, whereas four had had negative or mixed responses.

In summary, Episode 4 tended to be dominated by responses to the mother's absence, in contrast to Episode 2, dominated by exploration, and to Episode 3, dominated by responses to the stranger. Nevertheless, a substantial minority of infants played with the stranger in Episode 4. Of those who were distressed by their mothers' absence, however, few could be truly comforted by the stranger; ambivalence or outright rejection was more common.

EPISODE 5

It was expected that most infants would exhibit heightened attachment behavior in this reunion episode. Our analysis focused on greeting behaviors when the mother first enters, and upon the baby's attempts through the rest of the episode to establish or to sustain interaction, proximity, or actual contact with her. (We had also intended to examine the infant's response to hearing the mother call him before she actually opened the door to enter, expecting that the behavior of the average baby would clearly reflect the fact that he heard his mother's call. This "anticipatory" response, however, was infrequent, and because the observers could not hear the call, they could not link infant behavior to this auditory stimulus.)

During the first 15 seconds following the mother's entrance, 78% of the sample greeted her by approaching, reaching, smiling, vocalizing, or indeed by crying. The single most common form of greeting was approach; 22% made a full approach to contact the mother, and 8% a partial approach. Signaling desire for contact by reaching or leaning was shown by another 19%. Not all mothers responded to these behaviors by picking the baby up, but within the first 15 seconds, 33% of the babies had actually achieved contact. Some babies greeted their mothers across a distance, without an obvious signal for contact; thus 13% merely smiled and 3% merely vocalized. Some (32%) greeted the mother with a cry, or, if they were already crying, increased the intensity of their crying; but only 14% merely cried without mingling this distressed greeting with more active or more positive greeting behavior. Most infants greeted their mothers with a compound kind of greeting—smiling and approaching; crying and reaching; crying, smiling, approaching, and reaching; and many other combinations.

A substantial minority (22%) did not greet their mothers upon reunion. Nineteen percent merely looked, without giving another signal of acknowledgment, and 3% (excluding those who were crying so hard as to be oblivious to the mother's entrance) ignored her altogether. In addition to those who ignored the mother, 23% turned away or looked away from her after first looking at her or even after greeting her, and another 4% crawled or walked away from her. Thus 30% showed some initial avoidance behavior.

During the whole episode 51% showed some avoidance of the mother. Six percent moved away from her, and 24% turned away. Twenty percent conspicuously ignored the mother at some point in the episode, by failing to respond when she talked to him or by failing to acknowledge her presence with more than a momentary glance. Prolonged ignoring, lasting more than a minute, was infrequent however, occurring in only 8% of the infants.

Nearly all the crying in Episode 5 was linked to the preceding separation. Forty-two percent of the babies were crying when the mother returned, but most of them stopped crying with relatively little delay. The mean latency to stop crying after achieving contact with the mother was 12 seconds, and the mean latency without contact was 16.3 seconds.

Mothers differed in their behavior after the first 15 seconds, in part but not wholly because of the babies' initial behavior. Many (41%) went to their chairs immediately after entering the room. A few (5%) immediately attempted to reengage the baby in play with the toys. Others picked the baby up or continued to hold him if he had already been picked up, although there were great individual differences in the duration of the holding. Seventy-four percent of those who were picked up were held less than 30 seconds, whereas only 7% were held for over 120 seconds. Some mothers might have held their babies longer had it not been for the instruction to get the baby settled again in play with the toys.

At some time time during the episode, 50% of the infants approached the mother at least once, and some made several approaches. Only 37% actually achieved physical contact with her, however, and most of these did so during the first 15 seconds. Some babies did not seek proximity, others were content with mere proximity, and still others who obviously desired contact were not requited in this desire by their mothers.

Of the 37 babies who were held by the mother, six relaxed, sinking in or molding their bodies to adjust to the mother's; 20 put their arms around the mother; and 15 clung actively. When their mothers attempted to release them, 16 (43%) cried in protest, while 12 (32%) actively resisted release by clinging or otherwise attempting to regain contact.

Not all infants responded positively to being picked up. Two gave a little kick, and two either increased their level of crying or fussed intermittently while being held. Three either squirmed, trying to get down from the mother's lap, or leaned away from her while being held.

Acting in accordance with our instructions, mothers attempted to rekindle the baby's interest in the toys. Some showed sensitive timing in this, giving the baby a concentrated period of cuddling and soothing before trying to turn his attention away from her. Others tended to hurry the soothing and thus either prolonged the period during which the baby sought to maintain contact or elicited resistant behaviors. Five of the babies to whom the mother offered a toy dropped it, and 9 showed even stronger resistance, batting at it or throwing it away. Eight turned away from the toy.

In any event, the episode was prolonged if necessary until the baby had actually begun to play again. Consequently 96% of the infants managed some exploratory manipulation in this episode, although the amount of such activity was below that characteristic of Episode 2. We cannot know what proportion would have returned to exploratory play had their mothers not stimulated them to do so.

In summary, Episode 5 was dominated by the baby's response to his mother upon return after a brief absence. Although a majority of infants greeted the mother, only about half actively sought close proximity to her and/or physical contact, and about half showed some tendency to avoid her.

EPISODE 6

Distress was more frequent in the second separation episode than in Episode 4. Seventy-eight percent of the sample cried at some time during the episode, and 52% either cried through at least 150 seconds of the episode or were so distressed that the episode was curtailed. Curtailment was necessary for 53%. Forty-five percent cried immediately when the mother left the room, in contrast with 20% in Episode 4. (Indeed, some babies began to cry in Episode 5, as soon as the mother got up and made her way to the door and before she had actually left.) Of those who cried, the mean latency of the cry was 30 seconds, in contrast with 64 seconds in Episode 4.

A substantial minority (32%) went to the door immediately, whereas 59% in all made a full approach to the door at some time during Episode 6. Twenty-six percent banged on the door, touched it, or otherwise seemed to be trying to open it. Of the total sample, 47% both cried and searched strongly, 32% cried without strong searching, and 13% searched without crying. Thus 93% attempted to regain the absent mother either through following, through signaling (crying), or both. Weak forms of search behavior were also shown by the majority of infants: 77% looked at the door, and 31% looked at the mother's chair. Only 14% failed to show any search at all.

Most infants explored little or not at all in Episode 6. Only 44% showed exploratory locomotion, and only 21% showed as much as they had in Episode 2. Although 62% engaged in exploratory manipulation at least briefly, only 27% maintained at least the level they had shown in Episode 2. At least some visual exploration was shown by most babies, but 24% were too acutely distressed to explore even visually. In all only 4% seemed undisturbed by the mother's absence, maintaining exploration at preseparation levels and neither crying nor going to the door.

It is a safe assumption that these various manifestations of disturbance were activated by the mother's departure and continuing absence. That there was more disturbance in Episode 6 than in Episode 4 is perhaps attributable in part to the fact that the baby was left alone in Episode 6 rather than in the company of the stranger; but it is probably chiefly due to the cumulative effect of a second separation. The relative weights of these two factors cannot be ascertained, however, because they are confounded. On the other hand, it seems clear in retrospect that most of the babies who were distressed in Episode 4 were primarily protesting separation rather than manifesting fear of the stranger. Only one baby who cried in Episode 4 failed to cry in Episode 6.

EPISODE 7

The stranger's return in Episode 7 did little to reassure those babies who were distressed in Episode 6. This fact lends support to the interpretation that it was specifically the mother's absence rather than being alone that occasioned the distress in most instances. Of the 61 babies who were crying at the end of Episode 6, 35 continued to cry, and 13 stopped briefly as the stranger entered and then renewed their crying. Only 15 stopped crying altogether. Of the other 45 infants who were not crying at the end of Episode 6, four began to cry when they saw the stranger, as if disappointed that it was not the mother who entered. In only one instance did fear of the stranger seem to activate the cry, for this baby had cried in Episode 4 but not in Episode 6, and cried again when the stranger entered in Episode 7. In all, 71% of the sample cried at some time in Episode 7, a slight decrease from the 78% who cried in Episode 6.

Sixty-one babies were picked up by the stranger—twice as many as those picked up in Episode 4. Slightly more of these (23%) showed a totally positive response to the pick-up than did those picked up in Episode 4 (17%), and 57% showed a mixed response, in contrast to the 47% who did so in Episode 4. The incidence of totally negative responses was only 20%, in contrast with 37% in Episode 4. These findings suggest that under conditions of increased stress due to the second separation from the mother, infants tended not totally to reject contact, even with a strange person, but may derive some consolation from it even though they may be ambivalent.

Of the 61 infants picked up by the stranger, 35 increased their crying or at least cried at the same level as previously. Eight exhibited stiffness or rigidity while in the stranger's arms, and four kicked at the stranger while she was picking them up. Another 11 squirmed or arched back uncomfortably in the stranger's arms, signaling a desire to be put down. The percentage incidence of these resistant behaviors did not change significantly from that of Episode 4.

Of the 61 infants picked up by the stranger, 32 were later put down again. Of these, 11 protested the put-down—proportionately more than in Episode 4. About the same proportion of babies (11%) avoided the stranger's offer of a pick-up as in Episode 4. Of the 61 infants picked up, 22 reached or leaned in anticipation.

The stranger was somewhat less likely to offer a toy to a baby in Episode 7 than in Episode 4. She did so in 74% of the cases. Angry, resistant behaviors in response to these offers were more frequent, however. Of the 78 babies offered a toy, 16 actually pushed it away, and 33 refused the play offer altogether. On the other hand, 22 accepted the offer immediately, and 23 more did so after some delay.

Smiling at the stranger across a distance was less frequent than it had been in Episode 4, and very much less frequent than in Episode 3. Thirty-three percent smiled at the stranger. On the other hand, 25% vocalized to her—about the same number who had done so in Episode 4. Avoidance of the stranger was more frequent than in Episode 4; 25% turned or looked away from her.

The stranger's presence reduced the frequency of the more active forms of search. During the whole episode, only 17% approached the door, and only 6% approached the mother's chair. Forty-six percent showed no search behavior whatsoever.

Even though fewer babies showed active search in this episode than in Episode 6, this does not imply that they turned from a preoccupation with their mothers' whereabouts to a renewal of exploratory activity. Indeed the percentages of infants engaging even minimally in exploration remained about the same as in Episode 6.

In summary, Episode 7 was very much a continuation of Episode 6 for nearly all babies, and for most of them it was still dominated by their response to separation from the mother. Some were comforted by the stranger, but the distress of very few was truly alleviated. However, only a very few were more distressed in the stranger's presence than they had been when alone.

EPISODE 8

In this second reunion episode, more infants exhibited heightened attachment behavior than in the first reunion, even though some were too distressed to take as active a role in seeking contact with the mother as they had in Episode 5.

During the first 15 seconds following the mother's entrance, 81% gave some kind of greeting, positive or negative. The most common greeting was a cry or an increase in the intensity of crying (50%). This percentage is substantially higher than in Episode 5. Seventeen percent cried without mingling this with more active or more positive greeting behavior. Nevertheless 25% made a full approach, and another 6% a partial approach. Signaling a desire for contact by reaching or leaning was shown by 26%. More babies (78%) achieved contact within the first 15 seconds than had done so in Episode 5 (33%), either by themselves or with the mother's cooperation. Even in this second reunion episode, however, some babies greeted their mothers across a distance without an obvious signal for contact; 6% merely smiled in greeting, and 4% merely vocalized. A substantial minority (19%) did not greet their mothers at all. Fifteen percent merely looked at her without a greeting, and 4% totally ignored her entrance. In addition, 23% turned away or looked away from the mother after looking at or even greeting her, and one baby walked away from her.

During the whole episode, 47% of the babies exhibited some avoidance of the mother. Thirty percent either turned away or looked away from her, and another 15% ignored her, although only 8% ignored her for any substantial period of time (over a minute).

The instructions to the mother implied that she was to pick the baby up. Seventy-three percent did so at the beginning of the episode, and 84% did so at some time during it. Only 20% of the mothers went to their chairs immediately, in contrast with Episode 5 when 41% did so. At the beginning of Episode 8, 53% of the babies were crying, but most of them stopped with little delay, the majority immediately after being picked up. Only 18% of the crying babies stopped crying without physical contact, even after some delay.

Latency to stop crying was 9 seconds with physical contact and 11 seconds without.

Although only 25% of the sample approached the mother within the first 15 seconds, 46% did so at some time during the episode. Of the 94 who were held by their mothers, 44 clung actively, and 19 sank in against the mother's body—about the same proportion as in Episode 5, but involving a greater number of babies because twice as many were picked up.

Of the 94 who were held, 10 were not consoled and either increased the level of their crying or fussed intermittently during contact. Some babies also showed resistance to being held; five kicked at the mother, 18 squirmed to get down. three pushed away, and another four leaned away from her during the pick-up. Three were totally unresponsive to the contact.

Mothers were less likely to attempt to put their babies down in this episode than in Episode 5—perhaps because they sensed the baby would protest, or perhaps because they had not been instructed to reinvolve the baby in play with the toys. In all, 78 mothers (83% of those who had picked their babies up) attempted to put the baby down. Of these babies, 32 (41%) cried in protest at being put down, and 11 (14%) actively resisted release from the mother. Although the percentages exhibiting these behaviors are lower than in Episode 5, it must be remembered that more mothers held their babies and tended to hold them longer. Of those who were picked up, only 28% were held for less than 30 seconds (as contrasted to 74% in Episode 5) and 24% were in contact for over 120 seconds (as opposed to 7% in Episode 5).

About the same number of mothers (78) attempted to interest babies in toys, whether holding the baby or not, as had in episode 5 (76). Nine of the babies who were offered a toy dropped it, four rejected it actively by batting it away or throwing it down, and five turned away from the mother's toy. Only 82% of the sample manipulated toys even briefly in this episode, in contrast to 98% in Episode 5.

Hence Episode 8, even more than Episode 5, was dominated by baby's response to his mother upon her return after a brief absence, with the majority of these 1-year-olds seeking to achieve and maintain close contact with her.

5 Normative Trends Across Episodes

Whereas the previous chapter provided a detailed account of behaviors that commonly occur in each separate episode of the strange situation, the present chapter is concerned with the pattern of changes in a given behavior or class of behaviors from one episode to another. The intrinsic design of the strange situation was dictated by the hypothesis that 1-year-olds who are attached to their mothers will use her as a secure base from which to explore an unfamiliar environment when she is present. Consequently, it was expected that the array of toys would elicit exploratory behavior in the preseparation Episode 2, while at the same time the infant would display weak attachment behavior, if any. Although it was expected that the entrance of the stranger in Episode 3 would attract the baby's attention and therefore lead to a decrease in exploratory behavior directed toward the toys, no hypothesis was formulated in regard to normative trends in attachment behavior in Episode 3, because no advance prediction was made about the extent to which the presence of the unfamiliar person would activate fear (or wary) behavior and/or attachment behavior directed toward the mother. It was expected, however, that attachment behavior (crying and search) would be activated by the mother's departure and/or absence in the separation episodes, at the expense of exploratory behavior, which would thus decline. It was further expected that relevant forms of proximity- and contact-seeking behavior would be activated in the reunion episodes (at least initially), also at the expense of exploratory behavior.

The behaviors that are traced from Episode 2 through Episode 8 are all of those for which we have measures of frequency or strength. The frequency measures are: three measures of exploratory behavior (locomotor, manipulative, and visual), a measure of orienting behavior (looking), three measures of attachment and/or social behavior (crying, smiling, vocalization), and, finally, a measure of oral behavior. The measures of strength are the "interactive-behavior" scores. These are of two major classes: (1) attachment behaviors (or, in the case of the stranger, sociable behaviors)—namely, proximity and contact seeking, contact maintaining, search, and distance interaction; and (2) behaviors antithetical to attachment or sociability—namely, avoidant and resistant behaviors.

To supplement these measures of frequency and strength, we make appropriate reference to differences between episodes in the percentages of subjects showing the particular behavior at all (i.e., with minimal frequency or more). Full details of these percentage comparisons are given in Appendix IV, Tables 30 and 31. Finally, the "negative" behaviors—avoidant and resistant—seem best represented by percentage figures of infants at each score point, rather than by comparisons of mean scores across episodes.

INTERSAMPLE AND SEX DIFFERENCES

ANOVA tests, supplemented where relevant by t tests, were made for each of the behavioral measures of significance of differences among the four component samples. Of 26 ANOVAs, only four yielded significant intersample differences—exploratory locomotion, looking at the mother, total vocalization, and resistant behavior to the stranger. None of these behaviors is critical to the classification system; and the intersample differences in exploratory locomotion seem attributable to a change in a physical aspect of the room in which the strange situation was conducted, rather than to "true" intersample variabilty. The relative lack of significant intersample differences justifies combining the samples.

ANOVA tests were also made for each behavior of the significance of sex differences. No significant differences were found. Hence, the sexes are not considered separately in the cross-episode comparisons.

EXPLORATORY BEHAVIORS

In the home situation, it is difficult to ascertain whether it is the infant's mother or the whole familiar environmental context that provides him with the security necessary for him to be able to explore. In an unfamiliar situation, however, it is possible to determine the potency of the mother's role in supporting exploratory behavior. Will the baby explore a new environment readily with his mother present, but less readily when she is absent? How will his exploratory behavior be affected by the entrance of a third person who is benign but totally unfamiliar? An examination of changes in exploration from one episode of the strange situation to another is germane to these issues.

Exploratory Locomotion

A variety of attractive toys was provided in order to give strong instigation to active exploration. To test whether an infant would leave his mother to explore, the toys were placed at the maximum feasible distance from her. The infant could examine them from a distance, but to actively manipulate them, he had to leave the starting point where he had been put down and move toward them, by creeping, crawling, or walking. Of course, he might also move about the room, exploring its furniture or fixtures, or move in pursuit of a toy that had itself been moved (e.g., chasing a ball that was rolled by his mother, by the stranger, or by himself).

An analysis of variance shows a highly significant episode effect for exploratory locomotion $[F (6,612) = 15.072, p < .0001]$. Figure 2 shows the changes across episodes. Exploratory locomotion was most frequent in Episode 2, when the infant was alone with his mother. The stranger's entrance in Episode 3 sharply reduced locomotion, and this behavior remained at a low level of frequency in Episode 4 after the mother had departed. The mother's return in Episode 5 activated some increase in exploratory locomotion,

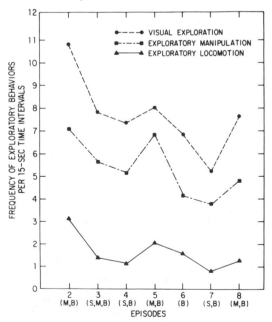

FIG. 2   Mean incidence of exploratory behavior in each episode.

although not nearly to the level of Episode 2. The second separation, beginning in Episode 6 and continuing through Episode 7, led to another decrease. The slight recovery in Episode 8 did not bring the frequency of exploratory locomotion up to the level of the first reunion episode, number 5.

These findings confirm the hypothesis that 1-year-old infants tend to move away from the mother to explore an unfamiliar environment as long as she is present and presumably perceived as readily accessible to him. The stranger's entrance dampened the vigor of exploratory locomotion even in the mother's presence—so much so that the subsequent separation episodes served to reduce it very little more.

There was a significant difference among the four component samples [$F(3, 102) = 7.13$), $p < .0005$] in the frequency of exploratory locomotion. This was almost entirely due to the fact that Sample 1 showed more exploratory locomotion than any of the other three samples. This finding is attributable to a change in the experimental conditions. A rug was on the floor for the first 13 subjects of Sample 1, but was subsequently removed so that the floor might be marked into squares to facilitate the recording of locomotion. In retrospect it is clear that the rug provided traction that made creeping, crawling, and early unsteady walking easier.

Exploratory Manipulation

An analysis of variance yielded a significant episode effect for exploratory manipulation [$F(6,612) = 4.47$, $p < .001$]. Figure 2 shows that the changes across episodes are similar to those for exploratory locomotion, although the frequency of manipulation is greater than locomotion in every episode. The highest frequency was in Episode 2. There was a substantial drop in Episode 3 and a further slight drop in Episode 4, the first separation episode. Manipulation increased in the reunion Episode 5—when indeed the mother intervened, if necessary, to reinvolve the baby in play—but it decreased to new lows during the second separation Episodes 6 and 7. It recovered little in Episode 8, despite the mother's presence.

Visual Exploration

Visual interest in the toys and in other features of the inanimate environment is both the most frequent form of exploratory behavior and the least active. It may be seen from Figure 2 that infants spend 10 or 11 of the 12 15-second intervals in Episode 2 visually examining one or another aspect of the physical environment. Although this behavior was less vulnerable to stress than the other two forms of exploratory behavior, its cross-episode trends are similar and significant [$F(6, 612) = 6.61$, $p < .0001$]. There was a decline in Episode 3,

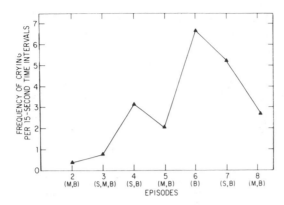

FIG. 3   Mean incidence of crying in each episode.

chiefly because the infants tended to look more at the stranger than at the toys, and a further decline in Episode 4. Visual exploration increased somewhat in the first reunion Episode 5, only to decrease again in Episodes 6 and 7. There was some recovery in Episode 8 when the mother returned.

CRYING

In general, distress behavior is incompatible with exploratory behavior, and hence it was expected that trends in amount of crying across episodes would be the reverse of trends in exploration. Indeed, as Figure 3 shows, such tends to be the case. Crying was minimal in the preseparation Episodes 2 and 3; it increased during the first separation Episode 4; decreased again when the mother returned in Episode 5; and reached a peak in Episode 6, when the baby was left alone. There was some decline in crying in Episode 7 when the stranger was present, but crying was nevertheless more frequent than in Episode 4, when the baby was previously alone with the stranger. When the mother returned again in Episode 8, crying declined to about the same level as in the first reunion Episode 5. Analysis of variance showed that these episode effects were highly significant [F (6, 612) = 67.38, $p < .0001$].

These findings suggest that separation from the mother in an unfamiliar environment tends to be distressing to 1-year-olds. It is not, however, as distressing as being left alone altogether, as is shown by a comparison between Episodes 6 and 7 ($t = 2.77$; $p < .01$). The decline of crying in Episode 7 suggests that the stranger is able to provide some comfort to at least some babies. At the same time this, together with a comparison between Episodes 4 and 6 ($t = 451$; $p < .001$), suggests that for most of these infants separation occasioned substantially more distress than did the presence of the stranger per se.

Crying in the reunion episodes is almost entirely interpretable as a continuation of the distress occasioned by the preceding separations.

Although the babies tended to be reassured by the mother's return, not all were calmed immediately.

SEARCH BEHAVIOR

This behavior peaked in Episode 6, when the baby was alone, and was relatively weak in the other separation episodes. An episode effect for search behavior was significant $[F(2, 204) = 8.06, p < .001]$. The stranger's presence is likely to have affected the baby's search for his mother in two ways. First, the arrangement of the experimental room was such that if the stranger was sitting in her chair, she was fairly close to the door, so that a baby who was wary of her might be deterred from passing by her to go to the door. Second, if the baby cried or seemed about to cry, the stranger tended to intervene either by distracting him or by picking him up; in either case any tendency to go to the door was thwarted. Furthermore, in Episode 4 babies tended to be less distressed, both because it was the first separation from their mothers and because they were not alone. Despite these complications, a hypothesis that following the mother is more strongly activated by being left alone than by being left in company receives support from findings in the home environment (Stayton, Ainsworth, & Main, 1973).

SEEKING PROXIMITY AND CONTACT

An analysis of variance yielded a significant episode effect for seeking proximity and/or contact to the mother $[F(3,306) = 26.87, p < .0001]$. Figure 4 shows that efforts to gain proximity to the mother were weakest in Episode 2 and increased only slightly after the stranger appeared in Episode 3. Hence, although the stranger's entrance slowed down exploratory behavior, it did

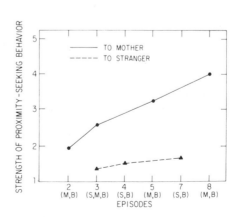

FIG. 4 Mean strength of proximity/contact-seeking behavior in each relevant episode.

not tip the balance between exploratory and attachment behavior strongly toward the latter. Separation, however, does so, as may be seen in the sharp increase in proximity and contact seeking in the first reunion Episode 5, and in the even more marked increase in the second reunion Episode 8.

An analysis of variance also yielded a significant episode effect for seeking proximity and/or contact with the stranger [$F(2,204) = 3.8, p < .025$]. Figure 4 shows that such behavior toward the stranger is especially weak in Episode 3, but increases somewhat in the separation Episodes, 4 and 7. Figure 4 shows clearly, however, that infants much more strongly seek proximity and contact with the mother than with a stranger.

MAINTAINING CONTACT

An analysis of variance shows a significant episode effect for contact-maintaining behavior directed toward the mother [$F(3,306) = 51.02, p < .0001$]. As in the case of the proximity seeking, contact maintaining was negligible in Episodes 2 and 3, but was intensified by separation experiences, increasing somewhat in the first reunion Episode 5, and then sharply increasing in the second reunion Episode 8. (See Figure 5.)

It may also be seen from Figure 5 that efforts to maintain contact with the stranger were negligible. Such efforts were virtually absent in Episode 3, and occurred in few cases in the separation Episodes 4 and 7. The mean for contact maintaining to the stranger was 1.01 in Episode 3 and 1.88 in Episode 7. Although absolute interepisode changes are small, an episode effect [$F(2,204) = 18.15, p < .0001$], is still highly significant.

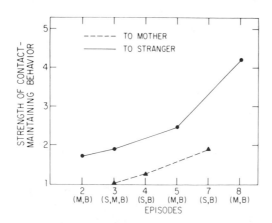

FIG. 5   Mean strength of contact-maintaining behavior in each relevant episode.

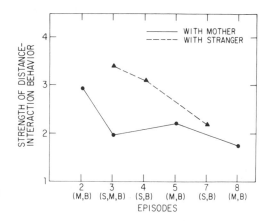

FIG. 6   Mean strength of distance interaction in each relevant episode.

DISTANCE INTERACTION

An analysis of variance shows a significant episode effect for distance interaction with mother [F (3,306) = 17.07, $p < .0001$]. It may be seen from Figure 6 that social interaction with the mother across a distance was highest in Episode 2; proximity-seeking and contact-maintaining behaviors were, in the same episode, lowest. In this episode, most babies are chiefly interested in toys, and they interact with their mothers mainly through signals across a distance, such as smiling and vocalizing, and occasionally by showing or pointing to a toy. Such interaction with the mother sharply decreases in Episode 3, when the stranger also is present. It will be recalled from earlier analyses that the entrance of the stranger increases proximity and contact seeking, but the major reason for the decline of distance interaction is that the baby's visual attention is shifted from the mother to the stranger. Although distance interaction increases slightly again in the first reunion Episode 5, it is clear that in both reunion episodes most infants seek proximity to or contact with their mothers rather than interact with them across a distance. Thus the behaviors included in the distance-interaction measure—chiefly smiling and vocalizing—seem to be low-intensity attachment behaviors; that is, they are most conspicuous when the attachment behavioral system is activated at relatively low intensity.

An analysis of variance also shows a significant episode effect for distance interaction with the stranger [F (2,204) = 24.50, $p < .0001$]. It may be seen in Figure 6 that the baby interacts at a distance with the stranger most in Episode 3, when his mother is also present, and more with the stranger than with his mother in that episode ($t = 8.79, p < .0001$). Indeed, he tends to interact across a distance more with the stranger in Episode 3 than he did with his mother

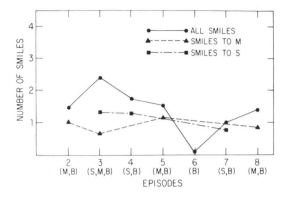

FIG. 7   Mean frequency of smiling in each episode.

when he was alone with her in Episode 2 ($t = 2.32$; $p < .02$). Nevertheless the baby's concern about his mother's accessibility is of greatest importance to him. Distress occasioned by the mother's departure overrides his interest in the stranger in the separation episodes, especially Episode 7.

In addition to the composite measure of distance interaction just described, a separate examination was made of the incidences of smiling, vocalizing, and looking.

SMILING, VOCALIZING, AND LOOKING

Smiling

Figure 7 shows the mean number of smiles emitted by the sample, as well as the number clearly directed toward the mother and the stranger. An analysis of variance shows a significant episode effect for total smiling, $F(6,612) = 13.22$, $p < .0001$. First it is evident that smiling was not a conspicuous behavior among these 1-year-olds in an unfamiliar situation. Even in Episode 2, the average baby smiled at his mother but once. Smiling was most frequent in Episode 3, when the babies smiled at both mother and stranger, but they smiled more at the stranger ($\overline{X}_s = 1.29$; $\overline{X}_m = .65$; $t = 3.96$; $p < .0001$). Separation from the mother in Episode 4 did not significantly lower the total number of smiles, nor those directed to the stranger. Smiling dropped quite precipitously, however, when the baby was alone in Episode 6.

Overall, babies smiled more at the stranger than at the mother in this unfamiliar situation, and they clearly smiled more when the stranger was present than when left alone. Bretherton and Ainsworth (1974) suggested that by 12 months of age, smiling, though still an attachment behavior, has also become a sociable behavior, directed toward "non-attachment" figures, including strangers. They also found that an infant who smiles at a stranger is also very likely to manifest signs of wariness. Therefore it seems likely that a smile to the stranger is not intended to invite her to come into proximity, but rather expresses friendliness as long as she stays at a distance. Even smiling at the mother may be a mode of interaction across a distance when a baby does not especially seek to be closer to her. Thus, at age 1, smiling seems to be an ambiguous signal. It by no means always signifies that the baby desires to draw the recipient into closer proximity, and therefore the frequency of smiling is an undependable criterion of attachment.

Vocalizing

One of the four significant intersample differences occurred in the case of total vocalizations, including both those judged to be directed toward persons and those that were not [$F(3,102) = 2.72; p < .05$]. Sample 4 differed from the other three in that more vocalizations were reported for the others. We had noted that Mary Main, who was one of two observers for all Sample-4 babies, was more adept than any other observer in receiving auditory input from the experimental room, simultaneously maintaining a continuous dictated record of what she observed. (For most observers the activity of dictation blocked auditory perception to a much greater extent than it did visual input.)

Nevertheless there was a significant episode effect for the sample as a whole for total vocalization [$F(6,612) = 12.71; p < .0001$]. As may be seen in Figure 8, vocalizing is most frequent in Episode 2, but decreases sharply in Episode 3, when the stranger is present ($\overline{X}_2 = 4.14; \overline{X}_3 = 2.51; t = 3.39; p < .001$). There is a further slight decrease in the first separation Episode 4, but it is in the second separation—including Episode 7, when the stranger is present, as well as Episode 6, when no adult is present—that vocalizing is least frequent. In contrast, vocalization increases in each of the reunion episodes, 5 and 8, although in neither does it regain its initial frequency of Episode 2. It was when these babies were alone with their mothers that they vocalized most.

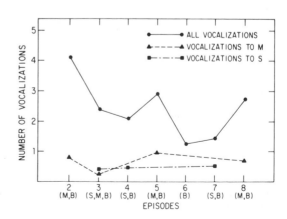

FIG. 8   Mean frequency of vocalizing in each episode.

A baby was considered to have vocalized to a person if he simultaneously looked at her and vocalized. Figure 8 shows that more vocalizations were directed toward the mother than toward the stranger, except in Episode 3. The mean number of vocalizations directed to the mother in all relevant episodes was .69, while the mean number directed to the stranger was .46 (t = 3.14; $p < .002$).

These findings are in striking contrast to those for smiling. It appears that infants in this unfamiliar situation tend to vocalize more frequently than to smile. For example, in Episode 2 the average baby vocalized 4.14 times, but smiled only 1.95 times (t = 3.1; $p < .002$). Whereas nearly all smiles were directed toward a person, relatively few vocalizations were so directed. Whereas the baby smiled somewhat more frequently at the stranger than at the mother, he vocalized significantly more frequently to the mother than to the stranger. Whereas smiles were most frequent in Episode 3, when both stranger and mother were present, vocalizations were most frequent in those three episodes in which the baby was alone with his mother. Indeed, because vocalizing to the mother was least frequent in Episode 3, and because total vocalizations were less frequent than they had been in Episode 2, it appears that the stranger's presence tends to inhibit vocalization. This inhibiting effect of the stranger is further reflected in a comparison of latency to vocalize between Episodes 2 and 3. For Episode 2, the latency is 78 seconds, but for Episode 3 it rises to 103 seconds (t = 3.61; $p < .001$).

Looking

Figure 9 shows the frequency of looking, per 15-second interval, at the mother and at the stranger. The figure clearly shows that babies tend to look more at the stranger than at the mother. Overall the mean frequency per episode of looking at the mother is 5.13, but the comparable mean for looking at the

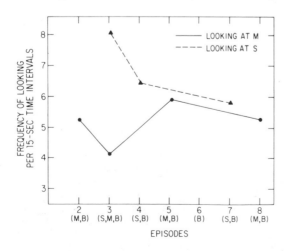

FIG. 9   Mean frequency of looking in each episode.

stranger is 6.76 (t = 8.31; $p < .0001$). That the baby's attention is captured by the stranger is shown further by an increase in latency to look at the mother, from 20.33 seconds at the beginning of Episode 2 to 43.64 seconds at the beginning of Episode 3. In short, looking serves many purposes— exploration, wariness, sociability, attachment, and so on. Because there is no evidence that looking is differential to an attachment figure at this age, it appears to be an unsatisfactory criterion of attachment. Bowlby (1969) identified looking as an orientation behavior. Ainsworth (1964, 1967) suggested that visual orientation may be differential to an attachment figure under one specific set of conditions: When held by an unfamiliar figure, Ganda babies tended to gaze persistently at the mother across a distance, while their muscular tension also suggested an intense kind of orientation. On other occasions, the baby tended only to glance at the mother occasionally, as though this were all that was necessary to keep track of her whereabouts.

In the strange situation no infant was held by the stranger, except momentarily, after the mother entered the room; consequently there was no opportunity to observe the tense visual-motor orientation noted in Ganda infants when held by strangers. On the other hand, in the strange situation, as in the Ganda homes, it appeared that infants were quite capable of keeping visual tabs on their mothers' whereabouts through the occasional glance. During Episodes 2 and 3, when the mother was stationary, the average infant seemed to take his mother's accessibility for granted, glancing at her infrequently. On the other hand (as reported earlier), when the mother got up to leave, most babies looked immediately, even at the end of Episode 3 when the mother attempted to leave unobtrusively and the stranger was doing her best to distract the baby into play with the toys. Furthermore, most babies looked immediately at their mothers when they returned in the reunion Episodes 5 and 8; and under these circumstances, failure to look—or a marked delay in doing so—has been characterized as gaze aversion, a form of avoidant behavior.

On the other hand, a 1-year-old has a strong tendency to monitor the location and behavior of an unfamiliar person. Bretherton and Ainsworth (1974) presented evidence that linked prolonged gazing at the stranger with wariness. In any event, it is likely that a baby feels less confident in his expectations about a stranger's movements and intents than he does of his mother's. All in all, frequency of looking at the mother in the strange situation is so greatly influenced by a number of factors that it is very difficult to interpret without a meticulous situational analysis, such as Bretherton and Ainsworth conducted for Episode 3.

There was significant intersample variability in the amount of looking at the mother [$F(3,102)$ = 3.30, $p < .05$]. Samples 3 and 4, more than Samples 1 and 2, looked at the mother in two or three 15-second intervals. This finding has no clear explanation. Intersample differences in looking at the stranger— and in visual exploration—were not significant, and therefore the intersample

TABLE 5
Percentage of Infants Who Exhibited Resistant Behavior
to the Mother or to the Stranger

Strength of Resistance	Resistance to the Mother				Resistance to the Stranger		
	Ep. 2	Ep. 3	Ep. 5	Ep. 8	Ep. 3	Ep. 4	Ep. 7
6–7	1%	1%	6%	6%	0%	8%	11%
4–5	1%	0%	6%	16%	7%	8%	19%
2–3	3%	1%	15%	21%	5%	66%	11%
1	95%	98%	73%	57%	88%	78%	58%

difference in looking at the mother does not seem attributable to greater alertness to looking behavior by one set of observers than by the other set.

RESISTANT BEHAVIOR

Analyses of variance indicate significant episode effects for resistant behavior, as directed to both the mother and to the stranger [to mother, $F(3,306) = 24.16, p < .0001$; to stranger, $F(2,204) = 17.09, p < .0001$].

Table 5 shows the frequency of various degrees of strength of resistant behavior directed toward the mother and toward the stranger. Unlike other behaviors discussed so far, resistant behavior is shown by a minority of subjects. Therefore, mean scores provide an inadequate impression of changes that take place across episodes.

Because the mothers were instructed not to intervene in Episodes 2 and 3, it is not surprising that extremely few infants were resistant in these episodes. The incidence of resistant behavior increases substantially in the first reunion Episode 5, and still more in the second reunion Episode 8. Separation activates angry resistance to the mother in some cases, but in only a few (6%) is this behavior strong. Nevertheless, 12% in Episode 5 and 22% in Episode 8 showed moderate to strong resistance. As reported earlier, there is also an increase in the strength of seeking to gain and to maintain contact in the reunion episodes, especially in Episode 8. Those children who resist contact and interaction also show moderate to strong proximity-seeking and contact-maintaining behavior. This combination of resistance and of seeking to gain and maintain contact cannot be interpreted from the scores alone. In some cases the baby's behavior suggests classic ambivalence: The baby seeks to be picked up, yet resists being held, and furthermore may resist being put down. In other cases the baby seems angry because his mother does not pick him up, and he manifests resistance to her efforts to interest him in play by batting away the toys she offers or perhaps by having a full-blown temper tantrum.

Slightly more infants show resistance to the stranger in Episode 3 than showed resistance to the mother in the preseparation episodes. This is scarcely surprising, for the stranger was instructed to approach the baby and to attempt to engage him in play; in 12% of the cases her overtures met with mild to moderate resistance. The percentage who showed resistant behaviors to the stranger increased somewhat in Episode 4, and more sharply in Episode 7. Even in Episode 7, however, only 42% of the sample showed any degree of resistance to the stranger. In most cases those who resisted the stranger were distressed by the mother's absence, and when the stranger attempted to distract them with toys they pushed or threw them away; or if she attempted to pick them up, they tended to push away from her or squirm to get down. Some of those who resisted also sought to gain or maintain some degree of contact with the stranger, and thus this behavior, like similar behavior directed to the mother, suggests an ambivalent reaction. In such cases it seems likely that resistance to the stranger can be interpreted as a redirection of the anger occasioned by the mother's departure. On the other hand, there are undoubtedly some infants, especially those who had taken no initiative in seeking contact with the stranger, whose resistance to the latter may be linked to fear or wary behavior.

Although there was no intersample difference in amount of resistance to the mother, there was a significant difference [$F (3,102) = 3.45$, $p < .05$] in resistance to the stranger. This difference was attributable largely to the fact that Sample 1 showed more resistance. It seems likely that this was due to the behavior of Sample 1's chief stranger, but it is unclear what aspect of her behavior might have evoked more resistance.

AVOIDANT BEHAVIOR

Like resistant behavior, avoidant behavior is entirely absent in a substantial number of infants. Table 6 shows the percentages of infants who showed various intensities of avoidance to the mother or of the stranger in the relevant

TABLE 6
Percentage of Infants Who Exhibited Avoidant Behavior
to the Mother or to the Stranger

Strength of Avoidance	Avoidance of the Mother		Avoidance of the Stranger		
	Episode 5	Episode 8	Episode 3	Episode 4	Episode 7
6–7	11%	12%	5%	1%	3%
4–5	29%	22%	12%	15%	14%
2–3	10%	13%	27%	8%	15%
1	49%	53%	55%	76%	68%

episodes. (Avoidance of the mother was not scored in Episode 2 or 3 because her noninterventive role obviated any instigation to avoidant behavior.) Although 51% show some degree of avoidance in the first reunion Episode 5, only 11% show very strong avoidance. Reunion Episode 8 yielded much the same percentages. Earlier we (Ainsworth & Bell, 1970) interpreted avoidance of the mother in reunion episodes as a defensive behavior. We are now inclined to believe that it is more useful to consider it as a conflict behavior when exhibited in a context in which most children seek proximity to or contact with their mothers. This is an approach–avoidance conflict, in which attachment behavior has been activated, presumably by the separation episodes, but in which avoidance behavior is also activated. In some cases approach and avoidance behavior alternate, but in those who score highest in avoidance we have reason to believe that the baby's previous experience in close bodily contact with his mother has been disappointing or aversive. This issue is discussed more fully in later chapters.

Avoidance of the stranger seems likely to stem from fear or wariness, without necessarily implying conflict. This is most frequent in Episode 3, when it was shown by 45% of the sample, although by only 5% to a strong degree. Relatively weak avoidance was scored for infants who merely looked away from the stranger, whereas strong avoidance was scored for those who moved away from her, usually to the mother. In the light of Bretherton and Ainsworth's (1974) analysis, it is by no means evident that all of those who retreated from the stranger to the mother in Episode 3 could be identified as showing strong fear, for nearly all of those few who approached the stranger went directly to the mother.

ORAL BEHAVIOR

Because infants can comfort themselves by sucking their thumbs or fingers, it seemed possible that they might do so in lieu of crying, perhaps especially in the separation episodes. This did not prove to be the case, however. There was a very high degree of variability in oral behavior, and in each episode in each of the four samples, the standard deviation exceeded the mean. It may also be seen from Appendix IV, Table 30, that there is little change across episodes in the frequency of infants showing oral behavior.

6

An Examination of the Classificatory System: A Multiple Discriminant Function Analysis

Whereas the findings so far discussed have focused on normative patterns of behavior as they are linked to the situational properties of the sequence of episodes, the findings we now report focus on patterns of individual differences in behavior—patterns that occur commonly enough to be recognizable when they recur. The normative findings presented in the previous two sections depict certain features of the species-characteristic organization of attachment behavior in the human 1-year-old and its interplay with other behavioral systems. We consider that the normative findings substantially support Bowlby's (1969, 1973) descriptions of the organization and function of infant attachment behavior.

As we have previously pointed out, however (Ainsworth, 1967, 1972, 1973), the infant–mother attachment relationship must be distinguished from the species-characteristic attachment behavior from which it develops and that continues to mediate it. To be sure, it is a characteristic of the human species to become attached to a mother figure. This attachment or bond has the same biological function as the attachment behavior from which it stems. Although the infant is predisposed to become attached, the attachment relationship develops only gradually and is influenced in its development by the specific patterns of interaction the infant has experienced with caregiving figures. It is a hypothesis impicit in ethological attachment theory that differences in early social experience will lead to differences in the development and organization of attachment behavior and hence in the nature of attachment relationships themselves.

In the classificatory system introduced in chapter 3, we presented certain salient features of strange-situation behavior in terms of which we identified three major patterns. These are hypothesized to represent qualitatively different attachment relationships on the basis of their correlates in behavior outside the strange-situation—correlates that are presented in later sections. We also presented data indicating satisfactory levels of interjudge agreement in the identification of these patterns. In this chapter we tackle the issue of reliability in more depth, using a multiple discriminant function analysis as our vehicle. The analysis was undertaken to test the significance of multivariate differences among the three groups and to test the hypothesis that the behaviors highlighted in the instructions for classification are indeed the major behaviors in terms of which three main groups differ. In later chapters we test the hypothesis that individual differences in the attachment relationship are stable across situations, in contrast to specific attachment behaviors, which our normative findings show to be sensitive to changes in context. This is accomplished by examining the relationship between patterns of behavior in the strange situation and patterns of behavior at home. We also test the hypothesis that the organization of the infant's attachment to his mother is influenced in its development by his mother's behavior in interaction with him. This is accomplished by examining the relationship between patterns of the infant's behavior in the strange situation and his experience of his mother's characteristic behavior at home.

MULTIPLE DISCRIMINANT FUNCTION ANALYSIS

Because we cannot assume that the reader is familiar with multiple discriminant function analysis (MDFA), we discuss certain of its features before reporting the way in which this procedure was used with our data. This procedure is useful when two or more groups are compared in terms of many variables, and when it is of interest not only to see whether the groups differ significantly from one another, but also to understand the nature of their differences. The MDFA (Tatsuoka, 1970, 1971; Tasuoka & Tiedman, 1954; Cooley & Lohnes, 1971) is a multivariate technique closely related to canonical correlation and to multivariate analysis of variance. For the purposes of evaluating our classificatory system, the MDFA has three features that offer distinct advantages over these other multivariate techniques, as well as over univariate techniques.

First, the MDFA allows us to test the significance of differences among groups of subjects with respect to multiple variables without the problems associated with repeated univariate tests (Tatsuoka & Tiedeman, 1954). Furthermore, it is not necessary to have equal numbers of subjects in each group.

Second, in the process of deriving and testing successive uncorrelated composites of the "predictor"[1] variables, the MDFA generates weighted vectors or discriminant functions (DFs), which, like the factors yielded by a factor analysis, may be interpreted as dimensions underlying group differences. The number of possible functions, however, is defined as the number of groups minus 1, which in our analysis is 2.

A third advantage of MDFA is related to the classification of individual subjects. The analysis allows us to evaluate differences between groups not only in statistical terms but also in practical terms. This is accomplished by means of classification functions based on distributions of DF scores. The DF scores of individuals in each criterion group are compared to see whether these scores can reproduce the classifications based on a larger set of variables. Finally, and more important, individuals from an independent sample can be classified to see whether the discriminant functions derived from one sample are applicable to another sample. This test with an independent sample is labeled "cross-validation." A high degree of classification and cross-validation success points to the generality of the descriptive aspects of the analysis on a subject-by-subject basis.

The MDFA procedure is a maximization technique—that is, it derives composite variables by maximizing the average degree of separation between groups relative to variance within groups. This being so, it has considerable potential for capitalizing upon variance that happens to be specific to a given sample. Just as in linear multiple regression (which is also a maximization procedure), the results of MDFA often "shrink" when functions derived from one sample are applied to another. In addition the descriptions of dimensions of group difference often vary from sample to sample. Two precautions can be taken to minimize the influence of sample-specific variance in the interpretation of the MDFA. The first precaution is to use large samples and to keep the number of predictor variables relatively small in relation to sample size. Tatsuoka (1970) suggested that total sample size should be at least two and preferably three times the number of variables used. He also suggested that the size of the smallest criterion group be no less than the number of groups used. These criteria prevent us from using MDFA to investigate the eight subgroups of our sample. Therefore we have concentrated on analysis of the three main groups. A second precaution that can help to reduce the influence of sample-specific variance is to employ cross-validation techniques to estimate the generalizability of results to an independent sample. The method of cross-validation that we employ is described presently.

---

[1]The "predictor" variables are used to predict the criterion variables. In our case the criterion is the classification into Groups A, B, and C.

TABLE 7
Distribution of Infants in the Four Samples Among
the Three Strange-Situation Groups

	Samples				
Groups	1	2	3	4	Totals
A	6	5	7	5	23
B	13	24	14	19	70
C	4	4	2	3	13
Totals	23	33	23	27	106

TABLE 8
Distribution of Infants by Sex Among
the Three Strange-Situation Groups

	Sex of Infant		
Groups	Male	Female	Totals
A	11	12	23
B	41	29	70
C	7	6	13
Totals	59	47	106

Procedure

As a preliminary to the application of MDFA, we first checked to see whether the four component samples differed in the proportions of infants classified in the three main groups, A, B, and C. (See Table 7.) They were found not to differ significantly (Chi square = 3.337; $df = p > .70$). We also checked the distribution of sexes among the three groups. (See Table 8.) There were no significant sex differences (Chi square = .99; $df = 2; p < .50$). It was necessary to drop one subject[2] from the sample for the MDFA, reducing the total sample to 105, consisting of 23 in Group A, 60 in Group B, and 13 in Group C.

---

[2]One male subject had to be omitted because the recording equipment broke down in Episode 6. Although it was possible to classify this baby (in Subgroup B₄) on the basis of a written record for the rest of the situation, insufficient detail could be included to permit us to score the measures for the later episodes.

TABLE 9
Means and One-Way ANOVAs for Strange-Situation Variables That Distinguish Among Groups A, B, and C

Variable	Episode	Persons Present	Means A	B	C	Total	F (2,102)
Interactive Behaviors with M							
Proximity Seeking	5	M, B	1.74	3.47	4.07	3.17	9.40
	8	M, B	2.30	4.68	3.38	4.00	21.24
Contact Maintaining	5	M, B	1.17	2.64	4.08	2.50	10.42
	8	M, B	1.98	4.98	4.69	4.29	26.26
Avoidance	5	M, B	5.02	2.16	2.08	2.78	30.88
	8	M, B	5.39	1.70	2.69	2.63	59.29
Resistance	5	M, B	1.09	1.55	3.54	1.69	15.85
	8	M, B	2.72	1.62	4.00	2.15	17.68
Interactive Behaviors with S							
Resistance	3	S, M, B	1.13	1.16	2.38	1.30	11.19
	4	S, B	1.00	1.56	4.23	1.77	25.89
	7	S, B	1.35	2.41	4.12	2.39	10.19
Distance Interaction	4	S, B	4.33	3.09	1.62	3.18	9.86
	7	S, B	3.87	1.92	1.04	2.24	16.84
Exploratory Behavior							
Exploratory Locomotion	3	S, M, B	2.65	1.18	.22	1.39	8.44[a]
	4	S, B	2.42	1.09	.15	1.26	5.74[a]
	5	M, B	3.28	1.92	.65	2.06	5.62[a]
	7	S, B	2.10	.47	.00	.77	14.85
	8	M, B	2.15	.82	.00	1.01	9.47[a]
Exploratory Manipulation	3	S, M, B	7.40	5.48	3.25	5.63	8.29[a]
	4	S, B	7.86	5.00	2.00	5.25	11.15
	5	M, B	8.52	6.70	4.52	6.83	9.24[a]
	7	S, B	6.85	3.33	.26	3.72	18.62
	8	M, B	6.19	3.49	1.67	3.85	9.46
Crying	2	M, B	.13	.15	2.19	.40	12.84
	3	S, M, B	.41	.52	2.19	.70	6.36
	4	S, B	.48	3.15	7.36	3.08	14.87[a]
	5	M, B	.74	1.78	6.00	2.08	18.89
	6	B	3.67	7.15	9.60	6.69	7.03
	7	S, B	1.00	5.92	9.20	5.25	17.25[a]
	8	M, B	.72	2.59	6.32	2.64	18.51

[a]Variables not included in the multiple discriminant function analysis.

The next preliminary step was the reduction of the number of variables from the original 73 that had been scored,[3] to a smaller set consistent with Tatsuoka's suggestions. Groups means were computed for each variable, along with one-way analyses of variance. Because only those variables in regard to which two or more groups differ can contribute to the discrimination among groups, we eliminated all variables for which the F-ratio yielded by the analysis of variance fell short of significance at the 1% level. This reduced the number of variables from 73 to the 30 shown, together with their group means and F-ratios, in Table 9.(See Appendix IV, Table 32, for the other 43 variables.)

A further reduction of the number of variables was desirable because the number of infants classified in Group C was so small. We did not wish to risk eliminating potentially important variables by specifying a more restrictive F-ratio as the criterion. Instead, all 30 variables were entered into 2-group discriminant function analyses—Group A vs. Group B, and Group B vs. Group C. (The rationale for omitting the A vs. C distinction was that the most interpretable differences among groups are those that contrast one of the smaller groups with the normative B group.) Any variable that did not contribute significantly to either one or other of these discriminations was eliminated from the analysis on the grounds that it contained little information about group membership that was not contained in the other variables, despite its significant F-ratio. It may be noted in Table 9 that each of the variables eliminated in this second step is represented in the analysis by its counterpart, as scored in other episodes, and by other variables scored in the same episode as the eliminated variable. This procedure reduced the set of independent variables to 22. No further reduction was attempted, for this could have defeated the descriptive goals of the analysis.

Using these 22 variables, the multiple discriminant function analysis was run on the Statistical Package for the Social Sciences, SPSS 6.0 (Nie, Hull, Jenkins, Steinbrenner, & Bent, 1975) at the University of Minnesota.

Results

Table 10 gives the statistics relevant to the degree of separation among the groups, the significance of each discriminant function, its relative contribution to the among-groups variance, and the proportion of variance in the total set of 22 variables attributable to group differences.

The two discriminant functions were significant in distinguishing the three groups. The conventional approach to testing the significance of the functions relies on the fact that the first DF derived will be the one that yields the greatest average difference among the groups. Subsequent DFs are successively smaller. When the maximum number of DFs has been extracted and the total

---

[3]The original 73 variables included separate scores for each episode and, of course, separate scores for behavior directed toward the mother and the stranger.

TABLE 10
Multiple Discriminant Function Analysis

	Function I	Function II
Eigenvalue	2.359	1.790
Canonical Correlation	.838	.801
Percentage of Trace	56.9	43.1
Wilks's Lambda	.107	.358
Group Centroids		
Group A	–2.816	.426
Group B	.917	.519
Group C	.115	–3.507

Notes: $N = 105$ (23, 69, 13)
Number of groups = 3
Number of independent variables = 22
Maximum number of functions = (n groups – 1) = 2
Significances:
Functions 1 & 2; Chi square = 207.01; $df = 44$;
$p = 1.39 \times 10^{-21}$
Function 2 alone; Chi square = 94.92; $df = 21$;
$p = 1.54 \times 10^{-10}$

discrimination afforded by them is significant, then at least the first DF must be significant. The discrimination due to the first DF is then set aside, and the same inference is made with respect to the second, and so on until the residual discrimination is not significant, or until the maximum number of functions possible has been derived—in our case, two. It may be seen that each of the two DFs yielded by the analysis is significant at a very high level of confidence.

The canonical correlations (R_c) presented in Table 10 are correlations between the entire set of predictor variables and the criteria of group classifications. As may be seen, they are very high. The eigenvalues (e_i) are related to the canonical correlations by the formula $e_i = R^2_{ci}$. The squared canonical correlation is the proportion of the variance of the group-membership variables accounted for by the set of predictor variables. Thus the eigenvalues are indices of the amount of among-groups variance.

The percentage of trace shown in Table 10 is the percentage of the total among-groups variance correlated with the respective discriminant functions. This figure for the first DF is 56.9%, somewhat larger than that for the second DF.

Wilks's Lambda is an inverse measure of the relative separation of the groups by the discriminant functions. It is distributed as an approximate chi square, with the degrees of freedom indicated. There was significant discrimination power in both functions.

Thus we may conclude that Groups A, B, and C differ significantly with respect to the set of predictor variables in the analysis, even when redundancies

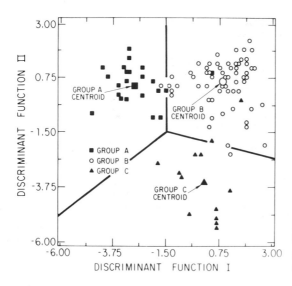

FIG. 10   Centour plot of discriminant scores. *Note:* Subjects whose scores were identical are represented by one symbol in this plot.

are removed. Evidence that the criterion groups are quite distinct is highly desirable in evaluating any classificatory scheme, and this one may be seen to meet the various tests satisfactorily.

CLASSIFICATION BY DISCRIMINANT SCORES AND CROSS-VALIDATION

The economy of describing Groups A, B, and C in terms of two uncorrelated functions instead of 22 correlated variables is considerable. Its practical advantage, however, depends on evidence that the two-factor description can reproduce the A-B-C classifications based on the criteria of our classificatory system. This was assessed by a centour analysis of the discriminant scores of each subject in each group, as plotted in Figure 10.

Development

Each subject was assigned three scores reflecting his proximity to the centroid of each group.[4] Proximity was defined relative to the members of a particular group, to take into account different dispersions of subjects around the three group centroids. Infants were assigned to the group to which they were closest.

---

[4]In classifying subjects from their scores on the discriminant functions—both for the development sample and in serial cross-validation—no a priori probability of membership in any group—A, B, or C—was specified. Thus, we did not take advantage of the fact that membership in Group B is most probable. As a consequence subjects were automatically classified in the group whose centroid their scores most closely approximated.

The results of this classification procedure are compared with our original classifications of each infant in Table 11. The extent to which the discriminant functions allow us to reproduce A-B-C classifications is presented in terms of "hit rates" and percentage agreement. Cohen's (1960) index of nominal-scale agreement (Kappa) was computed by correcting the observed rate of agreement for the rate of agreement expected by chance. It was tested as described by Fliess, Cohen, and Everitt (1969). Obviously there is a very high degree of agreement between the original classifications and those derived from the discriminant functions.

It is clear that description in terms of two discriminant scores conveys as much information about a subject's A-B-C classification as does description in terms of the 22 MDFA variables. The findings also suggest that the significant differences among Groups A, B, and C, as reported above, are not merely group trends. Indeed, most members of each group differ from most members of each of the other groups in the direction indicated by the discriminant functions.

Cross-Validation

Correct classification of the individuals of an independent sample would provide the best evidence that the discriminant functions developed on our sample have more general applicability. Because Groups A and C are small, however, there were not enough subjects in our total sample of 105 to provide both a "development" sample and an independent cross-validation sample for a 22-variable analysis.

As an alternative, we performed a "serial" cross-validation by repeatedly deriving classification equations for 104 subjects and applying them to a single "unknown" subject. The technique differs from independent cross-validation in that it provides an estimate of whether an independent cross-validation would reach statistical significance, rather than an estimate of the

TABLE 11
Discriminant Score Centour Analysis

Actual Classi-fication	Predicted Classification from Discriminant Scores			% Correct Classification
	A	*B*	*C*	
A	22	1	0	96%
B	5	63	1	91%
C	0	1	12	92%
Total	27	65	13	92%

Note: Kappa = .854 (z = 11.8, $p < .001$).

TABLE 12
Serial Cross-Validation of the Multiple Discriminant
Function Analysis

Actual Classi-fication	Predicted Classification of Unknown Subject			% Correct Classification
	A	B	C	
A	12	1	0	92%
B	1	11	1	85%
C	0	4	9	69%
Total	13	16	10	82%

Note: Kappa = .730 (z = 6.51, p < .001).

exact degree of success that would actually be achieved with an independent cross-validation sample.

Thirty-nine "unknown" subjects, 13 from each group, were used as cross-validation subjects. These included all of Group C and a random selection from each of Groups A and B. They were classified as previously described, using discriminant functions developed without reference to the scores obtained by the cross-validation subject on each of the 22 variables.

It may be seen from Table 12 that an almost entirely accurate match of actual classification and that predicted from DF scores was obtained for Groups A and B. The misclassification of 4 of 13 Group-C subjects suggests that the group is too small to yield the highly generalizable results obtained for the other two groups.

It may be seen in Chapters 9 and 11 that three investigations, including one by one of us (EW), used our sample of 105 infants as a development sample and then cross-validated the classifications on independent samples of their own. Although in each case the variables used for their MDFAs differed somewhat from our final list of 22, their findings nevertheless suggest that the level of generalizability indicated by our cross-validation procedure is indeed representative of the relevance of the classificatory system to samples of middle-class 1-year-olds.

THE CONTRIBUTIONS OF EACH OF 22 VARIABLES TO DISCRIMINATION AMONG GROUPS

As implied earlier, the multiple discriminant function analysis provides an alternative to the vagaries of multiple univariate testing of group differences, by taking into account the intercorrelations among our 22 independent variables. The analysis also leads us to think in terms of a small number of factors underlying the wide range of individual differences in strange-situation behavior. The scatterplot of the 105 subjects' scores on the two uncorrelated discriminant functions (Figure 10) points toward a clear relationship between these independent linear combinations of the behavioral variables and the A-B-C classificatory system. This relationship is evident from a correlation of –.918 between the first discriminant function (DF I) and the dichotomy A vs. non-A, and from a correlation of –.852 between the second discriminant function (DF II) and the dichotomy C vs. non-C.

To take advantage of this relationship in the analysis of individual variables, and to use the discriminant functions for an economical description of the three groups, we must determine the relative contribution of each variable to each discriminant function. This is essentially the same problem that arises in the interpretation of factor loadings and, more exactly, in the interpretation of multiple-regression "weights".[5]

Darlington (1968) has elaborated the difficulties involved in interpreting regression coefficients and has emphasized that there is no simple or single answer to the question: "What is an important variable?" In the present analysis, however, it would seem that an "important" variable would have some combination of the following characteristics:

1. The variable provides univariate discrimination between at least two of the classificatory groups—that is, it could be used to predict group membership.

2. The variable does not make a "trivial" contribution to group differences because of its correlations with or dependency on another variable. Thus, for example, smiling and exploratory variables reflect group differences, but these seem to be a product of the high negative correlations between these variables and crying, a variable to which they seem secondary—that is, crying babies do not smile or engage in exploratory play.

3. The variable is not largely redundant with information about group membership that is available from other variables. In the absence of such incremental validity, however, a variable that passes the first test (of providing discrimination) and the second test (of not being secondary or trivial) may be very important in summarizing the behavior of members of a given group, even though there is substantial redundancy with the information provided by other variables.

4. A variable that passes the aforementioned test may be especially interesting if a substantial proportion of its total variance is correlated with one or another or both of the discriminant functions (that is, if it is heavily saturated with the dimension in question.)

---

[5]The standardized partial discriminant coefficients in Table 13 are in fact proportional to the regression coefficients relating the individual variables to the discriminant scores.

The first characteristic of an "important" variable (univariate discrimination among groups) is reflected in the group means and F-ratios. Those for which the one-way ANOVA is significant at the 1% level or better were reported in Table 9; the nonsignificant data are reported in Appendix IV, Table 32.

The second characteristic (group differences not due to trivial dependencies) can be assessed by referring to the individual group means (in Table 9) and to the descriptions of behavior in each of the episodes of the strange situation reported in chapter 4. We must draw, however, on what we know about infant behavior to deal with such obvious dependencies as the one just cited—the negative relationship between crying, on the one hand, and smiling and exploratory play, on the other.

In regard to our third test, when group differences on several correlated variables are not "trivial," the interpretation of the partial discriminant coefficients presented in Table 13 can help to uncover redundancies in the information provided by the variables. For example, interactive behavior with the mother in different episodes can not be considered trivially dependent, even though the behaviors may be highly correlated. Under these conditions, any discrimination among groups or predictive relationship of the variable to groups membership will be "echoed" by the behavior as it appears in other episodes. The partial discriminant coefficients shown in Table 13 attempt to remove this type of redundancy by highlighting certain variables at the expense of their correlates. Thus a low value of the partial discriminant coefficient does not necessarily imply that the groups are indistinguishable in terms of this variable. Indeed the method of selecting variables for inclusion in the present analysis ensured that this was not the case. A low value of the partial discriminant coefficient may suggest that a subject's score on the discriminant function cannot be predicted from the variable in question and/or that the variable adds little to the predictive power of the other variables with which it is correlated. In general, the variable highlighted by the partial discriminant coefficients is the one that makes the greatest contribution to discrimination among the groups, *when the contributions of correlated variables are controlled for.*[6]

The semipartial (or part) correlations shown in Table 13 reflect the correlation between the discriminant functions and that part of the variance of the variable that is uncorrelated with the other variables in the analysis.

The Pearson correlations of the 22 variables used in the MDFA with the two discriminant functions are shown in Table 14. Because the discriminant functions correlate so strongly with the A vs. non-A and the C vs. non-C dichotomies, it is clear that the correlation of a variable with either

---

[6]The discriminant coefficients are dependent upon the variables included in any given analysis. If new variables were added, these coefficients might change substantially, even though the simple correlations of the individual variables with the discriminant functions might not change significantly.

TABLE 13
Multiple Discriminant Function Analysis of Strange-Situation Variables

Variable	Epi-sode	Persons Present	Standardized Partial Discriminant Function Coefficients		Semipartial Correlation with Discriminant Function		Commu-nality
			DF I	DF II	DF I	DF II	
Interactive Behaviors with M							
Proximity Seeking	5	M, B	.118	.152	.045	.065	.225
	8	M, B	.058	.304	.021	.123	.422
Contact Maintaining	5	M, B	−.284	.033	−.087	.011	.252
	8	M, B	.577	.050	.182	.017	.485
Avoidance	5	M, B	−.521	.060	−.183	−.023	.539
	8	M, B	−.922	.120	−.300	.043	.765
Resistance	5	M, B	.412	−.388	.157	−.162	.367
	8	M, B	−.294	−.388	−.124	−.179	.392
Interactive Behaviors with S							
Resistance	3	S, M, B	.107	−.256	.039	−.102	.281
	4	S, B	−.025	−.528	−.010	−.225	.522
	7	S, B	.070	−.204	.031	−.099	.252
Distance Interaction	4	S, B	−.153	.086	−.055	.034	.243
	7	S, B	−.255	−.033	.092	−.001	.361
Exploratory Behavior							
Exploratory Locomotion	7	S, B	−.190	.131	−.077	.059	.325
Exploratory Manipulation	4	S, B	−.100	−.055	−.032	−.019	.267
	7	S, B	−.031	.204	−.010	.072	.396
	8	M, B	.221	−.092	.084	−.039	.230
Crying	2	M, B	.008	−.750	.004	−.392	.314
	3	S, M, B	.058	.191	.023	.082	.172
	5	M, B	−.343	−.440	−.123	−.173	.297
	6	B	−.252	.225	−.092	.102	.495
	8	M, B	−.103	.020	−.037	.008	.408

discriminant function reflects a mean difference between groups on that variable. The vector of correlations of variables with a discriminant function (not the vector of partial discriminant coefficients) provides the most descriptive summary of the behavioral correlates of the discriminant function.

Finally let us consider the communality statistic in Table 13. Because the discriminant functions are uncorrelated, the sum of the squares of the correlations of a variable with each function indicates the proportion of variance associated with the two functions.

Thus in the description that follows, the relevant statistics are: the group means and F-ratios in Table 9, the standardized partial discriminant function

TABLE 14
Correlations of Strange-Situation Variables
with Two Uncorrelated Discriminant Functions

			Correlations With	
Variable	Epi-sode	Persons Present	DF I	DF II
Interactive Behaviors with M				
Proximity Seeking	5	M, B	.429[a]	−.203
	8	M, B	.625[a]	.177
Contact Maintaining	5	M, B	−.358[a]	−.352[a]
	8	M, B	.693[a]	−.070
Avoidance	5	M, B	−.719[a]	.148
	8	M, B	−.874[a]	−.040
Resistance	5	M, B	.168	−.582[a]
	8	M, B	−.313[a]	−.542[a]
Interactive Behaviors with S				
Resistance	3	S, M, B	.029	−.529[a]
	4	S, B	.183	−.699[a]
	7	S, B	.281[b]	−.416[a]
Distance Interaction	4	S, B	−.323[a]	.373[a]
	7	S, B	−.525[a]	.293[b]
Exploratory Behavior				
Exploratory Locomotion	7	S, B	−.525[a]	.223
Exploratory Manipulation	4	S, B	−.358[a]	.373[a]
	7	S, B	−.468[a]	.421[a]
	8	M, B	−.386[a]	.285[b]
Crying	2	M, B	.022	−.560[a]
	3	S, M, B	.041	−.413[a]
	5	M, B	.297[b]	−.457[a]
	6	B	.335[a]	−.619[a]
	8	M, B	.314[a]	−.556[a]

[a]$p < .001.$ [b]$p < .01.$

coefficients, and the communalities reported in Table 13; and the Pearson correlations of interactive behavior with the discriminant functions reported in Table 14.

CHARACTERIZATION OF THE DISCRIMINANT FUNCTIONS

The discriminant analysis highlights the importance of interactive behaviors in discriminating among the three classificatory groups. This is especially true of interactive behavior with the mother. The analysis also highlights the importance of the reunion episodes, numbers 5 and 8. These are also the behaviors and episodes that are most heavily emphasized in the criteria for classification (Chapter 3). Thus the multiple discriminant function analysis suggests that the instructions for classification do in fact dwell on the variables that convey the most discriminating information about an infant's classification. As indicated below, the analysis also casts some light on the role of strange-situation crying as an indicator of the nature of the infant–mother attachment relationship.

Discriminant Function I (A versus non-A)

As indicated by the –.918 correlation between DF I and the dichotomy A vs. non-A, the first discriminant function serves to distinguish Group-A infants from infants in Groups B and C. Variables that correlate negatively with DF I typify Group-A subjects; variables that correlate positively with DF I typify non-A subjects, especially those in the large B group.

Avoidance of the Mother. The variables most highly correlated with DF I are avoidance of the mother in Episodes 5 and 8 (r = .719 and –.874, respectively). This matches the criteria for classification of Group A, which give the first emphasis to "conspicuous avoidance of proximity to or interaction with the mother in the reunion episodes." Although avoidance in Episodes 5 and 8 are significantly correlated (r = .581, $p <$ .001), their substantial partial discriminant coefficients (–.521 and –.922, respectively) indicate that they are by no means entirely redundant. Even though avoidance in Episode 8 is especially noteworthy, avoidance in Episode 5 still ranks as a highly important variable for the discrimination of Group-A from non-A babies.

Seeking To Gain and Maintain Proximity To and Contact With the Mother. Both proximity- and contact-seeking and contact-maintaining behaviors in the reunion episodes are positively correlated with DF I, and thus are shown to be more typical of non-A than of A babies. Their relationship to classification is especially clear in the second reunion episode (r = .625 and .693), in contrast with the first (r = .429 and .358). These behaviors are also featured in the criteria for classification. Presence of such behaviors in the reunion episodes is given first place in the instructions for identifying Group-B infants and is second only to resistance in the instructions for identifying Group-C infants. Relative absence of such behaviors is second only to avoidance in the instructions for identifying Group-A babies.

Proximity- and contact-seeking and contact-maintaining behaviors reflect activity directed toward a common goal, and hence are positively correlated in both reunion episodes (r = .593 and .538). Proximity seeking is significantly but not strongly correlated from Episode 5 to Episode 8 (r = .244, $p <$ .01), reflecting the fact that infants who show weak proximity seeking in the first reunion episode may seek it strongly in the second, whereas some who seek it strongly in the first reunion may be too distressed to do more than signal for contact in the second—specifications detailed in the instructions for the classification of Group-B infants into subgroups. Contact-maintaining behavior, however, is somewhat more consistent across reunion episodes ($r = .452$), although very much more likely to occur strongly in Episode 8.

The low discriminant coefficients for proximity seeking in Episode 5 (.118) and Episode 8 (.058) and for contact maintaining in Episode 5 (−.284), as well as their small semipartial correlations, reflect the intercorrelations among these variables. They also reflect the fact that proximity seeking and contact maintaining in the reunion episodes are strongly and inversely correlated with avoidance ($r = -.485$ and $-.444$ respectively in Episode 5; $-.615$ and $-.574$ respectively in Episode 8). Despite these intercorrelations, contact maintaining in Episode 8 has a substantial discriminant coefficient (.577) and thus makes a relatively large contribution to the discrimination between A and non-A infants.

Resistance to the Mother.   Resistance to physical contact or interaction with the mother is significantly but not strongly correlated with DF I, and then only in Episode 8 ($r = -.313$). The group means in Table 9 indicate that the correlation is primarily due to the absence of resistant behavior in the large B group (as specified in the instructions for classification) and to the presence of some resistance in Group-A babies. Although it was specified in the instructions for classification that A babies tend to lack resistant behavior, it was also specified that A_2 babies, if picked up by the mother in Episode 8, tended to squirm to get down, a behavior scored as resistant.

Interactive Behavior With the Stranger.   Relatively little weight was given to behavior with the stranger in the instructions for classification. It was mentioned, however, that it was characteristic of Group-B babies to be more interested in contact and interaction with the mother than with the stranger, and of C_1 babies to be resistant to the stranger, whereas for Group A a tendency was noted to treat the stranger much as the mother is treated, although perhaps with less avoidance. Furthermore, it was specified that the A baby was not distressed when left with the stranger although he might be distressed when left alone.

The findings in Table 14 show that distance interaction with the stranger in the mother's absence (episodes 4 and 7) is characteristic of Group-A in distinction to non-A babies; it is significantly correlated with DF I ($r = -.323$ and $-.525$ for Episodes 4 and 7, respectively). It seems likely that this finding is secondary to the fact that Group-A infants are not distressed in Episodes 4 and 7; distance interaction with the stranger is not so much characteristic of A babies as it is of babies who are not distressed.

Exploratory Behavior and Crying. The instructions for classification placed relatively little emphasis on crying. As noted earlier, it was specified, however, that Group-A babies showed little or no separation distress, except possibly when left alone in Episode 6. For non-A babies the specifications in regard to crying differed from one subgroup to another. The instructions made no mention of exploratory behavior except by implication in the case of two subgroups—B_4 and C_2. Nevertheless the group means in Table 9 indicate that throughout the strange situation, Group-A infants explore more actively than either Group-B or Group-C infants and that they cry less in all episodes than the non-A infants, particularly less than Group-C infants. It could well be argued that lack of distress, whether due to the unfamiliarity of the physical environment and of the stranger or to separation, is the explanation of the ability of the A baby to sustain exploration throughout; crying babies do not explore. The dynamics of the Group-A pattern of behavior, however, are more complex than this, and are discussed after we have presented the findings of the behavior at home of infants and of their mothers in the three strange-situation groups.

In any event, even though the exploratory and crying variables have significant correlations with DF I, the standardized partial DF coefficients assigned to these behaviors are small, indicating that they offer little discriminative information not contained in the interactive variables. Furthermore, the signs of the coefficients for crying in Episodes 5, 6, and 8 contradict the direction of the group means and thus are best considered artifactual.

In summary, DF I is strongly correlated with the A vs. non-A dichotomy. Its strongest correlates are interactive behaviors displayed toward the mother in the reunion episodes, especially in Episode 8. It summarizes the dominant factor underlying group differences in terms of active avoidance of the mother in the reunion episodes (characteristic of Group A), and contrasts with proximity and contact seeking and contact maintaining in these same episodes (characteristic of non-A). In this respect the analysis confirms the match between the criteria for classification for Group A and the actual behavior of infants so classified.

Discriminant Function II (C versus non-C)

As indicated by the $-.852$ correlation between DF II and the dichotomy C vs. non-C, the second discriminant function serves to distinguish Group-C infants from infants in Groups A and B. Variables that correlate negatively with DF II typify Group-C infants; variables that correlate positively with DF II typify non-C infants, especially those in the large B group.

Resistance to the Mother. The criteria for classification of Group C give primary emphasis to "conspicuous contact- and interaction-resisting behavior." These criteria are reflected in the negative correlations of resistance to the mother in Episodes 5 and 8 with DF II ($r = -.582$ and $-.542$, respectively). Resistance in Episode 5 is significantly but not strongly correlated with resistance in Episode 8 ($r = .341$, $p < .001$). Neither variable is highlighted at the expense of the other in the standard partial DF coefficients in Table 13 (both are $-.388$). Thus resistance to the mother in each reunion episode adds to the information about group membership that is provided by the other. This belies the suggestion in the instructions for classification into Group that resistance might be especially telling in Episode 8.

Seeking to Gain and Maintain Proximity to and Contact With the Mother.   The criteria for classification specify that Group-C infants show, in addition to resistance to the mother, "moderate to strong seeking of proximity and contact and seeking to maintain contact once gained." The specifications for the two subgroups reflect the heterogeneity of Group C, however, stating that these behaviors are strong (active) in C_1 babies, whereas the C_2 babies, notable for passivity, tend more to signal their desire for contact than to seek it actively. On the other hand, the criteria for classification specify that proximity seeking and contact maintaining is characteristic of Group-B infants. Therefore it is not surprising to find that these variables do not clearly distinguish C from B infants, as the group means in Table 9 attest. There is one exception, however—one that was not included in the instructions for classification. Contact maintaining in the preseparation Episode 3 is negatively correlated with DF II ($r = -.328$, $p < .001$). The discriminant coefficients in Table 13 indicate, however, that it is largely redundant with other variables—probably with crying in Episodes 2 and 3.

Resistance to the Stranger.   The criteria for classification in specifying resistant behavior as characteristic of Group C did not limit the specification to the reunion episodes; and indeed in the case of subgroup C_1 they were explicit in specifying that resistance was likely to be shown to the stranger as well as to the mother. The findings of the discriminant analysis are congruent with the notion of generalized resistant behavior as characteristic of Group C. Resistance to the stranger in both preseparation and separation episodes (Episodes 3, 4, and 7) is strongly correlated with DF II ($r = -.529$, $-.699$, and $-.416$, respectively). Resistance to the stranger in the first separation episode is correlated $.415$ ($p < .001$) with resistance to the stranger before separation. The discriminant coefficients in Table 13 highlight the behavior during the first separation ($-.538$) rather than during the second. Because the means for these two episodes are not significantly different (4.23 vs. 4.12), this is not easily explained in terms of changes in the stranger's behavior, but probably can be accounted for in terms of redundancy of information contributed by

Episode-7 resistance. The only significant behavioral correlates of resistance to the stranger are crying and its correlates.

Crying. The criteria for classification included crying or its absence, but in a way that split the sample into two rather than three groups. Infants who did not cry in the separation episodes were generally to be classified either in Group A or in Subgroups B_1 or B_2 (and perhaps occasionally in B_3). Infants who cried in the separation episodes were to be classified in either Group C or in Subgroups B_3 or B_4 (or possibly in Group A if they cried only when left alone and otherwise fit into Group A). Furthermore, it was specified that B_4 infants might be distressed even in the preseparation episodes.

Nevertheless, five measures of crying were significantly discriminating among groups on the basis of the one-way analysis of variance to be entered into the MDFA; and in the case of all of them, the greatest frequency of crying occurred in Group C (Table 9). Crying in Episodes 2, 3, 5, 6, and 8 correlated significantly with DF II ($r = -.559, -.413, -.457, -.619,$ and $-.368$, respectively) as shown in Table 14. In addition, crying scores tended to be correlated across episodes.

Two crying variables were assigned substantial discriminant coefficients (Table 13). Crying when first introduced into the strange situation (Episode 2), although very rare, was assigned the highest discriminant coefficient of any variable of DF II ($-.750$). This implies that if an infant cries in Episode 2, he is likely to be best classified in Group C, even though not all Group-C babies do so. The correlation between crying in Episode 2 and in the subsequent preseparation Episode 3 was .311 ($p < .001$); but the latter was not assigned a significant discriminant coefficient (Table 13), probably because of redundancy with other variables. Crying in Episode 2 reflects inability to use the mother as a secure base from which to explore, and as such may be considered one of the ways in which Group-C infants may show the "maladaptive" behavior specified by the instructions for classification. Thus Group-C infants are clearly to be discriminated from non-C infants by the presence of even minimal unprovoked crying in the preseparation episodes. The other crying variable that received a substantial discriminant coefficient was crying in the first reunion episode 5; this is discussed later.

Crying during the separation episodes clearly distinguishes the C group from the others. Crying in Episodes 4 and 7 were, however, eliminated from the MDFA as a result of redundancies with the other crying variables. Crying in Episode 6, when the baby was alone, was retained, and as mentioned earlier was significantly correlated with DF II. It did not receive a large discriminant coefficient, however (.255). It was significantly correlated with crying in the reunion Episodes, 5 and 8 ($r = .458$ and .371).

Crying in the reunion episodes, while not explicitly specified as characteristic of Group C, is not inconsistent with the instructions for classification. This variable implies difficulty in being comforted when the mother returns—a difficulty that in part reflects extreme distress in the separation episodes, after which it takes a while to settle down, and in part reflects the ambivalence toward the mother that *was* specified for Group-C babies in terms of the simultaneous occurrence of both resistant and proximity- and contact-seeking behavior. In any event, crying in Episodes 5 and 8 is strongly associated with DF II ($r = -.457$ and $-.556$, respectively), and these two crying variables are significantly correlated with each other. It is clear that Group-C infants prolong the distress occasioned by separation into the reunion episodes and cannot be soothed easily by the mother's presence. The discriminant coefficients are $-.440$ and $.020$ respectively, which suggests that crying in Episode 8 is largely redundant with crying in Episode 5, although together or separately they are "important" descriptive variables. Furthermore, it seems plausible to class prolonged reunion-episode crying as one of the "maladaptive" behaviors characteristic of Group C.

Exploratory Behavior.   As noted in the discussion of DF I, the criteria for classification did not specify group differences in exploratory behavior, and indeed implied especial infrequency of such behavior with reference to two subgroups, B_4 and C_2. Nevertheless each of the exploratory behaviors included in the MDFA has a modest positive correlation with DF II, which indicates that Group-C infants explore less actively than do non-C infants. These correlations can be explained in part in terms of crying; crying babies do not explore. The correlations between crying and exploratory behavior are consistently negative and highly significant. Because of this redundancy, none of the exploratory variables in the analysis contributed in an important way to the discrimination between C and non-C babies.

In summary, DF II is strongly correlated with the C versus non-C dichotomy. Its strongest correlates are crying variables and resistance to both mother and stranger. It is difficult to summarize this second dimension underlying group differences in strange-situation behavior, except to repeat the rather imprecise and hence unsatisfying term "maladaptive," which was used in the criteria for classification. The findings to be reported later in regard to group differences in the behavior of infants and their mothers at home suggest that the attachment relationship of Group-C (and also Group-A) infants with their mothers is anxious. The small number of C infants—both in Sample 1, for which home data are available, and for the total sample involved in the MDFA—together with the nature of the MDFA cross-validation results, suggests that classification criteria for Group C should be left open to refinement in the light of new subjects who may be studied in the strange situation and, ideally, also at home.

CONCLUSION

The multiple discriminant function analysis does not, of course, prove that our present classificatory system is the best of all possible descriptions of individual differences in strange-situation behavior. It does, however, demonstrate that the ways in which the infants of our sample were classified is consistent with the stated specifications.

Furthermore, the MDFA helps us to assess the extent to which the range of individual differences was captured by classificatory system. It is clear that the groups A, B, and C differ markedly in terms of the dimensions described by the discriminant functions. It is also clear that the results of this analysis can be expected to generalize to new samples. Furthermore, the weighting assigned to each variable in the discriminant functions is for the most part highly congruent with the significance attached to each in the classificatory system. Only in regard to a few points relevant to the discrimination of C from non-C infants did the MDFA draw attention to the possible refinements that might be made in the classificatory system—preferably after obtaining a larger sample of infants potentially classifiable in Group C.

The MDFA has highlighted several interesting observations: the importance of interactive behavior, the importance of behavior in the reunion episodes (and indeed the importance of having a second separation so that there can be a second reunion episode), and the importance of assessing negative facets of interactive behavior, as well as the positive facets that may be classed as attachment behavior. These observations are not products of this analysis; they have been focal points of our strange-situation research for over a decade. The MDFA, however, removes from these observations the possible charge that they reflect our own bias in interpretation rather than the observable facts themselves. Ultimately, however, their importance and indeed the usefulness of the strange situation itself for the study of individual differences in infant–mother attachment and attachment behavior lie in the relationship between these observations and behavior outside the strange situation.

7

Relationships Between Infant Behavior in the Strange Situation and at Home

INTRODUCTION

In this chapter we address the issue of whether individual differences in strange-situation behavior are related to stable individual differences in behavior in the natural environment. Is the way a baby behaves in the strange situation significantly related to the way he characteristically behaves at home?

This issue can be examined for the 23 infants of Sample 1, who were among the subjects of an intensive, naturalistic study of mother–infant interaction throughout the first year of life. These infants and their mothers were observed at home in the course of 4-hour visits once every 3 weeks from 3 to 54 weeks of age. A responsive but noninterventive observer recorded a running account of the infant's behavior, especially his behavior in interaction with other persons, and this record was subsequently transcribed into a narrative report. The narratives were subjected to several coding procedures to yield measures of behavior. The findings of most of these analyses have already been published. Those that developed measures used in this section are: Bell and Ainsworth (1972) on crying and communication; Stayton, Ainsworth, and Main (1973) on behavior relevant to mother's leaving and entering the room; Stayton, Hogan, and Ainsworth (1971) on infant obedience to maternal commands; Ainsworth, Bell, and Stayton (1972) on behavior relevant to close bodily contact; and Blehar, Lieberman, and Ainsworth (1977) on behavior in face-to-face encounters. In addition, Main coded certain special forms of infant behavior relevant to close bodily contact, which had not been included in the earlier coding; she also coded infant behavior reflecting anger. The findings of Main's codings have not yet been published.[1] In this chapter we consider the relationship between strange-situation behavior and behavior during two periods of the first year—the fourth and first quarters.[2] Before considering these findings, however, we must briefly define the measures of home behavior used here.

MEASURES OF HOME BEHAVIOR

The fourth-quarter measures were based on the narrative reports of visits that took place when the infants were 39, 42, 45, and 48 weeks of age. (At 51 weeks the babies were observed in the strange situation. A home visit was also made at that time to some infants but not to all; so this visit was excluded from the fourth-quarter measures.) Individual first-quarter scores were the mean of the scores of the four visits that took place when the infants were 3, 6, 9, and 12 weeks of age, except for the measures of face-to-face behavior, which excluded the visit at 3 weeks.[3] The measures are as follows:

Crying and Communication.   Three measures were used. *Frequency of crying*—the number of crying episodes per infant's waking hour. A crying episode refers to any instance of a vocal distress signal, whether protest, fuss, or full-blown cry. *Duration of crying*—the combined length of all crying

---

[1]Particularly interested in the differences between Group-A infants and infants of the other strange-situation classificatory groups, Mary Main and some of her students have conducted additional analyses of the longitudinal home-visit data we collected for Sample 1, devising coding and/or rating systems for variables that she hypothesized to be likely to discriminate Group-A infants (and their mithers) from others. We are very appreciative of these additional analyses that she undertook on her own initiative, for they do indeed help to cast light on the dynamics of the development of babies who avoid their mothers in the strange situation. The results of these analyses are presented and discussed in Blehar, Ainsworth, and Main (1978). In the meantime we thank Mary Main for her permission for us to use her findings in this chapter.

[2]The first- and fourth-quarter comparisons are offered as samples of the kinds of relationships to be found between strange-situation behavior and home behavior. We are not including second- and third-quarter comparisons for three reasons: (1) they would be largely redundant with the comparisons we do present; (2) to include them might kindle the reader's interest in the nature of developmental changes in attachment behavior observed at home, but to present developmental data and to discuss the issues raised by them would unduly lengthen and complicate this report; and (3) we wish to present the detailed developmental data referring to behavior in the home environment, and to discuss the issues relevant to them, in other publications that will focus on them rather than on patterns of behavior in the strange situation and their significance.

[3]Blehar, Lieberman, & Ainsworth (1977) based their rerport on data from the visit at 15 weeks, in addition to those at 6, 9, and 12 weeks.

episodes (excluding those too brief to be timed), expressed in minutes per infant's waking hour. *Communication*—the subtlety, clarity, and variety of infants' facial expression, bodily gesture, and vocalization as signals and communications, rated on a three-point scale. (Fourth quarter only.)

Responses to Mother's Comings and Goings.   Four measures were used, all in the fourth-quarter only. *Crying when mother leaves room*—the percentage of leave-room episodes (in which the mother had not put the baby down just before leaving, and in which she left him in company rather than alone) in which a baby began to cry or increased the intensity of his cry at the time of her departure or shortly thereafter. Crying included the silent cry-face, as well as vocal protest, fussing, or full-blown crying. *Following when mother leaves room*—the percentage of leave-room episodes in which a baby, capable of locomotion and on the floor and free to follow, did in fact follow. He was judged to have followed only if he went spontaneously the full distance necessary to get into visual range of his mother, or as far as a barrier that prevented him from going farther. *Positive greeting*—the percentage of enter-room episodes in which a baby directed toward his mother the following behaviors singly or in combination: smiling, vocalizing, laughing, bouncing or jiggling, waving the arms, reaching toward her, leaning or straining toward her, and locomotor approach. *Crying or mixed greeting*—the percentage of enter-room episodes in which a baby cried, or if already crying increased the intensity of his crying upon his mother's entrance, or, in the case of mixed greetings, both cried and positively greeted her either simultaneously or in rapid succession.

Behavior Relevant to Close Bodily Contact With the Mother.   These include four classes of behavior, each of which was tapped by two or more measures.

1. *Responses to being picked up and held.   Positive response*—the percentage of episodes in which the mother picked the baby up in which he responded positively. In the first quarter smiling and/or being described by the observer as "happy" were the criteria for scoring a positive response. In the fourth quarter the following responses, singly or in combination, were identified as positive: smiling, laughing, kissing, hugging, clinging, "sinking in," exploring the mother's face or person, burying the face against her, and any response described by the observer as "delighted." *Negative response*—the percentage of pick-up episodes (undertaken by the mother) in which the infant's response was negative, as shown by crying, stiffening, or squirming in the first quarter, and in addition by pushing away, hitting, or biting in the fourth quarter.

2. *Responses to being put down.*   *Positive*—the percentage of episodes in which the mother put the baby down to which he responded positively; that is, he smiled or generally seemed content when contact with his mother was discontinued. *Negative*—the percentage of episodes in which the mother put the baby down in which he cried when put down, or, in the fourth quarter, made clear gestures that he wanted to be picked up again, such as reaching or clambering up.

3. *Initiation and termination of physical contact.*   The two measures included here were used for the fourth quarter only. *Initiation of pick-up*— the percentage of pick-up episodes that were initiated by the baby; that is, the pick-up was preceded by his spontaneous reaching, locomotor approach, or clambering up, in the absence of any invitation by the mother. *Initiation of put-down*—the percentage of put-down episodes that were initiated by the baby, by squirming, pushing away, sliding down, or otherwise actively indicating that he wanted down.

4. *Special forms of contact behavior.*   The three measures included here were defined by Mary Main and coded by her assistants, for the fourth quarter only. *Tentative contact behaviors*—the number of times in the quarter (corrected for variations in time of observation) that the baby used a tentative movement pattern in contacting his mother, such as touching, patting, or fingering, in lieu of (or in the absence of) close bodily contact. *Sinking in*—the number of times in the quarter (corrected for variations in time of observation) that the baby sank into the mother's person while she held him, or cuddled in, or adjusted his posture in order comfortably to conform to the contours of her body. *Active contact behavior*—the number of times in the quarter (corrected for variations in time of observation) that the baby engaged in active, even rambunctious, contact behavior, affectionately banging on, pulling on, wrestling with, hugging, or kissing his mother.

Behavior When Face-to-Face With the Mother.   These behavioral measures were scored only for the first quarter. *Smiling*—the percentage of face-to-face encounters with the mother (F/F) in which the baby smiled, either when initiating the interaction or when responding to his mother's behavior. *Vocalizing*—the percentage of F/F encounters in which the baby gave a noncrying vocalization, either when initiating the interaction or when responding to his mother's behavior. *Bouncing*—the percentage of F/F encounters in which the baby bounced, jiggled, or generally showed a marked increase of bodily activity. *No response*—the percentage of F/F encounters in which the baby made no response to his mother's initiative, not even looking at her. *Infant termination*—the percentage of mother-initiated F/F encounters that the infant terminated by turning away or by starting to cry or fuss.

Compliance and Anger.   The two behavioral measures included here were scored for the fourth quarter only. *Compliance to mother's commands*—the percentage of mother's verbal commands (such as "No!" "No!" "Don't touch!" "Come!" "Sit!" or "Give it to me!") with which the baby complied. *Anger*—Infants were rated on a nine-point scale devised by Mary Main for the extent to which anger appeared to direct their moods and activities.

Finally, it should be emphasized that the preceding list of measures constitutes a nearly complete list of all the measures developed and examined in the several component segments of data analysis of infant behavior at home. The few that were omitted either were highly redundant with measures included or dealt with behaviors manifested by a very small proportion of infants in the sample. In short, we have not edited our presentation of findings in such a way as to omit measures that do not relate to strange-situation patterns.

FOURTH-QUARTER HOME BEHAVIOR

Correlations With Strange-Situation Behaviors

The strange-situation measures used in this analysis were: proximity/contact seeking, contact maintaining, avoidance, resistance, a combined score of avoidance and resistance, and crying. Except for crying, the scores were based entirely on the reunion episodes, and combined the scores for Episodes 5 and 8. The crying score used here combined scores from all episodes. All of the aforementioned fourth-quarter measures of infant behavior at home were included in the matrix, except for compliance to mother's commands and infant communication—variables that had no apparent counterparts among the strange-situation variables. The intercorrelation matrix is shown in Table 15. (Table 15 also lists correlations of home behaviors with discriminant function scores—see Chapter 6. These are considered in another section.)

Let us deal first with a negative finding: In contrast with what might be assumed by those unfamiliar with our work, crying in the strange situation was not significantly correlated with any of the measures of home behavior in the fourth quarter. Because nearly all strange-situation crying is relevant to separation distress, the implication is that distress attributable to the brief separations from the mother that take place in the unfamiliar environment of the laboratory is not significantly related to the frequency or duration of distress experienced at home, either in relation to separation or otherwise. Those infants who are most frequently distressed by brief, everyday separations in the home environment are not necessarily those who show the greatest distress upon separation in the strange situation. If characteristic behavior at home may be taken as the criterion, crying in the strange situation is not a dependable indication of the quality of an infant's attachment to his mother. To be sure, distress when separated from a specific figure is a clear indication that the infant has become attached to that figure. Yet *absence* of such distress in very brief separations cannot be taken to mean that an infant is *not* attached to the figure who departed.

Crying in the home environment, including crying when the mother leaves the room, is most closely related to resistant behavior in the reunion episodes of the strange situation. Other responses to separation and reunion at home bear little relationship to behavior in the strange situation.

Two measures relating to physical contact are significantly related to four of the five measures of strange-situation reunion behavior—responding positively to being picked up and held by the mother at home, and "sinking in." These are positively correlated with proximity/contact seeking and contact maintaining in the strange situation, and negatively correlated with both avoidance and the composite score of "negative" (i.e., avoidant and resistant) behaviors. On the other hand, responding negatively at home to being picked up and held is significantly related only to the composite score of negative behaviors in the strange situation.

One of the two highest coefficients in the matrix is that between a positive response to being put down at home and the composite score of negative strange-situation behaviors—and the correlation is in the negative direction. Similarly a cheerful response to being put down is negatively related to mother-avoidance in the reunion episodes. Responding adversely (negatively) at home to being put down is positively related to avoidance in the strange situation, and also to the composite score of negative behaviors. Another measure with a similar pattern of correlations is tentative contact behavior at home; it is not only significantly correlated with avoidance and the composite of avoidance and resistance in the strange situation, but also negatively correlated with proximity/contact seeking. These findings are quite incompatible with any attempt to interpret avoidance of the mother in the strange situation either as an indication of greater maturity and independence of the mother or as being due simply to a greater genuine interest in exploratory play. At home, as Ainsworth, Bell, and Stayton (1972) have reported, the babies who enjoy close bodily contact with their mothers tend to respond cheerfully to being put down, and tend then to move off directly into independent exploratory play, whereas the babies who responded adversely to close bodily contact tend to object to being put down and are then less likely to move off into independent activity. Yet it is the latter who tend to be avoidant in the strange situation.

Finally, the infant anger measure is noteworthy for its high correlations with strange-situation behavior. It is negatively correlated with proximity/contact seeking in the strange situation, but positively correlated both with

avoidance and with the composite score of negative strange-situation behaviors. The implication is that babies who avoid their mothers in the reunion episodes of the strange situation are characteristically angry with their mothers.

It is clearly the "negative" behaviors in the strange situation, either avoidance or resistance or both, that are most strongly related to behavior at home. These negative behaviors are noteworthy because they are most strongly activated in the very episodes that also most strongly activate proximity-seeking and contact-maintaining behaviors in most infants. Later we develop the thesis that resistant and avoidant behaviors directed toward the mother in the strange situation reflect conflict in the infant–mother relationship, with a tendency for any strong instigation to attachment behavior also to activate those behaviors that are seemingly antithetical to it. In the present context, however, we merely wish to draw attention to a factor analysis of fourth-quarter infant behaviors displayed at home, reported by Stayton and Ainsworth (1973). The first factor was interpreted as representing a security versus anxiety dimension of the infant–mother attachment relationship. The measures with the highest loadings were crying when mother leaves the room and frequency and duration of crying in general. These are the very measures that are most closely associated with resistance to the mother in the reunion episodes of the strange situation. Therefore we suggest that such resistance reflects anxious attachment to the mother. Factor II was clearly related to response to close bodily contact. Avoidance of the mother in the reunion episodes of the strange situation is significantly related to behaviors relevant to close physical contact. We develop the argument that avoidant behavior reflects an approach–avoidance conflict in specific relation to close bodily contact with the mother.

Correlation with Discriminant-Function Scores

It will be recalled (from Chapter 6) that Discriminant Function I served mainly to discriminate Group A from the other two groups, and that Discriminant Function II provided discrimination between Group C and, especially, Group B. A score for each of these functions was calculated for each infant, and these were correlated with the measures of fourth-quarter home behavior. The findings are shown in Table 15. (It should be pointed out again that Group-A infants fell toward the negative pole of DF I, and Group-C infants toward the negative pole of DF II. Therefore the signs of the correlation coefficients are to be interpreted thus: Variables with a negative correlation with DF I are characteristic of Group A; those with a negative correlation with DF II are characteristic of Group C; and those positively correlated with either function are roughly characteristic of Group B.)

It may be seen that there are six significant correlations between the first discriminant-function scores and home behavior, and five of them clearly involve behavior relevant to close bodily contact. Positively related to DF I, and by inference characteristic of Group-B infants in distinction to Group-A infants, are a positive response to being held, relatively frequent incidence of "sinking in," and active behaviors when in close bodily contact. Negatively related to DF I, and by inference characteristic of Group-A infants, are a negative response to being put down and tentative contact behaviors, both of which we interpret as implying conflict about close contact with the mother. The behavior most highly correlated with DF I, however, is anger ($r = -.79$), which is, by inference, characteristic of Group-A infants.

There are six significant correlations between DF II and home behavior. Of these the three highest (all negative) are crying when the mother leaves the room, and the two measures of crying in general. By inference these are characteristic of Group-C infants. Positively correlated with DF II, and by inference characteristic of Group B in distinction to Group C, are modes of noncrying communication, following when the mother leaves the room, and positive response to being put down.

Difference Between Strange-Situation Groups

Table 16 shows the mean scores of each of the three strange-situation classificatory groups on measures of infant behavior at home in the fourth quarter. It may be seen that the means for Group B differ from the means of the other two groups in a regular way. In the case of 16 of the 18 variables, the Group-B means are either higher than or lower than the means of both Group A and Group C. (The exceptions are following when the mother leaves the room and tentative contact behaviors.) This general finding highlights the fact that Groups A and C resemble each other in regard to most home behaviors more closely than either resembles Group B. This finding seems paradoxical in view of the fact that the strange-situation behavior of Groups A and C differs strikingly; the paradox is discussed later.

Group B differed significantly from Group A in regard to 10 of the variables, and from Group C in regard to 13. These findings support the proposition that behaviors in the strange situation enable one to discriminate among infants who differ significantly from one another in regard to behaviors characteristic of their relations with their mothers at home. Babies who can be grouped together on the basis of their strange-situation behaviors also tend to resemble one another in behavior at home.

Crying and Communication. It may be seen that Group-B babies cried less at home throughout the last quarter of the first year than either A or C

TABLE 16
Measures of Behavior Displayed at Home by Infants
in the Three Strange-Situation Classificatory Groups
(Mean Scores for the Fourth Quarter)

Behavior at Home	Group A N = 6	Group B N = 13	Group C N = 4
Crying and Communication			
Frequency of crying (episodes per hour)	4.70	3.74	4.18
Duration of crying (minutes per hour)	5.60[b]	3.03	8.07[b]
Communication	1.83	2.63	1.25[a]
Responses to Mother's Comings and Goings			
Crying when M leaves room	20.33[b]	14.08	29.00[b]
Following when M leaves room	56.33	55.62	21.25[b]
Positive greeting when M enters	28.17[a]	39.08	23.00[a]
Crying and mixed greeting	12.33	9.46	17.25[b]
Behavior Relevant to Contact			
I. Responses to being picked up and held			
Positive response to being held	14.33[b]	40.00	20.75[a]
Negative response to being held	21.17[b]	6.15	23.00
II. Responses to being put down			
Positive response to being put down	59.83	68.69	50.25[b]
Negative response to being put down	39.17[b]	27.31	30.75[b]
III. Initiation and termination			
Initiation of pick-up	16.17	22.08	9.50[a]
Initiation of put-down	3.50	2.46	6.75
IV. Special forms of contact behavior			
Tentative contact behaviors	.76	.28	.19
Sinking in	.02[b]	.25	.20
Active contact behaviors	.02[a]	.40	.12
Compliance and Anger			
Compliance to mother's commands	54.00[b]	81.15	44.00[b]
Anger	7.83[c]	3.00	5.75[b]

[a] $p < .05$.
[b] $p < .01$.
[c] $p < .001$.

babies. The differences in duration of crying are significant, although the differences in frequency of crying are not. Group-C infants cried relatively longer than the others, both at home and in the strange situation. Group-A babies cried little in the strange situation; yet at home they cried more than the Group-B babies. Bell and Ainsworth (1972) reported negative correlations between crying (both frequency and duration) and level of noncrying communication. Group-B babies not only cried less but also had clearer, more varied, and yet more subtle modes of noncrying communication than did the other two groups—significantly more than Group-C babies, especially.

Responses to Mother's Comings and Goings.   Similar trends hold for responses to everyday separations and reunions at home. Group-B infants showed significantly less frequent distress when mother left the room than either A or C infants. Group-C babies showed the most separation distress both at home and in the strange situation. Group-A babies, who showed little or no distress in the separation episodes of the strange situation, were more frequently distressed than B babies in separation situations at home. It will be recalled that search behavior in the separation episodes of the strange situation did not significantly discriminate among groups. The equivalent measure of home behavior is following when the mother leaves the room. Group-C babies followed significantly less often at home than did B babies, whereas A and B babies did not differ significantly. Indeed, A infants followed slightly more frequently than B infants. These findings clearly negate the notion that A babies did not protest separation in the strange situation because they were not attached to their mothers or because they were relatively weakly attached. At home they unequivocally showed both the distress when mother departed and the following to regain proximity to her that are usually, and properly, believed to indicate that an attachment has been formed. Group-B babies, significantly more frequently than either A or C babies, gave the mother a positive greeting when she returned after a brief absence. Less frequently than either A or C babies they cried when greeting the mother upon her return (or mingled crying with positive greeting), although the difference was statistically significant only when comparing their behavior with that of C babies.

Behavior Relevant to Physical Contact.   Group-B infants, significantly more often than either A or C infants, responded positively when held by their mothers at home, and significantly less frequently responded negatively to being held. This finding is paralled by the strange-situation findings; in the strange situation, B babies sought to gain and maintain proximity and contact more strongly in the reunion episodes than did A babies, whereas C babies, who also sought proximity and contact, did so with less active initiative and sometimes with the simultaneous presence of resistant behaviors.

In the familiar home environment, Group-B babies were usually content to be put down after being held—significantly more frequently than C babies. Significantly less often than either A or C infants they protested being put down or tried to reinstitute contact. The finding that a positive response to being held is associated with acceptance of cessation of contact was discussed earlier. The apparent independence of the mother manifested by A babies in the strange situation is associated with avoidance; at home A babies are less frequently ready than B babies to cheerfully accept being put down, and by inference are less ready to shift to independent activity. In the strange situation, however, it was the Group-B babies who were conspicuous for contact-maintaining behavior in the reunion episodes—behavior distinguished by protest on being put down and especially active efforts to resist release and to reinstitute contact. It is suggested that separation in the unfamiliar environment activated attachment behavior to a higher pitch of intensity than did usual events in the home environment, so that infants not only sought contact more strongly but also sought to maintain it more actively and for a longer period than they ordinarily did at home.

In the familiar environment of the home, babies tended relatively infrequently to initiate either being picked up or put down, especially the latter. Nevertheless Group-B babies initiated being picked up more frequently than the babies of the other groups, and significantly more frequently than Group-C babies.

The three measures of special forms of contact behavior were added to the measures of home behavior by Mary Main in the expectation that they would differentiate mother-avoidant babies (i.e., Group A) from babies of the other groups. Indeed they tend to do so. Group-A babies significantly less often than Group-B babies "sank in" or showed "active contact behaviors" while being held by their mothers. Main's hypothesis about tentative contact behaviors was not supported, however; although some A babies were conspicuous for such behaviors, others were not, and thus the difference between Groups A and B was not statistically significant. Of the three special forms of contact behavior, one—sinking in—significantly distinguished A from C babies ($p < .03$).

Compliance and Anger. Main also assessed infant anger in the expectation that Group-A infants would emerge as more frequently angry than either B or C babies. This hypothesis was supported, in that C babies, despite being more overtly angry in the strange situation than the A babies, were significantly less angry at home ($p < .04$). Furthermore, Group-B infants at home were significantly less angry than infants of either Groups A or C. Finally, Group-B infants were conspicuous for their compliance with their mothers' verbal commands, obeying in 81% of the instances in which commands were issued, and were significantly more often obedient than the infants of either Groups A or C.

One further comparison was made of the three strange-situation classificatory groups in regard to home behavior—in terms of the balance between attachment and exploratory behavior in the home environment (Ainsworth, Bell, & Stayton, 1971). Because this analysis features differences among the subgroups, however, discussion of it is deferred until Chapter 12.

Let us now discuss in more detail the seemingly paradoxical behavior of the Group-A babies. A detailed analysis of their behavior at home led to the interpretation that they had developed a long-standing and pervasive approach–avoidance conflict relevant to close bodily contact with their mothers (Main, 1977a; Blehar et al., 1978). This proposition implies that their attachment behavior was activated by the same kinds of conditions, and to the same degree, as usual for their age-peers, so that they tended on occasion to seek proximity and contact, but that their previous experience had been such that close bodily contact—or even the anticipation thereof—activated avoidance behavior. (We consider the kind of previous experience that is common to Group-A babies in Chapter 8.)

At home the conflict between these two behavioral systems was manifested in a variety of subtle ways. Group-A babies tended to make a partial approach to the mother, then to halt, and then either to retreat or veer off in another direction. If their approach succeeded in bringing them near to the mother, they tended not to seek actual contact; if they touched her they were likely merely to touch her momentarily before withdrawing, and they were most likely to touch a peripheral part of her body—for example, her foot. If, nonetheless, they did achieve close bodily contact—either through clambering up or because the mother picked them up—they rarely responded positively (only in 11% of pick-up episodes), and were very unlikely either to show active contact behavior or to sink in, comfortably relaxed against the mother's body. Nonetheless, when put down they were more likely than infants of other groups to protest or to signal to be picked up again. Behaviors such as these give a very clear picture of conflict between antithetical behavior systems. (Indeed, avoidance itself suggests the presence of conflict, but we defer discussion of this assertion until Chapter 14.)

The presence of an approach–avoidance conflict implies that fear behavior may be involved in the conflict. It is perhaps not so obvious that angry behavior may also be involved. Yet if attachment behavior is chronically prevented from reaching its appropriate terminating conditions, it is reasonable to infer that anger is activated by the frustration implicit in these circumstances. Indeed, anger was found to occur significantly more frequently among Group-A babies than in babies of either of the other two groups. It must be pointed out, however, that the baby's angry behavior was rarely manifested in a direct attack on the mother, but in more subtle ways—for example, attack redirected toward physical objects or occasionally by biting or hitting the mother for no apparent reason and without the slightest indication of overt anger. Not only attachment behavior but also angry behavior tends to be inhibited by the approach–avoidance conflict.

These considerations pave the way for our interpretation of the strange-situation behavior of A babies. We propose that their attachment behavior was strongly activated in the separation episodes. This proposition is supported by the fact that they tended to search for their mothers as strongly as, and in some instances more strongly than, non-A babies, even though they tended to cry little or not at all. When the mother reappeared in the reunion episodes, it may be assumed that their attachment behavior was still at an unusually high level of activation, but the mother's presence also activated avoidant behavior, perhaps all the more strongly because of the high level of activation of attachment behavior. Subgroup-A$_2$ babies dramatically acted out their conflict by alternating approach and avoidance behavior, but even they— and, more conspicuously, the A$_1$ babies who seemed steadfast in ignoring the mother—turned to exploratory behavior, a third behavioral system that was also strongly activated in the strange situation as demonstrated in Episode 2. Under these circumstances, exploratory behavior serves as what ethologists call a "displacement behavior"—a conspicuous and readily available item of the behavioral repertoire that comes to the fore when two momentarily stronger behavioral systems are antithetical and block each other, as, for example, when a bird equally instigated to attack and to flee merely preens his feathers.

As for C babies, there also appears to be some conflict in regard to close bodily contact with their mothers. Like A babies they tend at home more frequently than B infants to respond negatively to being held and yet to respond negatively to being put down, but in this case, behavior in the strange situation is continuous with home behavior. In the strange situation the behavior of some C infants reflects conflict between wanting close bodily contact in the reunion episodes and, at the same time, resisting it. This is reminiscent of classical ambivalence. Some C babies, however, seemed to show their resistance more to their mother's efforts to interest them again in exploratory play; they wanted close contact and angrily resisted their mothers' efforts to interest them in a toy. Our hunch is that it is not so much that Group-C babies find close bodily contact with the mother aversive or disappointing (as is the case with A babies), but that they tend to distrust the mother's accessibility and responsiveness—that is, they are anxious in their relationship with her. Consequently, both at home and in the strange situation, they want more assurance of the mother's availability and responsiveness than do B babies, and probably more than their mothers are ordinarily able or willing to provide. Thus the problem of the C baby is one of getting more response—and perhaps especially more close bodily contact—than the mother is prepared to give, whereas the problem of the A baby is that he both wants and avoids such close contact. The C baby fears that he will not get enough of what he wants; the A baby fears what he wants. There is a difference.

Fourth-Quarter Developmental Quotients

Approximately every 9 weeks throughout the course of the first year, the Griffiths Scale of Infant Intelligence was administered to the infants in Sample

1. Although not of the same order as the other findings reported in this chapter—which were all measures directly pertinent to mother–infant interaction—it is convenient here to report the findings for test scores obtained in the fourth quarter. The mean for Group-A infants was 109.6, for Group-B infants 118.7, and for Group-C infants 106.9. Although the differences between the groups are not large enough—and the intragroup variability too large—to be statistically significant in this small sample, they clearly suggest that the Group-A infants are not more advanced in development than the infants of other groups. Therefore, it is not possible to interpret their relative lack of proximity seeking in the strange situation as reflecting greater "maturity" or more advanced cognitive development, as has sometimes been suggested. Likewise, B_1 and B_2 infants, who also show relatively little proximity seeking, cannot be judged more advanced in development, for their mean DQ is 118.0, whereas that of the B_3 subgroup is 119.0.

Summary

In summary, Group-B infants at home were conspicuous for little crying, infrequent separation distress, frequent positive greetings (and infrequent negative or mixed greetings) upon reunion, frequent initiation of close bodily contact, positive response to it once achieved, and yet positive response to cessation of such contact. In addition, B babies tended to have better-developed modes of communication than non-B babies, to be more compliant to the mother's wishes, and to be less frequently angry. In contrast, the infants of both A and C groups were characterized by relatively more crying in general, more separation distress, disturbances related to close bodily contact with the mother, and more anger.

We have already referred to the factor analysis of fourth-quarter home behavior of this sample, conducted by Stayton and Ainsworth (1973). This, together with the other considerations discussed above, leads us to interpret the strange-situation classifications as indicating that B babies have relatively secure attachment relationships with their mothers in comparison with A and C babies. Although both A and C babies may be described as anxious in their attachment to the mother, it is clear that they differ in the ways in which they manifest their anxieties—especially in situations, such as the strange situation, that activate attachment behavior at high intensity. We have also suggested that the source of the disturbance is different for Groups A and C. Whereas in C babies the source of the disturbance lies in the discrepancy between what they want and what they expect to receive, in A babies there seems to be a more basic conflict between the kind of comfort and reassurance that they want and are prompted to seek, and a fear or at least an avoidance of just that. Both A and C babies may be classed as anxiously attached; A babies are, in addition, more fundamental conflict than C babies.

FIRST-QUARTER HOME BEHAVIOR

Differences Between Strange-Situation Groups

In view of the fact that Group-B babies differed significantly from A and/or C babies in their fourth-quarter behavior at home, it is of interest to see to what extent differences occurred even earlier in the first year. Here we explore for differences in regard to home behavior in the first quarter. The roster of behavioral measures is shorter in the first than in the fourth quarter, however. It is too early for infants to respond to a person leaving or entering the room, to show active initiative in being picked up and put down, or indeed to show the special forms of contact behavior that were examined in regard to fourth-quarter behavior. Furthermore, it is too early for babies to be active enough for their behavior to be controlled by verbal commands, or for angry responses to be differentiated from distress. We consider only frequency and duration of crying, responses to being picked up and put down by their mothers, and behavior in response to face-to-face encounters with their mothers. Indeed, these three situations—episodes of crying, physical contact, and face-to-face interaction—account for most occasions for interaction between a baby and his mother in the earliest months. The only other common occasion for interaction is feeding, and this is largely comprehended by the three situations just mentioned.

In the previous section of this chapter it was apparent that, despite their striking differences in strange-situation behavior, babies in Groups A and C differed from each other less in their fourth-quarter behavior at home than they did from babies classified in Group B. It seems reasonable to assume that behaviors characteristic of Groups A and C would be even less differentiated from each other in the first quarter than they were in the fourth. Indeed, this proved to be the case. None of the differences between the means of Group A and Group C shown in Table 17 proved to be significant. If, however, we consider the differences between Group B and Groups A and C combined, some of the differences are significant. A and C babies, who by the end of the first year were identified as anxiously attached, cried longer and more frequently than B babies, who later were identified as securely attached. Bell and Ainsworth (1972) pointed out, however, that both frequency and duration measures of infant crying are confounded with measures of maternal responsiveness to crying within any given time period. Therefore, it seems likely to us that these significant differences between groups are attributable not so much to initial constitutional differences among the infants as to differences in maternal behavior, which we examine in Chapter 8. Thus if a mother is quick to respond to crying, that particular cry tends to be quickly terminated; moreover, the nature of the response may well tend to reduce the likelihood of another cry for some time. If a mother is slow to respond, the

TABLE 17
Measures of Behavior Displayed at Home by Infants
in the Three Strange-Situation Classificatory Groups
(Mean Scores for the First Quarter)

Behavior at Home	Group A N = 6	Group B N = 13	Group C N = 4	Significance of Difference Between B and A/C
Crying				
Frequency (episodes per hour)	5.4	3.4	3.8	.025
Duration (minutes per hour)	13.0	6.9	11.8	.01
Behavior Relevant to Physical Contact				
Positive response to being held	6.7	24.8	1.8	.02
Negative response to being held	16.3	19.5	32.5	ns
Positive response to put-down	5.3	11.4	6.5	ns
Negative response to put-down	46.7	36.0	61.2	.05
Behavior in Face-to-Face With Mother				
Smiling	39.3	45.3	26.3	ns
Vocalizing	26.7	23.9	6.9	ns
Bouncing	1.7	11.7	1.9	ns
No response	17.7	4.9	16.6	.05
Terminates face-to-face encounter	26.1	11.4	14.7	.05

baby tends to continue crying until she does respond, and if he does indeed stop spontaneously without her intervention, he may very well cry again soon. Therefore, we are inclined to view the differences in first-quarter crying between Group B and the combined Group A/C as reflecting differences in maternal responsiveness to crying. By the fourth quarter, however, Bell and Ainsworth suggest that amount of crying has become a fairly stable infant characteristic, and therefore the confounding of measures that concerned us about first-quarter behavior is less pertinent.

Measures of behavior relevant to physical contact are not similarly confounded. Therefore, it is of interest that Group-B infants more frequently than A/C infants responded positively to being held, and less frequently responded negatively to being put down—just as they were found to do in the fourth quarter. We are inclined to rule out the possibility of constitutional differences in "cuddliness" in this sample, because all infants were found to be capable of a positive response to being held—at least when held by the visitor if a positive response had not been observed toward the mother. In the light of the finding that A babies are in conflict about contact later on, it is of particular interest here that A and B babies differed very little in regard to negative response to contact in the first quarter. In the first quarter a positive response to being put down was uncommon in any group, although it was somewhat more frequent (insignificantly so) among Group-B infants.

In regard to behavior in face-to-face encounters with the mother, Group-B babies were more positively responsive—smiling, vocalizing, and bouncing more frequently—than A/C babies, although the differences fell short of statistical significance. Significantly less often, however, did B babies make no response to the mother's attempts to initiate face-to-face interaction—that is, not even looking at her—and significantly less often did they take the initiative in terminating the face-to-face encounter by either crying or looking away.

We undertook another analysis of our early face-to-face interaction data, sharpening the distinctions in regard to later attachment patterns by considering Subgroup B_3 in contrast to Groups A and C combined, with B_1/B_2 babies forming an intermediate group (Blehar, Lieberman, & Ainsworth, 1977). In this analysis the data base was also extended to include four rather than just three visits—including the visit at 15 months in addition to those at 6, 9, and 12 months. The differences between B_3 and A/C babies in regard to smiling and bouncing were significant in this comparison, and fussing was also significantly different, A/C infants fussing more than B_3 infants when face-to-face with their mothers.

The chief reason for mentioning the Blehar, Lieberman, and Ainsworth report here, however, is the interesting information it contains about the relationship of later attachment quality to early differences in responsiveness to attachment and nonattachment figures. A comparison was made between behavior to the mother and to the visitor-observer. B_3 infants vocalized and bounced significantly more in the presence of the mother than of the visitor in face-to-face encounters, whereas they merely looked at the visitor more frequently and more frequently terminated the episodes in which the visitor was involved. In contrast, the A/C babies showed no difference in responsiveness to the two figures, except for fussing, which was more frequently directed to the mother. These findings cannot be attributed to the fact that A/C babies were simply less socially responsive, because they were as responsive to the *visitor* as were the B_3 infants. The findings therefore suggest that babies who are later conspicuous for a secure attachment relationship with the mother—that is, B_3 babies—are during a very early period of life differentially responsive to an attachment figure in contrast with a nonattachment figure during face-to-face encounters, whereas infants who are later conspicuous for an anxious attachment relationship—that is, A and C babies—are not.[4]

Although it is not feasible here to cite similar differences in second- and third-quarter behavior in regard to any of the measures considered in this

---

[4]Here we have omitted reference to the intermediate group of four B_1/B_2 infants. They were indeed intermediate between B_3 and A/C in regard to most of the measures, but the group was too small for differences to be statistically significant.

chapter, these first-quarter findings should suffice to suggest that babies who later may be described as securely attached to their mothers have had a long history of interaction with their mothers in which they were more often positively responsive and less often distressed or unresponsive than were babies who later can be described as anxiously attached. To be sure—as is shown in Chapter 8—mothers of the babies in different groups may also be distinguished from one another along much the same lines. We do not attempt to argue here that the mother has a greater effect on the baby than vice versa; we merely argue that the infant's behavior in interaction with his mother forms a basis for distinguishing B from A/C groups, in several aspects, as early as the first quarter of the first year.

SUMMARY AND DISCUSSION

We have shown that 1-year-olds, classified into three groups on the basis of patterning of their behavior in the strange situation, may also be distinguished in terms of the behavior they display in interaction with their mothers in the familiar home environment. In particular, Group-B infants differ from Group-A and Group-C infants—the latter being less conspicuously different in their behavior at home than either are from Group-B infants.

Furthermore, specific classes of strange-situation behavior correlate significantly with specific classes of behavior at home. This does not imply that there is a one-to-one correspondence between strange-situation behaviors and home behaviors. Thus, an infant who cries relatively often at home may cry little or not at all in the strange situation; an infant who shows very little distress in brief, everyday separations at home is likely to show substantial distress when briefly separated in the unfamiliar laboratory situation. The laboratory situation, with its strong and repeated instigations to attachment behavior, elicits different behaviors to different degrees of intensity than are commonly displayed in the home environment. Nevertheless, the findings here reported suggest that one can establish a fair basis for predicting strange-situation behavior from home behavior and, perhaps more important, that one can assess certain general aspects of the infant's characteristic relationship with his mother from his behavior in the strange situation.

It is reasonable to conclude that the security–anxiety dimension of the infant's relationship with his mother is reflected in strange-situation behavior as it is in behavior at home. Evidence has been presented that suggests that certain patterns of behavior in the strange situation also reflect the nature and degree of certain conflicts an infant may long have been experiencing in his relations with his mother. The behaviors serving as the most conspicuous "pointers" to such conflicts are avoidant and resistant behaviors in relation to the mother in the strange situation, especially avoidance.

Nevertheless, no single strange-situation behavior, and indeed no list of behaviors considered separately, is adequate to describe the relationship with stable patterns displayed at home. It is the patterning of behaviors in the strange situation that "matches" the patterning of behaviors at home. Consequently, we conclude that the comparison of strange-situation and home behavior provides justification for viewing the strange-situation classificatory system as having continuing usefulness, and not merely as having being useful as an methodological step toward identification of dimensions of behavior that might then be assessed independently.

8

Relationships Between Infant Behavior in the Strange Situation and Maternal Behavior at Home

INTRODUCTION

Although in the previous chapter we presented evidence that strange-situation behavior reflects stable individual differences in the nature of the infant's attachment relationship to his mother, we did not concern overselves with how such differences might have arisen. In this chapter we examine the relationship between behavior of infants in the strange situation and the behavior their mothers displayed in interaction with them at home. It seems very likely to us that maternal behavior played a large part in influencing the development of qualitative differences in infant–mother attachment.

The subjects of this inquiry are the mothers of the 23 infants of Sample 1. Their behavior and its relationship to infant behavior at home has been dealt with in the same publications that were listed at the beginning of Chapter 7. In addition, we include several variables assessed by Mary Main and her students, which she hypothesized to be particularly relevant to the experiential background of Group-A babies, who avoided their mother in the strange situation (see Chapter 7). Furthermore, we refer to the detailed study of mother–infant interaction relevant to the feeding situation in the first quarter, as reported by Ainsworth and Bell (1969), and to an early analysis of the relationship between maternal fourth-quarter behavior and infant strange-situation behavior, as reported by Ainsworth, Bell, and Stayton (1971). Here for the first time all the available relevant data are brought together. Before presenting these findings, however, it is necessary briefly to define the measures of maternal behavior that we deal with in this chapter.

MEASURES OF MATERNAL BEHAVIOR

Two types of measures were devised: one based on ratings and the other derived from behavioral codings. Some of these refer only to fourth-quarter behavior, some only to first-quarter behavior, and some to both. Let us first consider the measures derived from codings. The relevant codings were of episodes of infant crying, leave- and enter-room episodes, pick-up and put-down episodes, face-to-face interaction, and episodes involving maternal commands to the infant. The fourth-quarter measures were based on the narrative reports of visits that took place when the infants were 39, 42, 45, and 48 weeks of age and represent the mean for these four visits. The first-quarter measures were based on the narrative reports of visits that took place when the infants were 3, 6, 9, and 12 weeks of age—except for the measures of face-to-face behavior, which excluded the visit at 3 weeks.

In the early stages of analysis of the longitudinal data, however, and before the very time-consuming codings had been completed, we worked with rating procedures. Nine-point rating scales were devised, with points 1, 3, 5, 7, and 9 anchored in detailed behavioral descriptions. These are not ordinary rating scales. Instead of being drawn up in a sketchy fashion in advance of data collection, they were devised on the basis of a careful examination of the behavior recorded in the narrative reports. (Indeed, we did draw up a set of a priori rating scales, but these were found inadequate to make the discriminations that it was possible to make once we knew more about mother–infant interaction than we did at the beginning of the project.) The precision and appropriateness of the behavioral definitions made it possible to achieve a very satisfactory level of interrater agreement among the two or more raters involved in each decision. Two sets of scales were devised, the first to deal with maternal behavior in the baby's first quarter-year, and the second referring to his fourth quarter.

Twenty-two rating scales were devised for the assessment of first-quarter behavior.[1] Of these we have chosen to present only the findings of the four that dealt with mother–infant interaction relevant to the feeding situation. These scales were based on a very detailed analysis of such behavior undertaken by Ainsworth and Bell (1969). A second set of scales was devised for the assessment of maternal behavior during the fourth quarter. Because using all 22 variables had seemed unduly redundant, we confined ourselves to four that seemed especially related to individual differences in the baby's response to the

---

[1] These 22 scales for rating first-quarter maternal behavior, as well as four scales for rating fourth-quarter maternal behavior, may be obtained in microfiche from the ETS Test Collection, Educational Testing Service, Princeton, N.J. 08540. Ask for the *System for Rating Maternal-Care Behavior* (008053). *Systems for Coding Infant Attachment and Reciprocal Maternal Behaviors* (008054) is also available there.

mother. (The procedure for rating these scales is described by Ainsworth, Bell, and Stayton, 1971.)

Let us consider the various maternal measures, whether derived from rating or coding, according to the following classes of behavior: responsiveness to crying, behavior relevant to separation/reunion, behavior relevant to close bodily contact, behavior relevant to face-to-face interaction, behavior relevant to infant obedience, behavior relevant to feeding, and general characteristics.

Responsiveness to Crying.   The two relevant measures, in fact, focus on unresponsiveness to crying. *Ignoring of crying*—the mean number of crying episodes per baby's waking hour to which the mother made no interventive response whatsoever. *Duration of unresponsiveness to crying*—the mean number of minutes per baby's waking hour that he spent in crying during which the mother made no response to him. This includes both the latent period after the baby began to cry before the mother intervened and the duration of episodes of crying in which the mother did not intervene at all.

Behavior Relevant to Separation/Reunion.   Only one maternal measure had been found to be related to infant response to separation and reunion. *Mother's acknowledgment of baby upon entering the room*—the percentage of enter-room episodes in which the mother smiled or talked to the baby, or approached him, or in other ways initiated interaction with him.

Behavior Relevant to Close Bodily Contact.   There were eight measures falling within this class. Only one of them deals with duration of contact. *Mean duration of a pick-up episode*—obtained by dividing the total holding time for each visit by the number of pick-ups that took place during the visit (first quarter only). Four measures deal with qualitative aspects of the mother's behavior. *Affectionate pick-ups*—the percentage of pick-up episodes in which the mother behaves affectionately toward the baby, kissing him, hugging him, or caressing him. *Abrupt, interfering pick-ups*—the percentage of pick-up episodes that constitute an active interference with the baby's ongoing activity (fourth quarter only). *Tender, careful holding*—the percentage of total holding time in which the mother was tender and careful in her handling of the baby. This behavior may be identified by a slowing of the mother's usual tempo of movement, a muting of her characteristic intensity of behavior, and a sensitive pacing of her behavior to the infant's response to contact with her. *Inept holding*—the percentage of total holding time in which the mother was inept or abrupt in her handling of the baby. Classed as inept was jerky maternal behavior, in which the baby's head was inadvertently banged against something or in which the baby was held in an obviously uncomfortable position. A further measure deals with the purpose of the episode of contact. *Routine holding*—the percentage of total holding time devoted to routines such as feeding, changing, transport, and the like (fourth quarter only).

Two of the four measures devised by Mary Main, according to the hypothesis that they tapped variables particularly relevant to the development of mother-avoidance, related specifically to close bodily contact. These took the form of nine-point rating scales in which careful behavior definition was given to each of the odd-numbered points. *Aversion to physical contact*—this scale measures the extent to which the mother appears to have an aversion to or dislike for physical contact, whether with people in general, with babies in general, or with this particular baby. A rating of 9 was given for strong aversion to contact with the baby if the mother was observed to withdraw from contact as the baby attempted to touch her, or if she actually said that she disliked or feared contact with him. A rating of 5 was given for inconsistent or moderate dislike of contact that may be inferred from frequent references to the "fact" that holding spoils a baby, repeated holding in unnatural ways that minimize close bodily contact, impatience in holding, and the like. A rating of 1 was given in instances in which there was no evidence of dislike of contact. Because the rating procedure has not yet been published (Blehar, Ainsworth, & Main, 1978), it is appropriate to say that ratings quarter by quarter were done by two pairs of raters, each member of the pair working independently. Interrater agreement was shown by correlations ranging from .90 to .99. Here we present only the first-quarter ratings, in the belief that it is in the first quarter that close bodily contact is of the most significance.

The second Main variable is providing the baby with *unpleasant experience in physical contact:* This scale dealt with the extent to which babies might be inferred to associate physical contact with the mother with unpleasant sensory experience. There was no outright child abuse observed in this sample, but nevertheless a rating of 9 was reserved for repeated experiences of a very unpleasant nature—the unpleasantness being inferred from the infant's strong negative response of screaming and/or struggling. The kinds of maternal handling that were relevant here tended to be highly idiosyncratic, including uncomfortable holding, rough handling, obnoxious overstimulation, pinching, and force-feeding; but the ratings were not so much geared to the type of handling as to its frequency and degree. Except for the extreme rating of 9, an inference could be made of "unpleasant experience" whether or not the infant overtly protested. Ratings were done by two pairs of raters; interrater agreement ranged from .95 to .99. Again we present only first-quarter scores here.

Behavior Relevant to Face-to-Face Interaction. We are using three measures of maternal behavior in face-to-face interaction with the baby, and all of these were scored for the first quarter only. *Contingent pacing*—the percentage of face-to-face episodes in which the mother paced her interventions slowly and gently, modifying them in keeping with the infant's cues and pausing if needed to allow him time to mobilize a response. *Silent, unsmiling*—the percentage of face-to-face episodes initiated by the mother in which she merely looked at him silently and impassively, rather than smiling or talking to him, or "jiggling" him. *Routine manner*—the percentage of face-to-face episodes in which the mother behaved in a "matter-of-fact" way— behavior more likely to occur during performance of routines such as changing than on nonroutine occasions.

Behavior Relevant to Infant Obedience.   Only two measures fall into this class, and both of these pertain only to the fourth quarter. *Frequency of verbal commands*—the mean number of verbal commands and prohibitions issued by the mother per visit. Only commands judged to be comprehensible to a baby were recorded (e.g., "No! No!" or "Give it to me"), and only those instances were tallied in which the baby was given an opportunity to comply without physical intervention. *Frequency of physical intervention*—the mean number of discipline-oriented physical interventions by the mother per visit. These included all instances in which the mother physically reinforced verbal commands by (or in lieu of verbal commands) trying to force the baby to do as she wished—for example, by dragging him away from a forbidden area or slapping him when he reached for something she did not want him to have.

Behavior Relevant to Feeding.   There are four first-quarter rating scales dealing with dimensions of maternal behavior relevant to feeding. *Timing of feeding*—concerned with the extent to which the mother synchronized her feeding interactions in accordance with the baby's rhythms. Implicit in this scale is the hypothesis that the optimal timing is when the baby is awake, active, and hungry, but before he has reached a peak of hunger and crying. A rating of 9 was given when there was adaptation of timing to the baby's behavioral signals, whether it came about through thoroughgoing and consistent demand feeding or sensitive and flexible schedule feeding. A rating of 1 was given when the intervention was very arbitrary—very badly geared to the baby's rhythms and in almost complete disregard of his signals. *Determination of the amount of food and the end of the feeding*—concerned with the mother's skill in perceiving the signal her baby gives when he is satisfied, gratifying him without giving him too much. The mother who receives a rating of 9 neither terminates a feeding abruptly when the baby stops feeding momentarily, nor coaxes him to take more when he seems not to wish to resume after she has waited a little. Mothers who received a rating of 1 terminate feedings in almost total disregard of the baby's signals. Some force-feed after the baby has signaled termination or carry coaxing to the point that it is aversive; others terminate the feeding prematurely and impatiently, so that the baby gets far too little food.

Two other scales relevant to feeding are as follows. *Handling of the baby's preferences in food*—this is pertinent only after "solid" foods have begun, although most mothers in this sample introduced them very early. A rating of 9 is given for great tact in presenting new or disliked foods, whereas a rating of 1 is given when the mother shows great disregard of the baby's preferences, forcing food on him even when he protests vigorously. *Synchronization of mother's rate of feeding to the baby's pace of intake*—this reflects the degree to which the mother respects the baby's autonomy and encourages him, to the extent that he is able, to take some initiative in the ingestion of food, both in suckling and in spoon-feeding. The mother receives a rating of 1 when she interferes unduly with the baby's own pacing. She may forcibly remove the nipple if he drowses, or she may provide him with so fast a nipple that he tends to choke. She may force-feed solids, or she may feed too slowly and inattentively.

Throughout all of these scales it is acknowledged that babies differ in the kinds of signals they give, that it may take some time before a mother can learn to read the signals of her baby, and that an approximation of the optimal synchronization with the baby's signals and rhythms requires a mutual adaptation. Nevertheless these ratings are included here as measures of maternal behavior because the mother, for better or for worse, has much more control than the baby over the whole feeding situation during the first few months.

General Maternal Characteristics.   There are six measures included here, all of them nine-point scales. The first four are fourth-quarter scales. *Sensitivity–insensitivity to the baby's signals and communications* is the first of these. The optimally sensitive mother is able to see things from her baby's point of view. She is alert to perceive her baby's signals, interprets them accurately, and responds appropriately and promptly, unless no response is the most appropriate under the circumstances. She tends to give the baby what he seems to want, and when she does not she is tactful in acknowledging his communication. Furthermore she makes her responses temporally contingent upon the baby's signals. A mother receives a rating of 1 when she gears her interventions almost exclusively in terms of her own states, wishes, and activities. She tends to distort the message the baby is sending, interpreting it in the light of her own needs or defenses, or she does not respond to his signals at all.[2] The second scale deals with *acceptance–rejection* —the balance between the mother's positive and negative feelings about her baby and the extent to which she has been able to integrate or to resolve her conflicting feelings. A highly rejecting mother frequently feels angry and resentful toward her baby. She may grumble that he interferes unduly with her life, or she may show her rejection by constantly opposing his wishes or by a generally pervasive mood of scolding and irritation. A mother would be

---

[2]This scale has been published in full in the chapter by Ainsworth, Bell, & Stayton, 1974.

rated as 9, or highly accepting, when she accepts her infant even when he is angry or unresponsive. She may occasionally feel irritated by his behavior, but she does not cast him in the role of opponent. She cheerfully accepts the responsibility of her maternal role, without resenting the temporary limitation this places on her other activities.

A third scale dealing with general maternal characteristics is *cooperation–interference.* The highly interfering mother does not respect her baby's autonomy and essential separateness. She tries to control him and to shape his behavior, or merely follows her own promptings without regard for his wishes or activity-in-progress. The highly cooperative mother respects her baby as a separate person and plans to avoid situations in which she might have to interfere with his activity or to exert direct control over him. When she does intervene, she is skillful at "mood-setting," so that the baby is persuaded that he wants to do what she wants him to do. A fourth scale is *accessibility–ignoring,* which deals with the mother's psychological accessibility to her infant when she is at home and in this sense physically accessible to him. The inaccessible or ignoring mother is often so preoccupied with her own thoughts and activities that she does not even notice her baby, let alone acknowledge his signals. She seems to notice him only when she deliberately turns her attention to do something to or for him. The accessible mother, on the other hand, seems able to attend to her baby's signals and communications, despite distraction by other demands on her attention

These four dimensions were rated separately for each visit to each mother–infant pair at 39, 42, 45, 48, 54, and (when possible) 51 weeks. Five judges participated, working independently. Although two of the judges unavoidably had knowledge of other assessments, the other three did not. A schedule of rating was designed to eliminate the possibility of halo effect, both across variables and across visits to the same dyad. The mean interrater correlation coefficients for each of the scales are as follows: sensitivity–insensitivity .89, acceptance–rejection .88, cooperation–interference .86, and accessibility–ignoring .87. Discrepancies between ratings were decided in conference. The final rating was the conferenced rating, which was almost invariably the median rating for all visits rated.

The other two measures were devised by Mary Main, according to the hypothesis that they tapped variables particularly relevant to the mothers of mother-avoidant babies. Both took the form of nine-point rating scales similar to those previously described. *Lack of emotional expression* is a scale concerned with the degree to which a mother lacks emotional expression in her face, voice, or bodily movements, making possible descriptions such as: poker faced, wooden, overcontrolled, monotone, mechanical, robotlike. A rating of 9 was given to mothers who were described in the narrative report in terms such as these, the descriptions not referring to specific incidents or to a single visit but implying a general characteristic of the mother's behavior. Main's hypothesis is that extreme expressionlessness implies repression of strong feelings, especially angry feelings, and/or inhibition of expression of negative emotions. A rating of 5 was given for a moderate lack of emotional expression, as for example when a mother is bland, phlegmatic, or matter-of-fact, but offers no reason to infer repression of feeling. A rating of 1 would be given to a mother who expresses herself freely, whether the resulting behavior is tender, playful, or angry or some mixture of these and other tendencies. Because our observer-visitors had not been briefed to make note of emotional expression or lack thereof, the raters often had to rely on general summary descriptions rather than on episode-by-episode reports of behavior. Because of this, Main thought it wise for the judges to rate the cumulative impression of the narrative reports for the whole of the infant's first year. Two judges independently rated each mother. Their interrater agreement was .88.

Finally, Main devised a scale of *maternal rigidity*. This variable rates the extent to which the mother is judged to be rigid, compulsive, and/or perfectionistic—not merely toward the baby, but toward other persons or "in general." The first step in assessment was a scoring sytem that combined frequency with degree of intensity of rigidity, the details of which cannot be given here.[3] The resulting scores were so greatly skewed that they were translated into ratings on a six-point scale in order to reduce the degree of spread between the most extremely rigid and the average nonrigid score. The original scoring was done by two coders working independently. As with the variable of nonexpressiveness, the score pertains to the first year as a whole, because the observer-visitors tended to comment at length on a rigid mother's characteristic behavior in the report of one visit and then perhaps not make specific reference to it again for some time, as though they assumed, quite properly, that such behavior was not subject to daily variation.

FOURTH-QUARTER MATERNAL BEHAVIOR

Group Differences in Fourth-Quarter Maternal Behavior

The mean scores for the fourth-quarter behavior of mothers of babies in each of the three strange-situation classificatory groups are shown in Table 18. It may be seen that Group-A and Group-C mothers, especially the latter, delayed significantly longer than Group-B mothers in responding to infant crying. They also tended to ignore more crying episodes altogether, although these differences were not large enough to be significant. Another behavior that reflects responsiveness to the infant is frequency of the mother's acknowledgment of the baby when she enters the room after an absence. Group-A mothers acknowledged their babies in a significantly smaller proportion of enter-room

---

[3]The scoring system, as well as the scales devised by Dr. Mary Main, may be obtained from her—Department of Psychology, University of California, Berkeley, Calif. 94704.

TABLE 18

Behavior Displayed at Home by the Mothers of Infants in the Three
Strange-Situation Groups (Mean Scores for the Fourth Quarter)

Maternal Behavior	Group A N = 6	Group B N = 13	Group C N = 4
Responsiveness to Infant Crying			
Ignoring of crying (episodes per hour)	2.06	1.50	2.35
Unresponsiveness to crying (minutes per hour)	3.26[d]	1.27	4.44[c]
Behavior Relevant to Separation/Reunion			
Acknowledging baby when entering room	17.83[b]	34.46	23.00[a]
Behavior Relevant to Close Bodily Contact			
% of pick-ups in which M behaves affectionately	8.83[b]	24.00	4.00[d]
% of pick-ups that are abrupt or interfering	20.33[c]	9.08	14.25
% of holding time in which M is tender, careful	8.67	21.62	3.00[a]
% of holding time in which M is inept	9.83[a]	3.85	15.00[b]
% of holding time occupied with routines	21.33	17.38	46.25[b]
Behavior Relevant to Infant Obedience			
Frequency of verbal commands	2.37	2.57	2.03
Frequency of physical interventions	1.32[a]	.58	1.33
General Characteristics (Ratings)			
Sensitivity–insensitivity to signals	2.42[d]	6.48	2.38[d]
Acceptance–rejection	3.75[d]	7.62	5.38[c]
Cooperation–interference	3.58[d]	7.30	4.25[d]
Accessibility–ignoring	3.83[c]	6.62	3.50[c]

Note: significance of *t* test comparing Group B with Group A or Group C

[a]$p < .10.$
[b]$p < .05.$
[c]$p < .01.$
[d]$p < .001.$

episodes than B mothers, and C mothers also tended to be less responsive than
B mothers.

Mothers differed also in their behavior relevant to close, bodily contact with
their babies. Group-B mothers were affectionate during bodily contact
significantly more often than either A or C mothers. They were also more likely
to be tender and careful in holding the baby than were A or C mothers, but the
variability of this behavior in the fourth quarter was too great for the
differences to be statistically significant. Earlier in the first year, tender, careful
holding seemed to have an important influence on the baby (Blehar,
Ainsworth, & Main, 1978), but by the time the baby is nine months old and
relatively big, strong, competent, and mobile, even a mother who had
previously been conspicuous for tender, careful holding may well increase the
speed and vigor with which she handles the baby. Group-A mothers,
significantly more frequently than B mothers, were abrupt and interfering
when they picked up the baby.

Correlations With Infant Discriminant-Function Scores

Table 19 shows the correlations between maternal behaviors and the two sets of discriminant-function scores assigned to infants on the basis of their strange-situation behavior. The findings are interesting in that they more clearly suggest differences between A and C mothers than did the findings reported in Table 18.

The coded behavior most characteristic of mothers of Group-A babies, in contrast with those of non-A babies, is picking the baby up in an abrupt and interfering manner. Especially infrequent among A mothers, in contrast with non-A mothers, is affectionate behavior while holding the baby. The behaviors most characteristic of mothers of Group-C babies, in contrast with those of non-C babies, are delay in responding to cry signals and occupying the time when holding the baby with routines. Also infrequent among C mothers is affectionate behavior during contact.

In regard to all the rated measures, the correlations are significant and substantial with the first discriminant function, although not with the second. Thus the characteristics of A babies that discriminate them from B and C babies in the strange situation are more closely correlated with maternal insensitivity, interference, ignoring, and especially with rejection than are the characteristics of C babies that discriminate them from non-C babies.

FIRST-QUARTER MATERNAL BEHAVIOR

Group Differences in First-Quarter Maternal Behavior

Table 20 shows the mean scores of first-quarter behavior of the mothers of the babies in the three strange-situation classificatory groups. The significance of the difference between mothers of B and non-B babies was assessed by means of t tests, and the results are also shown in Table 20. The significance of the differences between mothers of A and C babies was also assessed by t tests.

Perhaps the most extraordinary feature of the findings is that differences between B and non-B mothers were significant in 13 of 17 variables and reached a p level of less than .10 in 2 of the 4 nonsignificant variables. To be sure, there was a selection of variables for this analysis, but (except for the assessments provided by Mary Main) the selection was in terms of behaviors that had been proved significantly related to infant behavior at home either in the first or in later quarters. We have already pointed out that Main chose her variables in terms of theory-based hypotheses about behaviors that v ould discriminate Group-A mothers from Group-C mothers. The implication is that babies who differ qualitatively in their attachments to the mother at the

TABLE 20
Behavior Displayed at Home by Mothers of Infants in the Three Strange-Situation Classificatory Groups (Mean Scores for the First Quarter)

Maternal Behavior	Group A	Group B	Group C	Significance of Difference Between B and non-B
Responsiveness to Infant Crying				
Ignoring of crying	3.08	1.60	1.59	n.s.
Unresponsiveness to crying (minutes per hour)	6.77	3.64	9.35	<.01
Behavior Relevant to Close Bodily Contact				
Mean duration of a pick-up episode (in minutes)	5.20	8.70	7.80	<.10
% of pick-ups in which M behaves affectionately	6.50	16.90	8.75	<.05
% of holding time in which M is tender, careful	22.00	55.00	2.25	<.001
% of holding time in which M is inept	28.00	5.00	41.00	<.001
Aversion to physical contact[a]	7.30	2.28	1.73	<.01
Provides B with unpleasant experience[a]	5.68	1.45	2.90	<.005
Behavior Relevant to Face-to-Face Interaction				
Contingent pacing	20.70	52.90	10.90	<.01
Silent, unsmiling initiation	28.70	12.20	11.30	n.s.
Routine manner	29.70	11.00	25.50	<.01
Behavior Relevant to Feeding				
Timing of initiation[a]	2.75	6.40	2.38	<.001
Timing of termination[a]	3.17	6.54	2.83	<.001
Dealing with baby's food preferences[a]	3.87	6.70	3.83	<.01
Pacing according to baby's rate of intake[a]	3.42	6.85	3.33	<.01
General Characteristics				
Lack of emotional expression[b]	6.17	2.69	3.50	<.02
Rigidity[b]	4.33	2.15	2.75	<.02

[a]Ratings of first-quarter behavior.
[b]Ratings of behavior throughout the whole year.

end of the first year have mothers whose behavior and attitudes, as early as the baby's first 3 months, differ in salient ways.

It may be seen from Table 20 that Group-B mothers were more promptly responsive to infant crying signals in the first quarter, whereas non-B babies were allowed to cry for longer periods unattended. Bell and Ainsworth (1972) interpreted their longitudinal findings in regard to infant crying and maternal responsiveness to indicate that mothers who were promptly responsive early on had babies who cried relatively little by the end of the first year, whereas mothers who delayed for relatively long times before responding to crying signals in the first quarter had babies who cried relatively much later on. The present findings expand that interpretation: Mothers who are promptly responsive to crying signals in the early months have babies who later become securely attached.

Maternal behavior and attitudes relevant to close bodily contact in the early months also are significantly associated with later quality of attachment as reflected in the strange-situation classification. Group-B mothers, in the first quarter, handled their babies tenderly and carefully for proportionately much more time than did non-B mothers. Earlier we pointed out that by the fourth quarter, when the infants had become sturdier, more active, and more competent, there was a decline in tender, careful holding behavior—and indeed such behavior that did occur was not significantly related with the quality of infant–mother attachment. In the early months, however, tender, careful handling could easily be interpreted as sensitive responsiveness to the baby's behavioral signals in the context of physical contact. We suggest that a mother's muting of her usual speed and vigor of movement and her sensitive response to the baby's own bodily adjustments upon being picked up and held provides him with an initially secure experience of close bodily contact. In contrast, mothers of non-B babies, much more frequently than mothers of B babies, handled their infants ineptly in the first quarter. Affectionate behavior on the part of the mother was less common during the first quarter than was tender, careful behavior, and it had little relationship to the baby's concurrent response to close bodily contact. Nevertheless it proved to be significantly related to the baby's strange-situation behavior at the end of the first year.

Blehar, Ainsworth, and Main (1978) cite evidence suggesting that how much a mother holds her baby in the early months seems to be of far less significance than *how* she holds him—although this might not be the case in a sample including some infants who were grossly deprived of close bodily contact. Furthermore, the total time spent in holding seemed of less significance than the duration of the separate episodes of holding. There is a tendency for the mean duration of a pick-up episode in the first quarter to be associated with secure attachment at the end of the first year.

Clear support is found for Main's two hypotheses relevant to physical contact in the findings presented in Table 20. Non-B mothers have a significantly stronger aversion to physical contact with their babies than B mothers. The findings clearly suggest that this effect is entirely attributable to the strong aversion that Group-A mothers feel and express, and indeed they differ very significantly from Group-C mothers in this regard ($p < .0001$). It must be emphasized that such aversion is only rarely expressed openly, and could well have been missed had the home visits not been long and frequent enough to encourage mothers to behave naturally. Even so, Group-A mothers gave their babies a total amount of physical contact that was not significantly less than given by the mothers of non-A babies. They believed that babies needed to be held (especially while being fed), and did so even though they themselves did not enjoy it. As may be seen, they also, on occasion, behaved tenderly and affectionately—even though they did so less often than B mothers. Our hypothesis is that the underlying aversion and implied rebuff nevertheless communicates itself to the baby. It is also clear that non-B mothers in the first quarter more frequently and intensely than Group-B mothers provide their babies with unpleasant, even painful, experiences associated with close bodily contact. This effect also tends to be attributable more to the A than to the C mothers, although the differences between them proved not to be statistically significant ($p < .212$) for first-quarter behavior. However, the same measure for the entire first year did prove to be statistically significant ($p < .02$).

Main's other two hypotheses also gained some support. Mothers of non-B babies, in comparison with B mothers, tended to lack emotional expression when dealing with their babies. Again the effect seemed mainly attributable to the A mothers. Although they did not differ significantly from C mothers ($p < .148$), they did differ from B mothers ($p < .003$), whereas C mothers did not. Mothers of non-B babies, in comparison with B mothers, tended to be rigid and perfectionistic. This effect likewise seemed attributable to the A mothers, who differed significantly from the B mothers ($p < .01$), although not from the C mothers.

Group-B mothers were more likely than non-B mothers to pace their behavior in face-to-face situations in accordance with the tempo of the baby's responses. They were less likely to behave in a matter-of-fact, "routine" manner when face-to-face with their babies.

In regard to each of the four variables relevant to the feeding situation, Group-B mothers were also more likely to gear their behavior to the baby's signals than were non-B mothers. They tended to feed the baby rather than delaying when he gave signals implying hunger. They tended to terminate feeding only after the baby signaled that he was satisfied. They were tactful when presenting new foods. They carefully paced their feeding interventions to the baby's rate of intake.

SUMMARY AND DISCUSSION

The major implication of the findings reported in this chapter is that maternal behavior in both the first and the fourth quarters—and presumably in between also—is significantly associated with the security–anxiety dimension of an infant's attachment relationship with his mother, and that this association is evident even in the first quarter of the first year. The most important aspect of maternal behavior commonly associated with the security–anxiety dimension of infant attachment is manifested in different specific ways in different situations, but in each it emerges as sensitive responsiveness to infant signals and communications. The highly significant differentiation between B and non-B mothers in the fourth quarter that is provided by a global measure of this variable occurs, we believe, because of the pervasive effect of this quality of maternal behavior throughout many specific kinds of interaction. This and correlated measures of maternal behavior thus do not reflect maternal behavior in absolute terms, but they do tap the extent to which a particular mother is able to gear her interaction with a particular baby in accordance with the behavioral signals he gives of his states, needs, and, eventually, of his wishes and plans.

Although the sensitive responsiveness of mothers to infant signals and communications seems to be the key variable in accounting for environmental influences on the development of a secure versus an anxious attachment relationship (i.e., Group B versus non-B), some progress has also been made toward identifying aspects of maternal behavior that are implicated in a baby's developing an avoidant version of anxious attachment rather than a nonavoidant but perhaps resistant version (i.e., Group A versus Group C). So far, the four aspects of maternal behavior that are most closely associated with the avoidant solution are: (1) rejection; (2) especially rejection communicated through aberrant reactions to close bodily contact; (3) submerged anger; and (4) a generally compulsive kind of adjustment. Main (1977a) hypothesized that the relative lack of emotional expressiveness characteristic of Group-A mothers was attributable to an effort to control expressions of anger. Although the lack of expression has the consequence of withholding from the baby important feedback when in interaction with his mother—a consequence that may affect his own social development—it seems likely that it is the rejection implicit in the anger itself that affects the baby, despite his mother's attempt to hold it in. The most obvious consequence of a generally compulsive kind of adjustment is that it makes the mother less often aware of infant signals and hence less responsive to them. However, it also may be implicated in rejection, for the rigid and compulsive mother is reluctant to give precedence to the baby's needs and wishes, if only because she is so preoccupied with what is important to her outside of a purely motherly role.

Of all of these aspects, we are inclined to give major emphasis to interaction in the context of close bodily contact, if only because this seems most directly relevant to the origins in the baby of an approach–avoidance conflict about such contact. Although the findings yielded by a longitudinal study of Sample 1 have yielded much support for the account of the origins and dynamics of mother-avoidant behavior that we share with Main, it is too small a sample to yield wholly clear-cut distinctions. Main's independent work with a group of toddlers drawn from Samples 3 and 4 provides further evidence in support of her hypotheses, however; this we examine in Chapter 9.

9
A Review of Strange-Situation Studies of One-Year-Olds

INTRODUCTION

We believe that our strange-situation procedure will be very useful in research into the attachment of a child to his mother figure and its relationship to other facets of development. Indeed it has already been a point of departure for a substantial number of studies of attachment and/or attachment behavior.

In many of these projects, modifications in the procedure have been introduced that make it difficult to make direct comparisons between their findings and those presented in this volume. Attachment behavior can be strongly affected by the situation in which one attempts to observe it; some situations offer strong instigation to it, whereas others do not. As we have shown in earlier chapters, behavior toward the mother in Episode 8—whether this be attachment behavior or behavior antithetical to it, such as avoidance or resistance—particularly highlights the kind of qualitative differences in attachment that are reflected in our classificatory system. The most common modification of the strange-situation procedure has been to eliminate a second separation and consequently also a second reunion episode, thus omitting the very episode that we have found to be most crucial in highlighting individual differences that prove stable across a variety of situations. However interesting and fruitful it would be to review the findings of these studies in order to interpret each in the light of the whole, this enterprise would take us too far afield.

Here we review only those studies that were intended to be directly comparable to ours, in that the strange-situation procedure was used with little or no departure from our format—at least in the arrangement of the conditions under which observations were undertaken. These studies fall into two main classes: those that examined the strange-situation behavior of 1-year-olds and related it to behavior under other conditions, to other behaviors, or to antecedent factors that might have affected it; and those that dealt with the strange-situation behavior of 2-year-olds or older children. Some of the latter studies were directly concerned with age-attributable changes that may take place in strange-situation behavior itself, and demonstrated that such changes are substantial. Therefore we propose to defer a review of studies dealing with the older preschoolers to the next chapter and to consider here only those that focus on the strange-situation behavior of 1-year-olds.

The studies of 1-year-olds may be divided into five classes: (1) those that view qualitative differences in infant–mother attachment as a "dependent variable" and examine their relationship to antecedent conditions; (2) those that view either mother–infant interaction or infant–mother attachment as an "independent variable" and investigate other facets of infant behavior to which it may be concurrently related; (3) those that similarly view either mother–infant interaction or infant–mother attachment as an "independent variable" and investigate other facets of behavior *some months later;* (4) those that compare behavior in our standard situation with behavior in another situation of parallel design but with either the setting or the adult figure changed; and (5) those that are concerned with the stability of strange-situation behavior and/or classification over time. Because these last-mentioned studies are clearly relevant to the topic considered in Chapter 11, they are discussed there. This present chapter is concerned with the first four groups of investigations mentioned here. We consider first those that address the issue of antecedent conditions that may be related to qualitative differences in attachment.

PATTERNS OF ATTACHMENT AT ONE YEAR
RELATED TO ANTECEDENT VARIABLES

Neonatal Separation.   Hock, Coady, and Cordero (1973) compared the strange-situation behavior of 31 infants who had been born prematurely with that of 30 full-term infants when the latter were about 11 months old and the former of comparable age after a correction was made for prematurity. The mean birth weight of the premature group was 1,500 grams or less—that is, less than 3 pounds, 4 ounces. The antecedent condition of interest was the extent of separation from the mother experienced by the premature babies—a mean of 40 days following birth in contrast to only 3 or 4 days for the full-term neonates. The separation was complete in neither case, for the hospitals concerned encouraged the mothers of the prematures to visit them, to touch them, and later to participate in caretaking. Nevertheless the early mother–infant interaction was necessarily more limited with the premature than with the full-term babies. Because of the age correction, both groups had experienced about the same length of time with their mothers at home after discharge from the hospital and before observation in the strange situation— namely, about 46 weeks.

No significant differences were found between the premature and full-term groups. The authors concluded that the 46 weeks that the prematures had spent at home with their mothers after the prolonged neonatal separation had quite overcome any effects the latter might have had on either quality of mothering or on eventual infant–mother attachment.

Twins Versus Singletons.   In the premature sample studied by Hock, Coady, and Cordero (1973), there were 14 twins and 17 singletons. Significant differences were found between these two groups. Specifically, the premature twins showed more resistant ($p < .01$) and more avoidant ($p < .05$) behavior in the strange situation than the premature singletons. The authors suggested that it is plausible that the mothers of twins would be less able than mothers of singletons to respond promptly to infant signals—a suggestion that is clearly congruent with our findings of behavioral differences among the mothers of the babies in our classificatory groups.

Demographic and Other Variables.   Connell (1974) observed the strange-situation behavior of 46 infants from white, middle class families when they were approximately 51 weeks of age, and later (1976) added 55 more infants to his sample, making a total of 101. For this total sample, as well as for the original 46, he checked a variety of different variables that might have influenced infants' development or their behavior in the strange situation, in order to "rule them out." He indeed found that the following had no significant relationship to strange-situation classification in his sample: social class of parents, number of siblings, precise age at the time of observation, time of day of observation, and identity of the stranger in the strange situation.

It must be pointed out that Connell used a "multivariate classifier" based on the classificatory system we developed. It was devised by Connell and Rosenberg (1974) on the basis of the data from our total sample of 105. Their method of reduction of the variables from 72 to a more acceptable number for multivariate analysis differed substantially from the method we used for the same purpose (see Chapter 6). One step of their method involved cluster analyses, in the course of which they concluded that our Groups A, B, and C were highly distinct clusters, thus confirming our classificatory system, but noted "two minor anomalies." Subgroup-B_1 subjects seemed to fit better with Group A than with Group B, and B_4 subjects seemed to fit better with Group C. The subjects of these two small subgroups were, therefore, not considered in the development of the classifier.

After the reduction of measures had been completed, a discriminant function analysis was then undertaken to yield a set of discriminant weights that could be used to assign subjects of a new sample to Groups A, B, and C. A "design set" of 65 subjects randomly selected from our total data base (after removing B_1 and B_4 subjects) yielded a 97%-correct classification rate. The remaining set of 26 subjects, which had been held out of the classifier-design computations, was classified correctly at a 96.2% rate. When the weights were applied to Connell's own sample, the distribution into Groups A, B, and C was congruent with the distribution we reported in Chapter 6, Table 7.

Although we have chosen other methods of data reduction for our discriminant function analysis, it is evident that the data are sufficiently robust to withstand diverse methods of analysis without undue loss of information. As to the anomalies presented by B_1 and B_4 infants, we acknowledge that the discriminations between A and B_1 infants and between C and B_4 infants are the most difficult to make. We have chosen, nonetheless, to retain both subgroups in Group B, for reasons that are discussed in Chapter 12.

Low Birthweight and Low APGAR Scores.   Connell (1974, 1976) found a significant tendency for Group-C infants to have lower weight and lower APGAR ratings at birth than the A and B infants in his sample. One child in his sample weighed 4 pounds, 5 ounces at birth; otherwise none weighed less than 5½ pounds. Presumably, all of the low-birthweight infants in his samples were born at term, and none of them weighed as little as the prematures observed by Hock, Coady, and Cordero (1973). The two samples of low-birthweight infants are not comparable, therefore; Connell's were small for their gestational age, whereas Hock's were of a size appropriate for their gestational age. The implication is that low-birthweight infants in Connell's sample may have been retarded in intrauterine growth, and thus perhaps more predisposed toward postnatal developmental anomalies than the "normal" prematures of Hock's sample. If so, it is indeed interesting that one of these anomalies is related to the development of an anxious attachment relationship with the mother.

Maternal Attitudes and Mother–Infant Interaction.   Rosenberg (1975) undertook to evaluate the validity of our inference (Ainsworth, Bell, & Stayton, 1971) that the strange-situation classifications reflect the characteristic harmony/disharmony of mother–infant interaction. Because of this, we have included his study with those concerned with antecedent conditions. It should be emphasized, however, that he views mother–infant interaction as a highly reciprocal matter, to which both partners make an important contribution.

His sample consisted of 46 of the infants with whom Connell worked, and the identification of classificatory groups was done by means of the "multivariate classifier" (Connell & Rosenberg, 1974) to which reference was made earlier. In choosing measures of mother–infant interaction, he focused on Sander's (1964) concept of reciprocity, and therefore chose to use the Reciprocity Factor Scale of the Maternal Attitude Scale constructed by Cohler, Weiss, and Grunebaum (1970), which had been based on Sander's work. In addition, he observed mother–infant interaction in two laboratory situations: (1) a free-play situation lasting 6 minutes in which the mother was told to do whatever she wished; and (2) a directed-play situation, also lasting 6 minutes, in which she was instructed to administer three Bayley Scale items to her infant. Both situations could be described as low-stress situations in which the social interaction tended to be mediated through objects. In each situation the degree of sensitivity and reciprocity of the mother's behavior was rated on a nine-point scale adapted from our scale of maternal sensitivity to infant signals and communications (see Ainsworth, Bell, & Stayton, 1974), which had originally been designed for the rating of maternal behavior in the home environment. In each situation the infant's social responsiveness was also rated on another nine-point scale adapted from a three-point scale devised by Brody and Axelrad (1970). To tap the actual interaction between mother and infant, as well as to assess the separate contribution of each, he calculated the time spent in the laboratory situations in each of four mutually exclusive interaction states: reciprocal interaction (M+I+), reciprocal ignoring (M–I–), and two mixed interaction states (M+I–) and (M–I+).

Rosenberg focused on comparisons between Groups A and B. He considered the 6 Group-C infants in his sample to constitute too small and too heterogeneous a group for statistical comparisons. Group-B mothers scored significantly higher on the Reciprocity Factor of the Maternal Attitude Scale, and thus more strongly endorsed encouragement than discouragement of reciprocity with the infant. They were also rated significantly higher on reciprocity–sensitivity in the free-play situation, although they did not differ from Group-A mothers in the directed-play situation. Group-B and Group-A infants did not differ significantly, however, in their rated social responsiveness in either situation. Group-A infants increased significantly in social responsiveness from the free-play to the directed-play situation, however. In the free-play situation, Group-B infants showed more nondistress vocalizations than Group-A infants, whereas Group-A infants explored more than Group-B infants. Group-B mother–infant pairs had reciprocal-interaction states (i.e., M+I+) in significantly more 15-second intervals than did Group-A dyads, whereas the latter had significantly more reciprocal-ignoring states (i.e., M–I–).

The finding that Group-B infants were not found to be more socially responsive than Group-A infants, Rosenberg was inclined to attribute to an overly global measure of social responsiveness; he pointed out that Group-B babies vocalized more than Group-A babies—a behavior that is especially likely to elicit maternal social behavior and thus is conducive to reciprocal interaction.

The rest of Rosenberg's findings offer substantial support both to his hypotheses and to our findings. Group-B mothers emerged as more sensitively responsive to infant signals and more consciously geared toward establishing reciprocal interaction than Group-A mothers. Such sensitive responsiveness undoubtedly includes encouraging rather than ignoring or interfering with an infant's interest in exploring a novel environment, as well as responding to infant's bids for interpersonal interaction. Rosenberg's findings clearly show that mother–infant interaction is more harmonious in Group-B than in Group-A dyads.

Working Versus Nonworking Mothers.   Brookhart and Hock (1976) compared 18 home-reared infants with 15 who attended a day-care center for at least 2 consecutive months before the strange situation. The day-care babies were separated from their mothers for a mean of 33.6 hours per week, whereas the home-reared infants were separated for only 7.3 hours a week on the average. Both samples were middle class and aged 11 months when observed in the strange situation. (Brookhart and Hock, in the same study, investigated the differences for this sample between behavior in the strange situation conducted in a standard fashion in the laboratory and behavior in a parallel situation conducted in the home environment. This aspect of their study is discussed later in this chapter.)

The measures used were our measures of proximity and contact seeking, contact maintaining, resistance, and avoidance (all scored for behavior to mother and stranger), search, and crying. A multivariate analysis of variance was undertaken, with the main effects examined for groups (day-care versus home-reared), episodes, and sex. (The main effects attributable to location—i.e., laboratory or home—were also examined, but are considered in a later section.) There were no main effects attributable to rearing conditions, although there were significant group by sex interactions in regard to proximity-seeking and contact-maintaining behavior directed toward the stranger. These interactions were complex, and the groups were too small for firm conclusions about sex differences to be drawn. Therefore, the chief finding was a lack of difference between infants reared at home and infants with at least two months' experience in group day care.[1]

---

[1]Because significant effects were found for location, and because the effects attributable to rearing were based on observations in both home and laboratory contexts, it occurred to us that the effects attributable to rearing might have been obscured by the effects of location. Brookhart and Hock (personal communication) reported, however, that a separate analysis of variance based solely on the laboratory data also failed to yield significant main effects attributable to rearing conditions, and replicated the findings in regard to interactions.

In another report, Hock (1976) was concerned with a comparison of the effects of a variety of different types of infant care. The number of variables that might affect the results were several—including part-time vs. full-time work, age of infant when mother began work, how consistently she worked, whether the baby was placed in individual or group care, whether individual care was in the baby's own home or elsewhere, and how many different caretakers were involved. Hock attempted to control for (or test the effects of) these variables in her several analyses, but even a total sample of 83 working mothers was not large enough to deal with all variables.

Her first analysis of variance concerned a comparison of 74 nonworking mothers with the total sample of 83 working mothers. There were no significant main effects in regard to strange-situation variables, although both resistant and avoidant behavior directed toward the stranger approached significance. The infants of nonworking mothers were somewhat more disturbed in their behavior toward the stranger. The 27 babies whose mother worked part-time were not found to behave significantly differently from those whose mothers worked full-time, and there were no effects attributable to the baby's age at the time the mother began working.

Two samples of working mothers that met more homogeneous criteria were selected, both of which consisted of mothers who began working and placed the infant in some kind of substitute care before he was 7 months of age, but who stuck to one type of care within which the infant had no more than two caretakers. In other words, babies of these two samples experienced continuity and a reasonable degree of consistency in substitute care. One of these samples consisted of 31 infants who were cared for individually, whether at home or elsewhere. These infants showed significantly less resistance to the stranger in the strange situation than the infants of the 74 nonworking mothers, but otherwise there were no main effects attributable to mothers' working. No main effects were found within the individual-care sample attributable to whether infants were cared for in their own homes or elsewhere.

The second sample consisted of 28 infants who were cared for outside of their own homes, 17 individually and 11 in group care, whether in a day-care center or in a babysitter's home where at least three children constituted the group. Those in group care showed significantly more resistant behavior to the mother in the strange situation than those in individual care; they also showed somewhat more crying and less search behavior in the separation episodes. Hock suggested that they seemed to exhibit a disturbance best described as an angry mood. In this report, Hock did not compare the group care sample with a home-reared group because group care was confounded with care away from home.

Discussion. This group of five studies, primarily concerned with antecedent conditions that might influence the later quality of the infant–mother attachment relationship, tend to support our findings. In Chapter 8, which dealt with the relationship between maternal behavior and infant attachment, we emphasized that the pervasive variable of maternal responsiveness to infant signals emerged as the most important antecedent. We concur in the suggestion made by Hock, Coady, and Cordero (1973) that mothers of twins (and probably not merely mothers of premature twins) are likely to find it more difficult than mothers of singletons to respond promptly to infant signals. Rosenberg's (1975) findings about the importance of maternal reciprocity and sensitivity are also congruent with ours. Although Connell (1974, 1976) found no relationship with quality of attachment within his sample of either social class or number of siblings, this would not necessarily be the case for other samples in which these variables were related to conditions likely to reduce maternal responsiveness to signals or to make the mother relatively inaccessible to the infant. Thus, for example, Bell (1978) reported a higher incidence of secure attachment among white, middle-class babies than among black, disadvantaged babies, and attributed it largely to the chaotic substitute-care arrangements experienced by a number of infants in the disadvantaged sample. (Other findings of Bell's study are reported later in this chapter.) Similarly, one could expect that infants in large families might find their mothers less accessible than infants in small families if multiple births or other conditions of high "density" were associated with large family size.

We thought it a reasonable hypothesis that extended, early neonatal separation might affect the quality of mothering and hence the quality of the eventual attachment relationship, especially because evidence has been accumulating that close bodily contact immediately postpartum facilitates the emergence of the attachment of mother to infant and is associated with more harmonious mother–infant interaction in later months (Klaus & Kennell, 1976). It may be, however, that the encouragement given by the hospitals to the mothers of the prematures studied by Hock, Coady, and Cordero (1973) to visit and to interact with their babies, together with the long subsequent opportunity to interact with them fully at home, may have overcome any initial adverse effect of the extended but often partial neonatal separation—especially if the mothers of the full-term control babies were given no particular encouragement toward close interaction in the neonatal period.

The trends found by Connell for his small-for-date babies (i.e., those with low birthweight and low APGAR ratings, but who were not born prematurely) to be classified as Group C and hence as anxiously attached invites more intensive longitudinal research into the development of mother–infant interaction in the case of babies with this kind of "at risk" factor.[2]

Rosenberg (1975) has implied that infant responsiveness may itself be an antecedent variable that could influence strange-situation behavior and hence presumably quality of infant-mother attachment. It is indeed difficult to disentangle this variable from variables of maternal attitudes and behavior that influence the course of mother-infant interaction. It is, however, too complex a research issue to review and discuss here the question of the ways and extent to which an infant influences the behavior and attitudes of his mother in contradistinction to the ways and extent to which a mother influences the behavior and development of her baby.

The issues raised in Hock's (1976) study of working mothers are also very complex. Of these, most controversy has focused on the issue of group day care and its effect on the child–mother relationship. Research into this issue has been sparse, and it inevitably raises questions about the nature of the day-care experience itself. The larger issue of the effects of a variety of different methods of substitute care had scarcely been addressd before Hock's pioneer study. This study had a longitudinal design with mother–infant dyads selected at birth in terms of the mothers' declared intentions to work or not to work. Even though a large sample was initially assembled, it is clear that crucial comparisons between conditions of infant rearing are difficult to accomplish with a preselected sample. The chief difference between groups that emerged from Hock's comparisons was that infants in group care tend to be more resistant to their mothers than infants in individual care. Hock suggested that caretakers responsible for more than one infant are inevitably less prompt and consistent in their response to infant signals and communications than

---

[2]As we go to press, E. Waters, B. Vaughn, and B. Egland (personal communication) offer preliminary findings pertinent to Connell's in regard to the neonatal status of Group C infants. At the University of Minnesota, 72 of a projected sample of 100 infants from families of very low socioeconomic status have been studied. They were given the Brazelton Infant Scales on the seventh day of life and again three days later and were observed in the strange situation at about 12 months. Of the 72 infants, 12 were classified in Group A, 42 in Group B, and 18—an unusually high proportion—in Group C. Whereas the Day 7 mean Brazelton scores were normal for A and B babies, C babies departed from normal expectations in a number of ways. They were unresponsive to both auditory and moving visual stimuli. They had low muscle tone. When crying, they were difficult to soothe. When excited, their level of excitement was higher than average, and they built up to a peak of excitement faster. They were more irritable and showed more startle. There were, however, no "hard" signs of neurological damage; furthermore, three days later their performance on the Brazelton Scales was no longer significantly different from those of the other two groups. Nevertheless, these preliminary findings suggest some constitutional basis for difficulty in coping with moderate stresses that other infants do not find unduly difficult. Should such an infant experience insensitive mothering of the type given by the Group C mothers of our Sample 1, it is especially easy to understand that he would develop anxious attachment. Indeed, unless the mother were strongly predisposed to respond promptly and appropriately to infant signals, it seems likely that she would find such a baby "difficult" and react to him with less sensitivity than she might have managed with a less vulnerable child.

are caretakers of only one infant. This interpretation is obviously congenial with our position. The implication is that an anxious (i.e., Group-C) pattern of attachment is more frequent among the infants of working mothers who are cared for in groups than among those cared for individually, because resistant behavior is a cardinal characteristic of the strange-situation behavior of Group-C infants.

On the other hand, Brookhart and Hock (1976) concluded that there is no evidence that experience in day-care centers adversely affects the infant–mother relationship—a conclusion also reached by Caldwell, Wright, Honig, and Tannenbaum (1970) even though their day-care centers undoubtedly differed in their methods, and despite different bases of assessment of the infant–mother attachment relationship. It must be pointed out that Hock's (1976) group-care sample included infants cared for in informal groups away from home as well as those cared for in formally constituted day-care centers. Her contrast group was with infants cared for individually but also away from home, whereas Brookhart and Hock's contrast group consisted of infants reared by their own mothers at home. It is not clear which of these variables might have accounted for the discrepancy in findings—or indeed whether the network of potentially significant variables is so complex that critical comparisons of any two sets of conditions could only be made with samples much larger than those so far assembled. Brookhart and Hock's conclusions also differ from those of a study by one of us (MCB) of children who started day care at a later age; but a discussion of this discrepancy is deferred until Chapter 10.

It is inappropriate in the present context to discuss in further detail research into the effects of home rearing versus day care, or indeed the other alternatives that a working mother may choose. Nevertheless, we wish to point out that Hock (1976), in two of her analyses, selected samples that emphasized consistency of substitute care arrangements and continuity of caretakers. Moore (1964, 1969), in his longitudinal study of 223 London children, found many variations in child-care arrangements among the working mothers who constituted half of his total sample. He found that the degree of stability of the arrangements for substitute care was the chief variable to be associated with outcome. We have no doubt that the most adverse outcomes of substitute care stem from a sequence of arrangements, any of which in themselves might have been adequate, but that are disturbing because of discontinuities.

PATTERNS OF ATTACHMENT AT ONE YEAR
RELATED TO OTHER CONCURRENT BEHAVIOR

There are three studies that examine the relationships between patterns of attachment manifested in strange-situation behavior and other aspects of infant behavior and/or development assessd at or about 1 year of age—two studies by Silvia Bell (1970, 1978) and one by Connell (1974). All of these addressed themselves to the relationship between patterns of attachment and aspects of cognitive function. One of Bell's studies also investigated social behavior. It is convenient to discuss separately the relationships between attachment and cognitive function and social behavior. Because the three studies had their major focus on cognitive function, we consider that topic first.

Attachment and Cognitive Function at One Year of Age

Let us first consider Bell's (1970) study, in which she explored a suggestion of Piaget's (1936) that infants develop a concept of persons' existing independent of self, even when not present to perception, more quickly than they develop a homologous concept of the permanence of inanimate objects. Piaget suggested that the acquisition of person permanence would be accelerated because the baby finds persons, and especially the mother, the most interesting and important among objects. As Saint-Pierre (1962) showed, however, not all infants are more accelerated in the acquisition of person permanence. Bell hypothesized that the degree of harmony/disharmony in mother–infant interaction would affect the degree and direction of discrepancy between the developments of persons and of inanimate objects as permanent entities. Because such differences in the nature of interaction between mother and infant were also related to qualitative differences in the infant–mother attachment relationship, she further hypothesized that there should be a relationship between patterns of attachment and the development of the object concept. (Bell had access to our then-unpublished findings on the relationship between maternal behavior and subsequent quality of attachment in the first year of life, which are reported in Chapter 8.)

Bell devised parallel scales to assess the development of object and person permanence, based on the details of Piaget's own (1937) account of this development. These scales were administered to 33 infants from white, middle-class families (Sample 2 in the present report) three times between 8½ and 11 months of age; a fourth testing took place for a subsample at 13½ months. A week after the 11-months' testing, the infants were observed in the strange situation.

Infants who, with some consistency in the course of the three testings between 8½ and 11 months, were more advanced in the concept of persons than of inanimate objects as permanent were identified as having a "positive décalage." Those who, with some consistency, were more advanced in "object permanence" than in "person permanence" were identified as having a "negative décalage." Those who showed no consistency in this regard were identified as having "no décalage."

Twenty-three infants fell into the positive-décalage group; all of these were classified in Group B (securely attached) on the basis of their behavior in the strange situation. Seven babies fell into the negtive-décalage group; all were classified in either Group A or Group C, indicating anxious attachment. The three babies who had no décalage were distributed among all three strange-situation classificatory groups. Furthermore, infants in the positive-décalage group were significantly more advanced in the development of person permanence than were the infants in the negative- and no-décalage groups (combined) in the development of object permanence; and by 13½ months they were also more advanced in object permanance. It thus appears that the conditions of mother–infant interaction that foster the development of secure attachment also facilitate the development of the concept of the object—a facet of cognitive development that is generally acknowledged to be a highly significant one and an acquisition necessary for several other aspects of cognitive development.

In her second study, Bell (1978) began with a replication of her first study, using 33 black infants from socioeconomically deprived families; but she also observed infant exploratory behavior, maternal behavior relevant to it, and she assessed developmental quotients. She aimed to determine the relative importance of three variables in affecting cognitive development: the infant–mother attachment relationship, socioeconomic level of parents, and degree of environmental stimulation. The design was a short-term longitudinal study that began when the babies were 8½ months old and continued until they were 36 months old. Infants and mothers were seen together on 11 occasions, all sessions taking place in observation rooms in a local hospital. In this section we are concerned only with the sessions between 8½ and 15 months.

The schedule of sessions was as follows: (1) At 8½ months, infants were administered the object- and person-permanence tests and the Griffiths scale of infant development. After the testing the baby was observed for approximately 1 hour in a free-play session, with his mother present, in order to observe the baby's exploratory play and his mother's behavior with respect both to interaction with the baby and to the kind and degree of stimulation she gave to his play with toys. During part of the play session, a black research assistant engaged the mother in interview in order to obtain information about demographic variables and living conditions, history, attitudes toward infant-care practices, amount of mother–infant interaction, amount of home stimulation, daily separations, and the number and stability of substitute caregivers. (2) Three days later all of these procedures were repeated. (3) At 11 months the same procedures were again repeated. (4) One week later the strange situation was conducted in another experimental room using toys that were new to the child. (5) At 15 months the same procedures were repeated that had been used in Sessions 1, 2, and 3. (Later sessions are discussed in a later section.)

In regard to object and person permanence and its relation to infant–mother attachment as assessed in the strange situation, the findings of Bell's (1970) earlier study were confirmed in all essentials, despite the differences between a white, middle-class and a black, disadvantaged sample. Thirteen infants displayed a positive décalage in regard to person and object permanence; all of these were classified in Group B. Twelve showed a negative décalage; eight of these were classified in Group A and four in Group C. Eight showed no décalage, and these were distributed among all three strange-situation groups. The 13 who showed a positive décalage had, at all ages of testing, reached a level that was significantly higher than that reached by the negative- and no-décalage groups for the concept of the permanence of either inanimate objects or persons. Thus the relationships between quality of attachment and the development of the object concept that had been found for the middle-class sample held also for the black, disadvantaged sample.

On the other hand, there were more infants in the white, middle-class sample who had positive décalage. Furthermore, at 8½ and 11 months of age the middle-class whites were significantly superior to the disadvantaged blacks in person permanence, and at 11 and 15 months in inanimate-object permanence as well. These differences are attributable entirely to the negative- and no-décalage groups. There were no significant differences between the black and white samples when only the groups showing positive décalage were considered. It will be recalled that the latter consisted entirely of securely attached (Group-B) babies in both samples. Thus the differences between the samples may be largely attributed to the fact that there were more securely attached babies in the white, middle-class sample and more anxiously attached babies in the black, disadvantaged sample. Among the "living-condition" factors that may be involved in making for less harmonious mother–infant interaction in the dyads of the disadvantaged sample, and hence more frequent anxious attachments, are father absence, mother absence from the home for long daily periods, and multiplicity and discontinuity in regard to substitute caregivers.

The biserial correlations (Group B versus non-B) between the strange-situation classification and both person permanence and DQ were significant ($p < .01$) at 8½, 11 and 15 months, the former ranging from .65 to .61, and the latter from .55 to .45. The correlations of strange-situation classification and (inanimate) object permanence were lower and not significant—except for a coefficient of .39 at 15 months. It appears that the development of the concept of inanimate objects as permanent is not sensitive to mother–infant interaction in the same way as are person permanence and DQ.

Bell also correlated the cognitive measures with scores in the strange-situation behavioral variables. The "positive" variables, consisting of proximity seeking and contact maintaining, were not significantly correlated with any of the cognitive measures at any of the ages in question. On the other hand, the "negative" variables, consisting of resistance and avoidance directed to the mother, had substantial negative correlations with person permanence and DQ scores at every testing, and also with (inanimate) object permanence at

15 months. (This is another piece of evidence that meaningful individual differences in infant–mother attachment are not well reflected by strength of attachment behavior, even at high intensity of activation, but are reflected both by the negative behaviors of avoidance and resistance that supplant or accompany high-intensity attachment behavior, and by the strange-situation classification that depends heavily upon the patterning of both positive and negative behaviors.)

Infant–mother attachment, hypothesized to reflect the degree of harmony of mother–infant interaction, was not the only variable that Bell found to be significantly correlated with cognitive function. The amount of floor freedom the mother permitted the infant was substantially correlated with person permanence at all ages of testing, and significantly correlated but to a lesser degree with (inanimate) object permanence. A variable entitled "exploratory potential of the environment" had significant correlations with person permanence at all testing, but the correlations were weaker than those with either strange-situation classification or floor freedom. The amount the mother played with the baby was significantly correlated with object permanence at 11 and 15 months. Mother's educational level had negative correlations with cognitive measures, except with person permanence at 15 months.

Connell, in his 1974 study mentioned earlier in this chapter, was directed by the hypothesis that the quality of the infant's attachment relationship would affect his learning capacity, as indicated by response decrement to a redundant stimulus. He used a variant of the habituation paradigm designed by Schaffer and Parry (1969, 1972) to investigate the development of wariness, a variant that permitted infant manipulation of the stimulus object. A complex and attractive nonsense object emerged from a sliding door and moved within the infant's reach. This was presented for 30 seconds in seven trials separated by 20-second intervals. On an eighth trial a "novel" object was presented, which was identical with the first nonsense object except for its color. On the ninth trial the original object was shown again. Measurements included length of first visual fixation of the object, total visual fixation, latency to first manipulative approach, and total manipulation. The sample consisted of 46 white, middle-class 1-year-olds.

Let us consider the findings for the three strange-situation classificatory groups in turn, beginning with Group C. All six Group-C infants manifested so much distress in response to the repeated stimulus presentations that observations had to be discontinued, whereas only two of the 40 non-C infants evinced such responses. This finding is in line with Main's (1973) hypothesis, discussed in a later section, that the anxiously attached infants of Group C are too anxious to take advantage of opportunities to explore and thus to learn from their explorations. It should be recalled also that Connell had found that Group-C infants in his sample tended to have been small-for-date and to have low APGAR ratings at birth. On both scores it is a reasonable hypothesis that learning disabilities may emerge as more frequent among Group-C infants than among infants of either Group B or A.

The 12 Group-A infants tended to play with the stimulus-object throughout all nine trials, thus showing a low rate of habituation to the repeated stimulus. Although they showed a greatly increased initial fixation of the novel stimulus on Trial 8, they also had a very short latency to manipulate it—indicating a lack of wariness, by Schaffer's definition. At least on a superficial level, therefore, their behavior in the habituation–wariness test resembled their behavior in the strange situation, where they explored actively throughout and evinced little wariness of either the unfamiliar situation or the stranger.

The 28 Group-B infants showed marked habituation to the repeated stimulus, giving it long visual fixation in the early trials, but very little visual attention during the later trials. Indeed during the latter they showed some behavioral disruption—minor fretting, attempting to climb out of the chair, reaching for the mother, and the like. They showed a significant increment in visual response to the novel stimulus in Trial 8, but also substantial wariness in terms of a relatively long latency before manipulating it. The relationship between wariness defined as latency to manipulate a novel object and wariness of the stranger in the strange situation (indicated by withdrawal to the mother in Episode 3) was found to be significant.

Thus, both A and B infants showed dishabituation to the novel-stimulus object, but in different ways, the former by prolonged visual attention and the latter by inhibition of manipulative response. Only Group B infants showed the clear-cut habituation to the repeated stimulus that Lewis, Goldberg, and Campbell (1969) suggested to be indicative of higher learning capacity. However one may interpret the differences in habituation between A and B babies, Connell's findings demonstrate that infants who differ in the patterning of their responses to the strange situation—and hence, it is hypothesized, in the quality of the infant–mother attachment relationship—differ also in the patterning of their responses to an entirely different type of laboratory situation, which focuses on their responses to inanimate stimulus objects.

The findings of the studies by both Connell and Bell are congruent with our findings (see Chapter 7) that the Griffiths DQs of the infants in sample 1 were significantly correlated with maternal sensitivity to signals; and if other maternal variables, especially arrangements in regard to floor freedom, are also considered, they may be seen to account for about 50% of the DQ variance. Clearly, differences infants show in interaction with their mothers in the first year and in quality of the infant–mother attachment relationship are related to some, if not all, differences that emerge in their cognitive development and learning capacity.

A second important congruence between Bell's and Connell's findings is that not all aspects of strange-situation behavior were found to be related to various aspects of cognitive function. Connell used only the strange-situation classification as a variable. Bell used both classification and two sets of composite behavioral variables. Of these she found that the classification and the "negative" variables of avoidance and resistance were related to the cognitive measures, whereas the "positive" variables of proximity seeking and contact maintaining did not discriminate. Our interpretation of these findings is that seeking to gain and to maintain proximity and contact under even mildly stressful conditions is "built into" the behavioral repertoire of human infants, hence, even though there may be individual differences in the strength in which these behaviors are displayed under stress, these differences are not nearly as differentiating as those in the way in which and the extent to which these proximity/contact behaviors are interlocked with antithetical behaviors, such as avoidance and resistance. It is the patterning of the "positive" and "negative" behaviors that is important, and this is precisely what is reflected in the classificatory system.

Attachment and Quality of Mother–Infant Interaction at One Year of Age

Only Bell's (1978) study is reported here, although some aspects of Rosenberg's (1975) investigation, which was described in an earlier section, are also pertinent. Bell derived 14 measures of interaction between mother and child in the free-play sessions, at each of five ages: 11, 15, 24, 30, and 36 months of age. (Of these only those at 11 months are considered here.) These measures dealt with the number of "episodes" of interaction, prorated for the length of the session. They included: the proportion initiated by each to which the other responds (or resists or ignores); the proportion of responses that involve verbal/vocal behavior in distinction to bodily contact; the nature of the affect that might be inferred from the behavior of each partner; and the extent to which the mother attempted to prolong the interaction with the child and used this as an occasion to teach or to explain to the child about the things around him. These measures were correlated with three strange-situation variables: positive behavior (i.e., proximity seeking and contact maintaining summed), negative behavior (i.e., avoidance and resistance summed), and, biserially, strange-situation classification (i.e., B versus non-B).

Interaction measures at 11 months were all significantly correlated with negative behaviors in the strange situation that took place 1 week later, and all but one also with strange-situation classification. Only four were significantly correlated with positive behaviors. These findings suggest an impressive degree of congruence between the quality of mother–infant interaction (including both infant variables and maternal variables) and the child's behavior in the strange situation when the two are assessed at the same age. Even so, it must be noted that it was the avoidant and resistant behaviors (scored only in the reunion episodes of the strange situation) that were more strongly related to the interaction measures—and, of course, the strange-situation classification in which the negative behaviors are crucial.

Bell then undertook three principal components analyses based on correlation matrices of the behaviors of mother and infant in the free-play session at 11 months. In each, only the first factor was used in subsequent analyses. The first principal component analysis was based on intercorrelations among the measures of infant behavior. The first factor referred to the baby's social interactions with his mother, with the factor loadings ordered in terms of positive versus negative affective tone in these interactions. Factor scores significantly differentiated infants who had been classified as Group B from those who were not, in terms of their positively toned interactive behaviors. A second principal components analysis was based on intercorrelations among maternal behaviors in social interaction with the baby. The first factor was very similar to the first factor that emerged from the analysis of infant behavior, in that factor loadings reflected a range of behaviors from affectively positive and responsive to affectively negative and unresponsive. These factor scores also significantly distinguished the mothers of Group-B babies from mothers of non-B babies. The third principal components analysis was based on intercorrelations among maternal behaviors having to do with "teaching" the baby and/or stimulating his interest in exploratory play. The first factor to emerge from this set of "didactic" maternal behaviors was labeled the "Super Teacher" factor. It defined all the desirable things a mother might do to induce her young child to take an interest in the world about him and in how it works. This factor also clearly differentiated Group-B from non-B mothers, with the B mothers having significantly higher scores on the "Super Teacher" factor.

Discussion.   It is of interest to compare three sets of findings that consider differences among infants of different classificatory groups and among their mothers, in regard to behavior of both infants and mothers in other situations at about the same time as the strange situation was conducted or somewhat earlier. Our own findings are the most naturalistic, having been based on observation of mother–infant interaction in the home environment, without any intervention by the visitor. They also have the broadest data base. The fourth-quarter measures were based on approximately 16 hours of observation on four or five different occasions. Rosenberg's observations took place in the laboratory and included 6 minutes of highly structured interaction (his "directed-play" situation), as well as 6 minutes of unstructured free play immediately preceding. In terms of length of observation time, his study yielded the narrowest data base. Bell's study was intermediate between the two. It also took place in a laboratory, but there was no attempt to direct the mother's behavior and no intervention except that, for part of the time, the mother's attention was at least partially taken up with responding to an interviewer. Furthermore, her free-play session lasted for 60 minutes—substantially longer than Rosenberg's total observation time—and thus had a somewhat broader data base.

There were also differences in methods of recording observations and of subsequently reducing data. Rosenberg's sessions were videotaped, and subsequently two rating scales and one coding system were used for data reduction, all three of which had been devised in advance. Our records of home visits consisted of transcriptions of dictated "play-by-play" accounts of behavior originally recorded in the form of jotted notes. Because ours was a pioneer study, we did not commit ourselves in advance to rating or coding systems, but rather allowed the data themselves to suggest variables that seemed important to examine systematically. Again Bell's study was intermediate. She viewed the play session through a one-way-vision glass, and concurrently dictated a play-by-play account, thus managing to record more detail than our home visitors could with their jotted notes. She also did not commit herself in advance to coding systems or variables to be derived therefrom.

It is not appropriate here to discuss in detail the relative advantages and disadvantages of these different procedures. What is worthy of note in this context is that despite procedural differences, all three studies yielded data that distinguished between strange-situation classificatory groups in regard to mother–infant interaction; and the kinds of significant differences that emerged are highly congruent among the three studies. In each it emerged that interaction in Group-B dyads was more harmonious and that positive behaviors were generally characteristic of Group-B babies and mothers in contrast with those of non-B. The one exception to this generalization is that Rosenberg did not find support for his hypothesis that Group-B babies would be more socially responsive than Group-A babies. In the light of Bell's findings and ours, which do support Rosenberg's hypothesis, it seems likely to us that the very brief duration of his laboratory session did not yield a broad enough data base for stable measures of infant behavior to be derived from it. In addition, he himself questioned whether his predevised rating scale was an adequate instrument for assessing infant social responsiveness.

PATTERNS OF ATTACHMENT OF ONE-YEAR-OLDS RELATED TO OTHER CLASSES OF BEHAVIOR AT SUBSEQUENT AGES

Four investigations were concerned with the relationships between the patterns of attachment reflected in strange-situation classifications and assessments of performance or behavior made in the second or even the third year of life. Bell (1978), Connell (1976), and Main (1973) and her later associates assessed infants in the strange situation at 12 months of age. Matas

(1977), however, undertook her strange-situation assessments when the infants in her sample were 18 months old.

These investigations imply a degree of continuity and stability, whether this be in the child's development, in the mother's behavior, or in the development of the relationship between child and mother. Bell explicitly stated that her hypotheses were based on a concept of continuity of qualitative differences in mother–child interaction. Main and Connell implied continuity of qualitative differences in the attachment relationship itself, with effects on both cognitive and social development. Matas also implied continuity of qualitative differences in the attachment relationship.

Bell, Connell, and Main made assessments of both cognitive development and mother–child interaction. It is convenient to consider these two aspects of development separately, even though all investigators consider them interrelated. Matas assessed behavior in both a free-play session and in a problem-solving situation. Because it is difficult from preliminary reports to distinguish between findings derived from the free-play session and those derived from the problem-solving situation, we propose to consider them all in our section on mother–child interaction. Main and Connell were also interested in the child's behavior toward an unfamiliar person. The findings of these four investigations are considered in the next three sections—first findings relating specifically to cognitive development, then findings relating to mother–child interaction and social development, and finally findings related to responses to unfamiliar persons.

Attachment in One-Year-Olds and Cognitive Function at Subsequent Ages

Bell (1978) followed up her sample of black, disadvantaged infants until they were 36 months of age. Connell (1976) followed up his original sample at 30 months of age, and in addition followed through a new sample from 12 to 18 months. Main (1973) assessed her sample at 20½ and 21 months of age.

Bell (1978) used the Bayley Mental Scale with her sample of 33 black infants at 24 months, and the Stanford-Binet Scale at 30 and 36 months. (These tests were administered within 2 days of the free-play sessions, which occurred at each of these ages.) On the Bayley scale the mean scores of children who had been classified as B and non-B were not significantly different at 24 months. On the Stanford-Binet they were significantly different at 30 months but not at 36 months. (As reported in an earlier section, the two groups differed significantly in both Griffiths DQ and in object and person permanence at 15 months.)

Connell (1976) followed up 30 of the original sample of 46 infants who had been studied by Rosenberg (1975) and himself (1974) as 1-year-olds. On the Stanford-Binet scale administered at 30 months, the mean scores of children who had been classified into Groups A, B, and C 18 months earlier did not differ significantly, although there was a slight trend for Group-C children to have lower IQs than children of the other two groups. He also investigated a new sample of 55 children in a short-term longitudinal study from 12 to 18 months. The children were classified on the basis of their strange-situation behavior at 12 months. At 14 months the Cattell Infant Development Scale was administered at home, and at 18 months language was tested. Developmental Age, as measured by the Cattell scale, did not differ significantly between Groups A and B. The mean for each group approximated 16 months. (The three Group-C children in the sample were excluded from this analysis and from the language testing.)

Connell did, however, find significant differences between Groups A and B in respect to both maternal and child measures of language at 18 months. Group-B mothers had longer vocabulary lists, and Group-B children also had larger observed vocabularies. (Significant sex differences in vocabulary were also found, the details of which are not given here.) On a task involving repeating words spoken by the mother, B children were found to imitate her more frequently than A children, even when vocabulary size was controlled for. No differences were found, however, on a task involving language comprehension.

Earlier in this volume we emphasized the dynamic relationship between exploration and attachment; we have shown how even mild stress activates attachment behavior at the expense of exploratory behavior; and we have shown how the mother normally serves as a secure base for infant explorations. We have cited several studies in addition to our own that have shown that the mother's presence or absence has a strong effect upon exploratory behavior; in particular, her absence has a detrimental effect.

Main (1973, 1977b) hypothesized that when a mother characteristically behaves in ways that prevent her baby from having confidence in her accessibility and/or responsiveness (i.e., ways characteristic of the mothers of anxiously attached babies, as we have reported in Chapter 8), the baby is under chronic stress, and hence unable to devote full attention to objects in this environment other than his mother. She set out to test this hypothesis using our strange situation.

Forty infants who had been observed in the strange situation at 12 months (a sample selected from Sample 3 and 4 of our present study, to represent a reasonable distribution of sexes and strange-situation classifications) were tested on the Bayley Mental Scale at 20½ months of age, and then observed in an hour-long play session at 21 months. Twenty-five infants who had been identified as securely attached (Group B) at 12 months were compared in regard to their later behavior with the 15 who had been identified as anxiously attached (Groups A and C).

At 20½ months, the toddlers earlier judged as securely attached were significantly more advanced in Developmental Quotient than the insecurely-attached toddlers. These differences could certainly be mediated in part by the differences found in exploratory behavior (see later) or by differences in the amount of time their mother had spent with them as Super Teachers (to use Bell's term). But another mediating variable was simply the significantly greater cooperation that the securely-attached toddlers, in contrast with the anxiously-attached toddlers, showed in taking the Bayley examination ($p <$ .01). They were willing to be tested.

Main's primary interest in this study was, however, in the observation of unstructured exploratory behavior. The hour-long play session was divided into four episodes: a free-play session of 10 minutes in which the mother was present and responsive but noninterventive, play with an adult playmate for 20 mintues, another free-play session for 20 minutes, and finally a 10-minute episode in which the mother was to play with the child in any manner she found natural and preferable. Here we are interested in exploratory play behavior, and therefore we are concerned only with the 30 minutes devoted to free play. These episodes, as well as the others, were videotaped, and coding of preselected variables was made from the videotaped record.

Five measures of exploratory behavior were made. The securely-attached children spent longer in individual bouts of exploratory behavior (40 seconds vs. 29 seconds, $p < .02$); showed a more intense interest and attention to objects per bout ($p < .001$); attended more to the details of complex objects ($p < .02$); and more frequently laughed or smiled in relation to the toys and other objects in the room ($p < .01$). The total amount of time spent in exploration did not differentiate the groups significantly, although the secure children spent a longer time ($p < .13$).

Main also made six assessments of "semiotic function." Two measures dealt with the presence and level of symbolic play; differences between the groups did not reach significance. The secure toddlers showed some tendency to issue more Vygotskian self-directions than other toddlers ($p < .10$). Although sheer number of utterances in words did not significantly distinguish the groups, they differed in the number of different words used (15 vs. 9, $p < .09$) and in mean morpheme length (3.1 vs. 2.1, $p < .03$).

Main found avoidance and resistance, which we have found associated with different patterns of infant–mother attachment, associated to different degrees with exploration and cognitive functioning. Avoidance was not significantly related to any deficits in cognitive functioning, whereas resistance was significantly negatively related to DQ, to length of exploratory bout, and to the intensity of interest in and attention devoted to the object during the exploratory bout. As we see later in this chapter, avoidance, in contrast, was related to disturbances in social and emotional behavior. In a more recent analysis of her 1973 data, Main (personal communication) has found that it was the Group-C babies rather than the Group-A babies who were lagging behind in tested (and also, to some extent, in observed) levels of cognitive functioning.

In addition to avoidance, resistance, and classification, five measures of discrete strange-situation behavior were correlated with 20 variables of the testing and play session (Main, 1973). These five—crying, touching, vocalizing, smiling, and looking—are variables that have frequently been used by other investigators of attachment behavior in lieu of the scores of interactive behavior that we have found more useful. Only seven of the 100 correlations reached significance at the .05 level or better—findings congruent with chance expectations and not otherwise interpretable.

Discussion. At 14 months Connell found no differences between Group-A and Group-B babies in regard to Cattell Developmental Age. At 20½ months Main found significant differences between Group-B and non-B babies in regard to Bayley DQ, but later reported that this difference was attributable to Group-C infants and that there was no significant difference between Groups A and B, thus confirming Connell's findings. At 24 months Bell found no significant difference between B and non-B toddlers in regard to Bayley DQ. She found a significant difference to be yielded by the Stanford-Binet at 30 months but not at 36 months; but Connell did not find the same at 30 months.

These findings may be compared with those obtained toward the end of the first year or shortly afterward. Ainsworth and Bell (1974) reported a substantial multiple correlation coefficient ($r = .70$) between the mean fourth-quarter Griffiths DQ and several maternal variables, of which the two most important were maternal sensitivity to infant signals (a variable clearly characteristic of Group-B mothers in contrast to non-B mothers) and floor freedom permitted by the mother (which did not distinguish between B and non-B mothers). Beckwith (1971) reported similar findings for 24 adopted infants tested on the Cattell scale. Bell found significant differentiation between B and non-B infants in regard to Griffiths DQ and person permanence at 15 months.

There is thus substantial evidence that strange-situation classification and/or certain aspects of maternal behaviors are significantly related to measures of infant cognitive development when both sets of measures are obtained more or less concurrently. As for the value of strange-situation classification for "predicting" cognitive development, the findings are equivocal.

There are three major possibilities that might account for the fact that different investigators found different levels of "predictability" for different ages. One possibility, congruent with the test–retest findings reported in the literature, is that the correlation of performances at two different ages attenuates in proportion to the discrepancy in time between the two assessments. Although this explanation, by itself, does not wholly account for the discrepancies in the reported test findings, it seems likely to have had some effect on them. A second possibility is that different scales of infant "intelligence" tap different facets of cognitive function, and may even do so differentially at different age levels, and that some facets are more closely related than others to whatever is reflected by strange-situation classification. This argument resembles the oft-stated claim that the insignificant correlations between infant DQ and IQ later in childhood can be accounted for by the fact that the test instruments used test different functions. This argument does not altogether fit the facts here reported, but it may have some pertinence.

A third possibility is that the samples used by the various investigators differed sufficiently in regard to distribution of subjects among the three strange-situation groups, so that real differences in some may have been obscured by too few subjects representing one or other of the groups. Main's finding that her B vs. non-B differences were accounted for largely by Group-C subjects lends support to this possibility. The fact that Bell's disadvantaged sample contained a larger number of non-B subjects than her middle-class sample may have made it more likely that she could observe effects associated with strange-situation classification than did other investigators who used middle-class samples (e.g., Connell). (It will be recalled that Main selected her sample from a larger pool in order to include a larger proportion of non-B subjects than was the case in the pool from which she drew.) It seems likely that all three of these possible explanations have some pertinence in accounting for the discrepancies in the findings we have reported.

Both Connell and Main, however, did find differences between B and non-B toddlers in respect to language development—specifically, in regard to number of words used, and, at least in Main's study, mean length of morpheme. Only Main specifically reported assessments of exploratory behavior. Her findings that securely-attached infants differed from anxiously-attached ones (and especially from Group-C infants) in a variety of different measures reflecting involvement in and enjoyment of exploration not only supported her hypothesis that this would be so, but thus also yielded findings strongly confirming our interpretation of the dynamics of behavior in the strange situation.

The studies reported or cited in this section, together with those reported in the earlier section dealing with concurrent assessments, form part of a promising new trend of investigation into the interrelations between social behavior and cognitive performance. This particular set of studies has implied a direction of effects from quality of attachment and social experiences associated therewith to facets of cognitive development and function. At least one study reported in Chapter 10 implies an opposite direction of effects— namely, from developing cognitive processes to changes in the nature of the attachment of child to mother. We do not consider these two sets of studies incompatible in their emphases; but we feel that both represent highly significant new ventures in research that, we hope, will stimulate further investigations of the interlocking of social and cognitive development.

Attachment in One-Year-Olds and Quality of Mother–Child Interaction and Social Development at Subsequent Ages

Mother–child interaction was observed by Bell at 15, 18, 24, 30, and 36 months, by Main at 21 months, and by Connell at 30 months for one sample and at 14 and 16 months for another. Matas (1977; Matas, Ahrend, & Sroufe, 1978) assessed interaction at 24 months. All four studies used a laboratory play session in which social behavior was observed, although they differed in length of play session, in whether or not the session was repeated at different ages, and in the proportion of the session in which the mother either was instructed to be responsive but noninterventive or was left free to play and/or interact with the child as she wished. For one of his samples, Connell observed free play in the home environment. Matas used both a problem-solving situation and a free-play session.

Bell (1978) observed mother–child interaction in an hour-long free-play session in which no constraints were put on the mother's behavior, except for the distraction entailed in talking briefly with an interviewer midway through the session. We have already discussed the findings of the free-play session at 11 months. Here we are concerned with the repetitions thereof at 15, 24, 30, and 36 months, in which the same data-analysis procedures were used.

Each of 14 measures of the behavior of mother and child in interaction was correlated at each age level with three assessments of behavior in the strange situation that had taken place at 11 months: positive behavior toward the mother (proximity seeking and contact maintaining), negative behavior toward the mother (avoidance and resistance), and classification (Group B vs. non-B). As at 11 months, there were higher correlations of the 14 variables with strange-situation classification and negative behavior than with positive behavior. There were fewer significant correlations than there had been at 11 months, however. Moreover the variables fell into three groups.

One group consisted of variables that were not significantly correlated with strange-situation patterns at any of the later age points, although they had been at 11 months—specifically, the number of child's initiations of interactions to which the mother responds and the number of child's initiations to which the mother responds physically rather than socially or verbally. A second group of variables were correlated with strange-situation patterns at 15 months and in one case also at 24 months, but not at 30 or 36 months. These included total number of episodes of interaction, number of episodes initiated by the mother, the proportion of the latter to which the child responds, and the proportion that he ignores or resists. A third group of variables were correlated with strange-situation patterns at 24 months and in most cases also at 30 and 36 months, but not at 15 months. These were: child's positive verbal/social and physical behaviors toward the mother, ratings of mother's and child's affect (both interpreted as indicating warmth and affection), and ratings of mother's level of communication with the child in regard to interaction as a means of teaching the child about objects, playing with him, or in some way both expanding his awareness of things around him and keeping the interaction going. In addition one variable was significantly correlated with strange-situation patterns at all age points—namely, the proportion of maternal initiations of interaction that were positive, whether these were verbal or physical.

Bell's basis of interpretation of these significant correlations was that the strange-situation classification (together with avoidance and resistance, the relative absence of which is crucial in distinguishing Group-B infants from others) reflects clear-cut and lasting differences in mother–child interaction. On this basis, the correlations reported above may be summarized as follows. Throughout the second year of life, Group-B dyads will continue to be characterized by frequent interaction, usually initiated by the mother, in which the child is positively responsive, rather than resisting or ignoring. Throughout the third year of life (but, for some reason not immediately explicable, not at 15 months) Group-B dyads continue to be conspicuous for "positive" behaviors—both those that reflect mutual warmth and affection and those on the part of the mother that actively stimulate the child's interest in play and in objects in the world around him. Throughout the entirety of the second and third years, the social behavior of Group-B mothers toward the child continues to be positive, in both verbal and physical modes. In other words, the degree of harmony/disharmony in mother–infant interaction that was predicated by Bell to be reflected in patterns of strange-situation behavior is not a transitory phenomenon but rather tends to be stable over a long period of time.

Bell also found significant differences between Group-B and non-B dyads in the first-factor scores in each of the three principal components analyses done for behavior in the free-play sessions at 15, 24, 30, and 36 months. (See an earlier section for the findings at 11 months.) The factor reflecting positive versus negative affective tone in the child's behavior to his mother significantly differentiated B from non-B dyads at 15, 30, and 36 months. The difference was in the same direction at 24 months but fell below the .05 level of significance ($p < .07$). The factor reflecting affectively positive and responsive versus affectively negative and unresponsive maternal behavior significantly differentiated B from non-B dyads at all four age levels. The mother-as-super-teacher factor differentiated significantly between B and non-B dyads at 15 and 24 months ($p < .01$); at 30 months it yielded no discrimination between groups, but at 36 months again there was a tendency ($p < .09$) for Group-B mothers to be super teachers. Although Bell had originally discriminated "didactic" from social/affective modes of interaction with the child when she subjected them to separate principal components analyses, she found that they tended to be associated together; the mother whose interactive behavior reflects a positive affective tone tends also to display didactic features in her play with her child, taking care to interest him in learning how to cope with objects in his environment. Nevertheless, Bell proposed that the didactic features of mother–child interaction become increasingly important toward the end of the first year of life—continuing on throughout the second year at least—in stimulating her child's cognitive development.

Connell (1976) followed up two samples of children who had been observed in the strange situation at 12 months of age. One sample, consisting of 30 of the original sample of infants who had been studied by Rosenberg (1975) and himself (1974), were introduced at 30 months to a laboratory playroom with their mothers. The room was partitioned into a playroom section equipped with toys and a "livingroom" with a sofa and magazines. For 10 minutes they were left by themselves for the child to become accustomed to the playroom. Then the investigator placed a chair in which the mother was to sit, responding to the child's initiations of interaction but otherwise being noninterventive. After 5 minutes the mother was cued to move to the living-room sofa, where she was to behave in the same noninterventive but responsive way and where she remained for 5 minutes.

At 12 months, eight of the 30 children had been classified in Group A, 17 in Group B, and five in Group C. There were significant differences among these groups in regard to mother–child interaction at 30 months. The Group-B dyads had more interaction than the A dyads, and the mean length of a bout of interaction was longer. The C dyads had more interaction than the B dyads during the episode when mother was on the sofa. Group-B children spent more time within 6 feet of the mother than the A children, under all conditions. When mother was on the sofa, C children spent more time within 6 feet of her than did B children. It may be noted that the sofa was in the living-room area, out of sight of a child in the play area. Presumably the C children interpreted the mother's move to this more distant position as indicating a decrease in her accessibility, whereas the B children considered her still accessible.

Connell also examined the correlation of six strange-situation variables with the following four measures of interaction at 30 months: mean length of interaction, type of interaction, total proximity, and total vocalization. None of the strange-situation variables was significantly correlated with the proximity measure; only contact maintaining in the reunion episodes even approached significance. Both proximity/contact seeking and contact maintaining in the reunion episodes were significantly correlated with length of interaction, type of interaction, and vocalization. Exploration was significantly but negatively correlated with quality of interaction and vocalization. Crying in episodes 7 and 8 was significantly correlated only with vocalization. Neither avoidance nor resistance in the reunion episodes was significantly correlated with any of the later measures of interaction, although a negative correlation between resistance and vocalization approached significance.

Connell's second (1976) sample consisted of 55 infants observed in a short-term longitudinal study from 12 to 18 months of age. The strange situation was administered at 12 months. Two observers watched mother–infant interaction at home during a 1-hour session at 14 months and again at 16 months. At 12 months, 19 infants were classified in Group A, 33 in Group-B, and 3 in Group C. Because they were so few, the C infants were not included in the home observations.

A multivariate analysis of variance yielded significant ($p < .02$) effects for Group-A versus Group-B dyads for the following measures of interaction in the home visits: time spent in interaction, number of interactions initiated by the child, distance between child and mother, and mean length of bouts of interaction—at both 14 and 16 months. In each case the means for the B dyads were higher, except for distance between child and mother, which was less for the B dyads. No differences between A and B dyads were found for the following variables: mother's ignoring of the child's signal for interaction, child's crying, mother's restriction of the child, and either mother's or child's anger—at either 14 or 16 months.

Thus the findings for his two samples—one was observed at 30 months in the laboratory and the other at 14 and 16 months at home—are congruent. Children classified in Group B in the strange situation at 12 months, in comparison with children classified in Group A, maintained closer proximity to their mother and sought and maintained more interaction with them, both in terms of total time spent in interaction and longer bouts of interaction.

Main's 1973 report did not deal with maternal behavior or with mother-child interaction; these aspects of her study were subjected to later analysis by her students at the University of California at Berkeley. Tomasini (1975), Tolan (1975) and Tolan and Tomasini (1977) examined Main's play-session videotapes of her sample of 40 children, aged 21 months, and their mothers with respect to maternal behavior. Both Tomasini and Tolan (and later Main & Londerville, 1978; Londerville, 1977) compared three groups of mothers in terms of the strange-situation classification of their babies at 12 months of age: mothers of B_3 infants, mothers of B_1 and B_2 infants, and mothers of A and C infants.

Tolan (1975) focused on mother's facial expression, hypothesizing that differences in her "facial affect communication" should be related to differences in the security of the infant–mother attachment relationship. To test this hypothesis, slides were made of the faces of the mothers videotaped in Main's study at two points in the session—when the adult playmate first entered the room to invite the toddler to participate in a game of ball, and during the first minute of the game. The toddler's face was masked in the slides.

The slides were rated (by raters who were "blind" in regard to both the hypothesis and strange-situation classification) for expressiveness—the degree to which the mother's face seemed to express any emotion whatsoever—and for pleasure in her expression. Analyses were conducted using both the first slide taken and the mean rating over several slides. All eight resultant correlations were significant. Mothers whose infants were more securely attached (as assessed by the three-point measure implicit in the B_3 vs. B_1/B_2 vs. A/C groupings) had more expressive facial behavior and more frequently expressed pleasure than did mothers whose infants were less securely attached. Even ratings given to the first slide of the mother's face taken at the playmate's entrance differed significantly, even though at this moment the mothers were reacting to the adult playmate rather than to their (secure or anxious) toddlers.

Tomasini (1975) was interested in replicating our findings (see Chapter 8) that mother's degree of sensitivity to infant signals and communications and her degree of acceptance vs. rejection of the child were related to the patterns of strange-situation behavior that are reflected in the classifications. She adapted the two Ainsworth scales of sensitivity–insensitivity and acceptance–rejection to fit videotaped mother–child interaction for the two-year-old, and rated the mothers of Main's sample on the basis of repeated viewings of the play-session tapes—the first 10 minutes of free play and the last 10 minutes, which was made up of mother–child play. Both sensitivity ($p < .05$) and acceptance ($p < .01$) were positively related to the degree to which the child had shown secure attachment in the strange situation 9 months earlier.

Tomasini also made extensive and extremely detailed narrative descriptions of the mother's behavior with special reference to three variables of particular interest to Main; the mother's apparent attitude toward physical contact with her child, her general emotional (rather than merely facial) expressivity, and her anger. An assistant, unfamiliar with Tomasini's other ratings and any other assessments, rated these from Tomasini's narrative descriptions. The mother's apparent attitude to physical contact was not related to strange-situation classification, but mothers of more secure babies were significantly more expressive ($p < .05$) and much less angry ($p < .001$) than other mothers.

Main and Londerville (1978), in a new and elaborate analysis of the Main videotapes, were not so much interested in mother–child interaction as such as in toddler socialization—whether the toddler was developing into a cooperative, "easy" child, with internalized controls, or an actively disobedient, difficult, and antisocial child—and its relationship to strange-situation behavior in infancy. The three groups compared in their analysis were: B_3, B_1/B_2, and A/C. Londerville devised the coding system for each of six "socialization" variables: obedience to maternal verbal commands, active disobedience to such commands, "internalized controls" (shown by self-inhibition of forbidden behavior), "baby rescue" (acceding to the adult playmate's urgent request not to let a toy dog bite a baby doll), physical attack on the mother, and maternal description of the child as being very difficult vs.

easy to live with. Londerville undertook the coding of the videotapes (and rating of the maternal interview) without knowledge of strange-situation behavior. A seventh variable was a rating of the child's cooperation with the Bayley examiner (Main, 1973). A trend analysis was used to determine the presence of a linear ordering in the expected direction for each of the seven variables.

For six of the seven variables, the means for the B_1/B_2 toddlers fell between the means for B_3 and for A/C; the exception consisted of a minimal crossover between B_1/B_2 and B_3 with respect to active disobedience. Trend analysis showed five significant linear orderings. The more securely attached the toddler had been as a 1-year-old, the more likely he was as a toddler to self-inhibit forbidden behavior, to obediently "rescue" a toy "baby" when urgently asked to do so by the adult playmate, to be reported easy to live with by his mother and, to cooperate with the Bayley examiner, and the less likely to physically attack or threaten to attack his mother. There was also a positive association between degree of security of the attachment relationship and the percentage of maternal commands obeyed ($p < .10$), and a negative association with the percentage of maternal commands actively disobeyed ($p < .10$). When the seven variables were converted into standard scores and summed into a single "socialization score," trend analysis showed an extremely strong ordering in terms of the original security groupings: $F(1,33) = 21.13$, $p < .001$.

Main and Londerville also considered strange-situation avoidance and resistance in relation to toddler socialization. They entertained the hypothesis that these two variables might reflect some temperamental characteristic of the infant first manifested at 12 months, rather than be the outcome of important differences in mother–infant relationships. If this hypothesis were true then behavior with the stranger at 12 months should relate as strongly to toddler socialization as does behavior with the mother in the strange situation. Correlations between the toddler-socialization variables and strange-situation avoidance and resistance shown both to the mother and to the stranger were therefore computed. To summarize, the relationships between avoiding and resisting the stranger in the strange-situation and the toddler-socialization scores were insignificant. Avoidance of the mother, however, was significantly related to toddler socialization: $r(36) = -.54$, $p < .001$. Resistance to the mother was not significantly related to toddler socialization, except that it was related to failing to cooperate with the Bayley examiner at $20\frac{1}{2}$ months, whereas resisting the stranger in the strange situation was not related.

Finally, Main and Londerville computed the product-moment correlations between the five discrete attachment measures in the strange situation— crying, touching, looking, smiling, and vocalizing—and each of the toddler-socialization variables, and found none of them significant.

Matas (1977; Matas, Ahrend & Sroufe, 1978) observed a sample of 45 infants at 24 months of age in a free-play session and in a problem-solving situation, in both of which their mothers were present. The problems involved the use of tools, and some of them were very difficult for 2-year-olds. The mothers were instructed to let the child work on the problem for a while before giving whatever help they thought necessary. Both sessions were videotaped, and later both child's and mother's behaviors were coded or rated by two independent judges.

All children had been earlier observed in the strange situation and classified according to our procedure—33 on the basis of their performance at 18 months, and 12 at both 12 and 18 months. (In Chapter 11 we cite findings— Waters, 1978—of the degree of agreement between classifications at 12 and 18 months—and it is impressive.) Those who had been identified as securely attached (i.e., Group B) 6 and/or 12 months earlier, at 24 months of age were significantly more enthusiastic, affectively positive, and persistent. They showed less frustration behavior and less nontask behavior in the problem-solving situation than did those who had been classified as insecurely attached (Group A or C). In comparison to the latter, the securely-attached children also showed less ignoring of the mother and less noncompliance, negativism, and negative affect. It was the avoidant children (Group A) who were especially noncompliant. In addition the Group-A children tended to seek help from the experimenter rather than from the mother, and showed unprovoked aggression to the mother. Ambivalent babies (Group C) were conspicuous for showing extreme reliance on the mother, giving up quickly in the problem-solving situation, exhibiting such frustration behaviors as whining and stomping, and appearing generally incompetent. In the laboratory situation the mothers of anxiously-attached children (i.e., non-B) were rated as significantly less supportive and as offering a lower quality of assistance.

Discussion.   There are two ways in which the findings of these four studies may be interpreted. One is that the behavior of a 1-year-old in the strange situation reflects the degree of harmony/disharmony experienced in the interaction with his mother during previous months and that individual differences in the degree of harmony in mother–child interaction continue throughout at least the next year or two. The other interpretation is that the way in which an infant has organized his attachment to his mother, in response to the nature of his previous interaction with her, tends to persist and to influence his behavior in predictable ways. There is no way to distinguish decisively between these two interpretations, for none of the studies report changes in maternal behavior that might influence the nature of the child's attachment to her. As Sroufe and Waters (1978) have pointed out, however, assessments of the child's behavior in the strange situation are independent of maternal behavior, so that it is not merely mother–infant interaction that is being assessed in that situation.

Nevertheless, the implication of the first interpretation is that a securely attached infant continues to be securely attached not so much because the quality of attachment is an enduring characteristic as because his interaction with his mother continues to support a secure-attachment relationship. Both Bell and Connell reported more interaction among Group-B dyads throughout the second year of life, and Connell also reported more in the third year. He noted longer bouts of interaction among B dyads and a tendency for the child to maintain close proximity to his mother.

Three of the four investigators found that Group-B mothers differed from A and C mothers in the nature of their input into interaction with their children at times during the second and/or third year. Bell found that they initiated more interaction, were more positive in the affective tone of their behavior, and were more active in stimulating the child's interest in exploratory play. Main and her associates found that they expressed feelings and emotions more readily, showing more pleasure. They were also more sensitive in their response to the child's communications, as well as less rejecting and less angry. (Connell, however, did not find differences between A and B mother in terms of anger.) Matas found them more supportive to their children in a problem-solving situation, and as offering a higher quality of assistance than did A or C mothers.

All four investigators found that Group-B children differed from A and C children in terms of their input into interaction with their mothers. Bell found that Group-B children were more positive in the affective tone reflected by their behavior throughout the second and third years, and Matas reports the same finding for 24-month-olds. Connell found that they maintained less distance from their mother and initiated more bouts of interaction. Main and her associates found that they were more socialized—more capable of "self-inhibiting" forbidden behavior, easier to live with, more cooperative, and more empathetic. Both Main and Matas reported that Group-B children are less aggressive toward their mothers and more compliant to maternal commands. In addition Matas' findings that Group-B children showed less frustration and nontask behavior in the problem-solving situation are congruent with Main's findings that were reported in an earlier section.

Connell found no differences between Group-B and non-B dyads in terms of anger. Main found Group-B mothers less angry and Group-B children less aggressive. Matas found that Group-A children were particularly likely to display unprovoked aggression toward their mother. It will also be recalled that Main found more evidence of anger in Group-A mothers and babies in our Sample 1 than among Group-B dyads. The differences between Connell's findings and those of Main and Matas may reflect different lengths of observation, different conditions of observation, and differences in criteria of anger and/or aggression. We are sufficiently impressed with Main's and Matas' positive findings to urge future investigators to attend to this variable.

It may be noted that the four investigators used different degrees of refinement in their comparisons of variables with strange-situation classification. Bell limited herself to B vs. non-B comparisons; Connell compared A, B, and C groups in one sample, and A and B in the other. Matas compared both B and non-B groups, Group B with both A and C, and A and C with each other. Main compared B and non-B in some of her analyses and dealt indirectly with A and C groups in her analyses of avoidant and resistant behavior. In some of the comparisons of maternal behavior, Main's associates compared B_3, B_1/B_2 and A/C. It is of interest that the findings of these studies are congruent on the whole, and that Matas' differentiations between A and C and Main's differentiations between B_3 and B_1/B_2 were also significant.

Main, Bell, and Connell all considered strange-situation interactive measures in addition to classification. Bell pooled avoidance and resistance and found that, combined, they tended to correlate more significantly with later mother–child interaction variables than did the combined "positive" variables of proximity/contact seeking and contact maintaining. Main dealt only with avoidance and resistance, treating them separately; she found that avoidance was significantly (and negatively) related to toddler socialization, whereas resistance was not. Connell, on the other hand, found that both proximity/contact seeking and contact maintaining were significantly correlated with measures of mother–child interaction at 30 months, whereas avoidance and resistance were not. (The discrepancy between Connell's findings and those of Main and Bell is not immediately explicable.) Main also checked out five "discrete" measures of strange-situation interactive behavior and found them unrelated to later socialization.

Attachment at One Year and Behavior Toward Unfamiliar Adults in the Second and Third Years

Two studies, one by Main (1973) and another by Connell (1976), examined the extent to which strange-situation behavior or classification at 12 months was related to later behavior toward adult figures with whom the child had only slight familiarity. In the sample followed up at 30 months, Connell at the end of the mother–child free-play session invited the child to accompany him to another room to play some games. If the child would not leave with him within 1 minute, the child was asked if he would come with his mother. In either case the mother accompanied them to the other room, where a Stanford-Binet test was administered.

Scores were assigned to the response to the experimenter/stranger, as follows: a score of 1 for leaving with the stranger, without the mother and without urging; a score of 2 for leaving with the stranger, without the mother after urging; a score of 3 for refusing to leave without the mother; a score of 4 for uncooperative behavior in the test situation. Group-A children received the lowest mean score, and Group C the highest ($F[2, 27] = 5.2, p < .02$). Most of the Group-A children left without their mothers, whether with or without urging. Most of the Group-B children refused to leave the room without the mother, although they subsequently participated willingly in the test; a substantial minority did, however, agree to leave without their mothers. None of the group-C children left without their mothers, and most of them were uncooperative in the test situation.

Main's (1973) data came from two sources: from the child's interaction with the Bayley examiner at $20\frac{1}{2}$ months and from the 20-minute episode of her play session at 21 months, in which an adult playmate attempted to engage the child in a sequence of different kinds of play behavior. As we mentioned earlier, Main found Group-B toddlers to be significantly more cooperative with the Bayley examiner than the non-B toddlers. They were also more likely to treat the test as an opportunity for playful interaction with the Bayley examiner—that is, to show more of a "game-like spirit." This greater friendliness and playfulness was again affirmed 2 weeks later with another person, the female playmate, who also had entertained the child for a few minutes before the laboratory play session began. When the adult playmate invited Group-B toddlers to engage in a game of ball, they tended to approach her and to return the ball to her in a game-like manner, whereas non-B toddlers tended to avoid her. Main further found that avoidance of the mother in the strange situation was positively related to avoidance of the playmate 9 months later and negatively related to a game-like spirit in the episode with the playmate.

Main (personal communication) does not consider avoidance of the playmate in the play session to be the kind of fearful or wary avoidance young children may display toward a complete stranger. Although, like fearful avoidance, it was manifested by gaze aversion and/or turning away from the adult, it seemed to express merely unwillingness to interact with the playmate rather than fear/wariness. She further suggested that such avoidance seems to reflect an entirely different phenomenon from unwillingness to leave the mother to accompany an unfamiliar person. She based this suggestion on informal observation of the behavior of her sample in the 15-minute familiarization session, which preceded the formal laboratory play session and during which the adult playmate attempted to interact with the child in the investigator's office and in the adjoining hallway. As in Connell's sample, her Group-B toddlers were reluctant to leave their mothers to go into the hall with the playmate, although later in the play session they were friendly and playful with her; and as in Connell's sample, her Group-A toddlers were willing to accompany the playmate away from the mother, even though they were unwilling to enter into reciprocal play with her in the play session. One A toddler, alarmed by thunder during the familiarization session, dashed to the playmate rather than to his mother. Two A toddlers protested the playmate's departure at the end of the playmate episode of the play session, even though they had been unwilling to interact playfully with her; and one of these also protested when first left in the playroom with his mother for the beginning of the play session.

In conjunction with Main's findings pertaining to behavior toward the mother in the play session, reported earlier, it would appear that the willingness of the Group-A toddler to leave his mother with an unfamiliar person in an unfamiliar environment reflects disturbance in his relationship with her rather than greater friendliness toward other persons than Group-B toddlers tend to show. Indeed, as long as the mother is present, Group-B toddlers interact more positively with unfamiliar persons than do Group-A toddlers, just as they interact more, and more positively, with their mothers— as Bell and Connell, as well as Main, have shown.

COMPARISON OF BEHAVIOR IN THE STRANGE SITUATION WITH BEHAVIOR IN OTHER SITUATIONS OF PARALLEL DESIGN

Whereas the other studies that we have considered in this chapter have focused on individual differences in strange-situation behavior and their relationship to individual differences in other variables, the four studies that we consider in this section are normative in their thrust, concerned with the effect of variations in environmental conditions upon strange-situation behavior. One of these, by Brookhart and Hock (1976), is concerned with the setting in which the "strange" situation is conducted, whether in the unfamiliar setting of the laboratory or in the familiar setting of the home. The other three deal with the issue of whether the behavior directed by the child to the adult who accompanies him differs according to the identity of that figure.

Behavior in the Laboratory Versus Behavior at Home.   Brookhart and Hock (1976) designed a set of episodes, similar to those of the strange situation, that could be staged in the infant's familiar home environment. Some episodes had to be altered substantially in order to fit the conditions at home, although the investigators aimed to make them as closely matched as possible to those of the standard laboratory situation. (Obviously, however, the situation was not "strange" in the sense in which we originally intended it—as taking place in an unfamiliar environment.) Thirty-three infants were introduced to the home and laboratory situations, in counterbalanced order, with the first session occurring at a mean age of 11.3 months. The measures used were our measures of proximity and contact seeking, contact maintaining, resistance, and avoidance (all scored for behavior to mother and stranger), together with search and crying.

A multivariate analysis of variance was undertaken with main effects examined for location (i.e., home vs. laboratory), episodes, and sex. (Because the subjects included both day-care and home-reared groups, the main effects attributable to group were also examined as reported earlier.) Here we consider only the main effects attributable to location. Four of these emerged as significant: The infants showed more proximity seeking and contact maintaining toward the stranger in the laboratory than at home, and more avoidance of both mother and stranger at home. There were significant location by episode interactions for maintaining contact with both mother and stranger, indicating a greater increase across episodes in the laboratory than at home.

The findings relating to proximity and contact are readily explicable by the assumption that the separation episodes in the unfamiliar environment of the laboratory are more upsetting than those occurring at home; hence stronger instigation to attachment behavior occurs both in these and in the reunion episodes that follow them. The lesser avoidance of the stranger in the laboratory situation may be viewed in similar terms. The greater avoidance of the mother in the home environment has no such obvious explanation.

Brookhart and Hock acknowledge that avoidance of the mother at home could not be interpreted as a defensive "detachment" reaction, as Ainsworth and Bell (1970) had interpreted such avoidance in the reunion episodes in the laboratory. Rather, they interpreted it as an "independent gesture" by infants who had not become anxious about their mother's comings and goings at home. In Chapter 7 we reported that the securely-attached (Group-B) infants showed least separation anxiety at home; they were also notable for lack of avoidant behavior in the laboratory strange situation. On the other hand, Group-A babies, conspicuous for avoidance in the mother in the laboratory reunion episodes, show relatively strong separation anxiety in the home environment (in fact, A_1 babies did so, although A_2 did not). If indeed the securely attached babies were scored as most avoidant at home, we certainly agree with Brookhart and Hock that mother-avoidance in the two different situations must be interpreted differently. Indeed, we are not convinced that what Brookhart and Hock scored as avoidance of the mother in the home situation should be considered as such. It seems likely to us that the behavior of the securely attached infants at home would be comparable to behavior in Episode 2 in the laboratory, when the child is using his mother as a secure base from which to explore the world and is thus absorbed in his own activities. At home, he may be confident enough of his mother's accessibility so that even when she leaves the room he can continue to use her as a secure base and so that when she returns, attachment behavior may not be activated. Under these circumstances, to continue exploratory play and to make only brief acknowledgment (if any) of the mother's return seems unlikely to imply avoidance, for we have observed such behavior to occur commonly among securely attached infants in the course of our longitudinal study conducted in the home.

Comparisons of Two or More Figures as Accompanying Adults. Feldman and Ingham (1975) held that the "measures of attachment derived from the Ainsworth strange situation suffer from inadequate validation." If they are indices of attachment, it is necessary to demonstrate that they are exhibited more frequently or more intensely toward attachment figures than toward others. The fact that attachment behaviors are indeed exhibited differentially to the mother in comparison with the stranger in the strange situation was not considered to be adequate evidence of their specificity; the child might have behaved similarly to any accompanying adult. (We agree that the mother vs. stranger comparisons in the strange situation do not provide crucial evidence of specificity of attachment behavior, but we point out that the strange situation was not designed to explore the issue of behavior that is differentially directed to the mother in comparison with other figures.)

To examine this issue of differentiality, Feldman and Ingham undertook two comparable studies, one with 1-year-olds and another with 2½-year-olds, in each of which the subjects were randomly assigned to one of three conditions, in terms of whether the accompanying adult was the mother, the father, or a relatively unfamiliar acquaintance. The third was a woman whose total familiarity to the child was 1 hour's free play with him at home immediately before accompanying him to the strange situation. Only the 1-year-old findings are considered here; the findings for the older group are presented in Chapter 10.

The 1-year-old sample numbered 56. The procedure was intended to be identical with our strange situation (except for extending Episode 2 to 4 minutes, during the first two of which the adult was attentive to the child, and during the last two of which he filled out a questionnaire).[3] Feldman and Ingham used the same measures used by Maccoby and Feldman (1972), some of which differed substantially from our measures. Their measure of proximity was a composite score roughly comparable to our score of proximity and contact seeking. All of their other measures were frequency

---

[3]The summary of episodes given by Feldman and Ingham (1975) suggested that their procedures may have differed substantially from ours, but upon examination of their detailed instructions, which they kindly sent us, we are convinced that there were in fact no substantial differences.

measures: playing (similar to our exploratory manipulation), activity (which included all locomotion, whether exploratory or otherwise), crying, looks, and distance bids (a composite measure combining speaking, smiling, and showing a toy—roughly comparable to our measure of distance interaction). None of these measures was scored for the reunion episodes. Kruskal–Wallis analyses of variance were carried out for each of these measures for each relevant episode (excluding the reunion episodes). In the case of significant findings, Mann–Whitney U tests were performed to examine the differences between the mother, father, and acquaintance conditions.

For the reunion episodes a tally was made of the presence or absence of certain behaviors within 10 seconds of the reentrance of the accompanying adult, including the following: looking, smiling, talking, gaze aversion, increase or decrease of crying, movement toward the entering adult, and bids for comfort. Although the presence or absence of certain other behaviors was noted for the remainder of the reunion episode—for example, whether the child initiated physical contact, and whether he rejected a toy offered by the adult—nothing comparable to our measures of proximity and contact seeking, contact maintaining, avoidance, and resistance was undertaken for the reunion episode as a whole.

Let us turn to the findings. In regard to several measures, it seemed that mother and father were interchangeable as attachment figures. In comparison to those accompanied by an acquaintance, babies accompanied by a parent cried less in the preseparation episodes, were more active in all but one episode, more frequently acknowledged the stranger's first appearance in Episode 3, and sought more proximity in the preseparation episodes. There were some differences between mother and father as accompanying adults, however. Infants accompanied by the mother played more in Episode 2 than those accompanied by father or by the acquaintance, whereas there was no difference between the latter two groups. In Episode 3 those accompanied by the mother made more distance bids to her than did those accompanied by the father to him, but both groups in that episode made more distance bids to the stranger than to a parent.

Differences between conditions in regard to reunion behavior were examined by means of chi-square tests. Although approach and wanting to be picked up were both more frequent in the case of parents than in the case of the acquaintance, the differences were evidently not large enough to be significant.

Feldman and Ingham concluded that reunion behaviors in the strange situation fail to yield significant differences between accompanying figures and hence challenged our claim as to their significance as attachment behaviors. The ways in which they measured reunion behavior were so different from the ways in which we did, however, that we do not consider that they have properly tested our propositions.

Let us consider the ways in which our measures differ from theirs. First, our measures of interactive behavior recognize that even the 1-year-old is capable of goal-corrected behavior, so that different children (and the same children at different times) may adopt different and yet perhaps equally effective modes promoting contact and/or proximity—whether by approaching and clambering up, by reaching, or by other modes of signaling the adult to approach, or by some combination of these. To consider each of these modes as discrete behaviors, rather than as more or less equivalent alternatives, would tend to obscure differences in proximity and contact seeking that might well exist. Second, Feldman and Ingham (and Maccoby and Feldman in their earlier investigation, which is discussed in Chapter 10) did not attempt to take account of the contingencies of the adults' behavior, as did our systems for scoring interactive behavior. In the reunion episodes the adult's behavior is variable and largely uncontroled by instructions; they therefore felt it necessary to limit the use of most of their presence–absence measures to the first 10 seconds of the episode, which constitutes a very small segment of reunion behavior. Our measures of interactive behavior were, in contrast, designed to allow for differences in the behavior of the adult, and therefore could comprehend the entire episode instead of a fraction of it.

The fact that significant differences in behavior toward attachment and nonattachment figures were found in the preseparation episodes makes it seem likely to us that they would also be found in the reunion episodes if our scoring system had been used. It may be noted that it was proximity seeking rather than "distance bids" or looking that differentiated between figures in Episodes 2 and 3, and this would also be our expectation for the reunion episodes.

Furthermore, we have stressed reunion behaviors for their role in distinguishing qualitative differences in the attachment relationship with the mother rather than indices of "strength of attachment" in terms of which attachment toward one figure might be compared with another. In advance of undertaking a study such as Feldman and Ingham's our expectation would be that both seeking to gain and to maintain contact and/or proximity and the negative behaviors (avoidance and resistance) would tend to be greater when the accompanying adult was the mother rather than an acquaintance, and that although proximity and contact might be sought with the father as strongly as with the mother, babies would tend to show less avoidance of or resistance to the father than to the mother.

Lamb (1978) was concerned with Freud's assertion that the infant–mother relationship was "the prototype of all later love relations," because his previous work (e.g., 1976a, 1976b, 1976c, 1977a) supported the view that attachment to mother and attachment to father are qualitatively different. In one context and through one set of behaviors a child might show preference for his father, whereas in another context and through another constellation of behaviors he might show preference for his mother. Regardless of such differences, however, both attachment relationships in their own ways are significant for social and personality development. This being so, then one relationship could scarcely be the prototype for the other.

Lamb chose the strange situation as a procedure for further investigating this issue—for rounding out the picture presented by his earlier research into this complementary nature of an infant's attachments to father and mother. He used 32 1-year-olds who were brought to the strange situation twice, with an interval of 1 week, once accompanied by the mother and once by the father, half of the subjects coming first with mother, half first with father. Two strangers were also used in counterbalanced order, resulting in four procedural groups, each of which consisted of four girls and four boys.

He used videotapes rather than dictated narratives as records. He recorded the duration per episode for each of the following: crying, exploration, and oral behavior. His measure of distance interaction (with parent and with stranger) resembled ours. Perhaps because the videotape records yielded an overwhelming amount of detail (see our discussion of this issue in Chapter 13), he did not use our measures of proximity/contact seeking, contact maintaining, avoidance, resistance, or search behavior. Instead he tallied the presence or absence in each episode of a specific list of relevant behaviors, including protest, search, and soothability (by the stranger) in the separation episodes, and approach (full or partial, delayed or otherwise), touching, pick-up appeal, positive or negative greeting, resistance to the put-down, avoidance, and resistance to contact and to interaction in the reunion episodes. Finally each baby was classified in one of Groups A, B, or C, according to our classificatory criteria.

Sixteen infants were classified as secure (Group B) and seven as insecure (Group A or C) in the relationship to both parents, whereas nine emerged as secure with one parent and insecure with the other. It is not clear whether the counterbalanced design of the study confounded the order effects with differences in classification of attachment to the two parent figures. Lamb reported that he found no order effects for measures of behavior in the strange situation. Nevertheless, there was a marginally significant similarity of attachment relationships ($p < .055$).

We cannot go into the details of the findings in regard to differences in the percentage of babies showing and not showing each item of behavior to father vs. mother. There were a number of similarities in responses to parents in the first reunion episode, but very few in the second. In the separation episodes the only consistent similarity was distress so acute that the episode had to be curtailed. Lamb concluded that this study gave equivocal support to the hypothesis that attachment relationships to mother and to father are similar in nature. Indeed, we suggest that Lamb's earlier procedures, which compared the behavior of infant to each parent figure when both were present, did more than the strange-situation procedure to clarify differences (and similarities) in regard to attachment behavior to different parent figures in a variety of situations.

Willemson, Flaherty, Heaton, and Ritchey (1974) predicted, from their understanding of attachment theory, that various indicators of attachment should be intercorrelated not only with each other but also with indicators of exploratory behavior and furthermore that these correlations should be greater for the infant when with his mother than with his father, who may presumed not to be an object of strong attachment. Their subjects numbered 24 (12 boys and 12 girls), divided into four groups of six each. Two groups experienced the strange situation first with the mother, two first with the father; and each was exposed to two arrays of toys in counterbalanced order, one "more interesting" and one "less interesting."

Neither dictated narratives nor videotape records were kept. Instead, scoring was done "instantaneously" by two observers. For crying and exploratory behavior, presence or absence was scored for each 15-second interval. For our measures of proximity/contact seeking, contact maintaining (to mother and stranger) and search, there was a quick rating at the end of each relevant episode. Neither avoidant nor resistant behavior was scored, and exploratory manipulation (which we found to be the most useful of the three exploratory measures) was dropped from analysis because of low intercoder agreement.

The findings may be summarized as follows. There was a strong order effect; attachment behavior, especially crying, increased from Session 1 to Session 2. There were few significant differences in behavior toward mother vs. father. Slightly more exploratory behavior to toys and less attachment behavior to parent was evinced in the presence of the "more interesting" in comparison with the "less interesting" set of toys. Proximity-seeking and contact-maintaining behaviors were positively correlated with each other, but the two exploratory behaviors (locomotor and visual) were not significantly correlated with each other or with the attachment behaviors. There were no "main effect" sex differences, although there was an inverse relationship between attachment and exploratory behaviors for girls, but not for boys.

The findings that behavior toward mother and father is essentially the same the authors take to be inconsistent with ethological attachment theory, as is the finding of an inverse correlation between exploratory and attachment behavior (albeit only in girls), although the authors acknowledge that the latter was their own prediction. They perceive some basis for speaking of attachment behavior as an entity. On the other hand, their findings in regard to the two sets of toys lead them to conclude that attachment behavior is probably more a function of situational variables than evidence of a focused, specific bond with the mother.

Despite disparities in approach and hypotheses there are some similarities in the findings of these three studies. The first and most conspicuous is that 1-year-olds in the strange situation behave toward mother and father in much the same way. This finding is not surprising to us. we would have expected that any attachment figure could support exploration in the nonstressful episodes of an unfamiliar situation and that intensified attachment behavior would be directed toward such a figure under stress. Although Bowlby's concept of "monotropy" suggests that the principal attachment figure may be preferred under stress conditions to other attachment figures (and that the figure who plays the mother role is likely to be the principal attachment figure), such preference can scarcely be assessed unless the comparison figures are simultaneously present.

Furthermore, in our opinion, none of these studies provides an adequate basis for assessing the attachment relationship to mother and to father (separately) and then comparing them. Both Feldman and Ingham and Willemsen and associates implied in their hypotheses a trait theory of attachment, so that differences in behavior to mother and father might be indicators of different strengths of attachment, although their findings gave little support to these hypotheses. Lamb, on the other hand, expected to find qualitative differences in response to the two figures, but used measures too insensitive (in our opinion) to identify them if indeed they do exist. We think it is likely that the "main effect" of the strange situation is to progressively heighten attachment behavior toward an accompanying attachment figure, and this effect is so strong that it tends to overshadow quantitative and qualitative differences that might otherwise differentiate one figure from another in regard to specific attachment behaviors or their organization together.

It is of interest to consider Feldman and Ingham's findings regarding the behavior of children accompanied to the strange situation by a mere acquaintance. First, they attest to the efficacy of a "familiarization" period to turn a possibly alarming stranger into a comfortable companion. Second, they show that a barely familiar but benign figure can serve remarkably well as a substitute for an attachment figure in a stressful situation. (This matter is discussed further in Chapter 13.) Even so, high-intensity behavior (e.g., proximity seeking) was found more likely to be directed toward parents as accompanying figures.

Willemsen and associates are correct in our opinion to emphasize the situational variables in the strange situation. Our interpretation, however, is that the succession of episodes tends to progressively heighten attachment behavior, and that this heightening will tend to be expressed toward the accompanying adult, whether principal or secondary attachment figure, and whether attachment figure or merely benign conspecific. On the other hand, for reasons that we elucidate in Chapter 13, we acknowledge that the extent to which an unfamiliar situation is "interesting," and thus activates exploratory behavior, may modify the expression of attachment behavior toward the accompanying adult.

Finally, although Lamb did concern himself with the patterning and organization of behaviors insofar as he employed our A-B-C classificatory system, the other two mother vs. father studies ignored this consideration. We agree with Lamb that the crux of such comparison should rest with qualitative differences reflecting differences in the way attachment relationships are organized.

SUMMARY AND DISCUSSION

In summary, the findings of 13 different studies using our strange-situation episodes with little or no modification interlock to an impressive extent both with each other and with our findings as presented in Chapters 7 and 8. The evidence strongly suggests that our strange situation, at least when used with 1-year-olds, is a useful instrument for studying individual differences in infant-mother attachment as they relate to: (1) antecedent and possibly causative variables; (2) concurrent behaviors in a variety of different situations; and (3) subsequent development.

A number of studies found that strange-situation classification and/or avoidant and resistant behaviors in the reunion episodes were significantly correlated with other measures of infant behavior and with maternal behavior (as hypothesized); whereas attachment behaviors, such as proximity seeking and contact maintaining, were not. Frequency measures of discrete behaviors—for example, such as looking, touching, smiling, vocalizing, and crying—also tended not to be significantly correlated with other measures. Findings such as these have led us to conclude that strength and/or frequency of attachment behavior are not the crucial variables when relating strange-situation behavior to other variables external to the strange situation. The patterning of attachment behaviors with avoidant and resistant behaviors is of primary importance, however, and this is what is reflected in strange-situation classification. It is our hypothesis that qualitative differences in the attachment of infants to their mothers are significantly related to differences in antecedent experience and to differences in subsequent development. The strange-situation classification, we propose, highlights some of these qualitative differences in attachment, and is therefore a useful variable in research into their antecedents and consequences, together with the measures of avoidance and resistance, which are crucial to the classification.

Those studies that use strange-situation classification as a variable yield findings highly congruent with each other and with ours. Those that use measures of resistant and avoidant behavior in the reunion episodes yield findings that tend to be congruent with those that use classification. The patterning of behaviors that our classificatory system identifies is robust enough to be approximated by different multivariate approaches with different samples, as demonstrated by a comparison of our findings (Chapter 6) with the "multivariate classifier" devised by Connell and Rosenberg.

The findings of the studies reported in this chapter plainly show that 1-year-olds who are identified as securely attached on the basis of their strange-situation behavior have experienced and concurrently experience more harmonious interaction with their mothers than those who are identified as anxiously attached, whether avoidant or resistant. Their mothers are more sensitively responsive to their signals and communications and are more keyed to reciprocity. These findings emerge from studies representing a wide variety of conditions of observing mother–infant interaction. Furthermore Bell's findings (as well as our own) suggest that there are also comparable differences in infant responsiveness when interacting with the mother, although Rosenberg did not find such differences, perhaps because his observation time was too short.

The findings of these studies also suggest that the behavior of mother and child and the interaction between them differ in the second and third year in the case of children who had been identified as securely or anxiously attached at the end of the first year. These findings suggest that patterns of mother–child interaction established in the first year of life tend to persist.

Relatively little has yet been done to relate strange–situation behavior to the child's response to figures other than his mother, whether these be other attachment figures, more or less familiar nonattachment figures, or strangers. Main's and Connell's findings suggest, however, that securely attached and anxiously attached children behave differently to relatively unfamiliar figures who propose or initiate play.

Three studies reported here compared strange-situation behavior toward mother versus father, and these figures emerged as fairly interchangeable as attachment figures in the strange situation. Further research comparing behavior toward different attachment figures, as well as to different classes of nonattachment figures, would be highly desirable, although we do not consider the strange situation to be an ideal procedure for such comparisons.

It is clear that the environmental context makes a great difference in resulting behavior. One such context that has been considered here is that of the accompanying adult. However, as Brookhart and Hock have shown, the degree of familiarity of the environment (home vs. laboratory) affects behavior in episodes that are also "environmentally" defined. Furthermore, as Willemsen and associates have shown, the degree of "interestingness" of toys provided in the strange situation is a variable that should not be ignored.

Finally—and to return to individual differences—an impressive amount of evidence has accumulated to demonstrate that strange-situation classification and/or associated maternal behavior are related to various aspects and measures of infant cognitive development. Furthermore, both Main and Bell have reported findings that suggest that qualitative differences in attachment are associated with differences in subsequent cognitive development in the second and third years. These positive findings point toward the desirability of further intensive research intended to elucidate the effect of qualitative differences in infant–mother attachment in the development of cognitive processes, or vice versa.

10

Review of Strange-Situation Studies of Two- to Four-Year Olds

INTRODUCTION

The strange situation was designed especially for 1-year-olds. Because it depends on the baby's being old enough both to have become attached to a mother figure and to have become adept at some form of locomotion, it is not applicable to infants much younger than 11 months of age. Indeed, it has not been used—at least not without substantial modification—with younger infants. It has been used, however, for children older than 12 months—in particular, for children between the ages of 2 and 4 years, inclusive.

This volume has assembled all the available information known to us about the behavior of 1-year-olds in the strange situation, together with its correlations with behavior elsewhere. On the basis of this, we have a reasonably good normative picture of how white, middle-class American infants behave in it. Furthermore, the information contained in Chapters 7, 8, and 9 gives us a reasonably satisfactory basis for interpreting the significance of individual differences in strange-situation behavior. It could be assumed that the norms would differ with increasing age, however, if only because we could expect that developmental processes would bring about increasing tolerance for brief separations from an attachment figure, and that attachment behavior activated by the situation would be both less intense and somewhat different in form. This being so, it is by no means certain that individual deviations from the norm may be interpreted in the same way as they would be with 1-year-olds. We must rely on empirical evidence on both scores—both to establish norms for children aged more than approximately 12 months and to examine the correlates of individual differences among children of different ages.

Eight studies to date have yielded evidence relevant to these issues. They may be classified as follows, with some studies classifiable under more than one heading: (1) those that provide normative comparisons for different age groups; (2) those that explore the developmental processes associated with age differences; (3) those that are concerned with antecedent conditions that might influence attachment and hence strange-situation behavior; and, finally (4) those that use the strange situation as a basis for identifying qualitative differences in child–mother attachment, and consider these as antecedents possibly related to other aspects of subsequent development.

NORMATIVE STUDIES OF THE DEVELOPMENT OF STRANGE-SITUATION BEHAVIOR

Three studies have specifically addressed the issue of developmental changes in strange-situation behavior: Feldman and Ingham (1975), Maccoby and Feldman (1972), and Marvin (1972).

Marvin's (1972) study used a cross-sectional design to explore certain aspects of the development of child–mother attachment beyond 12 months of age. In particular, he was interested in the transition from Bowlby's (1969) Phase 3, in which the child is capable of active, goal-corrected behavior in maintaining his desired degree (set-goal) of proximity to his mother figure, to the Phase-4 level of "goal-corrected partnership." His sample included 48 young children from white, middle-class families, 16 of each of three age levels—2, 3, and 4 years. He used our standard strange-situation procedure, except that at the beginning of Episode 6[1] the mother said, instead of merely "Bye, bye!": "I have to make a phone call; I'll be back!" He employed the same measures as we, and attempted to use our classificatory procedure, although he found it necessary to modify this for 3- and 4-year-olds.

In general, Marvin (1972, 1977) found that his 2-year-olds behaved in much the same way as our 1-year-olds. They tended to cry in the separation episodes, especially in Episode 6, although somewhat less than the 1-year-olds, and tended to continue to cry in Episode 7, after the stranger returned. Even more strongly than the 1-year-olds, they sought proximity to the mother in the reunion episodes, although they were more content with mere proximity and did not seek to maintain contact as strongly. More than any other group, including the 1-year-olds, they sought proximity to the mother in Episode 3, after the stranger had entered. Avoidant and resistant behavior in the reunion episodes had about the same incidence as in our sample of 1-year-olds. (Indeed, this was also the case with 3- and 4-year olds, suggesting that these

---

[1]Marvin excluded the introductory episode when numbering his episodes, so that his Episode 1 is our Episode 2, and so on. We have adhered to our numbering in reporting his work here.

may be characteristics of individual children that change little during the preschool period of development.)

The 3-year-olds seemed little disturbed by the first separation episode, and maintained their exploratory behavior at a high level until Episode 6, when they were left alone. They tended to cry while alone, but, unlike the younger children, they were reassured when the stranger entered in Episode 7. Nevertheless, they sought proximity to the mother in the final reunion episode almost as strongly as the 2-year-olds.

The 4-year-olds were the least disturbed by separation, on the whole, and maintained their exploratory play well over all episodes. They seemed content to be with the stranger when the mother was absent, but some of them were indeed distressed when the mother left in Episode 6. These distressed children begged the mother to take them with her, arguing that they did not want to be left alone; but the mother, acting on instructions, had no option but to leave the child behind—which must have seemed very arbitrary to the child. Marvin suggests that it was this, rather than acute separation distress, that caused 4-year-olds to cry in Episode 6. Those who had not begged to go with the mother were not distressed in Episode 6, greeted the mother cheerfully in Episode 8, and then went on with their play, maintaining communication with her across a distance. The distressed group stopped crying when the stranger entered in Episode 7, but when the mother returned in Episode 8 they strongly sought proximity to her, whining, angry, and demanding.

Maccoby and Feldman (1972) undertook a longitudinal study of white, middle-class children, observed in the strange situation first at 2 years of age, then later at 2½ and 3 years of age. Forty-eight children were observed in at least two of these sessions, and 23 of them were followed through to nursery school. As mentioned in Chapter 9, in conjunction with the study by Feldman and Ingham (1975), they used different measures from either ours or those of other investigators reported in this volume. Therefore their findings are not entirely comparable with Marvin's, especially in the reunion episodes.

Those measures that seem comparable are manipulative play (our exploratory manipulation), crying, looking, and speak–smile–show (our distance interaction.) Finding avoidant and resistant behavior infrequent in their samples (or with their age groups), they did not score them as we did. Their measure of proximity was a composite measure, which proved to be highly correlated with ours in our sample when we checked it, but which they applied only in the preseparation episodes. In addition to their formal measures, they reported percentages of children showing specific, discrete behaviors in the first few moments of the reunion episodes, before the mother intervened.

They found that some behaviors increased with age: amount of manipulative play in Episodes 2, 4, 6, and 7, speak-smile-show to the mother in Episode 2 and to the stranger in Episodes 4 and 7, and attention span in play. Other behaviors decreased with age: proximity to the mother (i.e., in the preseparation episodes), crying, calling to the mother, going to the door, and proximity to the stranger in the separation episodes. In addition, in the reunion episodes "movement toward the mother" was most frequently seen at age 2, whereas 2½ and 3 the more "distal" forms of greeting were more common. These findings are generally congruent with Marvin's.

In an earlier review of attachment and dependency, Maccoby and Masters (1970) entertained the hypothesis that attachment might be a trait or central motive state, as dependency had originally been viewed. To establish the validity of such a hypothesis, it would be necessary to demonstrate intraindividual consistencies, across measures of attachment behavior, across episodes, and across time intervals. Measures of dependency have yielded equivocal evidence of such consistencies, but measures of attachment behavior might yield more. For such an analysis, Maccoby and Feldman confined themselves to five measures assumed to reflect attachment to the mother: proximity; frequency of speak-smile-show (both only in the preseparation episodes); frequency of looking at her; crying in Episodes 4 and 7, when the stranger was present; and crying in Episode 6, when the child was left alone.

They found that proximity to the mother in Episode 3 correlated significantly with crying when mother leaves in the next episode. Looking and speak-smile-show were not correlated with either proximity or separation protest, although these two distal modes were correlated with each other between ages 2 and 2½. Similar findings for behavior with the stranger led the authors to conclude that "proximal" and "distal" attachment behaviors are independent of each other.

Neither "distal" attachment behavior nor proximity in Episode 2 was stable across time (i.e., from 2 to 2½ to 3). Significant crossage stability was found for: crying in the separation episodes, proximity to mother in Episode 3, manipulative play in Episodes 3, 4, and 7 (between 2½ and 3), speak-smile-show to the stranger (between 2½ and 3), and looks at stranger (between 2 and 3). In general the authors concluded that the child's reaction to the stranger is more stable than "attachment to the mother."

They next examined their data for evidence of "transformations" from one age to another in regard to the form that attachment behavior might take. The implication was that forms of behavior characteristic of 2-year-olds were "immature," whereas those forms characteristic of older children were "mature." Consistency would be shown if those displaying immature forms of attachment behavior most strongly at age 2 showed mature forms most strongly at age 2½ or 3, thus demonstrating that the same children were among those most strongly attached to their mothers at all age levels. The findings were equivocal in regard to this issue.

Feldman and Ingham (1975), in a comparison of behavior toward mother, father and an adult acquaintance as adults accompanying the child to the strange situation, used a sample of 79 2½-year-olds, as well as their sample of 1-year-olds (discussed in Chapter 9). They expected the 2½-year-olds to show less attachment behavior toward parents than did the 1-year-olds because presumably a "process of progressive detachment" had begun.[2] Indeed there were fewer significant differences between the three conditions (mother, father, and acquaintance) in the case of the older sample. The exceptions are as follows: Children stood closer to their parents than to an acquaintance in Episode 2, and in Episode 3 they moved closer to the mother but not to the father; they also moved closer to the acquaintance in Episode 3, but did not achieve the same proximity to her as to the father or mother; children left by their mother with the stranger in Episodes 4 and 7 played less than those left by an acquaintance; and children accompanied by parents looked more at the stranger in Episode 3 than those accompanied by an acquaintance. There were no significant differences among the three conditions in regard to reunion behavior, nor were there such differences with the 1-year-old sample.

Discussion

In regard to the two groups in which there was overlap—namely, 2- and 3-year-olds—there seems considerable congruity between the normative findings of Marvin and those of Maccoby and Feldman, even though the findings for reunion episodes are not strictly comparable. It is clear that there are developmental changes in strange-situation behavior between the ages of 1 and 4. The general trend of these changes tends to be confirmed by the study by Feldman and Ingham, and also by the work of Blehar (1974), which is reported later in another context. In general older children manifest less distress in the separation episodes than the younger children. Although 2-year-olds seem to seek proximity as strongly as, or sometimes more strongly than, 1-year-olds, proximity seeking decreases in older children. Furthermore, the maintenance of physical contact seems less important with older children at all ages studied than it was with 1-year-olds.

Although the general trend of changes in normative behavior across ages seems common to all studies, there is no similar consensus for stability of

---

[2]Rheingold and Eckerman (1970) use the term "detachment" to refer to an infant's willingness to separate himself from his mother in order to enter and explore an unfamiliar room. Feldman and Ingham have adopted this term to refer to the decrease of "proximal" attachment behavior with increasing age. Both of these uses obviously differ from the term "detachment" first used by Bowlby (1953) to refer to the last of three phases of response to a major separation. Here a child, having previously shown intense separation distress, now seems indifferent to his mother's absence and, in her presence (or upon reunion), shows little or no attachment behavior, but instead avoids, rejects, or is indifferent to her. He interpreted this response as a defensive behavior, with perhaps an underlying repressive process. It is in this sense that in this volume and elsewhere (e.g., Ainsworth & Bell, 1970) we liken avoidance of the mother in the reunion episodes of the strange situation to the detachment response of young children in long and disturbing separations.

individual differences across ages. Marvin's design did not permit an examination of crossage stability of individual differences in response to either mother or stranger. Maccoby and Feldman noted some stability in response to the stranger, but not in response to the mother. It seems likely to us that the reason for their failure to find stability of individual differences in response to the mother was that they examined discrete measures rather than patterns of behavior. We found that their measures—especially looking, crying, and distance interaction—failed to discriminate in any important way among our strange-situation classificatory groups. Main (1973)—see Chapter 9—found that discrete measures, which included both "proximal" and "distal" measures, failed to predict behavior from 12 to 21 months. In Chapter 11 we note that we found no stability for discrete measures from 50 to 52 weeks of age and that Waters (1978), in an independent study, found no stability for them from 12 to 18 months.

In Chapter 11 we see that both Waters (1978) and Connell (1976) found stability in strange-situation classification from 12 to 18 months. No one, however, has searched for such stability among 2-year-olds and older. Marvin (1972) attempted to use our classificatory system with his sample, but found that modifications were necessary because of developmental changes in behavior patterns. The problem of "transformation," to which Maccoby and Feldman addressed themselves, would best be examined after devising new classificatory systems for older children and then investigating the relationship between our classifications at age 1 and later classifications.

Maccoby and Feldman's hypothesis that attachment might be a trait or central motive state is a complex issue, the discussion of which is deferred until Chapter 14. Likewise, the issue of strength of attachment behavior as an index of the strength of the attachment relationship—an issue raised in their discussion of possible transformations of behavior—is considered in Chapter 14.

DEVELOPMENTAL PROCESSES ASSOCIATED WITH AGE CHANGES IN BEHAVIOR

Marvin (1972, 1977) hypothesized important cognitive developmental processes as a condition both for changes in attachment behavior with age and for changes in child–mother communication. As the child moves from Phase 3 to Phase 4 in the development of attachment, he and his mother enter into a "goal-corrected partnership" (Bowlby, 1969). Although his attachment behavior becomes attenuated, the change in the nature of the child–mother relationship does not imply a weaker attachment.

Following Bowlby's original formulation, Marvin argued as follows. Although a Phase-3 child may become increasingly capable of modifying his "plans"—that is, intentionally adjusting his behavior—in accordance with the behavior of his mother figure, he is still too egocentric (in Piaget's sense of the term) to be able to take the perspective of another person. Consequently, in the course of his attempts to maintain his set-goal of proximity to his mother, he does not realize that she has plans and goals of her own that influence her behavior, sometimes in a direction antithetical to his own. Being unable to infer her plans, the Phase-3 child is unable to undertake any deliberate course of action designed to change her plans so that they are in greater harmony with his own.

The Phase-4 child, on the other hand, becomes increasingly capable of inferring his mother's plans and goals, and of coordinating them with his own, both conceptually and behaviorally. Whereas the Phase-3 1- or 2-year-old has his goal-corrected attachment behavior specified in terms of literal spatial and temporal proximity to his mother, the Phase-4 child is capable of transcending literal spatial–temporal proximity in his plans, in favor of maintaining a relationship with her in more "abstract" terms. This is not to say that a Phase-4 child no longer wants literal contact with and proximity to his mother. He does sometimes, but at other times he is content with maintaining communication with her, sporadically and across a distance, secure in the knowledge that the relationship continues to exist despite periods of absence and despite lack of actual physical closeness.

Foremost in the development of a mature partnership, according to Marvin, is the development of communicative skills, including but not limited to verbal communication. Thus, although one would expect proximity-promoting behaviors to decrease with age, this would not necessarily imply a disappearance or even an attenuation of the attachment relationship, provided that it could also be demonstrated that this decrease in overt attachment behavior is associated with increasing ability in communication and in perspective taking.

Marvin therefore examined his sample of 2-, 3-, and 4-year-olds in a variety of simple cognitive tasks that implied ability either to defer gratification in the face of frustration or to take another person's perspective (i.e., role-taking ability.) The frustration task was entitled the "Cookie Test." The mother showed the child a cookie and told him that he could have it as soon as she finished writing a letter. She then placed the cookie out of reach but still in sight. After 3 minutes she told the child he could have the cookie. Marvin was interested in whether the child could accept the mother's inserting one of her plans into his plan, and whether he could inhibit his goal-directed behavior (i.e., to get the cookie) in accordance with his mother's plan. Nearly all the 2-year-olds (81%) failed to inhibit their cookie-seeking behavior, and displayed some combination of crying, reaching for the cookie or attempting to disrupt the mother's letter writing. In contrast, 75% of the 3-year-olds and all of the 4-year-olds accepted the situation immediately and waited for mother to finish her letter. Marvin suggested that in these cases a mutual plan, incorporating the mother's, had been implicitly agreed upon.

Four perspective-taking tasks were used. In the simplest of these the children were asked four questions of the following type: "Which do you think your Mommy would like for her birthday—a toy doll or a new dress?" The child's response was scored as "egocentric," indicating failure to take the mother's perspective, if he chose the child-appropriate article instead of the adult-appropriate article in more than one case in four. None of the 2-year-olds answered any of the questions in a nonegocentric fashion, whereas 20% of the 3-year-olds and 75% of the 4-year-olds were judged nonegocentric. From this and other tasks, Marvin concluded that when a child is about 4 years old, he begins to be able to understand his mother's perspective, and consequently to realize that she has plans of her own, to infer something of what they are, and therefore to be able to communicate with her more effectively in his attempts to get her to accept a mutual plan compatible with his own.

Now, let us consider Marvin's interpretation of developmental changes in strange-situation behavior. He suggests that the child–mother attachment relationship is organized in much the same way in 2- and 3-year-olds as it is in 1-year-olds. Despite some obvious developmental changes, maintenance of a reasonable degree of proximity remains the major goal in relation to the mother. Separation from her, not initiated by the child himself, can disturb the goal of proximity maintenance. That this goal was disturbed by separation in the strange situation was shown not only by crying and by efforts to regain the mother in the separation episodes (especially in the case of children aged 1 and 2), but especially by the fact that they sought proximity to her in the reunion episodes. The 3-year-olds, however, may be perceived as capable of inhibiting a goal-directed behavior in order to fit in with the mother's plan—as shown in the Cookie Test. Although being left alone in the strange situation was disturbing to most of them, they tended to be able to inhibit their proximity seeking to the mother while the stranger was present, and to wait until the mother had returned before releasing it.

Four-year-olds—having begun to be less egocentric, more capable of perspective taking, and more able to sustain a relationship on the basis of communicative skills, sharing of mutual plans, and internalized models of self and mother and their relationship—should behave differently in the strange situation. They were expected to maintain exploratory play, show little separation distress, and display little proximity-seeking behavior in the reunion episodes, but rather to be content with communication with the mother across a distance. Indeed about half of the 4-year-olds behaved in accordance with these expectations, as though they no longer had physical proximity to the mother as the overriding goal in their attachment to her.

The other group of 4-year-olds—those, described earlier, who begged to go with their mothers, who subsequently cried in Episode 6, and who were angrily demanding in Episode 8—can also be accounted for by Marvin's model. The mother, through refusing to negotiate a mutual plan acceptable to both (when she arbitrarily left at the end of Episode 5), abandoned the very process through which the equilibrium of a goal-corrected partnership is maintained. The child cried, then, more in anger at her refusal to negotiate than in distress at being separated from her. When she returned he tried to reestablish the equilibrium that she had disturbed through behavior directed toward controlling her—in a sense reasserting her right to alter her plans by making demands on her that, under the circumstances, were impossible for her to agree to. It would be interesting to ascertain in further research whether this kind of behavior in the 4-year-old reflects an attachment relationship that is anxious despite the child's cognitive gains, or whether it is entirely situational as Marvin's account implies.

ANTECEDENT CONDITIONS POSSIBLY AFFECTING THE ATTACHMENT RELATIONSHIP

Three studies of preschool-age children were concerned with the possible effects of antecedent conditions. One of these, by Serafica and Cicchetti (1976), was concerned with the effect of retarded cognitive development attributable to a genetic anomaly. The other two examined the effect of different conditions of rearing. Maccoby and Feldman (1972) compared Israeli kibbutz-reared children with the home-reared children of their American sample. Blehar (1974) compared day-care and home-reared children.

The sample studied by Serafica and Cicchetti (1976) consisted of 12 children with Down's syndrome and 12 normal controls—all white, middle-class, and family-reared. The dyadic relationship between child and mother was explored through behavior in the strange situation when the children were about 33 months old. Few significant differences were found between the groups. The children with Down's syndrome cried less in the separation episodes than did their controls, and in Episode 8 they sought contact with their mothers less often. The children of the control group, on the other hand, vocalized more in Episodes 5, 6, and 7, and these vocalizations could be construed as relating chiefly to the separation.

These findings are surprising, for one would have expected the children with Down's syndrome, who were retarded in development, to behave more like 1- or 2-year olds and thus, in comparison with their 3-year-old controls, to cry more in the separation episodes and to seek more proximity to the mother in the reunion episodes. Serafica and Cicchetti discussed three possible interpretations of these findings: "(1) a lag in the development of attachment among Down's syndrome children; (2) a difference in the strength of attachment to the mother between the Down's syndrome and normal groups; and (3) differential interpretations attached by the two groups to being alone in the strange situation [p. 147]." We cannot here report their considerations, except to say that they believed the third explanation to be the most tenable.

Later, Cicchetti and Sroufe (1976) suggested that children with Down's syndrome are generally low in reactivity to stressful situations and that this appears to be related to their hypotonicity, so that more strength of external stimulation is necessary to produce a given amount of physiological excitation. They would be the last to argue that affective expression is unaffected by cognitive factors, but nevertheless it seems to us that in this study the role of the cognitive factors is obscured by the hypotonicity to which they have drawn our attention.

In the second part of their 1972 monograph, Maccoby and Feldman reported a study of the behavior of 20 Israeli kibbutz-reared 2½-year-olds and the 35 American home-reared children whom the authors had observed at 2½. The kibbutz children were accompanied by their mothers in the strange situation, and the procedure was essentially the same, except that the arrangement of toys was somewhat different and the room was smaller, so that the groups could not be compared in regard to the proximity measures.

Because of the substantial differences in rearing conditions, it might have been expected that the Israeli and American groups would differ significantly in their strange-situation behavior, but the similarities between the groups were much more impressive on the whole than were the differences. The differences were as follows: The kibbutz children tended to display less touch–cling behavior to their mothers in Episode 3, less vocalization in greeting their mothers in the reunion episodes, more activity in Episodes 3 and 4, less looking at the mother in Episode 2 but more in Episode 3, and less speak–smile–show behavior to the stranger in Episodes 3 and 7. Although it might have been expected that the kibbutz children would show less upset over separation than the Americans, this was not so. It might also have been expected that they would be more readily accepting of strangers, but the findings suggest that they accepted strangers less readily. The authors expected that kibbutz children would be more homogeneous in their strange-situation behavior than the Americans, but this did not prove to be the case. Maccoby and Feldman (1972) comment: "Either kibbutz environments are not as uniform as one might suppose, or else ... there are strong individual differences among kibbutz children that emerge despite the environmental uniformities that do exist [p. 80]."

In any event, Maccoby and Feldman confirmed the finding that has emerged consistently from research into kibbutz rearing—namely, that such rearing does not prevent a child from becoming attached to his parents. On the other hand, qualitative differences in the child–mother attachment relationships within either the American or the Israeli samples were not explored, nor were the groups compared in respect to such differences.

One of the reasons that there has been much interest in the effect of kibbutz rearing is that it is perceived as having some parallels with group day care, which has become a very significant political issue, as well as being a matter of much concern to mothers who wish or need to work in full-time jobs. One of the issues is the effect of full-time group day care on social development in general, and on the child's attachment to his mother in particular. Because there is a dearth of adequate measures of social development in infancy and early childhood, the strange situation suggests itself as a possibly useful instrument for the whole relevant age range, despite the fact that it was designed to investigate the attachment relationship in 1-year-olds.

One of us (Blehar, 1974) used the strange situation to assess the effect of day care on young children aged approximately 30 and 40 months at the time of observation, comparing their behavior with a matched control group of home-reared children. The total sample consisted of 40 middle-class children, 20 of whom were in full time group day care of a traditional nursery-school type, and 20 of whom were home-reared children matched in sex and age. Several checks were made as to whether the home background of the day-care children and their controls differed; all such checks were negative. The 20 day-care children were divided into two groups that differed in the age at which they first began day care, 10 children having begun at age 2, and 10 at age 3. Five months after day care had begun, and at an equivalent age for the home-reared controls, all groups were observed in the strange situation. Because the groups were initially equivalent in home-background variables, the implication was that any significant differences that emerged 5 months later could be attributable to the effects of day care.

The total day-care group was found to differ significantly from the home-reared group in regard to a number of strange-situation variables. The day-care children interacted less with their mothers across a distance in Episode 2; they cried more in the separation episodes; they displayed more oral behavior, especially in Episode 7; they avoided and resisted their mothers in the reunion episodes. Furthermore, they sought less proximity to the stranger, avoiding her increasingly from the earlier to the later episodes, whereas the home-reared children, having been more wary of the stranger in Episode 3, became increasingly accepting of her as the situation progressed.

Even more interesting than these main group differences was the fact that the 30- and 40-month-old day-care groups showed two distinct patterns of strange-situation behavior. The children in the 40-month group, who had started day care at age 3, were the most disturbed by separation. They cried more than children in any of the other groups, searched more for the mother in the separation episodes, and explored less. They sought proximity to the mother in the reunion episodes more than either their 40-month-old home-reared controls or the 30-months-old day-care children, and in this they resembled the 30-month-old home-reared children. Resistant behavior directed toward the mother in the reunion episodes was stronger in the older day-care group than in any of the others, and occurred in 60% of the children. Resistance to the stranger was also higher among the children of this group. In short, the older day-care children resembled Group-C 1-year-olds in the pattern of their strange-situation behavior; they were anxious, resistant, and conflicted in their relations with their mother, although the intensity of their reactions was less.

The 30-month-old day-care children were particularly conspicuous for avoidance of the mother in the reunion episodes. Furthermore, they tended to approach and touch their mothers less frequently than the home-reared 30-month-olds, whereas the 40-month-old day-care group tended to approach and touch their mothers more frequently than the 40-month-old home-reared children. In short, the 30-month-old day-care children tend to resemble the 1-year-old children of Group A in the pattern of their behavior in the strange situation.

Blehar pointed out that the strange-situation behavior of the two day-care groups paralleled the reunion responses of young children after major separations, in regard to which it is the younger children who are more likely to be detached on reunion, whereas the older children are more likely to respond in an anxious, ambivalent fashion with intensified attachment behavior. She suggested that the results of her study may imply that the many repetitions of minor separation that occur in full-time day care may have effects similar in form, although perhaps not in severity, to those of major separations.

Discussion

Each of the studies reported in this section raises more questions than it answers. These have already been discussed with reference to the study by Serafica and Cicchetti of children with Down's syndrome. In both rearing-method studies, we recognize two major lacks: (1) a classification of patterns of behavior, comparable to our classification of 1-year-olds, in terms of which the kibbutz and day-care groups could have been compared with their controls; and (2) a thorough study of the interaction of the child with both mother and substitute figures in the natural environments of the home, day-care center, or kibbutz children's house, as the case might be. In regard to Maccoby and Feldman's kibbutz group, one would like to know the characteristic interaction of children with the *metapelet* in the children's house (and in the strange situation), and with parents at home, as well as patterns of individual differences in all of these settings. In regard to Blehar's day-care group, one would like to know the characteristic interaction with each of the caregivers in the day-care center and with the parents at home as well as the patterns of individual differences in each of these settings. Basic to all of these considerations is the need to know the relationship between characteristic behavior at home and behavior in the strange situation for children of differing age levels.

Although Blehar found significant differences between home-reared and day-care 30- and 40-month olds, it will be recalled that Brookhart and Hock (1976) found no significant differences between home-reared and day-care 1-year olds. A crucial difference between their samples was the age at which day care began. Brookhart and Hock's sample consisted of those who had begun day care in infancy—at 10 months of age at the latest and in most cases much earlier. The children of Blehar's two groups began day care at 2 and 3 years of age, respectively. She suggested that 2- and 3-year-olds may interpret the long, daily separations from the mother, implicit in full-time day care, as rejection or abandonment. It is possible that an infant who begins day care in the first year of life, before he has become attached to his mother—or at least before attachment has become well consolidated—may accustom himself more readily than older preschoolers to long, daily separations and be less apt to experience them as implying rejection or abandonment by the mother. Should this prove to be the case, it would help to resolve the discrepancies between Blehar's clear-cut findings of disturbance in child–mother relationships attributable to day care and findings of lack of disturbance reported not only by Brookhart and Hock, but also by two other sets of investigators of the effects of infant day care (Caldwell et al. 1970; Ricciuti, 1974).

Significant though they may be, these research issues are tangential to the main issue that should concern us here—the suitability of the strange situation as a basis for assessing individual differences in child–mother attachment among 2- to 4-year-olds. Further research is clearly necessary. First, it is necessary to undertake extensive studies of the relationship between behavior in the strange situation and behavior toward the mother at home and/or in various seminaturalistic situations of children in various preschool-age groups. Second, especially in the light of the findings of these studies, it would seem wholly desirable to revise the basis of strange-situation assessment of older preschool children, preferably devising a new classificatory system better suited than the present one to behavior of these older children, or at least to redefine the measures of interactive behavior so that they are more sensitive to differences among older children. Finally, it would be desirable in a longitudinal study to examine the degree of continuity from the assessments we have used with 1-year-olds to these new bases of assessment. With an extension of validation studies of this sort, the strange situation might well prove to have a wider application as a method of examining the effects of rearing methods.

ATTACHMENT AS RELATED TO LATER BEHAVIOR

Two studies have used child–mother attachment as it is reflected in strange-situation behavior as an independent variable hypothesized to affect other aspects of development. Pentz (1975) was concerned with its relationship to language development, and Lieberman (1977) with its relationship to competence in peer play.

Pentz (1975) considered qualitative differences in the child–mother relationship to be an indirect indicator of the long-term nature of mother–child interaction, and examined its relationship to language acquisition. He observed 31 mother–child pairs in the strange situation when the children were 28 months old. In a free-play session at about the same age, tape recordings were made of the language of both child and mother in interaction with each other. At 36 months of age a second assessment of language was made in another free-play session, and, in addition, the child was given a test of language comprehension. Pentz's chief hypothesis was that mothers can facilitate the development of language in their children by providing a simplified model of language to the child, the complexity of which is tailored to the child's level of linguistic skill. To do so requires some sensitivity to the child's language level, and consequently Pentz further hypothesized that this sensitivity may be a continuation of sensitivity to infant signals and communications, which we have found to be related to many aspects of an infant's social development. Therefore, on the basis of strange-situation behavior, the children in his study were classified as either securely or anxiously attached to their mothers; their avoidance behavior in the reunion episodes was also scored.

His hypothesis that a simplified model of language would facilitate language acquisition in the child was confirmed. Another hypothesis was also confirmed—namely, that various "teaching devices" (such as expansions and recast sentences) were significantly related to language acquisition, although different teaching strategies seemed effective at different points in the child's development. The child was found to play a very active role in his own language learning by adopting learning strategies of his own, frequently reciprocal to the teaching strategies of their mothers. The hypothesis relating quality of attachment to language development was not confirmed, however. The securely and anxiously attached groups did not differ significantly in level of language acquisition at either age. Pentz offered two explanations for the failure of this hypothesis. Language development may be buffered against the emotional context within which it proceeds, as Chomsky (1965) and Lenneberg (1967) might argue from their postulation of an inbuilt language acquisition device. Furthermore it would appear that mothers who were sensitive to their infants' nonverbal signals and communications are not necessarily sensitive to the verbal abilities and signals of their children a year or two later.

Lieberman (1977) hypothesized that competence in play with age peers was related both to the quality of the attachment relationship with the mother and to the amount of previous experience in play with other children. The quality of attachment was assessed in two ways: (1) through measures of strange-situation behavior (the "interactive" behavioral variables, plus several frequency measures of discrete behaviors); and (2) through an Inventory of Home Behaviors. The latter was scored on the basis of a home visit, which consisted of both an interview with the mother and observation of mother and child in a semistructured, task-oriented play situation. The Maternal Attitude Scale (Cohler, Weiss, & Grunebaum, 1974) was given; two of the component scales were used—encouragement of widening reciprocal exchanges and control of aggression. Social competence with an age peer was assessed in a free-play session with an unfamiliar playmate of the same sex and age. The measures of interactive behavior derived from videotape records of this session were too complex and numerous to be described here.

The subjects were 40 white, middle-class children about 3 years of age, recruited from the waiting lists of nursery schools and day-care centers,[3] with 20 destined for each preschool group experience. All of the assessments, except for social competence with peers, were undertaken before the beginning of preschool. Four months after the children had begun their preschool experience, their social competence was tested in a laboratory playroom with which the children had been individually familiarized in advance.

In order to reduce the number of variables, two principal components analyses were undertaken, one of the social-competence measures of behavior in the laboratory play session, and one for the measures derived from both the home visit and the strange situation. Composite measures were constructed on the basis of these analyses: Scores were derived by adding the z scores of variables with high positive loadings and subtracting the z scores of variables with high negative loadings on each of the components yielded by the analysis. The three composite scores (and the components upon which they were based) for social competence with a peer were labeled reciprocal interaction, negative behavior, and conflict behavior. In addition two composite measures, not included in the principal components analysis, were responsiveness and number of chains of exchange. The three composite measures of quality of attachment were labeled low home anxiety, excessive mother-centeredness in the strange situation, and sociability in the strange situation. The low home-anxiety measure was further divided into two: experience with peers and secure attachment.

All of the measures of social competence, except conflict behavior, were correlated significantly with low home anxiety. Only one measure, responsiveness to the playmate, was significantly related to excessive mother-centeredness, and the relationship was negative. None of the social-competence measures was significantly related to sociability. Maladaptive maternal attitudes about the child's expression of aggression (as measured by the MAS) were correlated negatively with responsiveness, reciprocal

---

[3]Lieberman has not yet reported her comparisons between nursery-school children and those in full-time day care.

interaction, and number of exchange chains in peer play. A restrictive maternal attitude about the child's widening reciprocal exchanges was positively correlated with negative behavior and negatively correlated with the child's responsiveness to a playmate. Because the two components of low home anxiety—secure attachment and experience with peers—were substantially correlated with each other, partial correlations were done when examining the relationship of each to the social-competence measures. Secure attachment was positively related to reciprocal interaction and negatively to negative behavior, both measures dealing with nonverbal behavior. Experience with peers was positively related to number of chains of interaction and responsiveness to the playmate, both measures dealing with verbal behavior.

Lieberman concluded that both the quality of the attachment relationship and experience with peers are related to social competence with peers; but because both "independent" variables are substantially correlated, she suggested that mothers who promote secure relationships are also responsive to their children's growing interest in peers.

Neither of the two composite scores that consisted largely of strange-situation variables was significantly related to the peer-competence measures, except that excessive mother-centeredness was negatively related to responsiveness to the playmate. It is our opinion that somehow the key strange-situation behaviors may have been obscured through the principal components analysis, so that their relationship to social competence could not be assessed. Lieberman (personal communication) has supplied us with correlations of the following strange-situation measures—contact maintaining, proximity seeking, resistance, avoidance (each pertaining to behavior to the mother), search, and crying—with each of the five composite measures of peer competence. The most conspicuous finding is a positive correlation between resistant behavior in the strange situation and negative behavior in interaction with the playmate ($r = .57$; $p < .001$). Four other statistically significant correlations were found, but these were low and may reflect nothing more than chance relationships. Particularly interesting to us was that avoidant behavior in the strange situation had no significant correlations with the measures of social competence with peers. Resistant behavior in the strange situation was also negatively and substantially related to low home anxiety, as were search and crying.

Discussion

Lieberman concluded that quality of child–mother attachment was one of two major variables significantly related to later social competence in play with age peers; but it is clear that the significant attachment measure stemmed from home-visit data and not from the strange situation, except for the fact that resistant behavior in the strange situation was correlated with negative behavior in peer play. Pentz concluded that maternal language behavior had a significant influence on the child's language acquisition, but that attachment as assessed by strange-situation behavior did not. In both studies it is notable that avoidant behavior, which was related to many variables when assessed in 1-year-olds, was related neither to language acquisition nor to social competence with peers when assessed in the third year of life. Although Lieberman did not use the patternings of behavior that are reflected in our classificatory system, Pentz did, distinguishing securely from anxiously attached children; this distinction also failed to yield differences.

We can scarcely conclude that the mother–child relationship has no bearing on the development of language, especially because both Connell (1976) and Main (1973) found that Group-B toddlers were superior to non-Bs in language function. Connell's assessment of language took place at 18 months, however, and Main's at 21 months; Connell's strange-situation assessment was at 18 months, and Main's at 12 months. It could be either that the special influence of mother–child interaction on language acquisition is effective during the second year of life, but later wanes, or that the strange-situation procedure as an assessment of child–mother relationship is more valid and/or more sensitive at 12 to 18 months than it is after the child's second birthday.

DISCUSSION

There is no doubt from the developmental studies of Maccoby and Feldman (1972) and Marvin (1972) that there are substantial changes in strange-situation behavior from age 2 to ages 3 and 4. Older preschoolers find the strange situation much less disturbing than 1-year-olds. In particular they are better able to sustain their equilibrium during brief separations from their mothers, and consequently attachment behavior is less intensely activated in both the separation and reunion episodes. In 1-year-olds resistant and avoidant behavior toward the mother in the reunion episodes may sometimes be assumed to occur because the attachment-behavioral system has been strongly activated. Children who respond to strong instigation of attachment behavior either with avoidance (which is antithetical to attachment behavior) or with resistance (which, when it occurs, is likely to accompany intense attachment behavior) tend to be those whose experience in interaction with their mothers had been disharmonious, at least in the case of 1-year-olds. There is no reason to believe that avoidance and resistance occurring in the case of older preschoolers has dynamics different from those that occur in the case of 1-year-olds. Marvin found proportions of avoidant and resistant children in each of his three age groups similar to those groups that we found in each of our four samples of 1-year-olds, and that Connell and Rosenberg (see Chapter 9) found in their samples. It is nevertheless reasonable to assume that both avoidant and resistant behaviors may be shown less conspicuously by older preschoolers than by 1-year-olds or even 2-year-olds, for the older the child the less strongly attachment behavior tends to be instigated by the brief separation episodes of the strange situation.

Connell (1976) and Waters (1978) found that 18-month-olds could be classified without difficulty in accordance with our classificatory system and, furthermore that there was a high degree of congruence with the classifications they had received at 12 months of age. (See Chapter 11.) Marvin found that his 2-year-olds could be classified in terms of our scheme without undue difficulty, but that the system had to be modified for 3- and 4-year-olds. He resorted to a two-step classification; the first applied our criteria as strictly as possible, and the second attempted to transform our system into one applicable to child–mother interaction in which proximity/contact seeking was no longer the focus, in any literal sense of the term. Thus he sought to distinguish between wholly positive interaction and interaction showing avoidant and/or resistant complexities.

Pentz (1975) classified his 28-month-olds into securely versus anxiously attached. Maccoby and Feldman (1972) did not attempt to use our classificatory system, nor did they use our scoring system for any interactive behaviors including avoidance and resistance. They watched for avoidant and resistant behaviors, however, but reported them as occurring in very few children. It could be that they minimized the importance of momentary avoidant or resistant gestures that receive scores of 2, 3, or even 4 in our system, and that Marvin took into account when distinguishing avoidant and resistant children from those classifiable as securely attached. Feldman and Ingham (1975) have suggested that the strange situation does not yield a valid assessment of attachment among older preschoolers. This may be so, but before accepting this conclusion we must examine two other possibilities.

One possibility is that the strange-situation measures do yield valid distinctions among older preschoolers but that the behavioral differences among them are smaller and less obvious than they are among 1-year-olds, requiring measures that take small and subtle distinctions into account. We have found that our interactional-behavioral scores yield valid distinctions among 1-year-olds, whereas frequency measures of discrete behaviors, such as looking, vocalization, or even touching, do not. Indeed Blehar (1974) found significant differences between 30- and 40-month-old day-care children and their home-reared controls, using the interactional behavior scores— differences congruent with her hypothesis that the long daily separations experienced after attachment to the mother had become well established made for anxiety in the attachment relationship.

A second possibility is that instead of using the patternings of behavior that differentiate significantly among 1-year-olds there should be a search for new patternings among older preschoolers, these would then be "calibrated" against mother–child interaction in other settings and against other aspects of development. So far no one has attempted this—not even Marvin, who modified the classificatory system to accommodate the behavior of the older children in his sample.

In our opinion both of these alternatives are worth consideration, but both require further research. A third alternative is to search for entirely new methods of assessing the child–mother attachment relationship in children beyond the first 2 years of life. Because home observations are very time consuming (and also present special difficulties in observing and recording the behavior of the child beyond infancy), one would hope to find a laboratory situation that would bear the same kinds of relationships to mother–child interaction in the natural environment that the strange situation does for 1-year-olds. Two strategies suggest themselves as possibilities. One is greatly to increase the stress in the laboratory situation so that strong instigation to attachment behavior is provided for 3- and 4-year-olds—a strategy with obvious disadvantages. Another strategy is to capitalize—as Marvin and his associates are currently doing—on cognitive changes in the preschool years and to relate behavior in laboratory situations tapping cognitive abilities to mother–child interaction in natural and seminaturalistic situations (Marvin, 1977; Marvin, Greenberg, & Mossler, 1976; Mossler, Marvin, & Greenberg, 1976).

11

The Effects of Repetition
of the Strange Situation

INTRODUCTION

As Masters and Wellman (1974) have pointed out, laboratory studies to date have not demonstrated any significant degree of stability of attachment behaviors from one time to another or from one situation to another. Because of the significant degree of relationship shown by Sample 1 between behavior at home and behavior in the strange situation (see Chapter 7), it seemed unlikely to us that the kinds of behaviors highlighted by our strange-situation procedure could be grossly unreliable. Nevertheless, to select a way in which such stability could be tested, presented considerable difficulty. None of the conventional methods used to demonstrate stability of test performance seemed entirely satisfactory. Attachment behavior—and indeed behaviors antithetical to it, such as exploratory, avoidant, and resistant behavior—are demonstrably "situational." That is, they are activated to different degrees of intensity in different situations. Furthermore, at low levels of intensity of activation, one set of attachment behaviors is likely to be manifest, whereas at high levels of activation another set is more likely. Therefore, any search for stability (at least as simply conceived) that assumed interchangeability of episodes, much as odd and even items of a multiitem test are considered interchangeable, seemed foredoomed to failure. No comparable laboratory situation had been devised that could serve as an "alternate scale" in the same way that two forms of an intelligence test are considered to be alternatives.

The only conventional method that held any hope of being appropriate for our problem was the test–retest method of assessing the stability of the behaviors at issue, and it is not entirely satisfactory. Three drawbacks are evident. First, an unfamiliar situation is not unfamiliar when it is encountered a second time. If a short time elapses between "test" and "retest" it will surely be recognized the second time, and once recognized, there will be anticipation of what is scheduled to happen later, so that behavior, even in the early episodes, may be affected by what previously happened in the later episodes. This might be especially likely to happen in a situation, such as this, in which behaviors in the later episodes are activated at high intensity. Second, if one allows a long time to elapse between "test" and "retest," in the hope that memory of the first session will have faded, developmental changes may have taken place. If indeed such changes have occurred, one is faced with the problem of assessing stability in terms of "transformations"—that is, to assess the proposition that behavior at one age has "continuity" with behavior at a later age, despite possible substantial differences in the form of the behavior. Third, to the extent that one alters the situation enough that it would not be recognized when encountered a second time, one risks changing it enough that the situations, and hence the behaviors displayed therein, are not comparable from one session to another.

Nevertheless, we decided to undertake an assessment of stability using a test–retest method. We used an interval of 2 weeks. Later in the chapter we report two studies that used an interval of 6 months—the first by one of us (EW) that used a sample quite independent of our total sample of 106 infants, and the other by Connell (1976).

EFFECTS

Let us first consider the test–retest study designed for the present investigation. The 23 infants of Sample 3 were introduced twice to the strange situation, once at 50 weeks and again at 52 weeks. The procedure was necessarily the same. The experimental room was also the same. The stranger and the toys were different but, we believed, equivalent. We expected, nevertheless, that 1-year-olds would recognize the situation after a mere 2 weeks lapse of time (we did not want to make it longer, lest developmental changes obscure the findings); and it was anticipated that the first session would affect behavior in the second session. Specifically, we expected that infants who had been distressed by separation in the first session would remember their distress and, anticipating separation-to-come in the second session, would be distressed even earlier in the second session, and more intensely distressed in comparable episodes. On the other hand, it seemed reasonable to expect that the infants who had experienced the first session without obvious distress might feel even more comfortable in the second session. Nevertheless it was expected that the major behaviors displayed in interaction with the mother—proximity/contact-seeking, contact-maintaining, avoidant, and resistant behaviors—would be

TABLE 21
Comparison of Means[a] of Strange-Situation Measures for Sessions 1 and 2
and Correlations Between Sessions

Behavioral Measure	Episodes	Session 1 Mean	Session 2 Mean	Significance of Difference	r
Interactive Behavior to M					
Contact maintaining	2 & 3	4.15	5.33	n.s.	.05
	5 & 8	7.06	8.29	<.05	.56[c]
Proximity/contact seeking	2 & 3	4.75	8.29	<.05	.56[c]
	5 & 8	7.00	8.13	<.01	.17
Resistance	5 & 8	3.37	3.58	n.s.	.04
Avoidance	5 & 8	5.60	3.71	<.01	.66[c]
Search	4, 6, & 7	8.81	10.96	<.01	.47[b]
Interactive Behavior to S					
Contact maintaining	4 & 7	3.69	3.87	n.s.	.26
Proximity/contact seeking	4 & 7	3.77	3.75	n.s.	.31
Resistance	4 & 7	3.71	4.85	<.05	.42[b]
Avoidance	4 & 7	3.96	4.27	n.s.	.24
Crying	4, 6, & 7	14.01	22.06	<.01	.62[c]
	All eps.	19.52	30.44	<.01	.74[c]
Discrete Behaviors					
Smiling at M	5 & 8	2.11	2.53	n.s.	.18
Vocalizing to M	5 & 8	3.71	3.79	n.s.	.39
Touching M	2 & 3	.99	1.16	n.s.	.24
	5 & 8	1.68	1.97	n.s.	.21
Smiling at S	4 & 7	1.27	1.73	n.s.	.61[c]
Vocalizing to S	4 & 7	3.20	2.55	n.s.	.26

[a]These are means of scores summed across the episodes in question.
[b]$p < .05$.
[c]$p < .01$.

correlated across the two sessions. Infants relatively high on one of these variables in the first session would also tend to be relatively high in the second session.

A comparison between the two sessions was made in terms of these four behaviors, scored for the stranger as well as for the mother. The following behaviors were also compared: search behavior, crying, smiling at mother and at stranger, vocalizing to mother and to stranger, and touching the mother. Instead of dealing with each episode separately, scores for each of the two preseparation episodes were combined, as were scores for each of the two reunion episodes and, where relevant, scores for the separation episodes. It is clear from an examination of Table 21 that an infant's behavior during the second session was affected by his experience during the first session. The following behaviors showed a significant increase from Session 1 to Session 2: seeking proximity and contact with the mother in both preseparation and reunion episodes, maintaining contact with the mother in the reunion episodes, search for her in the separation episodes, and crying both in the separation episodes and in the situation as a whole. Thus both attachment behavior and distress were more intense in the second session.

Resistant behavior toward the mother did not increase significantly in the second session. Avoidance of the mother in the reunion episodes decreased significantly in the second session. Resistance to the stranger in the separation episodes increased in the second session. This increase seems to be linked to intensified separation distress; more babies cried during the second session and they cried more often; consequently the stranger intervened more in an effort to give comfort, offering more occasion for resistance to be manifested.

These findings are not the result of large changes in a few children and of little or no change in most of the others. An examination of individual cases showed that for 21 of the 23 infants, attachment behaviors were stronger in the second session than in the first. Thus our initial expectations were not wholly borne out. Infants who had manifested little or no distress during the first session did not feel more comfortable in the second; rather they, like those who had been distressed during the first session, were more anxious in the second. This suggests that our gross behavioral assessment of distress in Session 1, in terms of crying, was inadequate to identify all infants who experienced disturbed affect. Indeed, as reported in Chapter 13, Sroufe and Waters (1977) observed heart-rate acceleration in those strange-situation circumstances expected to introduce some stress both among infants who cried and among those who did not.

Two other investigations, both discussed in Chapter 9, included two strange-situation sessions within 2 weeks of each other, one session with the mother as the accompanying adult and the other with the father, with counterbalancing for order. Willemsen, Flaherty, Heaton, and Ritchey (1974) reported significant increases from Session 1 to Session 2 in proximity/contact seeking, contact maintaining, and crying, especially in the separation episodes and in Episode 3. This is congruent with our findings. (They did not assess avoidant or resistant behavior, however.) Lamb (in preparation) did not use our measures of proximity/contact seeking or contact maintaining, but found no order effects for crying or for any of his measures that reflect response to parent figures. It is possible that differences in measures account for the fact that his findings in regard to Session 1 vs. Session 2 differ from ours and from those of Willemsen and associates, although the fact that crying did not significantly increase in Session 2 tends to belie that explanation.

Table 21 also presents evidence of substantial stability from Session 1 to Session 2 in regard to interaction with the mother. A significant positive correlation was found for contact-maintaining behavior with the mother in the reunion episodes. Babies who sought to maintain contact during Session 1 also tended to do so, although more strongly, during Session 2. Those babies who sought proximity or contact with their mothers in the preseparation episodes of Session 1 also tended to do so, but more strongly, in Session 2. In addition, some babies who had not sought proximity during the first session did so during the second—a fact that makes the correlation coefficient of .56 seem remarkably high. Proximity and contact seeking in the reunion episodes did not emerge as stable, however. Not only did babies who had shown little or no proximity seeking in the first session show more in the second, but some babies who received high scores in the first session were so upset in the second that their proximity seeking became less active, and they resorted to signaling behavior, which received lower scores.

Conspicuous in Table 21 is the correlation for avoiding the mother. Although the mean avoidance score for Session 2 was lower than that for Session 1, the correlation between the two sessions is substantial. Babies who avoided their mothers during the reunion episodes of Session 1 tended to do so also in Session 2, although during Session 2 their avoidance behavior was weaker and more intermingled with attachment behavior. Resistant behavior directed toward the mother was, however, essentially uncorrelated from Session 1 to Session 2.

The amount of crying during the two sessions was highly correlated even though there was significantly more crying during Session 2. Furthermore, infants who searched strongly during the separation episodes of Session 1 also tended to do so in Session 2. Resisting the stranger during the separation episodes also emerged as fairly stable and, as we suggested earlier, may be viewed as another measure that reflects separation distress.

Smiling, vocalizing, and touching are labeled as "discrete" behaviors in Table 21, to distinguish them from our scaled measures of interactive behavior. In light of the review by Masters and Wellman (1974), we did not expect these to show stability from Session 1 to Session 2, and as may be seen from Table 21, five of the six correlations, although positive, were too low to be significant. The one exception was a substantial positive correlation for smiling to the stranger in the separation episodes. (Maccoby and Feldman, 1972, who likewise used frequency measures of discrete behaviors, also found that behavior directed to the mother showed no substantial stability across ages, but that some behaviors directed toward the stranger did.) Furthermore, although five of these behavioral measures were higher in Session 2 than in Session 1, none of them was significantly different from one session to another.

In summary, the first strange-situation session seemed to sensitize the infants of this sample to separation from their mothers, so that they were more distressed and anxious in the second session than in the first. Nevertheless, certain of the behaviors examined were reasonably stable from the first to the second session. It was shown in Chapter 6 that most of these behaviors—specifically, avoidance in the reunion episodes, proximity seeking in the preseparation episodes, contact maintaining in the reunion episodes, and resistance to the stranger in the separation episodes—are significant in discriminating the classificatory groups, A, B, and C, from one another. The only highly discriminating behavior that was not stable from Session 1 to Session 2 was resistance to the mother in the reunion episodes, a behavior characteristic of Group C. Only two babies in Sample 3 were sufficiently resistant during Session 1 to be classified in Group C; therefore the apparent lack of stability in this behavior may be due merely to the relatively small amount of resistant behavior shown by infants of this particular sample. In general, the correlations are remarkably high when viewed as test–retest coefficients for behavioral measures in a situational test, for such tests are notorious for yielding low test–retest reliability (Block, 1972).

Infants were also classified independently according to their patterns of behavior in each of Sessions 1 and 2. The teams of judges who classified behavior in one session were "blind" as to the behavior in the other session. The unexpected outcome is shown in Table 22. It may be seen that none of the seven infants classified in Group A on the basis of their behavior in Session 1 was so classified in Session 2; instead they were classified in Group B in Session 2—that is, with a 0% hit rate. Of the 14 infants classified in Group B in Session 1, 12 were so classified in Session 2; two had moved to Group C—an 86% hit rate. Of the two infants classified in Group C in Session 1, one was classified in Group B in Session 2—a 50% hit rate. Overall the stability of classification was 57%. This does not, however, suggest a random pattern of change. The Group-A babies tended to move into Subgroups B_1 or B_2 in Session 2, the B_1 babies to B_2, and the B_2 babies B_3. There was only one Group-C infant who was an exception to the trend toward more "normative" classification in Session 2.[1]

From this and the direction of the differences between the means of the interactive-behavioral scores themselves, it is clear that the effect of the repetition of the strange situation after a brief 2-week interval was to increase distress and the intensity of attachment behavior, while at the same time the "negative" behaviors of avoidance and resistance decreased or remained at about the same level of intensity. Nevertheless, the substantial correlations between sessions for some of the scores of interactive behavior toward the mother, and for crying both in the separation episodes and overall, suggest substantial stability of individual differences across the span of two weeks. On

---

[1]Lamb (personal communication) also reported some slippage between A and B groups, but no consistent direction of slippage such as ours. He found the greatest instability in his small group of C babies. His investigation (in preparation) was intended, however, to compare the attachment relationships of the infant to mother and father. The fact that the attachment figure in Session 2 differed from that in Session 1 introduces a variable that tends to obscure any effect attributable to session.

TABLE 22
Stability of Strange-Situation Classification at 12 Months When Compared
with Classifications Obtained from a Second Testing[a]

Classifications at a Second Testing		Classifications at About 12 Months			
		Group A	Group B	Group C	Totals
Our data	Group A	0	0	0	0
Second Testing	Group B	7	12	1	20
2 weeks later	Group C	0	2	1	3
	Totals	7	14	2	23
Connell's data	Group A	11	3	0	14
Second Testing	Group B	4	26	1	31
6 months later	Group C	0	1	1	2
	Totals	15	30	2	47
Waters's data	Group A	9	0	0	9
Second Testing	Group B	1	30	1	32
6 months later	Group C	0	0	9	9
	Totals	10	30	10	50

[a]Our data compared with those of Connell (1976) and Waters (1978).

the other hand, the shifts in classification suggest, at least at first glance, that
patternings of behavior are not stable. The Group-A infants yield the most
important evidence relevant to this issue. In Session 2, Group-A babies were
still avoidant, but their attachment behavior in the reunion episodes had
intensified to an extent that judges perforce paid more attention to
proximity/contact seeking and contact maintaining than to avoidance when
making classifications. This does not suggest so much that individual
differences were unstable as that the classificatory system did not provide for
temporary stress-induced shifts in behavioral patterning. There are thus two
issues: the short-term effects of separation in an unfamiliar situation, and the
long-term stability of individual differences in the organization of the
attachment relationship. Let us defer a discussion of these issues, however,
until after examining Connell's and Waters' findings.

Connell (1976) followed up 49 infants of his second sample (see Chapter 9)
from 12 months of age until they were 18 months old, at which time he
administered the strange situation a second time. The means of interactive-
behavioral measures for each of the two sessions are shown in Table 23. It may
be seen that for most of the measures the means at 12 and 18 months are very
similar. Although Connell did not cite the significance of the differences
between pairs of means, it is perhaps worth noting that the average child at 18

TABLE 23
Comparisons of Means of and Correlation Between Strange-Situation
Measures at 12 and 18 Months[a]

Behavioral Measure	Episode	Session at 12 mos.	Session at 18 mos.	r
Interactive Behavior to M				
Contact maintaining	3	2.3	2.8	.06
	5	2.9	2.9	.55[c]
	8	4.3	3.6	.57[c]
Proximity/Contact seeking	3	2.8	3.8	.04
	5	3.8	3.8	.62[c]
	8	4.0	4.8	.45[c]
Resistance	5	1.3	1.5	.51[c]
	8	2.4	1.3	.53[c]
Avoidance	5	2.5	2.0	.33[b]
	8	2.3	1.8	.52[c]
Interactive Behavior to S				
Contact maintaining	4	1.6	1.3	00
	7	1.5	2.7	.04
Proximity/Contact seeking	4	1.3	1.6	−.06
	7	1.7	2.6	.37[c]
Resistance	4	1.8	2.4	.34[b]
	7	2.4	3.5	.64[c]
Avoidance	4	2.7	2.8	.37[b]
	7	2.0	3.6	.62[c]

[a]Data from Connell (1976).
[b]$p < .05$.
[c]$p < .01$.

months sought proximity to and contact with his mother (in Episodes 3 and 8) more strongly than at 12 months. The average child at 12 months showed both more avoidance of and resistance to the stranger at 18 months than at 12 months, and also manifested more contact-maintaining behavior to the stranger. The only noteworthy decrease from 12 to 18 months was in resistance to the mother in Episode 8. It seems likely that these differences reflect developmental changes. The 18-month-old shows somewhat stronger attachment behavior than the 12-month-old and somewhat more disturbed behavior toward a stranger. On the whole, however, the changes were not great, and one gains the impression that 18-month-old toddlers behave similarly to 12-month-old infants in the strange situation.

Of perhaps more interest is that such a large proportion of the measures were significantly correlated between 12 and 18 months. This was especially the case for measures of interactive behavior directed toward the mother; only proximity/contact seeking and contact maintaining in preseparation Episode, 3 showed no correlation between the two sessions. There were also significant correlations for interactive behaviors directed toward the stranger, except for contact maintaining in the separation episodes and proximity/contact seeking in Episode 4. In short, individual differences in behavior toward the mother in the reunion episodes showed a substantial degree of stability, whereas behavior toward the stranger also showed some stability, especially resistance and avoidance in the second separation episode.

Of major interest, however, is the remarkable degree of consistency that Connell found between the classifications of his infants at 12 months and those at 18 months. For his classifications he used his "multivariate classifier" (see Chapter 9). The results are included in Table 22. It may be seen that 38 of the 47 children—or 80.9%—were classified into A-B-C groups as before. Thus the stability of patterning of strange-situation behavior emerged as even greater than the stability of the individual scores that entered into the patterning.

Waters (1978) also used the strange situation at 12 and 18 months with a sample of 50 infants. He also correlated the interactive-behavioral measures in Sessions 1 and 2 to ascertain their stability over the intervening 6 months. These findings, including those for search behavior, are shown in Table 24. It

TABLE 24

Correlations Between Measures at the 12-and 18-Month Testings
for Interactive Behaviors[a]

	Pearson Correlation Coefficients Between Sessions 1 and 2			
	Behavior to Mother		Behavior to Stranger	
Interactive Measure	Episodes	r	Episodes	r
Contact maintaining	2 & 3	.720[c]	3	–.020
	5 & 8	.300[b]	4 & 7	.320[b]
Proximity/contact seeking	2 & 3	.423[c]	3	.033
	5 & 8	.303[b]	4 & 7	.286[b]
Avoidance	5 & 8	.621[c]	3	–.207
			4 & 7	.229
Resistance	5 & 8	.508[c]	3	–.056
			4 & 7	.274[b]
Distance Interaction	2 & 3	.065	3	.180
	5 & 8	.308[b]	4 & 7	.319[b]
Search	4, 6, & 7	.147		

[a]Data from Waters (1978).
[b]$p < .05$.
[c]$p < .01$.

may be seen that the correlations for behavior directed toward the mother are positive and significant, except for distance interaction in the preseparation episodes, and search in the separation episodes. The highest correlation was found for contact-maintaining behavior in the preseparation episodes ($r =$ .720), a finding that perhaps reflects the fact that Group-C infants are discriminated from both A and B babies in terms of this behavior. Substantial correlations were also found for avoidant and resistant behavior in the reunion episodes—behaviors that had previously been found (Chapter 6) important in the discrimination among groups. To a lesser extent proximity/contact seeking in the preseparation episodes was also fairly stable.

Four of 10 correlations for behavior toward the stranger reached the .05 level of significance. All of these were low, and all seem related to the presence or absence of separation distress, for all occurred in the separation episodes— proximity/contact seeking, contact maintaining, resistance, and distance interaction. It is plain that behaviors directed toward the mother show more stability over time than behaviors directed toward the stranger.

Waters was particularly interested in comparing the stability of our measures of interactive behavior—which he calls "categorical scores"—with those of "discrete" behaviors based on frequency measures and considered independently of one another rather than in combination and/or as alternatives as in the interactive measures. The correlations based on discrete measures, for 30 subjects randomly chosen from his total of 50, are shown in Table 25.

In contrast to the categorical scores of interactive behavior toward the mother, shown in Tables 21, 23, and 24, it may be seen that these discrete measures tended to have no stability from one session to another. Exceptions were vocalizing to the mother and touching her in the preseparation episodes. As for the behavior toward the stranger, there was no apparent stability across time. Waters' measure of crying, like ours, was also a frequency measure and is not included in Table 25. It showed some indication of stability. Crying (including fussing) in the separation episodes ($r = .397$), reunion episodes ($r = .416$), and all episodes ($r = .394$) were significantly correlated ($p < .05$) between 12 and 18 months.

In striking contrast to his findings for the "discrete" measures, Waters obtained a very high degree of consistency between the classifications at 12 and 18 months. (See Table 22.) Using our standard classificatory instructions, he found an even more precise match between the two sets of classifications than Connell did in his sample. Of 10 Group-A infants at 12 months, nine were still so classified at 18 months, and the same was true of the 10 Group-C infants at 12 months. All of the 30 Group-B infants at 12 months were still so classified at 18 months. Forty-eight of the 50 infants—96%—were classified as before.

TABLE 25
Correlations Between Measures at the 12- and 18-Month Testings
for Discrete Behaviors[a]

Discrete-Behavioral Measures	Behavior to Mother		Behavior to Stranger	
	Episodes	r	Episodes	r
Looking at	2 & 3	.072	3	−.047
	5 & 8	.224	4 & 7	.109
Vocalizing to	2 & 3	.357[b]	3	.119
	5 & 8	−.073	4 & 7	.240
Smiling at	2 & 3	.143	3	−.165
	5 & 8	−.048	4 & 7	.194
Gesturing to	2 & 3	−.116	3	−.083
	5 & 8	−.107	4 & 7	−.103
Approaching	2 & 3	−.151	3	.106
	5 & 8	.043	4 & 7	.085
Touching	2 & 3	.435[b]	3	___[c]
	5 & 8	.105	4 & 7	.255
Baby holding onto	2 & 3	___[c]	3	___[c]
	5 & 8	.263	4 & 7	−.032

Pearson Correlation Coefficients Between Sessions 1 and 2

[a]Data from Waters (1978); N = 30.
[b]$p < .05$.
[c]Mean = 0 at one age level.

Although Table 22 shows the results only for the main groups, Waters' match even held quite well for subgroups.

In summary, both Waters and Connell found a remarkable degree of stability of A-B-C classification between 12 and 18 months, even though they used different methods of arriving at the classifications. The degree of stability over a 2-week period appeared less in our own data, but there was nevertheless a striking trend toward normative Group B in the second session—a trend that belies any argument that there were random shifts in classification attributable to "error." In addition, all three studies showed a substantial correlation between Sessions 1 and 2 in regard to interactive behaviors directed toward the mother, and somewhat less stability in interactive behaviors directed toward the stranger. In particular all studies yielded evidence of stability for contact maintaining and avoidance in the reunion episodes, and Connell and Waters also found stability for proximity/contact seeking and resistance in the reunion episodes. The evidence of stability for the separate interactive scores was very much less striking than the evidence for the stability of classifications in Connell's and Waters' studies. As for the stability of discrete-behavioral measures, neither Waters nor we found as much evidence as for the stability of interactive-behavioral scores. Both studies found vocalizing to the mother to be marginally stable—Waters for the preseparation episodes, we for the reunion episodes. Waters obtained a significant cross-session correlation for touching mother in the preseparation episodes, and we for smiling to the stranger in the separation episodes. Neither of these sets of findings, separately or together, can be described as offering adequate evidence of stability.

Leaving the lack of stability of the discrete measures out of consideration, there still remains a remarkable paradox in that there is extremely high stability of the classifications (in Waters' and Connell's data) and yet evidence of only moderate levels of 12-to-18-month stability of the interactive-behavioral measures on which the A-B-C classifications were based. Especially because the stability of classifications was demonstrated in samples independent of ours in laboratories other than the one in which we developed our scoring system, we cannot question Connell's and Waters' findings. There are some changes in patterns of interactive behavior, some of them perhaps attributable to developmental changes; and yet there emerges this remarkable consistency in classifications. How are we to interpret this paradox?

One possibility is that the A-B-C classifications are so broad that they are insensitive to all but the most extreme changes in actual behavior. Under such circumstances it is not surprising to find stability of classification, and indeed such findings might be characterized as exaggerating the stability of the infant–mother attachment relationship during the period from 12 to 18 months. This seems unlikely in view of the shifts of classification when the intersession period lasts only 2 weeks—shifts that clearly are not attributable to random error. Another possibility is that the shifts during the period of 12 to 18 months nevertheless leave the patterning of the interactive behaviors more or less intact, and thus the A-B-C classifications remain relatively stable. In any event it appears that the patterning of interactive behaviors as represented in the classifications are stable in contrast with repeated failures to find stability in a variety of "discrete" variables, studied independently of one another (e.g., not only in the findings reported in this chapter but also in findings reported by Coates, Anderson, & Hartup, 1972b; Maccoby & Feldman, 1972; and as reviewed by Masters & Wellman, 1974).

To clarify the paradoxical nature of his findings, Waters (1978) performed an auxiliary analysis of his 12-to-18-month data to test the hypothesis that the A-B-C classifications are relatively insensitive to random variation in the interactive behaviors. Each interactive variable (e.g., contact maintaining, proximity/contact seeking, avoidance, etc.) scored at 12 months was randomly and independently transformed to produce a set of scores that reproduced the correlation between the 12- and 18-month data. The new data thus reproduced were in effect error analogues of the 18-month data. Data from our 105 12-month-olds and his 50 12-month-olds were used to develop classification equations that were then applied to the error data and the 18-month data. If the A-B-C classifications were insensitive to random variation in interactive behavior, the patterns of predicted classification should be the same in both sets of data. In fact, the "real" data and the error data produced strikingly different patterns of classification. In the "real" data, Group-B classifications were highly stable, and changes in the A and C classifications reliably drifted toward B classifications. In the error data, Group-B classifications often changed (46% vs. 13% in the real data), producing 16% A classifications and 30% C classifications from the 12-month Group-B data. In addition, when A and C classifications changed (48% and 45% respectively vs. 33% and 36% in the real data), the predicted classification was equally likely to be Group B or the other group (C or A as the case might be). The hypothesis that random variation in the interactive behaviors could underlie the stability of the A-B-C classifications was thus not confirmed.

DISCUSSION

The correlation data in our study, as well as in Waters' and Connell's, show a substantial degree of stability over time in regard to the measures of interactive behavior toward the mother in the strange situation—both behavior in interaction with her when she is present and behavior reflecting distress when she is absent. On the other hand, there is somewhat less stability in regard to measures of interactive behavior toward the stranger. These findings are the reverse of those reported by Maccoby and Feldman (1972) (see Chapter 10), who found little stability in behavior directed toward the mother but more stability in response to the stranger. The discrepancies between their findings and those reported in this chapter may be attributable to either one or both of two factors: (1) that there is more stability between 12 and 18 months than between 24 and 30 or 36 months—namely, that relevant developmental changes are greater in the third than in the second year of life; and (2) that their measures were less suited than ours to the task of uncovering underlying continuities in behavior. Although it seems likely to us that both factors have played a part in making for discrepancies, here we wish to focus on differences in measures.

Except for their measures of "proximity" and "speak-smile-show," Maccoby and Feldman used discrete, frequency measures. With the possible exception of crying, their frequency measures tended not to be stable between age levels and not to relate to other variables. In regard to this lack of stability of frequency measures, both our findings and Waters' tend to confirm theirs. Furthermore, Maccoby and Feldman did not score proximity in the reunion episodes, and although they kept an eye open for discrete behaviors that might be related to proximity/contact seeking, contact maintaining, avoidance, and resistance (and indeed tallied them), they apparently found no evidence of stability across age. Waters' examination of the stability of approach and touching in the reunion episodes bears out their impression of lack of stability when these behaviors are represented in separate frequency measures. The very measures that we find most stable across time (as well as most discriminating among individuals)—namely, the "categorical" measures of interactive behavior to the mother, especially in the reunion episodes—were plainly not adequately represented in the Maccoby and Feldman study. Coates, Anderson, and Hartup (1972b) not only used laboratory procedures that differed from those of the strange situation, but also focused on discrete measures. They also reported little stability over time. Because they relied chiefly on these two studies, it is perhaps not surprising that a conclusion of Masters and Wellman's (1974) review was that attachment and attachment behavior lack stability over time.

Let us discuss the differences between discrete behavioral measures such as Maccoby and Feldman and Coates and associates used and our interactive-behavioral measures. There are two main differences. First, our interactive behavioral measures cover a variety of separate behavioral components, considering them interchangeable to some extent. Thus, for example, in the reunion episodes an infant may make a bid for increased proximity to his mother through active approach (perhaps making contact with her on his own initiative), or by gesture, or by other signals, (such as crying), or by some combination of these. Waters examined the stability of these separate behaviors from 12 to 18 months and found that none of them, except for crying, was significantly correlated across time. Both Waters and Connell, however, found evidence of stability of our proximity/contact-seeking measure. By 12 months of age, normal infants are capable of goal-corrected behavior, and this implies ability to use alternate means to achieve a set-goal, or to implement a plan. It seemed to us that the appropriate measures would be those that assessed the degree of initiative in achieving the set-goal and the degree of strength implicit in the behavior or sequence of behaviors adopted. On the other hand, there seems no reason to suppose that a baby will always use the same means to his ends. Indeed within one session a baby who actively approached in one reunion episode might merely reach and cry in another, although in both episodes he sought closer proximity to his mother. Presumably similar variations of means toward ends might well occur from one session to another. Frequency measures of component proximity-promoting behaviors, considered separately, do not take into account the fact that these behaviors are to some extent interchangeable.

Second, let us consider proximity-promoting behaviors, such as vocalizing and smiling. Maccoby and Feldman differentiated between these "distal" behaviors and "proximal" behaviors, such as those involved in active proximity seeking and contact maintaining, hypothesizing that a developmental shift from proximal to distal modes might occur over time, and that those who scored high in proximal behavior at one age point might score comparably high in distal behavior at another age point—implying that the "strength" of attachment thus remained constant. (Their data did not support the hypothesis.) A more useful distinction between the two sets of behaviors is in terms of the intensity of activation of the attachment-behavioral system. Vocalizing, smiling, and the like are most likely to occur under conditions of low intensity of activation of attachment behavior, and thus differ from the more active and/or intense proximity-seeking and contact-maintaining behaviors that tend to occur under conditions of high intensity of activation. Consequently the former are not increased in incidence by the conditions implicit in the strange-situation procedure that were intended to activate attachment behavior at high levels of intensity.

Furthermore, at low levels of activation of the attachment system attachment behaviors of all kinds, including vocalizing and smiling, are of relatively infrequent incidence. It will perhaps be recalled that in the "free-play" episode, Episode 2, infants smiled only once at the mother, on the average, and the mother's noninterventive role undoubtedly offered little special instigation to vocalizing or smiling. Thus in regard to these low-intensity behaviors, laboratory studies encounter the problem of inadequate behavioral sampling. The 6 minutes of the two preseparation episodes together constitute too brief a time to yield an adequate sample. Thus for some of the discrete behaviors, stability between sessions cannot be adequately assessed because of the sampling problem. Even considering these to be interchangeable in some way, as in our categorical measure of distance interaction or in Maccoby and Feldman's speak-smile-show measure, did not result in stability across time.

Of more concern to us than the stability of behavioral measures over time is the issue of the stability of the patterning of behaviors that is reflected in the classificatory system. Our hypothesis is that qualitative differences in the child–mother relationship, which are reflected in the patternings of strange-situation behavior and which in turn are reflected in the A-B-C classifications, tend to be stable over time. To be sure, we can conceive of shifts in the security/anxiety dimension of this relationship that are attributable either to substantial changes in the pattern of interaction between mother and child or to gross changes that influence that interaction (such as severe separation experiences) or to both in combination. Nevertheless our longitudinal study of mother–infant interaction throughout the first year of life (see Chapters 7 and 8) has led us to expect continuity to be more frequent than discontinuity. Certainly within a period as short as two weeks, discontinuities could be expected only in a very few special cases in which circumstances had intervened grossly to change the quality of the child–mother relationship. Over a period of six months, however, it might be expected that more such changes might occur.

Therefore, it is paradoxical that Waters and Connell found a high degree of stability in the nature of the child–mother attachment relationship over a period of six months, whereas we found less apparent stability over a period of two weeks, when the criterion of stability was a match in regard to strange-situation classification from two sessions separated by a lapse of time. When the two sessions are separated by only two weeks, there is clear-cut evidence that anxiety engendered by the first session carries over to influence behavior in the second. We interpret the findings to suggest that the anxiety pertains to the issue of the mother's accessibility, and we believe that this issue is more or less restricted to the particular circumstances of the strange situation itself. In any event babies are more disturbed when they encounter a second strange situation shortly after they encountered the first, and this disturbance tends to break down the distinctions implicit in the classificatory system.

On the other hand, if the second session is some months after the first (as in Waters' and Connell's studies), the disturbance attributable to the first session seems to have dissipated, so that qualitative differences in the child–mother attachment relationship emerge as highly stable. To be sure, some of the few instances of instability may have been due to error in assessment or to chance variability in strange-situation behavior, but some may conceivably have come about because the relationship between child and mother had indeed undergone a qualitative change. With both of these possibilities open, it is indeed extraordinary that both Connell and Waters independently found such a high degree of stability over a 6-month period.

In conclusion, it appears that the individual differences that are stable over time are differences in the qualitative nature of the child's attachment relationship to his mother. These are reflected in our system of classifying the patterns of his behavior in the strange situation. The components of the patterning are tapped chiefly by the categorical measures of interactive behavior, not all of which are attachment behaviors, and those behaviors that are most closely related to the patterning as well as being most stable over time occur under conditions of activation of the attachment system at high levels of intensity. This means that the mother-directed behaviors are best observed in the reunion episodes, for only in the case of a relatively few infants did the preseparation episodes offer high-intensity activation. Discrete behavioral measures neither relate to the patterning of behaviors that reflect quality of attachment nor tap stable separate aspects of behavior in themselves. As Tracy, Lamb, and Ainsworth (1976) found for approach behavior observed at home, it is not only the environmental context of approach behavior that enables one to judge whether it serves attachment or some other behavioral system, but also the behavioral context in which approach appears. Discrete frequency measures, by their very nature, ignore behavioral context. The categorical measures of interactive behavior, in contrast, take both environmental and behavioral context into account. Of all our methods of assessment, however, it is the classificatory system, including the subgroups, that through its focus on patterns of behavior gives most scope for considering behavioral context. We consider the issue of classification into subgroups in the next chapter.

12 Subgroups and Their Usefulness

INTRODUCTION

The findings so far reported have tended to omit reference to the subgroups of the strange-situation classificatory system. None of the three major groups—A, B, and C—is large enough to support a discriminant-function analysis for its component subgroups. Within Sample 1, for which measures of infant and maternal behavior at home are available, the number of infants in each of the subgroups is too small to make it reasonable to expect significant differences among them. Therefore, it is difficult to assemble convincing evidence of the validity of the distinctions between subgroups that are made by the classificatory system. This being so, the reader may wish to conclude that such distinctions might well be ignored.

We are, however, reluctant to abandon subgroup distinctions at this stage of our knowledge, even though the accumulation of a large enough sample for the proper investigation of subgroups is a task for the future, probably contingent on the pooled findings of a number of independent investigators. Our reasons for reluctance are as follows. First, some of our findings with Sample 1 strongly suggest that infants in different subgroups within the same major classification may have had different kinds of experiences, and that these may make for different patterns of interaction with their attachment figures and for qualitatively different attachment relationships. Some evidence pertinent to this point is reported shortly. Meanwhile let us merely state our conviction that a more refined identification of "outcome" patterns offers more aid to the identification of relevant antecedent variables than does a cruder kind of identification.

Second, the specifications for classification into subgroups are more explicit than those for classification merely into one of the three major groups. Therefore, the use of the classificatory system is likely to be more reliable for classification even into the major groups if the judges in question first make (or attempt) a subgroup classification. At the same time it seems wise to think of any classificatory system as openended. It is inconceivable that any system based on a relatively small sample could comfortably accommodate all patterns represented in the total population from which the sample is drawn. We conceive of it as being relatively easy to extend the number of subgroups, if required, in order to comprehend new patterns encountered in further samplings, and indeed this was once done in our study in order to comprehend the infants now classed in Subgroup B_4. So far our experience has encouraged us to believe that the three major classificatory groups can, in fact, cover the variety of patterns of infant–mother attachment relationships commonly encountered. This is so, we believe, because the specifications for the classification into subgroups have enabled us to abstract the specifications for the three major groups in ways that are more incisive than they would have been had subgroups not previously been identified.

Finally, we consider the subgroups to be the foundation of the classificatory system. It may not be relevant that the subgroups were identified first, in the process of grouping together strange-situation protocols that were maximally similar. Nevertheless, it was through examination of the similarities among members of each subgroup that our attention was first drawn to those variables whose patterning reflected important qualitative features of the infant–mother attachment relationship.

Because of these considerations, we proceed to present our findings relevant to subgroups.

DISTRIBUTION OF INFANTS
AMONG STRANGE-SITUATION SUBGROUPS

Table 26 shows the distribution of infants in each of the four samples and in the total sample among the subgroups. It may be seen that Subgroup B_3 is the largest in the sample, and accounts for 42% of the total sample. We consider it to be the normative group, not merely because it is the largest, but also because, as we subsequently show, it is the subgroup whose members have had the most harmonious interaction with their mothers and who have established the most secure attachment relationships. The rest of the subgroups are small, especially B_4, C_1, and C_2.

TABLE 26
Distribution by Sample of Infants Among
Strange-Situation Subgroups

	Samples				Total	
Subgroup	1	2	3	4	N	%
A_1	4	3	2	3	12	11
A_2	2	2	5	1	10	9
$A_0{}^a$	0	0	0	1	1	1
B_1	1	3	1	5	10	9
B_2	3	4	4	0	11	10
B_3	9	14	8	14	45	42
B_4	0	3	1	0	4	4
C_1	2	2	1	1	6	6
C_2	2	2	1	2	7	7
Totals	23	33	23	27	106	

[a]This indicates Group A, but unclassified as to subgroup.

SUBGROUPS AND MATERNAL BEHAVIOR

Perhaps the major piece of evidence to date that has confirmed our decision to retain subgroup distinctions is the set of subgroup means for Sample 1 in regard to the fourth-quarter ratings of maternal behavior—first reported by Ainsworth, Bell, and Stayton (1971) and shown in Table 27. Here Subgroups B_1 and B_2 were combined, because there was only one infant in B_1, and her mother's scores were similar to those of the B_2 mothers.

On each of the four scales, the mothers of B_3 babies received the highest mean score, and one each of the mothers of the B_1/B_2 babies came next. This consistency is reflected in a coefficient of concordance significant at the level beyond .01. All of the mothers of the A and C infants were conspicuously insensitive to infant signals and communications. Group-A mothers, especially A_1 mothers, were more rejecting than C mothers. A_2 and C_2 mothers were the most inaccessible and ignoring. A_1 mothers were the most interfering. We consider these differences so important that we discuss them in more detail.

The mothers of B_3 babies are sensitively responsive to the baby's signals and capable of perceiving things from his point of view. The B_3 mother views her baby as a separate individual; she respects his activity-in-progress and therefore avoids interrupting him. She accepts the intermittent attachment behavior that leads him to her.

The mothers of B_1 and B_2 babies may be described as inconsistently sensitive in their responsiveness. For various reasons they were also inconsistently accessible to the baby, sometimes giving him much attention and sometimes ignoring him. During the periods of attention, the four mothers in these subgroups were somewhat interfering, tending to interrupt exploratory play. In two cases there was clear mismatch in regard to timing of desire for close bodily contact; the mothers sometimes interrupted the baby to cuddle him when he was interested in play, only to rebuff him later when he himself sought contact.

The mothers of A_1 babies were more rejecting and interfering than the mothers of the babies of any other subgroup. They were quite unable to see things from the baby's point of view or to respect his autonomy. They did not so much ignore the baby's communications as they discounted them as relevant guidelines, and thus were very arbitrary in their interventions.

The mothers of A_2 babies were inaccessible for prolonged periods. They were bored with the maternal role and found other interests to occupy them both at home and away from home. When they entered the room in which the baby was, they were usually so preoccupied with their own thoughts or activities that they failed to acknowledge his presence. They tended to respond only to very strong and persistent signals from the baby. Because they paid the baby so little attention, they were infrequently interfering, although they could not be described as cooperative or "codetermining." They seemed to reject the baby along with the maternal role.

The mothers of C_2 babies were also highly inaccessible and ignoring. Unlike the A_2 mothers, however, they had a strong investment in the maternal role. They were severely disturbed women. Multiple demands on their time provoked fragmented behavior. To hold themselves together, they often had to ignore the baby and "tune out" his crying. Especially in the first quarter, they left the baby alone to cry for prolonged periods. When the C_2 mother did intervene, she did so arbitrarily, even though the intervention itself might be pleasant. Because the C_2 infant could rarely experience a consequence contingent on his own behavior, it is not surprising that he behaved very passively both in the strange situation and at home, whereas A_2 infants, whose

TABLE 27
Subgroup Means on Scales of Maternal Behavior
in the Fourth Quarter

Maternal Behavior	Strange-Situation Subgroups					
	B_3	B_1/B_2	C_1	C_2	A_2	A_1
Sensitivity–insensitivity	7.36	4.50	2.50	2.25	2.50	2.75
Acceptance–rejection	8.00	6.75	5.50	5.25	4.25	3.50
Cooperation–interference	7.66	6.50	4.00	4.50	5.50	2.63
Accessibility–ignoring	7.39	4.88	4.50	2.50	2.25	4.63
Mean Scores	7.60	5.66	4.13	3.63	3.63	3.38

TABLE 28
Subgroup Means on Further Scales of Maternal Behavior[a]

Maternal Behavior	Strange-Situation Subgroups					
	B_3	B_1/B_2	C_1	C_2	A_2	A_1
Aversion to physical contact (1st Q)	1.61	3.80	1.65	1.80	6.80	7.55
Providing baby with unpleasant experience in physical contact (1st Q)	1.65	1.00	1.00	4.80	3.80	6.62
Lack of emotional expressiveness (whole year)	2.17	3.88	4.25	2.75	6.50	6.00
Rigidity (whole year)	1.89	2.75	2.00	3.50	3.50	4.50

[a]Data provided by Mary Main.

strong persistent signals eventually evoked a response, developed more active modes of coping.

The mothers of the two C_1 babies were disparate, except that both were highly insensitive to infant signals. One was highly interfering, although not rejecting. She continually interrupted her daughter to train her, to show off her accomplishments, or merely because she herself felt like playing with the baby or showing her affection. The other C_1 mother was compulsive, preoccupied, and generally unresponsive to all but emergency signals. On the other hand, she scored mid-scale in cooperation–interference, being excessively controling in the feeding situation but not otherwise. Although both little girls behaved similarly in the strange situation, the background of mother–infant interaction differed, and to a much greater extent than in the case of any other subgroup.

To this account we can add the findings for Main's four variables, shown in Table 28. Again it is clear that B_3 mothers emerge with the best ratings on the whole—in this case, the lowest ratings. They neither provided their babies with unpleasant experiences when in close bodily contact nor did they themselves find contact aversive. They showed no substantial lack of emotional expressiveness and were not rigid or compulsive

As shown in chapter 8, Main's hypotheses were supported by the high scores Group-A mothers received on these four variables, but there are interesting individual and subgroup differences. A_1 mothers were high in aversion to physical contact and in providing the baby with unpleasant experiences in contact. The two A_2 mothers were similar except that one of them was judged not to have provided the baby with unpleasant physical-contact experiences, which of course lowered the A_2 mean. Both A_1 and A_2 subgroups have relatively high means on lack of emotional expressiveness, which Main linked with suppressed or repressed anger. The A_1 mean would have been even higher had it not been for one mother whose anger toward the baby was quite overtly expressed.

For one variable—aversion to physical contact—the B_1/B_2 mean is higher than those of any but the two Group-A subgroups, and it is also relatively high in lack of emotional expressiveness. One B_2 and the one B_1 mother suffered from postpartum disturbance during the baby's first quarter-year—a disturbance that left them less responsive to their babies than they might otherwise have been, and indeed less responsive than they later became. This, we believe, is why they both scored relatively high in lack of emotional expressiveness. In addition, the B_1 mother received a high rating on aversion to physical contact.

As Main hypothesized, Group-C mothers differ from Group-A mothers in regard to three of the four variables here under consideration. Indeed, most of the mothers—and it must be recalled that there were only four—resembled Group-B mothers on the whole. None of them showed any substantial aversion to close bodily contact. One C_2 mother gave the baby highly unpleasant physical-contact experiences, but this was for reasons quite different from those that seemed pertinent with A_1 mothers—reasons associated with ignoring and neglect rather than interference, anger, or rejection. One C_1 mother was very bland and hence received a high score for lack of emotional expressiveness. C_2 mothers were more rigid and compulsive than C_1 mothers, and indeed received the same mean rating as A_2 mothers. Their compulsiveness seemed to be a mode of coping with their tendencies to become fragmented when exposed to any degree of stress, and was less consistently shown than the rigidity–compulsiveness of Group-A mothers. However, only research with future samples that include larger numbers of C_1 and C_2 babies can clarify our understanding of the patterns of maternal behavior associated with these subgroups. Meanwhile the evidence from our small sample of Group-C mothers suggests that they differ from Group-A mothers in regard to Main's four variables.

We have also examined subgroup differences in regard to the fourth-quarter measures of maternal behavior derived from the coding of the narrative reports. We do not present a table comparable to Tables 25 and 26, because for the most part the subgroups tend to reflect the trends characteristic of the three main groups, A, B, and C. However, we do report a few subgroup differences that override group trends, but only in instances in which there was minimal variation within the subgroups themselves.

A_2 mothers, much less frequently than the mothers of other subgroups, including A_1, acknowledged their babies upon returning from an absence from the room. C_1 mothers, more frequently than those of any other subgroup, picked up their babies primarily in order to play with them. Most of the other notable differences pertain to maternal interference. Although on the whole B_1/B_2 mothers resemble B_3 mothers more closely than the mothers of any of the A or C subgroups, they more frequently picked up their babies in an abrupt and interfering way than did B_3 mothers, and they were also more often inept in their holding. C_1 mothers, more frequently than others, and especially more frequently than C_2 mothers, intervened physically to back up their verbal commands to the baby. Both B_1/B_2 and C_1 mothers issued more frequent verbal commands than mothers of infants in other subgroups. A_1 mothers, however, were the most interfering in the context of physical contact.

Finally, let us consider three studies that offer evidence to justify the distinctions between B_1/B_2 and B_3 subgroups in light of maternal behavior. In Chapter 9 we reported the findings of Tolan (1975) and Tomasini (1975). In their analyses of the behavior of the mothers of toddlers in Main's (1973) laboratory play session, they distinguished the behavior of three groups—B_3, B_1/B_2, and A/C—as representing three degrees of security–insecurity in the attachment relationship. Tolan found significant correlations between maternal facial expression and degree of security–insecurity of the infant's attachment to his mother, and Tomasini found significant correlations of maternal sensitivity–insensitivity and acceptance–rejection with security–insecurity of attachment. We assume that the intermediate degree of security–insecurity provided by the B_1/B_2 subgroups contributed to the magnitude of the correlations reported by these investigators. Blehar, Lieberman, and Ainsworth (1977), in their study of early face-to-face interaction, also considered the same three groups, with B_1/B_2 intermediate between B_3 and A/C. Only one difference emerged as significant for either maternal or infant behavior—namely, B_3 mothers were more likely than B_1/B_2 mothers to be contingent in their pacing of their behavior to mesh with infant behavior. Nevertheless, for most of the measures—pertaining both to mother and infant—the B_1/B_2 subgroup was truly an intermediate group. Especially noteworthy is that it differed from the B_3 subgroup.

Thus, even though the subgroups in Sample 1 are too small to support estimates of significance of intersubgroup differences, the observable differences are impressive in that they suggest different forms of mother–infant interaction that tie into different dynamic processes affecting infant development. Our accounts of these processes must remain tentative, however, until they can be tested in other samples. Nevertheless, subgroup differences do suggest different processes, and this we consider to be a potent justification for continuing to distinguish subgroups.

SUBGROUPS AND THE ATTACHMENT–EXPLORATION BALANCE AT HOME

Ainsworth, Bell, and Stayton (1971) also reported on the congruence between subgroup classification of strange–situation behavior and classification of Sample-1 infants in terms of their behavior at home. The classificatory system was geared toward an assessment of the balance between attachment behavior and exploratory behavior in the home environment. Five groups were identified, and their behavior may be summarized as follows:

Group-I infants showed an optimum balance between attachment and exploratory behavior. They used the mother as a secure base from which to explore the world. The Group-I infant could freely move away from his mother to explore, but he would keep track of her whereabouts, and from time to time would gravitate back to her again, perhaps to gain physical contact with her, if only briefly.

Group-II infants at times showed a disturbance of this balance. This disturbance seemed to be in reaction to maternal behavior and to represent a mismatch between mothers' and infants' wishes for contact. Thus, the Group-II infant sometimes behaved precisely as a Group-I infant would; at other times he avoided his mother; at still other times he sought contact with her more anxiously than Group I-infants usually do.

Group-III infants tended to display active exploratory behavior with much less frequent or intense interest in either proximity or in close bodily contact with the mother than is characteristic of either Group-I or Group-II infants.

Group-IV infants seemed conflicted about proximity to and close bodily contact with the mother. The Group-IV baby did explore, although perhaps more briefly than infants of Groups I, II, and III. He was anxious about his mother's whereabouts and actively attempted to keep in proximity to her. On occasion he actively sought contact with her; but he did not seem to find pleasure in it once achieved, and indeed may have been markedly ambivalent about it.

Group-V infants tended to be passive either in attachment behavior or in exploration, or in both—some only intermittently and others more consistently. Stereotyped, repetitive, autoerotic activities were more frequent in this group than in any other.

We are now not altogether satisfied with this classificatory system and we believe that it can be improved through revision in light of data analysis that has subsequently been completed—a revision that we will not attempt to gear primarily to the concept of attachment–exploration balance. Nevertheless, a comparison between the strange-situation classification into subgroups and this present classification yields highly suggestive results. (See Table 29.) Let us discuss the congruencies and discrepancies between the two classifications. In fact, there are only four instances in which the members of a strange-situation subgroup do not all fall into the same attachment–exploration balance classificatory group. In the case of three of these, mother–infant interaction had deteriorated during the last few months of the first year. The classification in terms of home behavior seemed to better reflect this deterioration, whereas the strange-situation classification seemed to better reflect an earlier state of affairs.

TABLE 29

Classification of Strange-Situation Behavior and
Classification of Attachment–Exploration Balance in Behavior at Home[a]

Attachment–Exploration Balance at Home	Strange-Situation Behavior Classification						
Groups	B_3	B_1/B_2	A_2	A_1	C_1	C_2	Totals
I	8	—	—	—	—	—	8
II	1	3	—	—	—	—	4
III	—	1	2	—	—	—	3
IV	—	—	—	3	1	—	4
V	—	—	—	1	1	2	4
Totals	9	4	2	4	2	2	23

[a]From Ainsworth, Bell, & Stayton (1971, p. 37).

It may be seen from Table 29 that Subgroup B_3 is nearly coincident with Group I. One B_3 infant, however, was classified in Group II in regard to home behavior. The mother was conspicuously sensitive to her baby's signals throughout the first 9 months, but then became anxious and depressed because of marital difficulties that suddenly surfaced. Consequently, in the fourth quarter this mother alternated between responsiveness to the baby and impatient rebuff.

B_1/B_2 infants tend to fall in Group II. Both A_2 babies, as well as one B_2, were classified in Group III—the groups that emphasized exploratory behavior at the expense of proximity seeking. The exceptional B_2 baby enjoyed much interaction with his mother during his first 5 months or so. At this point a family crisis put the mother under such strain that she could not tolerate the baby's recently acquired and active seeking both for interaction and for floor freedom. She confined him in his crib alone in his room for most of the day, and thus was conspicuous for inaccessibility and ignoring. It is therefore not surprising that at home he behaved like the A_2 babies whose mothers were also highly ignoring.

Most A_1 infants, as well as one C_1 baby, fall into the conflicted Group IV. Finally, Group-V, which may be the most disturbed of all, included both C_2 infants as well as one each from A_1 and C_1. The split of the C_1 subgroups between Groups IV and V should arouse no surprise, for it has been acknowledged from the beginning that the two Sample-1 C_1 mother–infant dyads were disparate. The A_1 baby classified in Group V is worthy of mention, however. Although his mother had been both rejecting and ignoring from the beginning, she became in addition anxious and inconsistent during the fourth quarter, again presumably because of severe marital difficulties. Because of disruption in the home, the baby underwent several separation experiences, and the marriage broke up soon afterwards.

In brief, these findings indicate that classification in terms of strange-situation behavior is strikingly congruent with classification in terms of behavior at home in the fourth quarter, even though the former may be "phenotypically" different from the latter. Perhaps more important, especially for our present consideration of the value of retaining subgroup distinctions, it is clear that B_3 babies behave differently from B_1/B_2 babies at home, and that A_2 babies are strikingly different from A_1 babies. Furthermore, the passivity of C_2 infants is borne out in their home behavior.

SUBGROUPS AND OTHER MEASURES OF INFANT BEHAVIOR AT HOME

In regard to the infant-behavioral measures derived from the coding of the narrative reports, there are a few subgroup means that deviate from the general trend of the group means, although we do not present a table comparable to Tables 16 and 17. It is clear that B_1/B_2 infants differed from B_3 infants in regard to some measures of behavior relevant to close bodily contact; they were less frequently positive (and more frequently negative) in their response to contact, although they were more often positive than Group-A infants. They also more frequently initiated being put down than any other subgroup except C_1. These findings are consistent with the fact that B_1/B_2 infants tended to fall into Group II of the home-behavior classification—the group in which there tended to be a mismatch between mother's and infant's timing of desire for close bodily contact. In addition, B_1/B_2 infants were found by Blehar, Lieberman, and Ainsworth (1977) to be intermediate between B_3 and A/C infants in regard to a number of features of behavior in face-to-face situations between 6 and 15 weeks of age.

C_1 infants were more often negative to being picked up than the infants of any other subgroup, and less often responded positively to being put down. In these respects they differed strikingly from C_2 infants. It would appear that C_1 infants were overtly ambivalent about physical contact with their mothers—as indeed they were also in the strange situation—even though they showed much less evidence of approach–avoidance conflict than A babies.

The passivity of C_2 infants is reflected in a number of behavioral measures. Less often than any other subgroup did they initiate either being picked up or being put down, and less often did they follow their mothers when they left the room. They received a zero score on compliance to mother's commands, but the major discriminator here is that they moved about so little that their mothers issued few or no commands. Perhaps related to their passivity is the fact that the C_2 infants received lower DQs in the fourth quarter than the infants of any other subgroup, although A_1 babies also lagged in this respect.

Finally, A_1 infants more frequently followed when the mother left the room than did babies of any other subgroup, whereas A_2 infants did so less frequently than Group-B infants. More frequently than A_2 infants, A_1 babies cried or gave mixed greetings when the mother returned from an absence.

In summary, even though the subgroups are too small to assess statistical significance of differences between them, there is suggestive evidence that intragroup subgroup differences in the strange situation correspond to differences in behavior at home. This being so, we have somewhat more justification than we otherwise would have for examining strange-situation behavior for evidence of differences between subgroups.

SUBGROUP DIFFERENCES IN INTERACTION WITH THE MOTHER IN THE STRANGE SITUATION

Figure 11 shows the mean scores of each of the subgroups for each of 5 measures of interactive behavior in each of the episodes from 2 to 8. (Appendix IV, Table 33, gives the means and standard deviations for the subgroups, based on the total sample of 106.)

It may be seen at a glance that the differences between A_1 and A_2 infants are confined to the reunion episodes, and that these differences are clearly in line with the criteria for classification. A_2 infants, in comparison with A_1 infants, show stronger proximity seeking and somewhat weaker avoidance in the reunion episodes. In addition, in Episode 8 (when A_2 but not A_1 infants were picked up by their mothers) they showed some contact maintaining and resistance.

Subgroup B_1 is of particular interest as a group intermediate between Group A and the rest of Group B. This subgroup was originally included in Group B because of the positive reaction the infants showed to the mother's return in the reunion episodes. This was specified as a positive, undelayed greeting to the mother when she returned, followed by little or no avoidance and by interaction with her across a distance, even though the baby did not seek proximity or contact. Figure 11 reflects these specifications, except that there is a moderate amount of avoidance shown in the reunion episodes—in Episode 5, it is almost as much as that shown by Subgroup A_2. Furthermore although the distance-interaction measure was introduced specifically because of this subgroup, even it does not adequately take into account greeting behavior. In retrospect, we are inclined to conclude that some infants were classified in Subgroup B_1 who might more appropriately have been classified in Group A, probably because the avoidance behavior (which is the hallmark of Group A) was mistakenly given lesser weight than the pleasant distance interaction

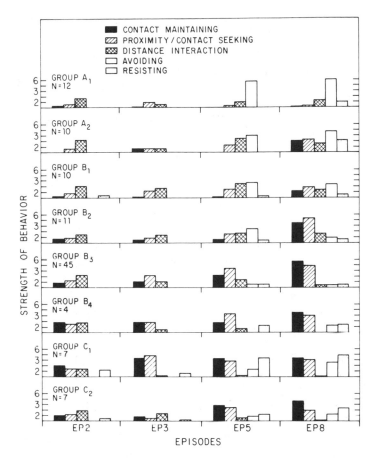

FIG. 11   Means of subgroups on five measures of interactive behavior
directed toward the mother.

characteristic of these babies. If this is indeed true, then Connell and
Rosenberg (1974), as a preliminary to their multiple discriminant function
analysis based on our data, had some justifiable grounds for excluding B_1
infants from Group B—although surely only a minority of our B_1 infants could
have been misclassified.

Subgroup B_2 matches the specifications very well. Up to Episode 8 they are
indistinguishable from B_1 infants, but then they show strong proximity-
seeking and contact-maintaining behavior with a minimum of avoidance. In
Episode 8 they resemble B_3 infants more strongly than they do B_1 infants.

The behaviors of B_3 infants very closely match the criteria for classification.
They are particularly conspicuous for seeking to gain proximity to and contact
with the mother in the reunion episodes and to maintain contact once
achieved, especially in Episode 8. What especially distinguishes them from the

other subgroups, however, is their almost complete lack of avoidant and resistant behavior.

Subgroup C_1 differs from B_3 in a number of respects, chiefly consistent with criteria for classification. The major difference, however, is that C_1 infants show strong resistance in the reunion episodes, whereas B_3 infants show little or none. The major surprise is that C_1 infants were scored as high as they were in avoidance in Episode 8, although the mean is substantially less than that of Group-A infants. It is possible that one or two infants classified as C_1 primarily because of strong resistant behavior might better have been classified in Group A. Indeed, the infant who appears as A_0 in Table 24 (i.e., unclassified as to subgroup) was originally put into Group C and then reclassified. As a result of the MDFA, with its great emphasis on avoidance behavior following reunion with the mother as the main discriminant between A and non-A behavior, we are inclined in retrospect to give more emphasis to strong avoidance behavior than to the combination of proximity-seeking, contact-maintaining, and resistant behaviors; thus, if all of these behaviors appear, the strong avoidance would call for classification in Group A.

A cardinal characteristic of C_2 infants was specified as passivity. Because our scoring of interactive behavior (except for distance interaction) reserved the highest scores for behavior showing strong, active initiative, it might be expected that C_2 infants would score lower on these measures than C_1 infants—and indeed this is borne out in Figure 11. Nevertheless it is clear that C_2 infants resemble C_1 infants much more closely than they resemble infants of any other subgroup, except for B_4.

Subgroup B_4, although the smallest in the sample, is of special interest. It was introduced into the classificatory system because Bell (1970) found three infants in her sample of 33 who seemed "wholly preoccupied with their mothers throughout the strange situation." They were clearly more anxious in the infant–mother attachment relationship than other Group-B babies. From what information Bell could gather in the course of home visits undertaken for other purposes, it appeared that these infants had all recently undergone an anxiety-provoking experience, such as major separation, but that both mother and infant were positively oriented to each other, and appeared to be in the process of mending their relationship. It is clear from Figure 11 that B_4 is intermediate between B_3 and Group C and is closer in the pattern of scores to C_2 than to C_1. In the reunion episodes, B_4 babies resemble Group-C babies, except that they show less resistance to the mother than do C_1 infants, and more active proximity-seeking behavior than C_2 infants.

Finally, it is clear that distance interaction with the mother is less differentiating among groups and subgroups than any of the other four interactive variables. It appears that for 1-year-olds in an unfamiliar situation, with cumulatively increasing instigation to high intensity attachment behavior, behaviors relevant to proximity and contact (both positive and negative) are more conspicuous and more differentiating than the so-called distal behaviors.

In summary, the finding for five behavioral measures of infant initiative in interaction with the mother match the criteria for classification into subgroups very well on the whole, with but few exceptions.

GROUP AND SUBGROUP DIFFERENCES IN GREETING THE MOTHER UPON REUNION

The baby's initial greeting to his mother when she entered in the reunion episodes was specifically represented in the criteria for classification, but was not scored separately from the interactive behaviors that characterized each reunion episode as a whole. Consequently, greeting behaviors were not represented in the multiple discriminant function analysis. Because positive greeting (without proximity seeking) was especially crucial in the identification of Subgroup B_1, as one of the behaviors that were specified to distinguish B_1 from Group-A infants, a descriptive ethological analysis was undertaken of responses to the mother during the first 15 seconds of each of the reunion episodes. The findings of that analysis are summarized here.

Group-A infants were conspicuous for the relative absence of proximity-seeking greetings; if they greeted the mother at all, it tended to be with a mere smile or vocalization, and many did not greet her. In Episode 5 35% greeted her with a smile or vocalization across a distance, whereas only 9% approached her. Most conspicuous, however, was failure to greet; 45% merely looked at the mother and 9% did not even look. In Episode 8 these avoidant tendencies seemed even stronger; 59% merely looked, and again 9% did not even look. Only 18% greeted the mother across a distance, and only 9% made even a partial approach.

The B_1 infants could not be distinguished from B_2 infants by their behavior in the first 15 seconds of the reunion episodes. Of all subgroups B_1/B_2 babies were the most conspicuous for smiling and vocalizing in greeting across a distance; 45% did so in Episode 5 without any proximity-seeking behavior, although fewer did so in Episode 8. In Episode 5, 29% reached, leaned toward, or approached the mother; in Episode 8, more (43%) did so, suggesting that their attachment behavior was more intensely activated by the second separation than by the first. In contrast with Group A, only 14% of B_1/B_2 infants merely looked at the mother without greeting her in Episode 5, and 23% did so in Episode 8. None ignored the mother altogether. After the first 15 seconds were over, B_2 babies, especially in Episode 8, showed proximity-seeking behavior, whereas B_1 infants did not. On the other hand, more B_1 than A_2 babies greeted their mothers across a distance, and fewer subsequently mingled proximity-seeking with avoidant behaviors. The hallmark of B_1

infants, therefore, is not so much in the fact that they greet the mother with a smile or a vocalization rather than with proximity-seeking behavior (or with a cry), but that they tend subsequently not to follow the initial greeting with either proximity-seeking or avoidant behavior.

The majority of B_3 infants clearly showed a desire for close bodily contact or at least for increased proximity. In Episode 5, 33% approached the mother as soon as she entered, and 43% more reached or leaned toward her. Only 11% were content merely to smile or to vocalize across a distance. In Episode 8, 36% approached the mother, 40% reached for a pick-up, and 20% were so distressed that they merely signaled their desire for contact by renewing the intensity of their crying. Thus, in the second reunion episode 96% indicated a desire for closeness in their initial greeting. Although 4% merely greeted the mother across a distance, even in Episode 8, no B_3 baby in either episode failed to look up when the mother entered.

The four B_4 infants were less active than B_3 infants in their greetings. In Episode 5, three continued or increased crying, and only one reached toward the mother for a pick-up. Their relative passivity continued in Episode 8. None gave smiles or vocalizations across a distance, but none failed to greet.

Only one Group-C infant greeted the mother merely with a smile in Episode 5, and none failed to give some kind of greeting in either episode. In Episode 5, only 3 (12%) approached the mother when she entered, and 2 of those were C_1 babies. Nevertheless all but one (93%) indicated a desire for contact or proximity because they either approached the mother, or reached toward her, or cried. In Episode 8, 14% approached and 36% reached toward the mother, but 50% merely cried. It appears that they were more severely distressed than B_3 infants, and less capable of active proximity seeking in their initial greeting responses. In this they resembled B_4 infants.

Thus, in summary, initial responses to the mother's return seem useful for distinguishing among subgroups. They are particularly useful in distinguishing B_1 and B_2 babies from Group-A babies on one hand and from B_3 babies on the other hand, and for distinguishing B_3 from both B_4 and Group C.

SUBGROUP DIFFERENCES IN OTHER BEHAVIORS

Subgroup Differences in Interaction With the Stranger.   A detailed analysis was conducted, but only a summary of findings is reported here. Subgroup means and standard deviations are shown in Appendix IV, Table 34.

Subgroup B_1 showed less distance interaction with the stranger than Group A in Episode 7, and whereas Group-A infants manifested no resistance, some B_1 infants showed some resistance. Indeed, in regard to the means of all behaviors in all three episodes—3, 4, and 7—B_1 babies closely resembled B_2 and B_3 babies.

Avoidance of the stranger occurred most frequently in Episode 3, while the mother was still present, but was conspicuous only among B_4 and C_1 babies. However, subgroup B_4 can be distinguished from both C subgroups in terms of resistant behavior. C Babies were conspicuous for resistance to the stranger in the separation episodes, whereas B_4 babies showed almost none. On the whole, therefore, B_4 infants resembled the infants of the other B subgroups more closely in their behavior to the stranger than the infants of Group C.

A_1 and A_2 babies cannot be distinguished by their behavior to the stranger, which featured a moderate amount of distance interaction. C_2 infants resembled C_1 infants, except that they showed little avoidance of the stranger in Episode 3, in contrast to the strong avoidance shown by C_1, and that they did not show the marked resistance to the stranger in Episode 7 that is such a conspicuous feature of C_1 behavior.

Subgroup Differences in Search Behavior.   The means and standard deviations for each subgroup in regard to search behavior in the separation episodes are given in Appendix IV, Table 35. The findings are easily summarized. Subgroups B_4 and C_2 showed very weak search behavior even in Episode 6, when the babies of all other subgroups tended to show moderately strong to strong search.

Subgroup Differences in Exploratory Behavior.   The means in Appendix IV, Table 36, show that exploratory behavior was maintained relatively well across all episodes by four subgroups A_1, A_2, B_1, and, to a lesser extent, B_2. B_3 infants were slightly less exploratory, even in the preseparation episodes, than the infants of these four subgroups. The babies of three subgroups—B_4, C_1, and C_2—explored less throughout than any of the other subgroups, and they explored almost not at all in the second separation and reunion episodes.

Subgroup Differences in Crying.   Crying was very infrequent among the infants of subgroups A_1, A_2, B_1, and B_2, especially in the preseparation episodes and in the first separation and reunion episodes. Indeed it was only in Episode 6, when the baby was alone, that other than minimal crying occurred. (See Appendix IV, Table 36.) B_3 babies cried little except in the separation episodes, and cried clearly more in the two second-separation episodes than in the first. Crying was much more characteristic of Subgroups B_4, C_1, and C_2. Furthermore, these infants cried more in the reunion episodes than did the infants of other subgroups, suggesting that they were less readily soothed.

Summary.   Exploratory behavior and crying scores differentiate between B_1/B_2, B_3, and B_4, but they distinguished neither B_1/B_2 from Group A nor B_4 from Group C. Search behavior merely differentiates B_4 and C_2 babies from the rest. Interaction with the stranger, however, tended to distinguish B_1/B_2

from Group A and B_4 from Group C, although it yielded little differentiation among the Group-B subgroups, or indeed between the Group-A subgroups. It did, however, yield some distinction between C_1 and C_2.

DISCUSSION

In this chapter we have assembled evidence pertinent to the issue of retaining the distinctions among subgroups in our classificatory system. The patterns of behavior reflected in the subgroup means of measures of interactive behavior and in initial greeting responses in the reunion episodes differentiate among the subgroups in close approximation to the specifications of the instructions for classifying into subgroups. Although crying, search, and exploratory behavior provide relatively little differentiation among most of the subgroups, findings match the specifications for classification in the few instances in which references were made to these behaviors. Responses to the stranger yielded some intersubgroup differences, but none had been specified by the instructions for classification. In general these findings demonstrate not only that the distinctions in the classificatory system could be objectified in quantitative measures, but also that the various judges who undertook the classifications could and did make the distinctions in accordance with specifications.

Although it is of obvious relevance to note ways in which the subgroups may be distinguished from one another in terms of strange-situation behavior this does not in itself demonstrate that the distinctions are worth making. Of all the evidence reviewed here, we attach most importance to that which shows that babies in different subgroups behave differently in interaction with their mothers in other situations, and especially in the natural environment of the home. This evidence is so far of limited extent, but it suggests that it is worth making distinctions between A_1 and A_2, between Group A and B_1/B_2, between B_1/B_2 and B_3, and between C_1 and C_2. It does not help us with distinctions between B_1 and B_2, between B_4 and B_3, or between B_4 and C_2. A major difficulty is, of course, the size of the subgroups in any one sample, which is too small for an extensive and intensive investigation to be made of mother–infant interaction in other situations, especially longitudinal investigation of the development of such interaction. Indeed the whole issue of the usefulness of subgroups in our classificatory system is an empirical issue that depends on a number of replications of research that relates patterns of strange-situation behavior to behavior in other situations and/or to differences in mother–infant interaction.

The issue of Subgroups B_1 and B_4 presents somewhat different problems from other subgroup issues. These are clearly "borderline" subgroups—B_1 clearly being intermediate between B_2 and Group A, and B_4 equally clearly being intermediate between B_3 and Group C. Connell and Rosenberg (1974) suggested that B_1 properly belonged in Group A, and B_4 in Group C; they excluded both of these subgroups from their discriminant-function analysis on this account. This, we believe, is still an open question, which can be settled only by further research with behavior in other situations (especially mother–infant interaction at home) that provide external criteria. In the meantime, B_1 babies also closely resemble B_2 infants; combined into a group intermediate between B_3 babies on the one hand and A/C babies on the other, they have been found to show clear-cut differences in mother–infant interaction. Even though much less is known about B_4 infants, they are clearly less resistant to their mothers in the reunion episodes of the strange situation than the Group-C infants whom they otherwise resemble in many ways. In view of these considerations, we are inclined to keep both B_1 and B_4 in Group B until the issue is settled through further research.

Finally, for the reasons stated in the introduction to this chapter, we believe that retention of subgroup distinctions serves useful purposes in the present state of our knowledge. Foremost among these purposes is the forwarding of "etiological" research. Here we refer to research geared toward identifying patterns of antecedent variables that are associated with different "outcome" patterns. Some of these outcome patterns may suggest incipient pathology, but probably even more important is research into the antecedent variables associated with healthy outcomes. Indeed, we propose that the major heuristic value of the strange-situation procedure is that assessments based on it may themselves serve as criteria—a set of outcome criteria—through which the effects of different patterns of infant experience may be evaluated. The research reported in this volume—we refer especially to the research reported in Chapters 7, 8, and 9—suggests that the strange-situation classificatory groups are likely to prove even more useful as outcome criteria than the "behavioral category" scores implicit in our interactive behavioral variables, and certainly more useful than scores of separate, "discrete" attachment behaviors. Furthermore, we believe that the refinements of classification offered by distinctions among subgroups will in time prove even more useful than classification into the three major groups themselves.

IV

DISCUSSION

13

Discussion of Normative Issues

INTRODUCTION

Despite our conviction that normative trends in behavior across episodes and that findings pertinent to individual differences in attachment and attachment behaviors throw light upon each other, it is convenient in our final discussion to focus first on one and then the other. In this chapter we discuss issues related to normative trends, and in Chapter 14 we turn to issues pertinent to individual differences. Nevertheless, where relevant, we refer to individual differences when discussing normative issues, and similarly we must on occasion refer back to normative trends when discussing individual differences.

Let us first consider the three sets of phenomena that the strange situation was primarily devised to examine: use of the mother as a "secure base" from which to explore, responses to a stranger, and responses to separation from the mother. In conjunction with these three topics, it is also convenient to consider the following: use of the mother as a "secure haven," differential behavior to mother versus stranger, and the issue of interchangeability of attachment figures. Later we consider a variety of other issues: activation and termination of attachment behavior, the effect of the intensity of activation of the attachment system on the behaviors elicited, and the interplay between attachment behavior and other behavioral systems.

EXPLORATORY BEHAVIOR AND
THE SECURE-BASE PHENOMENON

An unfamiliar or strange situation might be expected to activate three behavioral systems in varying degrees of strength: exploratory behavior, wary/fearful behavior, and attachment behavior. Exploratory behavior is antithetical to attachment behavior in that it leads the infant toward interesting features of his environment and thus usually away from the attachment figure. If, however, the baby is alarmed, attachment behavior as well as wary/fearful behavior tends to be activated (Bowlby, 1969, 1973), and commonly (although not invariably) these two systems work in concert. Thus behavior that promotes proximity to the attachment figure also tends to lead the baby away from the alarming stimulus or at least to reduce its impact (see Chapter 4). To the extent that exploratory behavior is activated more strongly than the other two systems in combination, a child could be expected to explore the new environment. Should the unfamiliar situation activate wariness/fear more strongly than the exploratory system, a child would not be expected to explore. Rather, he would be expected to direct attachment behavior toward his mother, for attachment behavior tends to be activated under circumstances of alarm. Episode 2 was intended to provide strong instigation to exploratory behavior through a massed array of toys. With the mother present and with the toys the most salient aspect of the unfamiliar environment, it was expected that the typical 1-year-old would approach the toys with little delay, rather than approach or signal his mother. The findings support these expectations. On the other hand, when the mother is absent (in Episodes 4, 6, and 7) nearly all infants explored much less than they had in Episode 2. This had been predicted to occur because attachment behavior is strongly activated under circumstances when the attachment figure is inaccessible and/or unresponsive. In the strange situation the mother's departures and brief absences provided strong enough activation of attachment behavior to override even the strongly activated exploratory system. This is an aspect of the phenomenon that we have referred to as "using the mother as a secure base from which to explore" (Ainsworth, 1963, 1967).

We consider it important to view this phenomenon as reflecting the relative strength of activation of the relevant behavioral systems. It does not imply that the physical environment did not activate wariness/fear at all—merely that its novel features activated exploratory behavior more strongly. Similarly, it does not imply that the attachment system was altogether inactive in Episode 2 but merely that it was relatively less intensely activated. In the separation episodes, on the other hand, the fact that exploratory behavior tended to be overridden by attachment behavior does not imply that the exploratory system was totally deactivated. At such a time that attachment behavior was terminated (or sufficiently reduced in intensity), one might expect exploratory behavior to reemerge, as indeed it did to some extent in many infants in the reunion episodes. Furthermore, one ought to expect individual differences in the relative strengths with which the relevant behavioral systems are activated even in this standardized situation.

Cohen (1974) objected to a comparison of behavior in the mother-present and mother-absent conditions as demonstration of the secure-base phenomenon. She pointed out that separated infants often cry and that a crying baby does not explore; crying inhibits exploration. This is essentially another way of saying that when attachment behavior is activated strongly enough, it overrides exploratory behavior. When a baby uses his mother as a secure base from which to explore, his attachment behavior is not activated strongly enough to interfere with exploration; the mother's presence is one of the conditions that operate to keep attachment behavior at low intensity.

Nevertheless it is conceivable that the mother's mere presence might not be enough under some circumstances or in the case of some individuals to hold attachment behavior down to a lower level of activation than that of exploratory behavior. This was the case with some of the Ganda infants who were observed at home (Ainsworth, 1967). There are three points of differences that must be considered when comparing the Ganda and Baltimore samples. The first, and perhaps least important, is that the Ganda infants were observed in the familiar home environment, where there was no massive instigation to exploration provided by a novel array of toys. Second, the Ganda infants tended to be more intensely afraid of strangers, and the relatively unfamiliar observers were present throughout the observations. Third, some of the Ganda 1-year olds who seemed least able to use the mother as a secure base from which to explore had had their relationship with her disrupted by recent weaning from the breast (Ainsworth, 1967, pp. 456–457). These conditions, separately or together, might be expected to lead to relatively more intense activation of attachment behavior and/or relatively less intense activation of exploratory behavior. Individual differences are evident both in the home behavior of Ganda infants and in the strange-situation behavior of our Baltimore sample. These are not discussed here, except to point out that distress in Episode 2 emerged as a conspicuous feature in discriminating Group-C from non-C babies. It could be argued that a baby who is distressed, even minimally, in Episode 2 and who is presumably alarmed by the unfamiliar but benign situation that does not alarm the majority of other children does not experience his mother as a secure base.

Cohen's (1974) discomfort with the concept of the secure base might be alleviated by the use Sroufe and Waters (1977b) made of heart-rate measures in conjunction with strange-situation behavior. Exploratory behavior was typically associated with heart-rate decelerations. All infants showed heart-rate acceleration in the separation episodes, including those who did not cry, and thus presumably including those who maintained some exploration in the separation episodes, albeit at a lower level than in Episode 2. Full recovery of exploratory behavior in the reunion episodes is associated with the disappearance of the acceleration characteristic of separation distress; and a return to basal tonic heart-rate levels is associated with the episodic decelerations characteristic of exploratory behavior. These findings throw light on the significance of both the lack of conspicuous distress in some children and the exploratory behavior of infants who avoid their mothers in the reunion episodes. With the convergent use of heart-rate and behavioral measures, we may become attuned to subtle behavioral clues that indicate when a baby is using his mother as a secure base from which to explore and when anxiety underlies his exploratory activity. We shall return to this point in the next chapter in the context of individual differences in the attachment relationship.

There is more to the secure-base phenomenon, however, than exploring when the mother is present and diminishing exploration when she is absent. Our previous discussion of secure-base behavior among the Ganda (Ainsworth, 1967) specified that the infant who explored away from his mother nevertheless monitored her whereabouts by glancing at her from time to time, perhaps occasionally interacted with her across a distance, and returned to her after a while, perhaps clambering up for a moment's close contact before making another foray away from her. Harlow's (1961) rhesus infants were briefly separated from their surrogate mothers before being placed in an open field, and hence initially rushed to the surrogate. After a few moments, however, their behavior in the open-field situation matches our description of Ganda infants very well.

Bowlby's (1969) concept of set-goal is highly relevant to this second aspect of the secure-base phenomenon. According to his theory, attachment behavior is activated when the distance between an infant and his attachment figure exceeds a certain point, whether it was the movement of the mother or of the infant that increased the distance between them. Consequently a baby, having moved away to explore, would be prompted to return to the attachment figure after exceeding the distance specified by his set-goal. The set-goal differs from time to time, however, according to circumstance. Two researches have been relevant to the concept of a spatial set-goal. Anderson (1972) observed that toddlers in a London park kept within a distance of approximately 200 feet from their mothers. They tended to move away from the mother slowly, with intermittent stops, but to return to her quickly from time to time on their own initiative. During a typical sortie away from his mother, the child looked at her occasionally, and when he returned he tended to make physical contact with her. Rheingold and Eckerman (1970) observed young children aged from 1 to 5 years in a large yard. The mean farthest distance that the 1-year-olds went from their mothers was 23 feet; for 2-year-olds, 50 feet; and for 3-year-olds, 57 feet. Both these researches imply that the strange-situation room (and indeed the usual room at home) tends to be too small for an infant to exceed his spatial set-goal while still remaining in the room. Consequently, in Episode 2 it was a reasonable finding that few infants returned to their mothers after beginning to explore, because they perforce remained well within the limits of their spatial set-goals for relatively nonalarming situations.

The baby's perception of his mother's relative accessibility or inaccessibility also may alter the set-goal. Carr, Dabbs, and Carr (1975) have shown that when the mother is faced away from the child or behind a screen proximity-seeking behavior much more frequently overrides exploratory behavior than when the mother is both visible and faced toward the child. Apparently a turned back, in addition to being a physical barrier to vision, gives the impression of relative inaccessibility. Individual differences in long-term interaction with the mother may also make for individual differences in the baby's perception of his mother as accessible and responsive, and thus influence the set-goal for proximity maintenance.

Bowlby (1969) suggested that there was also a temporal set-goal, so that, having been at some distance from his mother for a certain time specified by the set-goal, a child tends to return to his mother, whether or not he had exceeded the spatial set-goal. The only research with relevance to this concept is by Brooks and Lewis (1974). They divided a 15-minute free-play session (comparable to our Episode 2 except for duration and for number and placement of toys) into five 3-minute periods. Proximity to or touching the mother was of much shorter duration during the first 6 minutes than during the last 6. One possible interpretation of their findings is that the temporal set-goal was not exceeded by most infants during the first 6 minutes, but that attachment behavior was later activated. Brooks and Lewis do not report behavioral sequences, however. If a return to the mother tended to be succeeded by further exploration, this would fit with the set-goal interpretation.

Brooks and Lewis suggest another explanation—namely, that the novel features of the toys were exhausted during the earlier periods of the session. According to our paradigm, this would imply that the toys initially activated the exploratory system more strongly than the attachment system, but that as the novelty wore off exploratory behavior became weaker until it was no longer more strongly activated than the attachment system. Under these circumstances the infant might be expected to return to the mother and to remain close to her rather than resume exploration. Weight for this explanation is provided by previous research by Rheingold and Eckerman (1970), who found that how quickly 10-month-old infants left their mothers to enter a new environment (an adjoining room), how far they went, and how long they stayed away were influenced by the number and location of the toys that had been placed in it. Further evidence is provided by Willemsen and associates (1974), who found a differing amount of exploratory behavior in the strange-situation in two sessions differing in the degree to which they were judged to be "interesting."

All of these considerations suggest that the relative balance between exploratory and attachment behavior, and thus the way in which an infant uses his mother as a secure base from which to explore, are influenced by a variety of circumstances—including the size of the room; the length of the observational session; the nature, diversity, and complexity of the stimuli that activate and maintain exploration; the orientation and behavior of the mother, as well as the internal condition of the infant (e.g., whether tired, hungry, or ill); and the influence his previous experience has on his expectations of his mother's accessibility and responsiveness. In Episode 2 of our strange situation, the combination of the following circumstances seems to have kept the balance tipped for most infants in the direction of exploratory behavior: the large number of toys placed at a maximum distance from the mother, the small room (so that most infants' spatial set-goals for proximity to the mother were not exceeded), and brief duration of the episode (so that most infants' temporal set-goals were not exceeded). Consequently, the main evidence from the strange situation that supports the concept of an infant's using his mother as a secure base from which to explore necessarily rests on the comparison of the mother-present and mother-absent conditions. Further research on the spatial and temporal set-goal aspects of the secure-base phenomenon is obviously needed.

RESPONSES TO A STRANGER

Wariness/Fear Versus Friendliness.   The design of the strange situation implied that the entrance of a stranger into the unfamiliar environment would be more alarming to most infants than the unfamiliarity of the strange environment itself. Thus it was expected that the wariness/fear system would be more strongly activated in more infants in Episode 3 than in Episode 2. This expectation was confirmed by the fact that more infants cried in Episode 3 and that more gained proximity to the mother. Furthermore, only 3% spontaneously and fully approached the stranger in Episode 3, whereas 80% spontaneously and fully approached the toys in Episode 2. Indeed only 4% of the sample failed to show some sign of wariness in Episode 3 (Bretherton & Ainsworth, 1974). Nevertheless, we found that fear of stranger was neither as intense nor as ubiquitous as Spitz (e.g., 1965) implied. In Episode 3 of the strange situation, very few 1-year-olds cried when the stranger entered, and less than one-quarter of the total sample showed distress at any time during the episode. Even less distress was reported by Rheingold and Eckerman (1973) in their observations of somewhat younger infants in a laboratory setting. Indeed their findings highlighted friendly behavior to a friendly stranger.

Our findings provide some support for Rheingold and Eckerman. In our sample 89% of the subjects showed friendly behavior toward the stranger in some form or degree in Episode 3. In only 30%, however, was such behavior more conspicuous than wary behavior. Both friendly and wary behaviors tended to be mild rather than intense in our strange situation. Most babies smiled at the stranger or accepted a toy that she offered them, but very few approached her spontaneously or actually entered into interactive play with her during Episode 3. Eighty-five percent of the sample showed signs that both friendly and wary/fearful behavior were activated by the stranger.

In using "eight-month anxiety" as the criterion that "true object relations" (i.e., attachment) have been achieved, Spitz implied that stranger anxiety is an essential milestone in normal social development. However, he tested for stranger anxiety with the mother absent, thus confounding it with separation anxiety. Indeed he interpreted fear of strangers as a manifestation of underlying separation anxiety.

Bowlby (1969) also implied that alarm when faced by unfamiliar situations and persons was to be expected among infants in the second half of the first year, although he acknowledged that novelty also aroused exploratory interest and that the presence of the mother tended to dampen the intensity of alarm. He later identified the strange as a natural clue of danger, emerging without any necessary conditioning experience, although not until the infant had accumulated enough experience with the familiar to be able to distinguish it from the unfamiliar (Bowlby, 1973).

Our sample of Ganda infants (Ainsworth, 1967) so regularly showed fear of strangers that it was judged to be a normal phase of development, although one that came somewhat later than the phase during which an infant's active initiative in seeking proximity and interaction with his mother first made it clear that he had become attached to her. In most instances these Ganda infants showed more intense fear of strangers than did our sample of white, middle-class infants observed at home (Ainsworth, 1977). According to Konner's (1972) report, infants and young children of the Zhun/twa Bushmen show much more intense and persistent fear of strangers than either the Ganda or American infants whom we have observed.

How may one reconcile the apparent discrepancies between theory and findings, and among various sets of findings? Several variables seem to affect the intensity of activation of wary and/or fearful behavior in the presence of a specified stranger or class of strangers: the characteristics and behavior of the stranger, length of exposure to this stranger, previous experience with strangers or its lack, the context in which the stranger is encountered, and the degree of anxiety characteristic of the infant's attachment to his mother.

Some strangers may be more strange than others, in that their characteristics depart more widely from the characteristics of persons with whom the child is familiar. Thus a child chiefly familiar with female adults may find male strangers more alarming than females. Ganda infants may have found the skin color and dress of the visiting European especially strange (Ainsworth, 1967). The behavior of one stranger may be more alarming than the behavior of another. In most systematic studies of infants' responses to strangers, there is an attempt to control for this variable, either by using more than one stranger or by strictly controling the behavior of the stranger through instructions. Furthermore some studies (such as ours) attempt to have the stranger behave in what is assumed to be a minimally alarming way, so that any fear reaction may be attributed to unfamiliarity.

A stranger can remain a complete stranger for only a limited period of time. Thus Bretherton (1978) demonstrated that 1-year-olds' wary behavior declined and friendly behavior increased over a period of 8-minutes' exposure to a friendly stranger who attempted to interact with the baby through the intermediary of toys. Rheingold and Eckerman (1973) provided a period of familiarization with the stranger before systematically observing babies' responses to her—a fact that undoubtedly had some influence on their findings of infrequency of full-blown fear responses.

Children reared under widely differing conditions of opportunity to encounter strangers may differ in the intensity of wary/fearful behavior with which they respond to strangers. Our sample of middle-class American babies was taken to supermarkets, restaurants, and pediatricians' offices and experienced the visits to their homes of delivery men, meter readers, postmen, and appliance-repairers (to say nothing of babysitters). This relative familiarity with people in the general class of strangers may well have accounted at least in part for the fact that they found strangers less alarming than did the infants of the Ganda sample reared in villages with much less exposure to strangers (Ainsworth, 1977). Ganda infants, however, experienced visits from unfamiliar friends and relatives of their parents, whereas Konner's Zhun/twa Bushmen very rarely encountered persons other than members of the small group of families to whom they were exposed daily. It seems likely that the extent of a child's previous experience with unfamiliar people plays a role in determining his response to strangers, even though minor differences in such experience within a sample of children reared similarly (e.g., Bronson, 1972) may not correlate significantly with range of response to strangers.

The context in which a stranger is encountered has been demonstrated to influence infants' responses to him, as Sroufe, Waters, and Matas (1974) have pointed out. Thus Morgan and Ricciuti (1969) showed that a baby held on his mother's lap was more likely to respond positively to a stranger's advances than one seated some feet away from his mother. Bowlby (1973) suggested that natural clues to danger, including the strange, may be more alarming under conditions when a child is also anxious because his mother is inaccessible. It must be recalled that Spitz tested for stranger anxiety when the mother was absent, whereas the mother was present throughout the sequence of episodes observed by Rheingold and Eckerman (1973).

Finally some individual children are chronically anxious about their mothers' accessibility and responsiveness and are thus identified as anxiously attached. Such children may be expected to show more intense fear of strangers than children who are securely attached. The present study yields evidence pertinent to this point; Group-C infants are more likely to cry and to approach their mothers in Episode 3 than are the securely-attached infants of Group B. Ainsworth (1967) reported that some Ganda infants whose attachment to the mother had been made anxious by recent weaning from the breast demonstrated much more intense fear of strangers than they had before weaning. Any sample in which anxiously attached children are especially numerous might be expected to show more intense fear of strangers than a more "normal" sample. In this context it is pertinent to point out that Spitz's core sample consisted of infants of delinquent mothers in a correctional institution. It is unlikely that such a setting could provide optimum conditions for the development of a secure attachment of infant to mother, especially because the conditions of such an institution do not permit mothers to be regularly accessible to their infants (Arsenian, 1943). Blehar (1974) found that 30- and 40-month-old day-care children showed significantly more avoidance of the stranger in the strange situation than their home-reared controls; she attributed this to anxious attachment fostered by their very long daily separations.

These considerations go a long way toward accounting for the apparent discrepancies between theory and findings, and among findings of different studies; but there is also the matter of the indicators used in the identification of wariness/fear aroused by strangers. Rheingold and Eckerman (1973) recorded crying and approach (retreat) to the mother as signs of fearfulness, but did not record any of the more subtle indices of wariness that we (Bretherton & Ainsworth, 1974) employed. Whereas Spitz, too, focused on crying and withdrawal, he also mentioned looking and turning away as behaviors characteristic of stranger anxiety. Waters, Matas, and Sroufe (1975) employed a number of low-intensity indicators of wariness, such as gaze aversion, and found these as well as crying to be associated with heart-rate acceleration.

In conclusion, we suggest that the response of an infant to strangers can best be understood as determined by the relative strength of potentially conflicting behavior systems. On the one hand, we accept the proposition that the strange and strangers tend to activate wary/fearful behavior. On the other hand, it has been well demonstrated that exploratory behavior may be activated by the strange and lead to approach and investigation. Both sets of responses may be viewed as adaptive in an evolutionary sense. In any species whose behavior is not largely determined by fixed action patterns, it is of obvious advantage for the young to explore the environment and to learn ways of coping with it. Yet because such exploration may well be hazardous for the inexperienced infant, it is also of advantage for wary/fearful behavior to be activated by the strange—particularly in the absence of the mother, who can ordinarily provide protection. Furthermore, it seems likely that in social species such as man there is a survival advantage to friendly behavior toward conspecifics other than the mother or other attachment figures. Indeed there is more evidence of friendly behavior toward strangers among young humans than there is of exploratory behavior activated by strangers. Waters, Matas, and Sroufe (1975) suggest that even gaze aversion serves an adaptive function when an infant encounters a stranger. Such behavior may be analogous to the "cut-off" behaviors described by Chance (1962), when permitting the child to remain in proximity to the stranger rather than moving away, and thus enabling him a few moments later to entertain the possibility of friendly interaction. Waters and associates suggest that through such wary, cutoff behaviors the infant modulates arousal and prevents the disorganization of acute distress and crying, which would greatly delay the process of becoming acquainted.

In any situation, it seems reasonable to suppose that the response to an unfamiliar person will be determined by the interplay between the wary/fearful system and the exploratory and/or affiliative (friendly) systems (and, indeed, by the conflict among them). (Conflict behavior is discussed in more detail later.) It is reasonable to suppose that the relative strengths of the several behavior systems activated by strange conspecifics depend on a variety of circumstances, including those discussed above—environmental and behavioral context and experience with both attachment figures and strangers. Indeed there is every reason to believe that the state of activation of the attachment system is among the most important of the contextual variables and enters into the interplay among the other relevant systems in determining a baby's response to a stranger.

Use of the Mother as a "Secure Haven."   Because attachment behavior tends to be activated in an alarming situation, it was expected that when the wariness/fear system is more strongly activated than other relevant systems (such as exploratory or friendly behavior), the attachment system would simultaneously be activated so that the baby would tend to move away from the stranger and toward the attachment figure. It was not necessarily expected that he would remain close to his mother, however. Harlow (1961) showed that once an infant monkey had fled to his surrogate mother and clung, he thereby gained courage to approach a fear-producing stimulus object and even to explore it. In Episode 3 of the strange situation, a substantial minority of infants were sufficiently alarmed so that strong attachment behavior was activated; these infants moved away from the stranger into close proximity to or actual bodily contact with the mother. This movement can legitimately be identified as "retreat to the mother," for these infants did not approach the mother intending to interact with her; on the contrary they tended, as soon as they had reached her, to turn back to stare or even smile at the stranger from the secure haven provided by the mother.

Although 96% of the sample showed some wary behavior, by no means all of these wary infants approached their mothers. It seems likely that the mother's mere presence in the same room provided a "secure haven" for many, for she was sufficiently close that most babies probably felt confident of her accessibility. They could reach her if they wished or at least signal her to come closer; her mere presence provided security enough that attachment behavior was not strongly activated.

It might be argued that the concept of the mother as a secure haven is essentially the same as the concept of her as a secure base from which the child can venture forth to explore. There is no doubt that the two concepts are similar. Nevertheless it seems desirable to retain a distinction between them. When a baby uses the mother as a secure base from which to explore, there is no necessary implication of wariness/fear. Whatever fear might have been evoked by an unfamiliar stimulus object or situation is overridden by the security provided by the mother's presence. On the other hand, when a baby seeks to come or to remain in proximity to his mother as a secure haven, the implication is that he is at least somewhat alarmed. If, subsequently, his alarm is sufficiently moderated by proximity to this attachment figure so that he can venture forth to explore, as Harlow's infant monkeys did, then the attachment figure shifts from being a secure haven to being a secure base from which to explore. The implication is that proximity to it has reduced the activation of the wariness/fear system to a level of strength lesser than the activation of the exploratory system attributable to novel features of the alarming stimulus object.

Perhaps we also need a concept of the attachment figure as a secure base from which to make a friendly approach to a conspecific; for infants who, in the presence of their mothers, approach an amiable stranger or even accept her overtures do not seem impelled to explore the stranger as much as to interact with her. In the last minute of Episode 3 of the strange situation, however, a baby's approach to or acceptance of the stranger seems to combine friendly and exploratory behavior, because the stranger attempts to evoke interaction by inviting the baby to play with a toy that she offers him.

Differential Behavior to Mother Versus Stranger.   Although proximity-promoting (attachment) behaviors tend to be nondifferential in an infant's earliest weeks or months, it may be expected that as he learns to discriminate his attachment figure(s) from others, his attachment behaviors would become increasingly differentiated, in that they would be directed more frequently, more readily, and/or more intensely toward the persons to whom he is becoming or has become attached than toward others. We have proposed (Ainsworth, 1963, 1964, 1967) a variety of "patterns of attachment behavior" as a set of criteria for judging when and to whom a baby had become attached.

Implicit in these criteria is that the behavior would be manifested differentially (i.e., selectively or preferentially) toward an attachment figure in comparison to others.[1]

Others (e.g., Cohen, 1974; Feldman & Ingham, 1975) have assumed that we proposed attachment behaviors as measures of attachment, implying that the more strongly (and/or more frequently or longer) the behavior is manifested the stronger the attachment might be judged to be. Before identifying a behavior as an attachment behavior, therefore, they argue, it must be demonstrated that the behavior in question is indeed differential to attachment figures in comparison with others to whom the infant is not attached. Specifically, Feldman and Ingham, as well as Cohen, have criticized the strange situation as a "measure of attachment," because the comparison figure is a stranger rather than a nonattachment figure with whom the child has some familiarity.

Although we consider it useful to consider the differentiality of attachment behaviors as criteria for ascertaining the onset of attachment, the ethological-evolutionary theory of attachment that serves as our framework does not define attachment behavior in terms of either exclusiveness or relative strength or frequency of manifestation toward an attachment figure. Furthermore, as we have pointed out before (e.g., Ainsworth, 1967, 1972; Ainsworth & Bell, 1970), there are grave flaws in the assumption that the strength with which attachment behavior is manifested reflects the strength of any underlying attachment relationship. (This point is discussed more fully later in this chapter.) Finally, we did not intend the strange situation to provide the basis for identification or "validation" of behaviors as attachment behaviors, nor indeed to measure the strength of an infant's attachment to his mother.

Attachment behavior is defined as a class of behaviors that have the predictable outcome of gaining or maintaining proximity to a caregiver or later to an attachment figure. They are conceived as playing an important role in the development of attachment and in mediating the attachment once it has been formed. At least some of these behaviors—perhaps, indeed, all of them—may sometimes serve behavioral systems other than the attachment system, as Tracy, Lamb, and Ainsworth (1976) have argued in the case of locomotor-

---

[1]There is general agreement that before a baby may be described as having become attached to a figure, he must discriminate that figure from others. It can only be demonstrated that such discrimination has been acquired through the fact that he behaves differently toward that figure than toward a comparison figure. There is, however, difference of opinion as to whether mere discrimination of and preference for a figure constitute attachment to that figure or whether attachment emerges first in a later stage of development. (See Chapter 1.) Even at such a later stage of development, however, the differentiality with which attachment behaviors are manifested toward various figures serves as a useful criterion for the identification of those figures to whom an infant has become attached.

approach behavior. It is only with consideration of the context—both environmental and behavioral—in which the behavior appears that we can assert that the behavior in question is operating in the service of the attachment system or in the service of some other behavioral system at the time it is observed. To demand that the label "attachment behavior" be reserved for a discrete action that is displayed exclusively, or even more frequently, toward an attachment figure rather than toward others is to distort our understanding of the function of attachment behavior.

Nevertheless, a study of the selectiveness with which proximity-promoting behaviors are displayed toward different figures in various contexts throws light on what we consider to be a more fundamental task of research into the development of attachment—namely, the ways in which such behaviors become organized together to serve the attachment system and the ways in which the attachment system itself interacts with other behavioral systems. In this context let us consider the degree of differentiality shown by various behaviors in the strange situation. It must be kept in mind, however, that the sequence of episodes in the strange situation was designed to progressively intensify proximity-promoting behavior directed toward the attachment figure, and that the only figure with whom the attachment figure can be compared is a stranger—circumstances that facilitate maximum differentiality.

It is therefore of no great import to find that in the strange situation a number of proximity-promoting behaviors are sharply differential to the mother in comparison with the stranger, and thus identifiable as serving the attachment system rather than another behavioral system. These include approaching, touching, clinging, resisting release, and all of the behaviors that are comprehended in the measures of proximity/contact seeking and contact maintaining. They also include following and some (but not all) greeting behaviors. Furthermore, vocalizing was found to occur more frequently when the infant was alone with his mother than when the stranger was present. Of these approach, following, and touching in the home environment were not strikingly differential to the mother in comparison with a relatively unfamiliar figure (Tracy, Lamb, & Ainsworth, 1976). There it was found that approach was strongly differential to the mother only when it was acompanied by distress or when it ended in a pick-up appeal, and touching only when in the context of a pick-up appeal. Stayton, Ainsworth, and Main (1973), in a similar study of home behavior, were not able under the circumstances of their analysis to identify the contextual features of differential following.

It is of more interest in regard to strange-situation behavior to highlight behaviors that did *not* emerge as differential to the mother—namely, smiling and looking. Indeed, smiling was more *frequent* to the stranger than to the mother, although a measure of *intensity* of smiling favored the mother

(Bretherton & Ainsworth, 1974). Similar findings for greeting behavior at home were reported by Stayton, Ainsworth, and Main (1973) and for face-to-face behavior by Blehar, Lieberman, and Ainsworth (1977). Thus it is apparent that smiling not only serves the attachment system but also serves in sociable interaction with persons who are clearly not attachment figures. We suggest that it may also occur as a propitiatory behavior when wariness/fear is activated at a relatively low degree of intensity (Bretherton & Ainsworth, 1974).

A moment's consideration suggests that looking, too, must serve many systems other than the attachment system. Certainly in Episode 3 of the strange situation, infants looked much more frequently at the stranger than at the mother—whether this was in the service of exploratory behavior, wary/fearful behavior, or sociability. Furthermore, our composite measure of distance interaction (comparable to the smile-speak-show measure of Maccoby and Feldman, 1972) was stronger in regard to interaction with the stranger than in interaction with the mother. Although a child—or an adult, for that matter—may interact with an attachment figure across a distance, and this may serve the attachment system under conditions of low-intensity activation, it is clear that all the various modes of interaction across a distance commonly serve other purposes as well. It would plainly be a mistake to focus entirely on such behaviors when studying attachment and attachment behavior.

It might have been predicted that avoidant and resistant behaviors—which are antithetical to proximity promotion—would be directed more frequently and more intensely to the stranger than to the mother. This did not prove to be the case. Both are relatively uncommon behaviors, even at low intensity. In the case of avoidance there was effectively no overlap between those who avoided the mother and those who avoided the stranger. In the case of resistance, however, those who resisted the mother also tended to resist the stranger, and vice versa.

Finally, it is of interest to compare mother and stranger in regard to the termination of attachment behavior once it had been activated at high intensity, as it had been for most infants, especially in the second separation episode. Whereas most infants who had been distressed during separation calmed quickly when reunited with their mothers in Episodes 5 and 8, the stranger's return in Episode 7 reduced the distress of very few. Although some infants who were distressed by separation stopped crying when the mother merely entered the room, for most attachment behavior was terminated only by close bodily contact for varying lengths of time. Close bodily contact with the stranger in Episode 7, however, scarcely reduced the intensity of activation of attachment behavior—and the stranger offered such contact to all who continued to be distressed after she returned.

RESPONSES TO SEPARATION

Crying when briefly separated from the mother in the unfamiliar environment of the laboratory was not as ubiquitous as anticipated. Barely half of the babies cried during the first separation, although over three-quarters did so during the second. To judge from the babies of Sample 1, for whom extensive longitudinal data were available, failure to show separation distress in the strange situation may not be interpreted to mean that an infant has not become attached to his mother. Group-A babies, for example, showed relatively frequent separation protest at home even though they showed little or no distress in the strange situation. Furthermore, we have long believed that failure to show distress in very brief or everday separations at home is an undependable criterion of attachment—or the lack thereof (Ainsworth, 1963, 1967, 1972, 1973).

Nevertheless there is evidence that separation in the strange situation activated the attachment-behavioral system strongly enough in most infants that it competed with—and in many infants overrode—exploratory behavior, which had been so strongly activated in Episode 2. Furthermore, as mentioned earlier, Sroufe and Waters (1977b), using both behavioral and heart-rate measures, reported: "It appears that virtually all 1-year-olds are stressed by separation in the 'strange situation,' but that infants differ in the behavioral resources available to cope with the stress (i.e., the degree of distress is not the only or necessarily the crucial variable)."

As reported in Chapter 10, studies of 2- to 4-year-olds (Blehar, 1974; Marvin, 1977; and Maccoby & Feldman, 1972) showed that overt distress as evidenced by crying declines with age. Whereas 2-year-olds still tend to be distressed in the separation episodes, 2½-year-olds cry less frequently, and 3- and 4-year-olds do so little or not at all. Blehar's study suggests that 3-year-olds who cry in these brief separations may have been sensitized to separation anxiety by long, frequently daily separations. Marvin suggests that 4-year-olds who cry may do so not so much because they are distressed by separation as through frustration in not having persuaded the mother either to stay or to take them along—that is, frustration in having been unsuccessful in arriving at a mutual adaptation of "plans." Common sense experience suggests that as they grow older, children can sustain increasingly longer periods of separation from attachment figures without distress. Undoubtedly, increasing cognitive capacities enable a child to better understand the circumstances of even involuntary separations, and to have established well-based expectations that mother will return soon, unless some traumatic separation experience has led them to doubt that she will.

The miniscule separations in the strange situation, as well as little everyday separations occasioned by mother's leaving the room in the home environment, constitute situations much less anxiety provoking than "major" separations. A "major" separation might be defined as an involuntary separation either of very long duration (or permanent) or one that is at least long enough to greatly exceed a young child's expectations of the likely period of time that must elapse before reunion. Such major separations are the more anxiety provoking if he has no information about or understanding of the reasons for the separation or the conditions of its termination, or if he is at the same time separated from other attachment figures, especially if he has no opportunity for interaction with any figure who might substitute for his absent attachment figures.

At home, an infant may cheerfully accept separation because his past experience has engendered confidence that either his mother will return soon or that he can gain access to her if he wants to (Stayton & Ainsworth, 1973). Consequently some children are trusting at first, and only gradually become distressed when the mother's absence is longer than expected, or when their efforts to reach her are frustrated. Such confident anticipation may be expected to be characteristic of the baby who is securely attached. Some secure infants apparently carry their confident expectations over to an unfamiliar environment. This, we believe, accounts for the fact that some Group-B infants in Episode 4 are not apparently distressed at first, and only later begin to cry when their efforts to regain access to the mother are unavailing or when her absence is longer than expected. Indeed, some weather the entire first separation episode without distress, only to become distressed during the second separation when, it seems reasonable to suppose, their confidence in the mother's accessibility in *this* environment has been shaken.

Brief separations from the mother in an unfamiliar environment may evoke no distress if the baby is left with another attachment figure (e.g., Kotelchuck, 1972), and indeed the same phenomenon may be observed at home (Ainsworth, 1967). Even a relatively brief (i.e., 8-minute) previous play interaction with a stranger may diminish the distress manifested when the mother departs leaving the baby with a stranger (Bretherton, 1978). Also, in major separations, the presence of responsive substitute parent figures greatly reduces the distress occasioned by temporary loss of parents (Robertson & Robertson, 1971).

Whether a separation is voluntary or involuntary can strongly affect a child's initial responses to it. Infants and young children may quite cheerfully leave an attachment figure to explore elsewhere (Ainsworth, 1967; Rheingold & Eckerman, 1970) and show no distress if they are not prevented from an equally voluntary return to that figure. Nurses in hospitals often show an intuitive knowledge of this phenomenon; they know that many young children may be lured away from mother and will only later become distressed when they are prevented from returning to her.

Previous separation experiences may, however, make an infant or young child all the more alert to the likelihood of separation in a given situation. A child who has once been fooled by a nurse will not be so trusting a second time when invited to leave his mother to do something "interesting." Similarly, a child with a history of major (or even a series of seemingly minor) separation experiences is not likely to be as trusting as a child who has had no previous unhappy separations. Thus, for example, one child in Sample 1 could not tolerate separation in the strange situation. Throughout the first year he had been left by his working mother with a responsive housekeeper. Until he was about 10 months old, he accepted his mother's departures in the morning, but then began to protest them. In the strange situation, the moment his mother got up to go at the end of Episode 3 he was undone. Ganda infants (Ainsworth, 1977) showed more intense distress in everyday separation situations at home than did the American babies of our Sample 1. Most of them had been left with other caregivers every day for 4 hours or more while their mothers worked in the garden, whereas when the mother was at home she tended to take the baby with her as she moved from room to room. It would seem that when the Ganda mother did leave the baby behind, this signified to him a much longer absence than that expected by most of our American sample babies when the mother left the room. Similarly, we found (Blehar, 1974) that children in full-time day care, having been previously home reared, showed significantly more distress in the separation episodes of the strange situation than home-reared age peers—a finding that may be due to their having become sensitized to separation by their frequent, long absences from home. On the other hand, it would seem likely that these same day-care children might have left the mother's side voluntarily in order to approach other children when introduced to a new play group, as Ricciuti (1974) found with a sample of young children who had been reared in a day-care center.

The Interchangeability of Attachment Figures.   Because of contemporary interest in the role of the father, we have often been chided because we have used the mother as representative of the class of attachment figures in our strange-situation research. We do not consider the mother as the only figure who can provide a secure base from which to explore or, indeed, whose departure could arouse distress. Three sets of studies (viz., Cohen & Campos, 1974; Kotelchuck, 1972, and Lamb, 1976c), which have used modifications of our strange-situation procedure, have demonstrated that a baby can tolerate the departure of either mother or father without distress, as long as he still has the other figure available to him. Kotelchuck also (Kotelchuck, Zelazo, Kagan & Spelke, 1975; Ross, Kagan, Zelazo, & Kotelchuck, 1975; and Spelke, Zelazo, Kagan, & Kotelchuck, 1973) has shown, in contrast, that when either figure departed leaving a 1-year-old with a stranger, he tended to protest the separation and to decrease his exploratory behavior.[2] Whereas these studies used situations in which response to the departures of mother and father could be compared in the same children in the same laboratory session, Willemsen and associates (1974) and Lamb (1978) compared the responses of the same children in two sessions of the strange situation, once accompanied by the mother and once by the father. Feldman and Ingham (1975) used two groups of children but only one session for a similar comparison. (See Chapter 9.) The findings of all three studies showed minimal differences in responses to the two figures.

Arsenian (1943) investigated the behavior of young children under conditions of presence and absence of a mother figure in a laboratory situation. The children had been reared with their mothers in a facility for delinquent women. If the mother was not available to participate in the study, her role was assumed by a substitute caregiver who was responsible for the child in the mother's absence. The children explored when the substitute figure was present and protested her absence, just as did the children whose mothers were available for the experiment. These findings are quite in line with our Ganda findings (Ainsworth, 1967) that infants tended not to cry when the mother departed if another attachment figure remained in the same room.

Such findings have sometimes been interpreted as a refutation of Bowlby's (1958, 1969) concept of "monotropy," in that they demonstrate that an infant or young child is not necessarily attached solely to his mother. Bowlby, however, did not mean that there could be only one attachment figure, but implied that there was one principal attachment figure, to whom the others were secondary. This implies a hierarchy of attachment figures. Presumably for some purposes and in some situations, attachment figures can be interchangeable—as they tended to be in the studies just cited. But for other purposes and in other situations (e.g., when ill or fatigued), the principal attachment figure would be required, or at least preferred.

There has been very little research relevant to this issue. Lamb, however, in a series of recent articles, has addressed himself specifically to the question of whether, under what circumstances, through which attachment behaviors, and at what ages a child will express preference for his mother over his father or vice versa (e.g, Lamb, 1976a, 1976b, 1976c, 1977a, 1977b, 1977c). In summary, his findings indicate that under some circumstances infants express preferences for the father, but under other circumstances the preference is clearly for the mother. Furthermore, he has made a distinction similar to ours between behaviors that emerge with high-intensity activation of the

---

[2]Kotelchuck found this to hold for infants in his 12-, 15-, 18-, and 21-month-old age groups, but not for those 6 or 9 months old. The latter two groups showed no crying that was clearly associated with the departure of a specific figure.

attachment system, for which he reserves the term "attachment behaviors," and behaviors that emerge with low-intensity activation, which he terms "affiliative behaviors." At home, at age points from 7 months until at least 2 years of age, infants show preference for their fathers through "affiliative" behaviors in stress-free situations, whereas in stressful situations (including a situation as minimally stressful as the presence of a stranger in an unfamiliar laboratory situation) the preference tends to shift to the mother.

On the whole, Lamb confined himself to an examination of normative trends, although in one paper (1977b) he looked at individual differences.[3] In some cases it seems likely that an infant might fairly consistently prefer one figure to the other under both stressful and nonstressful circumstances, as for example when the father has played the maternal role, and/or the relationship with the mother is extremely disturbed, or when the father has estranged himself from the family. These exceptional cases, as well as the more usual trends reported by Lamb, are not incompatible with Bowlby's concept of monotropy—or, as more accessibly worded, his concept of a hierarchy of attachment figures—for he would identify the principal attachment figure as the one preferred under stress. Lamb's main point, however, is that although the relationship of a child to his mother is likely to differ qualitatively from his relationship to his father, both attachments are significant determinants of social and personality development.

It is possible that in the absence of any attachment figure, the child may direct even high-intensity attachment behavior to someone else. Both Maccoby and Jacklin (1973) and Rosenthal (1967) have shown that children in fear-arousing situations may direct attachment behavior toward an unfamiliar figure when the mother is not available, even though the intensity of such behavior may be somewhat muted in comparison with the behavior of children who faced the same situation with an attachment figure present. Fleener (1973) suggested that he had experimentally produced attachment within 3 days during which a young child was separated from his mother during the daytime and played with and cared for by a research assistant. At the end of the experimental period the subjects demonstrated differentiality of approach to the familiar surrogate in preference to another research assistant who was unfamiliar to the child, and manifested distress when the familiar person left but not when the unfamiliar person did. Nevertheless, when a subsample of children was faced with preference for the mother (or distress when separated from her) in contrast with the surrogate, it was clear that the mother was the preferred figure.

---

[3]This analysis was based on his longitudinal observation of infants in the relatively nonstressful environment of the home. Some, but by no means all, infants at 7 and 8 and 12 and 13 months showed clear preference for one parent over the other. During the second year of life, significant sex differences emerged, with boys preferring their fathers ($p < .02$). Although five of the six children who preferred their mothers were girls, some girls preferred their fathers. This analysis did not, however, examine preference in stressful environments.

Can such temporary relationships be classed as attachments? There is no doubt that they can play an extremely useful role during periods of separation from other figures with whom the child has more enduring attachment relationships, as the Robertsons have plainly demonstrated (Robertson & Robertson, 1971). Perhaps it is best to consider them as incipient attachments. Should circumstances permit a continuing relationship, they might well be consolidated as attachments, but when circumstances make the relationship of short duration they do not become sufficiently well consolidated to endure. However, should such relationships become well enough consolidated that they result in distress when the child is returned to his original attachment figures, even though the distress may be of relatively short duration and even though the child may reestablish his original attachment relationships without undue delay, surely one could identify the attachment to the temporary surrogate as more than merely incipient.

OTHER NORMATIVE FINDINGS

Although the strange situation was originally designed to investigate the secure-base phenomenon, response to strangers, and response to separation in an unfamiliar environment, its yield of findings has by no means been limited to these three areas of interest. Without doubt, the most interesting additional findings pertain to individual differences, which are discussed in the next chapter; but some of them may be classed as "normative"—specifically, findings pertaining to the activation and termination of attachment behavior, shifts in specific attachment behaviors that emerge at different levels of activation of the system, and the interplay between attachment behavior and other behavioral systems, including conflictful interplay.

Activation of Attachment Behavior. Of the several manipulations intended to activate attachment behavior, the one that activated it at highest intensity was separation from the mother. The presence of a stranger in Episode 3 effected observable activation of attachment behavior in some infants, but these were in a minority. The unfamiliar environment per se was the least effective, even though Sroufe and Waters (1977b) observed small-magnitude tonic heart-rate increases, which they interpreted as signs of wariness, upon first entering the room in the introductory Episode 1. Of course, this generalization is weakened by the fact that these three manipulations occurred in a fixed order. We do not, however, believe that an experiment that attempted to control for order effects would throw significant additional light on the relative effectiveness of the three relevant conditions in activating attachment behavior.

A comparison between responses to brief separation at home (Stayton, Ainsworth, & Main, 1973) strongly suggests that the unfamiliar features of the physical and social environment interacted with brief separations to create what Bowlby (1973) identified as a compound situation. Alarm occasioned by the strange environment (however minimal) and by the stranger interacted with the anxiety occasioned by the inaccessibility of the attachment figure in the separation episodes to activate attachment behavior at a higher level of intensity than would have been occasioned by any of the three sets of stimulus variables separately—indeed at a substantially higher level than their separate intensities summed. Furthermore, as Cohen (1974) has also suggested, cumulative stress has its effects. Once attachment behavior has been activated at high intensity in one episode, it does not subside to what might be conceived as "base-level" in the next episode, but rather tends to remain at a relatively high level, to be intensified easily by the next instigation. Or, as Cohen would put it (and as Fleener & Cairns, 1970, found), once a baby begins to cry in one episode the likelihood that he will cry again in later episodes is significantly increased. Finally, a strange situation by necessity is undertaken in an unfamiliar milieu. This background unfamiliarity would enter into every episode, whether the mother and/or stranger are present or absent.

We did not intentionally introduce any (nonseparation) conditions other than the merely unfamiliar that might be expected to activate attachment behavior. Indeed we discarded three babies from our analyses in which such conditions existed—two whose mothers brought them to the laboratory despite the fact that they were ill, and one who was intensely disturbed by the whirr of a fan in the experimental room. We did not control in advance either for individual differences in expectations relevant to brief separations or strangers, or for individual differences in the quality of the attachment relationship itself. Both undoubtedly accounted for individual differences in strange-situation behavior, but qualitative differences in attachment clearly emerged as the crucial variable. Furthermore, as mentioned previously, the limitations provided by the spatial features of the experimental room, together with the brief duration of the episodes, probably prevented us in most instances from observing the activation of attachment behavior attributable to a child's exceeding a spatial or temporal set-goal.

Our firmest conclusion, therefore, is that the combination of an unfamiliar physical environment, a stranger, and separation from the mother provides very strong instigation to attachment behavior.

Behaviors at Different Levels of Activation of the Attachment System. Because it is evident that attachment behavior was activated at different levels of intensity from one strange-situation episode to another, an examination of behavioral changes across episodes throws light on the specific attachment behaviors characteristic of different intensities of activation of the system. At low levels of intensity of activation, as in Episode 2, some infants manifested no attachment behaviors except an occasional smile or vocalization directed toward the mother. As we previously suggested, the set-goal for proximity for most infants was set at wider limits than would be exceeded in the episode. Because his mother seemed settled in her chair, there was little need for the infant even to check her whereabouts through occasional glances. Such behavior is entirely characteristic of what happens much of the time at home, when both mother and baby are occupied with their own activities and each is confident of the whereabouts of the other.

A few infants alternated in Episode 2 between exploratory play and initiating interaction with the mother, although such behavior seemed more characteristic of the young children observed by Maccoby and Feldman (1972) and Marvin (1977). At home, however, when the mother was free to initiate interaction herself, and also probably able to respond more naturally to infant initiations, episodes of interaction—whether playful, tender, or merely sociable—occur intermittently.

When attachment behavior is activated at somewhat higher intensity—whether because of a spatial or temporal set-goal being exceeded or because of a mildly alarming environmental stimulus—active proximity seeking is likely. The child approaches his attachment figure and may make contact, perhaps only momentarily and without apparent urgency. In our sample a few children behaved in this way toward the end of Episode 2, but more in Episode 3.

Still higher levels of intensity of activation seem to change the set-goal itself so that mere proximity is no longer sufficient and close bodily contact is required. Such a shift may be occasioned by an alarming environmental stimulus, or by separation or the threat thereof. Under these circumstances approach is likely to be quicker and accompanied or ended by active attempts to achieve close contact or by signals such as reaching and crying. Indeed crying may supplant active approach. If the intensity of activation is extremely high, an infant may abandon active behavior in favor of full-blown crying, as seemed to be the case with some infants who actively sought proximity and contact in Episode 5 but who abandoned themselves to intense signaling in Episode 8.

If, as in separation situations, the mother is not accessible when attachment behavior is intensely activated, there may be either an active attempt to follow her, or crying, or a combination of both. The frustration implicit in unsuccessful efforts to regain the absent mother can be expected to arouse attachment behavior to a still higher level of intensity, so that when the mother returns her mere presence is unlikely to terminate the behavior. Indeed attachment behavior at the moment of reunion and for a short time afterwards is likely still to be intense.

Thus, a variety of different attachment behaviors have the same predictable outcome—namely, gaining or maintaining proximity to an attachment figure or, under higher degrees of activation, gaining or maintaining bodily contact. One infant may cry and reach and thus induce his mother to come and pick him up, whereas another may make a beeline toward her and then clamber up on her. In this sense attachment behaviors are interchangeable to a degree. Because of this we had from the beginning more confidence in our scaled measures of proximity/contact seeking and of contact maintaining than in discrete measures of the frequency of the component behaviors that enter into these measures (e.g., approaching, crying, reaching, touching, and the like).

The difference between behaviors commonly emitted at low intensity of activation of the attachment system and those emitted at high intensity is so great that it seems useful to consider them as two subclasses of the general class of attachment behavior. Both promote proximity but they do so in different ways and under different circumstances. Bowlby (1969) proposed that attachment behavior has evolved because its predictable outcome of proximity of infant to mother favors protection and hence survival. High-intensity behaviors are easy to perceive as promoting a protective function. Whether because he is alarmed or because he is anxious about being separated from his mother, a child who does his best to get close to his mother may even have gaining protection as his conscious intent, although we do not posit that this is necessarily so. Low-intensity behaviors seem to serve the function of attachment behavior more indirectly.

Bowlby described how smiling and vocalization tend to attract the caregiver to the infant and to induce him or her to linger close by. These, and enthusiastic greeting behaviors, do much to evoke from the adult the parental behaviors that are the reciprocal of attachment behaviors, even though they are emitted under circumstances that are not crucial for the infant's survival, as indeed Sroufe and Waters (1977a) have suggested. Crying might be described as implying: "Come, I need you desperately!" Smiling and vocalizing might be interpreted as implying: "Stick around, I enjoy your company!" To the extent that the caregiver does remain reasonably close, for whatever reason, the protective function of attachment behavior is served. Furthermore, the reciprocal bond of caregiver to infant tends to be cemented thereby. Even after the infant becomes increasingly capable of maintaining proximity through his own efforts, and relies less on signals to attract people to come to him and to "stick around," a good proportion of the behavior he directs toward attachment figures is low-intensity attachment behavior. Smiling becomes supplemented by many nuances of facial expression and gesture, and vocalization begins to shade into the early stages of language. These forms of communication support interaction with attachment figures, and there is no doubt that they continue to maintain the attachment bond. Therefore, they indirectly continue to serve the biological function of this bond, even though they seem on the face of it to have little to do with protection.

Another distinction between low- and high-intensity attachment behavior is that the components of low-intensity behavior are not reserved for attachment figures. As we pointed out earlier, smiling frequency is scarcely differential to the mother in contrast with relatively unfamiliar figures even after the infant has learned to discriminate between them. Vocalization and other modes of nonverbal communication are surely used in interaction with nonattachment figures, even though they tend to be differential to attachment figures longer than smiling is. Even approach, as Tracy, Lamb, and Ainsworth (1976) have shown, is barely differential in frequency to the mother in contrast with a relatively unfamiliar visitor in the last quarter of the first year. What remains sharply differential is high-intensity attachment behavior—the approach when crying, the approach to be picked up, and, in general, behavior directed toward achieving and maintaining close bodily contact, whether it be signaling or a more active initiative.

A comprehensive study of attachment must include observation of both high- and low-intensity behaviors, as well as those that might be identified as characteristic of intermediate levels of activation. The strange situation comprehends the gamut from low to high intensity, but obviously focuses on the high-intensity behaviors. It is only because the infants in our samples, especially in Sample 1, were also observed under more extensive circumstances of low-intensity activation of attachment behavior that we have been able to appreciate the vast differences attributable to the situational context. The issues raised here have profound implications for the study of stability of individual differences in behavior at different times and in different kinds of situations, but these implications are discussed in a later section.

Finally, we do not consider measures of the strength of proximity and contact seeking—let alone measures of the frequency of smiling, vocalization, or looking—as measures of the strength of attachment. The very fact that there is such a shift in the nature and intensity of attachment behavior under different conditions and levels of activation suggests that the strength of attachment behavior reflects the situational intensity of activation rather than some postulated underlying strength of the bond between infant and attachment figure. We have said this repeatedly (Ainsworth, 1963, 1967, 1972, 1973; Ainsworth & Bell, 1970) but have had difficulty in convincing others—so ingrained in various current psychological paradigms is the notion that any construct such as attachment must have a high–low dimension of strength or intensity. Without wanting to imply that attachment is a drive—which it is not—it is useful to compare it with the hunger "drive." The more that is known about hunger, the more evident it becomes that there are many conditions, both internal and external, that influence the strength of food-seeking behavior and of food intake at any given time. Even hypo- and hyperphagia can be accounted for in terms of these conditions. It is no longer useful—if, indeed, it ever was—to think of strength of hunger drive as a significant dimension of an individual's personality.

Termination of Attachment Behavior. The conditions for termination of attachment behavior activated at a high level of intensity differ from those sufficient to terminate low-intensity behavior. Most of the relevant facts are implicit in our previous discussion. When attachment behavior is strongly activated, it is likely that only close bodily contact with an attachment figure will terminate it. Indeed, in the reunion episodes, especially in Episode 8, infants who had been distressed by separation needed to be picked up by their mothers before they were soothed, but most of them were quickly soothed by close bodily contact. This did not necessarily imply that attachment behavior was terminated, because a significant number of babies resisted or protested release if the mother attempted to put them down soon after they had been picked up. Apparently some prolongation of close bodily contact was necessary to terminate attachment behavior to the extent that exploratory behavior could again take over, even though it was unusual for this prolongation to involve more than a minute or two.

The concept of set-goal suggests that, unless the set-goal itself has shifted, the mere restoration of the limits of proximity in spatial terms may terminate attachment behavior. Thus, for some infants, perhaps especially those older than the 1-year-olds of our sample, the mother's return to the room seems to be sufficient, although this might not be the case if the mother did not acknowledge or greet the child when she returned. Still others seem to require closer proximity to the mother than before, as though their set-goal had narrowed, even though it did not shift to requiring close bodily contact.

Interplay Between Attachment Behavior and Other Behavioral Systems.
The chief behavioral systems activated in the strange situation appear to be: exploratory behavior, wary/fearful behavior, attachment behavior, sociable behavior, and angry/resistant behavior. Exploratory behavior is antithetical to attachment behavior in the sense that approach to the toys decreases proximity to the mother, although it is not uncommon for toddlers to compromise by bringing the toys closer to the mother and playing with them there, or by involving the mother in play. We are assuming that wary and fearful behaviors are manifestations of the same behavioral system, with wariness resulting from low-intensity activation, and fearfulness from activation at higher levels of intensity. At all levels of intensity of activation, however, wary/fearful behavior is antithetical to exploratory behavior and sociable behavior in that it militates against approach to and manipulation of (or interaction with) those features of the unfamiliar physical or social environment that have activated the wariness/fear system. Wary/fearful

behavior is *not* antithetical to attachment behavior, and at levels of activation beyond mild and brief wariness, it is usually congruent with attachment behavior. Indeed the same stimulus situation that activates wariness/fear at a moderate to high level of intensity tends simultaneously to activate or to intensify attachment behavior. The child is likely to move away from the alarming stimulus and/or toward the attachment figure, provided that one is accessible; or he may signal to the attachment figure, perhaps by crying.

We are distinguishing between attachment behavior, directed toward the mother as representing the class of figures to whom an infant has become attached, and sociable or friendly behavior, directed toward the stranger as representing the class of figures to whom he has not become attached. These two systems of behavior are antithetical in the sense that when a child directing behavior toward one figure, he usually can not simultaneously direct behavior toward the other. As we suggested earlier, the particular behaviors that serve the attachment system may also enter into sociable behavior with a nonattachment figure, especially low-intensity attachment behaviors. High-intensity attachment behaviors tend to be reserved for the attachment figure.

When two antithetical systems are activated simultaneously, they may be said to be in conflict. This conflict may not be readily apparent if one system is activated at a level of much greater intensity than the other; the more strongly activated system tends to determine the overt behavior. The other system may not become manifest in behavior until either the overriding behavior is terminated (or becomes less strongly activated) or some shift in the situation increases the activation of the system until it overrides the behavior of the previously stronger system. When two conflicting systems are more nearly equal in level of activation, there may be alternation of behaviors, "compromise" behaviors in which behavioral elements of both systems are combined, or intention movements or other fragmentary behavioral representatives of one or the other system. Furthermore, the behavior activated by one stimulus object may be redirected toward another that is not involved in the conflict—as in "displacement," as the psychoanalysts would label it. Finally, overt behavior may be determined by a third system, which is also at a moderate level of activation, although at not as high a level as the two conflicting systems that tend to block each other—a phenomenon that ethologists label "displacement *behavior*."

The interplay between exploratory, wary/fearful, and attachment behavior may be seen in Episode 2; certain aspects of this have already been discussed relevant to the use of the mother as a secure base from which to explore. For most infants exploratory behavior overrode both wary/fearful and attachment behavior, either with or without a brief delay during which one may presume wary behavior was dominant at first but soon weakened when the child perceived nothing really alarming about the toys that he was also stimulated to approach. A few infants approached the mother toward the end of the episode, perhaps because their temporal set-goal for this situation had been exceeded, thus intensifying attachment behavior enough to at least temporarily override exploratory behavior.

The interplay between wary/fearful, sociable, and attachment behavior may best be seen in Episode 3—exploratory behavior directed toward the toys having been overriden in most infants by some combination of the other three behavioral systems that were activated (or intensified) by the entrance of the stranger. Most infants could be described as being in a state of conflict between wary/fearful behavior and sociable behavior, both of which were activated by the stranger. Some behavior could be interpreted as expressing both of the conflicting systems simultaneously—for example, coy behavior, intention movements, and tentative responses to the stranger's offer of a toy. In other behavior, the competing tendencies alternated, as for example when approach to the stranger was followed immediately by rapid movement away from her usually toward the mother. In the latter case, attachment behavior was clearly involved in the conflict, as it was also in instances in which the infant,wary/fearful of the stranger, retreated to the mother as a secure haven from which vantage point he turned to examine the stranger, still wary of her. Attachment behavior was eventually overridden by sociable behavior (or possibly by a combination of sociable and exploratory behavior) in most infants, who were attracted away from the mother by the stranger's inviting him to play with the toy she offered. Wary behavior continued to conflict with exploratory and/or sociable behavior, however, for few infants in Episode 3 did more than tentatively reach toward the stranger's toy.

In the separation episodes, attachment and exploratory behaviors were in some conflict. Attachment behavior was intensified by the mother's departure and/or continuing absence. In many children attachment behavior was activated so strongly that it quite overrode exploratory behavior; the child explored little but cried, or searched, or did both in an attempt to regain his absent mother—especially in the second separation Episodes 6 and 7. In Episodes 4 and 7 attachment and sociable behavior were also in conflict, with wary/fearful behavior also likely to have been involved.

Especially in Episode 7 attachment behavior, possibly supported by the wariness/fear system, overrode sociable behavior in most cases. The conflict of most interest occurred in infants whose attachment behavior was activated to such a pitch that they seemed about to accept the stranger as a substitute attachment figure; yet in nearly all cases an approach or a signal for contact was succeeded by resistance or avoidance. The conflict in such cases seemed to be an approach–avoidance conflict with the stranger as focus. It could be hypothesized that attachment behavior was manifest in the approach but that wariness/fear and/or anger (prompted by the fact that the stranger was not an attachment figure) were manifest in the resistance or avoidance.

Conflicts in the reunion episodes are of particular interest. To be sure, conflict seemed at a minimum in Group-B babies. Attachment behavior, having been activated at high intensity by separation (especially by the second separation), overrode all other behavioral systems when the mother returned, and for varying periods afterward until attachment behavior was terminated—or at least sufficiently reduced in intensity so that (perhaps with the mother's cooperation) exploratory behavior was again activated. But in A and C babies, conflict was evident even in the reunion episodes. We should like to defer discussion of these instances of conflict to the context of individual differences, because they are at the nub of the whole issue of individual differences.

SHORTCOMINGS OF OUR NORMATIVE RESEARCH

The strange-situation procedure has proved to be useful far beyond our initial expectations. Even after the thorough analysis of our findings that we are reporting here, there is very little in our procedure that we would like to change. In regard to normative behavior, however, a few refinements of the procedure would make it a more powerful instrument for future research. Begun in 1964, our use of the strange situation antedated most ethological studies of facial expression, postural orientation, and gesture. Although the most obvious of these did not escape our observers' attention, there is much in the findings of ethological research on nonverbal communication in infants and young children that would have enriched the narrative records of our observers had they been trained to take account of them. In part this implies desirable further training in observation, but in part it merely implies a consistent vocabulary in terms of which observation can be reported. Without a lexicon of such communicative behavior (e.g., Blurton Jones, 1972; Brannigan & Humphries, 1972; McGrew 1972), it is difficult for an observer to quickly put into words a description of the facial expression, posture, and gesture that he sees.

One of the categories of behavior that our observers sometimes reported was "tension movements," including fingering clothing, repetitive movements such as pulling at an ear lobe, tense movements such as hunching the shoulders, putting the hands behind the neck and tensely cocking the head, and so on. It was our clear impression that such tension movements signified stress, both because they tended to occur chiefly in the separation episodes and because they tended to be prodromal to crying. Indeed, our hypothesis is that they occur when a child is attempting to control crying, for they tend to vanish if and when crying breaks through. Sometimes our observers noted such behavior clearly, characterizing it as a "tension movement;" sometimes they noted such behavior in purely descriptive terms, which made it difficult to identify as reflecting tension; and sometimes undoubtedly they did not mention it at all. In any event, such behaviors were not reported frequently enough, clearly enough, or in enough detail for us to be able to code tension movements or to devise a measure thereof.

Another closely related class of behavior that is not represented in our analyses is "displacement behavior." As ethologically defined, this behavior occurs when two other strongly activated behavioral systems conflict, effectively blocking the full expression of either; then a third moderately activated behavior (usually commonly appearing in the individual's repertoire) may find expression, this being the displacement behavior. We suspect that some exploratory behavior, especially in the separation and reunion episodes, operated as a displacement behavior. We had the impression, for example, that some Group-A babies (who neither evinced separation distress nor sought to be close to their mothers upon reunion) "explored" in a hyperactive way in such episodes, showing no investigative interest in the objects that they were either manipulating or moving toward, but rather banging them about repetitively or throwing and retrieving them repeatedly. Such an impression was very rarely recorded by the observers, however, who tended to confine themselves to a descriptive account of the locomotor and manipulative movements. Thus, although we have a hunch that displacement exploration might be qualitatively distinguished from more genuine investigative exploration, it is impossible to make the distinction in our present data in any systematic way. Another type of displacement behavior may have been thumb- and finger-sucking (which in Episode 7 was especially characteristic of Group-A infants).

Heart-rate records, such as those used by Sroufe and Waters (1977b), might very well have been a useful "convergent measure" to enable us to identify both tension movements and displacement behavior. Indeed, such a measure used in one crucial strange-situation study might lead to the sharpening of the behavioral criteria of tension and displacement to the extent that subsequent studies could rely solely on detailed behavioral records.

Finally, no videotape equipment was available to us throughout our strange-situation research; had it been available we would undoubtedly have used it. Certainly for a record of facial expression, postural orientation, gesture, resistance, avoidance, and tension movements, it would have enabled us later to retrieve detail not included in the observers' narrative accounts.

There are advantages and disadvantages to each kind of record. Narrative records depend for their usefulness on the observational and narration skills of the observer-narrators. Transcribing the dictated narratives is time consuming if done by research personnel (and expensive if a typist is employed), the more so if two or more observer-narrators are used, as of course they should be. Once transcribed, however, dictated narratives require relatively little time to examine for coding and scoring. Furthermore the transcriptions are permanent records that can be stored, available for reexamination. New variables can emerge from dictated narratives—and indeed in our research all of our measures of interactive behavior did so emerge—through reading the narratives over and over again, an enterprise that requires a fraction of the time required for viewing videotapes repeatedly.

Videotapes require a skilled cameraman who is alert to precisely what is of critical interest for the analysis of strange-situation behavior. A single camera may not be able to pick up behavior of both child and relevant adult when they are at a distance from each other, as well as from the observer-narrator. If one can use a split-screen technique, this disadvantage may be overcome by having two or three cameras focusing on the action from different vantage points and/or with different persons as targets. This requires a skilled and knowledgable person monitoring all cameras and combining their records to the best advantage. Coding and scoring require the same skill of the observer-coders as the other method requires of the observer-narrators, but training toward acquiring such skill is easier than training in the "live" situation. Coding and scoring are infinitely more time consuming for videotapes than for transcribed narrative records. Repeated viewing is possible, however, and through this it is entirely possible that new variables can emerge—indeed, with more confidence than for transcribed narratives. Videotape records may be permanent and thus available for reexamination; on the other hand, this is expensive, and often the tapes must be erased after the initial coding, thus eliminating the possibility of later reexamination. Finally, for better or for worse, videotape records can substantially alter the measures that can be derived. In lieu of frequency per 15-second interval measures, precise measures of duration of a behavior can be obtained, although this would be most useful for measures that are not very important components for our classificatory system. In the case of our interactive measures, an overwhelming amount of detail can be provided by videotape records, which might lead the investigator to short-cut methods of scoring and classification.

Only one of us (EW) has used videotape records of strange-situation behavior, supplementing them with transcriptions of dictated narratives. He has come to rely mostly on the videotape record, in the conviction that a good videotape record can comprehend all of the essentials of a dictated narrative, as well as provide more detail that may be very useful for resolving discrepancies in scoring and for elucidating behaviors not at present included in our scoring system. Otherwise, all of the studies reported or reviewed here (except Lamb, 1978) have relied solely on dictated narratives for recording the strange situation. The choice of methods of recording, we believe, can be left up to the individual investigator who wishes to use our strange-situation procedure, in accordance with his own preference, experience, and resources. The fact that our procedure was founded on dictated narrative records rather than on videotape recording should not discourage those who have come to rely on videotaping. In our opinion the dictated narratives make it easier to use our procedures and to make use of our findings, but the videotape records facilitate the extension of our work toward a more detailed and subtle understanding of attachment and attachment behavior.

14

Individual Differences: In Light of Contrasting Paradigms

INTRODUCTION

Most of the criticisms of attachment theory that have arisen since Bowlby (1958) offered his preliminary formulation of it have focused on the issue of individual differences. If we may liken the programatic theories that have so far guided psychological research to what Kuhn (1962) calls paradigms, the controversies about individual differences in attachment and attachment behavior constitute a good example of what he describes as the difficulties that face the adherents of an earlier paradigm when trying to come to terms with a new paradigm. The new paradigm in this case is Bowlby's evolutionary–ethological attachment theory, and the earlier paradigms are variants of social-learning theory.

In Chapter 1 we sought to summarize the basic components of the new paradigm as it applies to the attachment of an infant to his mother figure. Elsewhere (Ainsworth, 1969) we reviewed two major variants of the social-learning-theory view of the origins and development of a child's relationship to his mother, a relationship characterized, before Bowlby's 1958 paper, as "dependency." Since then, some social-learning theorists have adopted Bowlby's term "attachment" for the child's tie to his mother, but have attempted to rework attachment theory so that it is in harmony with the earlier dependency paradigm. Among the first of these were Maccoby and Masters (1970), whose review includes both an authoritative account of dependency research and theory and a discussion of attachment theory from a social-learning point of view—a discussion that has had substantial influence in shaping a type of social-learning attachment theory differing in important respects from Bowlby's ethological–evolutionary theory.

Before considering some of the influential implications of the view suggested by Maccoby and Masters, let us very briefly summarize some essentials of an earlier social-learning dependency paradigm. Following Hullian theory, dependency was initially viewed as a secondary or learned drive, derived from such primary drives as hunger, cold and pain. Because his mother is associated with the reduction of such drives, the infant learns to attach strong reinforcement value to her proximity, and thus to be dependent on her. This learned dependency drive was held to generalize readily from the mother to other people. (Indeed most research into dependency focused on the child's relations with nursery-school teachers and age peers.) Behavioral indices of such dependency in young children were generally held to be: seeking physical contact, seeking to be near, seeking attention, seeking approval, and seeking help. Research focused on individual differences in the strength of the dependency drive.

The drive model eventually lost ground, in part because of the criticisms implicit in other emerging variants of learning theory, perhaps particularly Skinnerian theory. Bijou and Baer (1965) and Gewirtz (e.g., 1969) described the origins of the child's relationship with his mother in terms of her acquisition of positive reinforcing function as a result of her association with primary reinforcers, such as food, relief from pain, stimulus change, and the like. They considered dependency as a convenient label for certain kinds of learned behavior, and as neither a drive nor a trait. We consider the implications of this view for attachment later in this chapter. Here we are concerned with those who shifted from a view of dependency as a generalized acquired drive to viewing it as a generalized personality trait. Focal to the trait view is the matter of measuring the strength of the trait in different individuals. The shift from drive to trait made little apparent difference in either measures of dependency or in the criteria considered necessary to validate the concept.

When attachment theory emerged, it was immediately perceived to be somewhat akin to dependency theory. Both theories were concerned with the origins of a child's tie to his mother, and contact and proximity seeking were focal to both formulations. Maccoby and Masters (1970) suggested that attachment might be viewed as a trait or central motive state, thus obviously attempting to assimilate attachment to the dependency paradigm. This implied that a major dimension of attachment was its strength, and this was to be inferred from the strength of attachment behavior. They suggested 10 possible measures of behavior strength, including the number of persons toward which the behavior is shown—a criterion obviously at variance with evolutionary-ethological attachment theory—as well as frequency with which the behavior is shown. The traditional criteria for testing the validity of the concept of a generalized trait were conceived as applicable to attachment. Thus, to support a trait hypothesis of attachment, Maccoby and Masters suggested that the following criteria should be met: (1) that all the behavioral indices of attachment should be positively correlated; (2) that there should be stability of measures of attachment across situations; and (3) that there should be stability of such measures across time (i.e., stability in the course of development).

Because the theoretical base from which we are working does not conceive of attachment as a personality trait (or central motive state), these criteria are not applicable to it. Indeed they are largely irrelevant. We can see no theoretical basis for expecting all attachment behaviors to be positively correlated—in other words, that a baby who cries much, for example, should also smile, vocalize, approach, and cuddle in when picked up significantly more often than others. This is not to say that we view the ways in which a baby mediates his attachment to his mother as unrelated to one another; but we view their intercorrelations as complexly patterned rather than in any simple, unidimensional relationship implying strength of attachment. We do not believe that attachment behaviors, considered as individual measures, should necessarily be positively correlated across situations. Thus, we can see no reason to expect that a baby who seeks contact with his mother when his attachment system is at a relatively high level of activation will necessarily do so proportionally often when his attachment system is at a low level of activation. On the other hand, we *can* expect that two infants who differ in the patterning of their behavior to the mother in one situation may well also differ in the patterning of their behavior in another situation, and that through research we can discover how different patterns of attachment manifest themselves in behavior across a variety of situations. Thus, it is obvious that our position implies stable individual differences; but these differences concern the ways in which several forms of behavior—including behaviors other than attachment behavior—are organized. Thus, in the strange-situation research described in this volume, we have reported the ways in which proximity-seeking and contact-maintaining behaviors are organized vis-à-vis angry, resistant behaviors and avoidant behaviors that are also directed to the mother; vis-à-vis wary/fearful behaviors and friendly affiliative behaviors directed to a stranger; and vis-à-vis exploratory behavior.

Let us consider the evidence for such stability of organization, as well as the evidence for the competing theory of attachment as a trait.

STABILITY OF INDIVIDUAL DIFFERENCES REFLECTED IN STRANGE-SITUATION BEHAVIOR

As reported in Chapter 10, Maccoby and Feldman (1972) noted that they found no evidence that "attachment" to the mother could be considered stable across time—that is, from 2 to 2½ and from 2½ to 3 years of age—and that more stability was found in regard to reactions to the stranger. Their measures of attachment consisted of "distal" behaviors, except for one "proximal" behavior—proximity—in the preseparation episodes only.

Coates, Anderson, and Hartup (1972a, 1972b) observed attachment in a laboratory situation using two samples and two periods of observation. The first sample was observed first at 10½ months of age and again at 14½, the second sample at 14½ and later at 18½. At each age there were two sessions and two conditions. One condition was a "nonseparation" condition consisting of 10 minutes when mother and infant were together under circumstances similar to our Episode 2. The other condition, the "separation" condition, consisted of three episodes: a 3-minute preseparation episode similar to the nonseparation condition, a 2-minute separation, and a 2-minute postseparation episode. The infants were randomly assigned to one of the two conditions in the first session at the first age point, and then the next day experienced the other condition; at the second age point the conditions were experienced again in the same order. The measures of attachment were time-sampled frequency measures—visual regard, vocalizing, smiling, touching, crying, and proximity—the last indicated by the child's presence in or absence from the same cell of a floor-grid as that occupied by the mother.

Stability of behaviors was assessed in three ways (Coates et al., 1972b): (1) within a session—which, in the nonseparation condition, compared each third of the session with the other thirds, and which, in the separation condition, compared pre- and postseparation behavior; (2) between sessions, which compared behavior in the nonseparation condition in one session with behavior in the preseparation episodes of the other, and (3) long-term stability, which compared behavior at one age with that at a later age—that is, 10½ vs. 14½ months for the first sample and 14½ vs. 18½ months for the second—both for the nonseparation and for the separation conditions. Neither visual regard nor vocalizing was consistently stable in the three comparisons for the two samples. Smiling was apparently too unstable for the authors even to report. Touching the mother and proximity to her were "moderately stable," with coefficients of correlation that were mostly significant. The measures relevant to separation behavior (crying and orienting to the door) were essentially unstable.

Masters and Wellman (1974), reviewing the two studies just cited, as well as a study of home behavior over 9 months of the first year (Stayton & Ainsworth, 1973), counted the proportion of significant to nonsignificant correlations in each study and concluded that "there is little stability and functional equivalence among many attachment behaviors ... it is their [the authors'] conclusion that the correlational analysis of human infant attachment behaviors does not provide substantial support for the concept of attachment as a psychological trait or central motive state [p. 228]."

In contrast, let us consider the evidence presented in this volume for the stability of both attachment behaviors (and certain behaviors antithetical to attachment behavior) and the patterns of behavior that we have proposed as indicative of qualitative differences in the infant–mother attachment relationship. This evidence is of three main kinds: evidence from repeated administrations of the strange-situation procedure, evidence of the relationship between strange-situation behavior and prior or contemporary behavior in other settings, and evidence of the relationship between strange-situation behavior and subsequent infant behavior in other settings.

Stability of Strange-Situation Behavior and Classification.   In four studies the strange situation was repeated after varying lapses of time with the mother as the accompanying adult. One of these was Maccoby and Feldman's (1972) study, which has already been discussed. The other three were reported in Chapter 11. All of these three first administered the situation at 12 months. In our study it was repeated 2 weeks later; in Connell's (1976) and Waters's (1978) it was repeated 6 months later. From these studies we may conclude that our four chief measures of interactive behavior were stable during periods of the second year of life- -contact maintaining, proximity/contact seeking, avoidance, and resistance, as directed toward the mother, especially in the reunion episodes. In addition, there was some evidence, especially from Waters, of stability of contact maintaining and proximity/contact seeking in the preseparation episodes. Waters and we also found some stability for crying; Connell did not report findings for crying. Our analyses and Waters's further showed that the "discrete" behaviors so commonly used by others in attachment research—looking, smiling, vocalizing, gesturing, approaching, and touching—tended not to be stable across sessions (with the exception of crying, mentioned earlier). We refer to these as "discrete" behaviors because the measures thereof are simple frequency measures that do not take into account the fact that different behaviors may serve the same purpose (i.e., gaining or maintaining proximity/contact) or allow for the contingencies of the situation, including the reciprocal behavior of the adult(s) in question. We consider our "categorical" measures of interactive behavior superior to frequency measures because they take into account the way behavior is organized with reference to the situation.

Furthermore, some of these discrete behaviors are also "distal" behaviors—looking, smiling, vocalizing, and gesturing. Not only were these unstable across time, but so was our categorical measure of distance interaction (Waters, 1978). Looking, as we have often pointed out (e.g., Ainsworth, 1973) probably should not be classed as an attachment behavior, for it serves so many behavioral systems from birth onward. As for smiling and vocalizing, we suggested in Chapter 13 that these may be considered to belong to a subclass of attachment behaviors that appear chiefly when the attachment-behavioral system is activated at low intensity. Under such conditions of activation, attachment behaviors tend to appear intermittently and irregularly. Without much longer periods of observation than were undertaken in the laboratory studies under consideration, there is no reason that one could expect them to appear stable; and one should especially not expect them to be stable when comparing a preseparation or nonseparation condition in which attachment behavior is only weakly activated with a separation or reunion condition in which it is intensely activated.

In contrast with Coates and associates (1972b) and Maccoby and Feldman (1972), Connell (1972), Waters (1978), and we also examined the stability of A-B-C classifications, these reflect the way in which an infant's behavior is organized toward his mother and hence, we have suggested, qualitative differences in attachment. Although there was too much carryover of anxiety (with a time interval between sessions of only 2 weeks) for us to find stability in classifications, both Waters and Connell reported a very impressive degree of stability over the 6-month period from 12 to 18 months. Individual differences in quality of attachment of infant to mother thus appear to be strikingly stable over a relatively long period of time and despite the possibility of occurrence of life events that might have intervened to change the attachment relationship in some cases.

We have already suggested three reasons for the apparent discrepancy between the findings of Coates and associates and Maccoby and Feldman, on the one hand, and those of Waters, Connell, and ours, on the other hand:

1. Use of measures of discrete behaviors vs. measures that reflect some degree of organization and interchangeability among behaviors.
2. Emphasis on attachment behaviors that are characteristic when the system is activated at low levels of intensity (which tend to be "distal" behaviors) vs. those characteristic when the system is activated at high levels of intensity (which tend to be "proximal").
3. Search for stability of separate measures vs. attention to the stability of patterns of behavior such as those reflected in our classificatory system.

There are several other possible sources of discrepancy:

4. Neither Coates and associates nor Maccoby and Feldman capitalized on the fact that repeated separations raise the level of activation of attachment behavior to especially high intensity. Coates and associates used only one 2-minute separation. Maccoby and Feldman, although using the standard strange-situation procedure with two separations and two reunions, used only discrete and/or distal measures for behavior in the reunion episodes.
5. Neither Coates and associates nor Maccoby and Feldman used our measures of resistance and avoidance when reporting a child's interaction with his mother, whereas Connell and Waters found these measures especially stable over time.

6. Maccoby and Feldman dealt with children older than those of other studies.

Let us comment on the last two points of difference. Studies that examine the stability of the A-B-C strange-situation classifications across time intervals inevitably examine avoidant and resistant behavior, which, although antithetical to attachment behavior, feature conspicuously in classification. It is not merely the way in which *attachment* behaviors are organized together that is of moment for individual differences, but, more saliently, the way in which *behavior as a whole* is organized vis-à-vis the attachment figure; and avoidant and resistant behaviors have emerged to be especially important among the nonattachment behaviors.

In Chapter 10 we considered developmental changes in strange-situation behavior between the ages of 12 months and 4 years. These developmental changes undoubtedly affect the ways in which a young child interacts with an attachment figure, and hence may well affect the behavior that mediates the relationship, including attachment behavior. Of perhaps crucial importance is that the features of the strange situation that activate the behavior of 1-year-olds at high intensity tend not to do so as the child grows older. This is not to imply that the degree of activation can be judged solely in terms of overt behavior, for heart-rate studies (e.g., Sroufe & Waters, 1977b) suggest that there may be quite intense activation internally while overt behavior appears to remain in a low key. Nevertheless, the "strange" or unfamiliar may have become less strange to the older preschooler, and, especially, cognitive development is likely to have enabled him to endure his mother's absence over longer periods of time. From Waters's and Connell's work it appears that 18-month-old infants respond to the strange situation in much the same way as 12-month-olds. Marvin (1972) found that 2-year-olds also organized their behavior in much the same way as did 12-month-olds, but that 3- and 4-year-olds did not. This being so, we must know much more about how preschoolers from 2½ onwards organize their behavior toward their mothers, both in situations in which attachment behavior is activated at high intensity and in situations in which it is activated at low intensity, before we can assess the stability of individual differences in their attachments to their mothers.

The Relationship Between Strange-Situation Behavior and Prior or Contemporary Infant Behavior in Other Settings.   The evidence presented in Chapter 7 that infant behavior at home, both in the first and in the fourth quarters of the first year, is significantly related in many ways to strange-situation assessments is of even more importance for our proposition of stability of organization or patterning of behavior than is the test–retest evidence cited above. Behaviors at home that were found by Stayton and Ainsworth (1973) to reflect a secure attachment to the mother bear a significant relationship to the patterning of strange-situation behavior that we have identified as characteristic of Group B. Mother-avoidant behavior in the strange situation, characteristic of Group A, is significantly related not only to the cluster of home behaviors that signify anxious attachment, but also specifically to another cluster of home behaviors not shown by nonavoidant but anxiously attached infants—namely, Group C.

Bell's (1978) finding that Group-A and Group-C babies, more frequently than Group-B babies, in a free-play situation showed a cluster of behaviors judged to display negative affect in interaction with their mothers is congruent with our findings; it seems likely that her positive vs. negative affect factor is equivalent to our secure vs. anxious attachment factor. Rosenberg's (1975) findings that Group-B infant–mother dyads had more reciprocal interaction than Group-A dyads in a free-play situation, and fewer reciprocal-ignoring states, are also congruent.

Despite these close relationships between strange-situation patterning of behavior and behavior in low-stress situations, separate behavioral variables are not necessarily positively correlated across settings. Thus, for example, crying in the strange situation is not significantly correlated with crying at home. In particular, crying in the separation episodes of the strange situation is not significantly correlated with crying in the brief, everyday separations that occur in the home environment. Securely attached infants show little separation distress in the familiar environment of the home but tend to protest separation in the strange situation—especially the second separation. Group-C infants protest separation in both settings, especially intensely in the strange situation. Group-A infants, however, who behave anxiously when mother leaves the room, tend not to cry when separated in the strange situation. On the other hand, behaviors related to close bodily contact with the mother *are* positively correlated with comparable behaviors in the strange situation.

Significant relationships between cognitive measures and individual differences in the organization of strange-situation behavior were found by Bell (1970, 1978) and Connell (1974). Connell found striking differences among the A-B-C groups in terms of behavior in his habituation experiment. Bell found that Group-B infants in both her white, middle-class and black, disadvantaged samples were significantly advanced in comparison with non-B infants in the development of the concept of the object, especially the concept of a person as having permanence. She also found that Group-B infants had a significantly higher mean DQ than non-B infants, although in our smaller Sample 1 this difference fell short of statistical significance (Ainsworth & Bell, 1974).

The only separate strange-situation measures that consistently yield significant correlations with behavior in other settings are our scores for resistant and avoidant behavior in the reunion episodes, which are themselves "categorical" rather than "discrete" measures. In Chapter 7 we reported positive correlations between resistance in the strange situation and amount of crying, including separation distress, at home. We also reported significant correlations between avoidance in the strange situation and both anger and various measures of behavior relevant to close bodily contact at home. Bell (1978) combined avoidance and resistance into a measure of "negative" behavior, and found this to show essentially the same relationships with behavior in other settings as did the B vs. non-B comparisons. It may seem paradoxical that these two classes of behavior, which are clearly not attachment behavior because they do *not* promote proximity/contact to attachment figures, are more closely related to attachment behavior in other settings than are separate components of strange-situation attachment behavior. The paradox is resolved, however, when one considers that these two measures give important clues to the way in which behavior is organized to mediate the infant's attachment to his mother, and are indeed key behaviors in our classificatory system.

The Relationship Between Strange-Situation Behavior and Subsequent Behavior in Other Settings. In Chapter 9 we reviewed evidence by Bell (1978) Connell (1976), Main (1973, 1977; Main & Londerville, 1978), and Matas (1977) that the patterning of strange-situation behavior is significantly related to social, emotional, and cognitive development in the second year of life, and in the case of studies by Bell and Connell the third year of life as well. In regard to social and emotional development, the evidence is plentiful. In summary, Group-B children, in comparison with non-B children, emerged as more responsive to and initiating more interaction with their mothers, directing more positive behavior and less avoiding, ignoring, aggressive, and/or resistant behavior to their mothers, displaying more positive affect, maintaining more proximity to mothers, and being more cooperative and willing to fit in with their mothers' wishes, and generally easier to live with. In addition, B children, in comparison with non-B children, are friendlier, more cooperative, and more participant in interaction with relatively unfamiliar persons.

Although there were nonsignificant relationships between strange-situation classification and developmental test scores at some age points, there was nevertheless suggestive evidence of a relationship between quality of infant–mother attachment and subsequent DQ or IQ. In addition, Bell found that Group-B babies at 14 months continued to be more advanced in the development of person- and object-permanence, while Connell and Main both found Group-B toddlers to be more advanced in language acquisition. Main reported that B toddlers engaged in superior exploratory activity.

Matas found them to be more enthusiastic and persistent in a problemsolving situation, and to show less frustration behavior and less nontask behavior than non-B children.

Furthermore Main, Connell, and Matas all found some significant differences between Group-A and Group-C children. Connell found that whereas A children clearly maintained more distance between themselves and their mothers than B children, C children did not, and indeed in an episode in which the mother moved to a less accessible place, C children showed more proximity seeking than B children. Matas found that C children showed extreme reliance on the mother in a problem-solving situation and were also likely to give up quickly and show frustration behavior, whereas A children sought more help from the experimenter than from the mother and were aggressive to the mother. Main reported that resistant strange-situation behavior, which is characteristic of Group C, was negatively correlated with DQ, intensity of exploratory play, and length of play bouts, whereas avoidant behavior (characteristic of Group A) was not significantly related to these variables. Matas identified Group-C children as relatively incompetent in problem-solving situations, whereas Group-A children were especially noncompliant. The dynamics that we believe to underlie these differences are discussed in Chapter 15.

Conclusions Regarding Stability of Individual Differences. Whereas Masters and Wellman (1974) found so little evidence of individual differences in attachment behavior that they suggested that these ought to be disregarded in studies of attachment, the evidence that we have reported here leads us to conclude that there is substantial stability of individual differences in attachment across time and across situations. It is clear that the A-B-C classifications of strange-situation behavior yield the most striking evidence of stability. This implies that it is the way in which an infant organizes his behavior in directing it toward his mother figure that is stable. Individual differences in such organization reflect what we have termed differences in the quality of the infant–mother attachment relationship. The focus is on the organization—the attachment—rather than on the separate components of behavior that enter into the organization.

There is substantial evidence also for the stability of our "categorical" measures of strange-situation behavior, such as proximity/contact seeking, contact maintaining, resistance, and avoidance, across time in similar situations. This stability we attribute to the fact that in dealing with classes of behavior that have the same "predictable outcome" (Bowlby, 1969), we take into account the goal-corrected nature of behavior. Thus in the category of contact-maintaining behavior, we acknowledge a variety of ways in which a baby can maintain close bodily contact with his mother when there is a threat of interruption, rather than consider clinging, clambering up, holding on, and crying in protest to the interruption as separate behavioral items.

There is little evidence, however, for the stability of what we have termed "discrete" behaviors. As our previous discussion has implied, we attribute this to the fact that measures of such behaviors do not take into account either the way in which behaviors are organized or their goal-corrected nature. When, in addition, context is ignored—as it often is when testing for stability across situations—it is small wonder that such isolated behavioral items tend to emerge as unstable. This tends especially to be the case with "distal" behaviors that tend also to be "low-intensity" behaviors characteristically but intermittently occurring when the attachment system is at a low level of activation and especially subject to competition from other behavioral systems, such as exploratory behavior or affiliative behavior directed toward persons other than attachment figures. As suggested earlier, the intermittent nature of such behaviors would require much longer samples of time than afforded by the usual laboratory study for their stability to be tested.

We conclude therefore that individual differences in the quality of attachment tend to be stable across time and across situations because they reflect underlying differences in the organization of behavior. Nevertheless we cannot expect to find similar consistency across situations in the behaviors that mediate attachment unless we take into account the way the exigencies specific to the situation interact with the underlying organization of attachment. Sroufe and Waters (1977a) have also emphasized that our concept of attachment is an organizational construct. According to this view the specific behavior toward an attachment figure in any given situation will be determined both by the underlying organization and by the situational context.

COVARIATION OF ATTACHMENT BEHAVIORS

In addition to stability of the behavioral indices of attachment, covariation of these indices must be demonstrated, according to Maccoby and Masters (1970) and Masters and Wellman (1974), to validate the concept of attachment as a trait or central motive state. Although we consider this criterion—at least as narrowly conceived—to be irrelevant to the ethological–evolutionary theory of attachment, it is useful to consider some of its implications. There may be at least three ways in which two or more behaviors might be conceived as covarying: (1) they tend to occur together; (2) they are positively and significantly correlated; and (3) they are organized together in stable ways, which may result in a complex matrix of positive and negative correlations. We consider that only (3) is relevant to our concept of attachment.

Concurrence of two behaviors would certainly satisfy the requirements of a trait model (although one of the behavioral indices would be redundant if concurrence was invariable or nearly so). Thus, proximity to the mother and touching her concur; it is impossible for a baby to touch his mother if he is not already close to her, although of course he may be close to her without actually making physical contact. Another example comes from face-to-face behavior in the early months (Blehar, Lieberman, & Ainsworth, 1977). Smiling, vocalizing, and bouncing often occur together when an infant is face-to-face with his mother. However, if one accepts the definition of attachment behavior as behavior that promotes proximity to an attachment figure (or caregiver), it is evident that concurrence cannot be required as a criterion. Thus it can be demonstrated that both crying and smiling promote proximity, but they are obviously unlikely to occur at the same time.

Maccoby and Masters (1970) specified positive correlation among behavioral indices as their criterion of covariation. Obviously concurring behaviors, even when the concurrence is only partial, will be positively correlated more or less strongly. Even though behaviors never concur, they might nevertheless be positively correlated if the same individuals who show one behavior in one kind of situation also tend to show the other in another kind of situation. Thus, for example, babies who respond positively when picked up and held by the mother also tend to greet her positively when she returns after a brief absence from a familiar environment (Stayton & Ainsworth, 1973). In our strange-situation findings, other examples may be found. For example, infants who seek proximity/contact with their mothers in the reunion episodes also tend to resist any attempts by their mothers to put them down after being held for "too short a time."

On the other hand, there are many instances in which behaviors that may be classed as attachment behaviors (in that they are proximity-promoting) are negatively rather than positively correlated, and hence speak against the concept of attachment as a generalized trait. For example in the strange situation, measures of distance interaction are negatively correlated with both proximity seeking and crying, even though they include such obvious proximity-promoting behaviors as smiling and vocalization. At home both positive and negative greeting of the mother after an absence may be considered proximity promoting, for behaviors such as smiling, vocalization, reaching, and approach are classed together as positive, while crying is the essential feature of the negative greeting. Nevertheless, positive and negative greetings are negatively correlated; not only are they rarely concurrent, but the children who tend to show negative greetings, relative to other children, infrequently tend to show positive greetings (Stayton & Ainsworth 1973). Furthermore, some attachment behaviors are positively correlated with behaviors antithetical to proximity promotion; thus at home positive response to being held is positively correlated with positive response to being put down (Ainsworth, Bell, & Stayton, 1971), and in the reunion episodes of the strange situation, proximity/contact seeking is positively correlated with resistant behavior (because they concur in Group-C babies). These few examples suffice to reflect the complex pattern of intercorrelations that may be found among the behaviors infants and young children direct toward their attachment figures.

It is nevertheless possible to conceive of covariation in terms of behavioral organization rather than as a matter simply of concurrence or positive correlation among all behavioral indices. As Blurton Jones and Leach (1972) commented: "Ethologists, asking themselves what they mean by words like 'attachment', find that the only use for such a term is as shorthand for a number of behaviour items which vary together, *or are found to be related together in a more complex way in a causal system* [italics ours] [p. 218]." We believe that the data presented in this volume indeed suggest that the behavioral items relevant to attachment are related in a complex but systematic way that suggests an underlying "causal system." They do not, however, suggest a unitary, generalized trait.

Let us not, however, belabor the issue of attachment as trait. It is now generally agreed that attachment cannot be conceived as a trait or central motive state (e.g., Coates et al., 1972b; Masters & Wellman, 1974), although it is erroneous to conclude that the concept of attachment is therefore an invalid concept, as others have done (e.g., Rosenthal, 1973). We should like, however, to pursue the issue of covariation in order to discuss further the implications of intercorrelational analysis of behavioral measures of attachment. We have three main points to make.

First, the dimension of strength of attachment (or strength of attachment behavior), which is so focal to the trait concept, is of relatively little importance for ethological–evolutionary attachment theory. We can think of only two contexts in which strength of attachment is relevant. If one were attempting to distinguish a principal attachment figure from other supplementary and secondary attachment figures, we can at present conceive of no criterion other than the strength of preference for one over the others, and no way to assess the strength of preference except the strength of attachment behaviors displayed to one in comparison with another in a free-choice situation. (Even then, one could argue that one set of attachment behaviors is more relevant than others for an assessment of such preference.) Or in a practical situation in which the issue is whether or not to remove a child from his natural parents and place him in a foster or adoptive home, it might be of moment to ascertain whether he has become strongly enough attached to his parent(s) that it would be more traumatic to him to be separated from them or to remain with them. Certainly, in the context of a paradigm that views attachment as specific to the figure to whom one is attached, it is not pertinent (as Maccoby and Masters suggested) to consider the *number* of figures to which attachment behaviors are directed as an index of the strength of attachment. Clinical findings suggest that the relationship a child has with his principal attachment figure may to some extent color his subsequent relations with other attachment figures, but this is a proposition that requires further research. In the meantime the conservative position would be to assume that the relationship with each attachment figure depends upon the history of the interaction between the child and that figure.

Second, the most conspicuous dimension that has emerged so far in our attachment research is not strength of attachment but security vs. anxiety in the attachment relationship. This does not imply substitution of degree of security for degree of strength in a unidimensional concept of attachment. On the contrary, insofar as individual differences are concerned, we conceive of security–anxiety as being only one dimension in terms of which an attachment relationship might be assessed. Our concept of patterning has implicit in it that there may well be several other dimensions relevant to such assessment. Obviously, from the data reported in this volume, avoidance and conflict relevant to close bodily contact constitutes a second dimension. Only our limited number of subjects has held us back from identifying other dimensions. In short, our concept of attachment is multivariate insofar as individual differences are concerned. A multivariate model implies complexity in the correlations among behavioral indices of attachment and not a simple "positive correlation" model.

Third, any frequency measure of behavior implies an assumption that all instances of the behavior in question are equivalent. This assumption is highly questionable in many cases. Let us consider approach behavior, for example. As Tracy, Lamb, and Ainsworth (1976) have pointed out, it cannot be assumed that a given instance of approach behavior serves the attachment-behavioral system rather than some other system, such as food seeking, exploration, or mere friendly affiliation, unless the context—both behavioral and environmental—is taken into account. We cannot even assume that all instances of approach to an attachment figure serve the attachment-behavioral system; a child may approach his mother for a variety of reasons on different occasions—for example, because she offers him food, because she shows him an interesting toy, or because he wants to be near to her. Even among instances of approach that may be assumed to serve the attachment system, there is a miscellany of contexts in which approach might appear— for example, following a departing figure, greeting a returning figure, approaching when frightened, and approaching because the current proximity set-goal has been exceeded. A total score consisting of the frequency of all approaches within a given period of observation tends to contain a great deal of "noise." Because frequency measures have commonly been used in studies of both attachment and dependency, it is not surprising to find that intercorrelations among behavioral indices tend to be low.

Such difficulties may be reduced in several ways: (1) by controling the context in which behavior occurs, as in the design of the episodes of the strange situation; (2) by taking context into account when devising measures, rather than relying on frequency alone, as in our categorical measures of strange-situation behavior; (3) by including within one measure several behaviors that may be considered equivalent, as we have done both in our categorical measures of strange-situation behavior and in some of our measures of behavior at home—for example, responses to being picked up and being put down; and (4) by using ratings rather than frequency measures of behavior, presumably because an intelligent rater using a well-designed rating scale tends *not* to give equal weight to all instances of a behavior but to take context and behavioral equivalents into account; and finally, and infinitely more difficult, (5) by abandoning correlational methods in favor of a detailed analysis of the environmental and behavioral contingencies of each item in a prolonged sequence of interactions—a type of analysis that Gewirtz (1961) has proposed. So far such detailed analyses have been undertaken only for very brief sequences of interaction between mother and infant in a face-to-face situation (Brazelton, Koslowski, & Main, 1974; Stern, 1971). Considering the bewildering complexity of data yielded by such detailed analyses, it seems reasonable that they be confined to behavior in specific contexts and that, for a study of attachment behavior, they be confined to contexts known in advance to elicit such behavior with fair consistency.

Giving no credence to the concept of attachment as a trait, some of those approaching attachment from a social-learning position (e.g., Cairns, 1972; Gewirtz, 1972a, 1972b; Rosenthal, 1973), rather than turning toward attachment as an organizational construct, have argued that the study of the phenomena of attachment requires no construct at all but can best be understood as stimulus-response contingencies in the interaction of an infant with his mother or other caregiver. Before discussing this proposal let us review the findings earlier reported in Chapters 8 and 9 on the relationship between strange-situation behavior and maternal behavior.

RELATIONSHIP BETWEEN STRANGE-SITUATION BEHAVIOR AND MATERNAL BEHAVIOR

Because our hypothesis is that different experiences in interaction with the mother are largely responsible for qualitative differences in infant–mother attachment, the relationship between maternal behavior and patterns of strange-situation behavior is of particular interest. Of most relevance to our hypothesis are studies of maternal behavior prior to or at least contemporaneous with the strange-situation assessments of patterns of infant behavior. Here we are concerned solely with maternal behavior at home or in other "uncontrolled" situations, for the behavior of the mother in the strange situation was at least partially controlled by instructions and by the structure of the situation, so that there was relatively little scope for individual differences to be manifested.

The findings reported in Chapter 8 for our Sample 1 are of particular importance because they are based on extensive observations of mother–infant interaction at home throughout the first year of life. In comparison with the mothers of A and C babies, the mothers of Group-B infants were found to be more sensitively responsive to infant signals and communications, including crying signals. In the first quarter of the baby's first year, their sensitivity to signals was specifically shown in their behavior relevant to feeding, in their contingent responsiveness in face-to-face situations, and in their "tender, careful holding" when in close bodily contact with the baby. They were relatively mobile in emotional expression and tended to lack rigidity and compulsiveness in dealing with the baby throughout the first year. When rated in regard to fourth-quarter behavior, they were also found to be psychologically accessible to their infants, accepting rather than rejecting, and cooperative rather than interfering. They continued to be responsive to infant crying signals, and showed more affectionate behavior when in contact with their babies than did the mothers of non-B babies.

Group-A mothers were clearly more rejecting than non-A mothers; they more frequently had their positive feelings toward the infant overwhelmed by anger and irritation. They also expressed their rejection in terms of aversion to close bodily contact with their infants. They gave them more unpleasant experiences in the context of bodily contact. They showed a relative lack of emotional expression, which was interpreted as reflecting a way of controling the expression of anger. They were rigid and compulsive in dealing with their babies. Their insensitivity to infant signals, as well as their rigidity, seems to have fed their frequent tendencies to interfere with the baby's activity in progress.

Group-C mothers, like Group-A mothers, were relatively insensitive to infant signals, but they were clearly less rejecting. They showed no aversion to close bodily contact; yet they were inept in holding their babies and manifested little affectionate behavior when in contact with them, but rather used holding time largely for routines, even in the fourth quarter.

Studies that followed mother–infant dyads beyond the strange situation into the babies' second or third years of life report subsequent maternal behavior that is highly consistent with our reports of maternal behavior during the first year. Thus Bell (1978) reported that Group-B mothers, in comparison with non-B mothers, tended to be more positive and appropriate in their interactions with the child, to manifest more positive affect, and to have superior communication. Tomasini (1975) found that maternal anger, rejection, insensitivity, and lack of emotional expressivity when the child was 21 months old were significantly correlated with strange-situation classification at 12 months; A/C mothers showed these behaviors most conspicuously and B_3 mothers the least. Tolan (1975) confirmed that the facial expressions of B_3 mothers while watching their toddlers were more expressive of both pleasure and a wide range of emotions than were the expressions of mothers of A/C babies. Main (1977a) found mother avoidance in the strange situation to be positively correlated with the following maternal behaviors at 21 months: anger, avoidance of proximity to and contact with the child, and lack of emotional expressivity.

Connell (1976) found that Group-B dyads had more interaction and longer bouts of interaction than did non-B dyads. In this follow-up of one sample at 14 and 16 months, he found no differences between Group-A and Group-B mothers in restrictiveness, ignoring the child's signals for interaction, or anger. The latter two findings are disparate with the findings of the other studies. In regard to ignoring signals, we would suggest that Connell's mothers, who were visited for 1 hour on two occasions, may have been making an effort to "do a good job" and hence may have been more than usually responsive to signals, whereas our mothers, who were observed more frequently and for longer periods of time (as well as Bell's mothers, observed in the course of eight long visits), could not keep up such unusual effort; hence significant differences in maternal responsiveness to signals and to initiations of interaction were more likely to emerge. As for anger, Main (personal communication) acknowledges that maternal anger is very difficult to assess. Overt angry display tends to be inhibited in the presence of observers, and this is especially the case in the relatively brief span of a laboratory session or in a first or even second home visit. When anger is under tight control, it can only be inferred through subtle or indirect cues, as was the case in Tomasini's study.

In summary, we may conclude that different patterns of infant strange-situation behavior are associated with different constellations of maternal behavior both before the strange situation and subsequent to it. During the strange situation, however, maternal behavior was controled both through instructions and through the structure of the episodes themselves. Therefore, in that situation infant behavior was largely freed from its usual contingencies with maternal behavior. Nevertheless individual differences in infant behavior emerged under these circumstances that, although consistent with individual behavioral differences shown in previous interaction with their mothers, could not be attributed to individual differences in the contingencies provided by maternal behavior in the strange situation. This kind of continuity in patterns of infant behavior, despite control of maternal behavior, suggests that the determinants of infant behavior toward an attachment figure include an inner organizational component, as well as situational determinants. We have no doubt that the long experience an infant has in interaction with his mother in the course of his first year of life is chiefly responsible for the way in which he organizes his behavior toward her; but the resulting organization becomes to some extent independent of the particulars of his interaction with her in any given situation.

ATTACHMENT AS DISTINGUISHED
FROM ATTACHMENT BEHAVIOR

In Chapter 1 we distinguished between infant–mother attachment and an infant's attachment behavior. By *attachment* we mean the affectional bond or tie that an infant forms between himself and his mother figure—a bond that tends to be enduring and independent of specific situations. By *attachment behavior* we mean the class of behaviors that share the usual or predictable outcome of maintaining a desired degree of proximity to the mother figure— behaviors through which the attachment bond is first formed and then later mediated, maintained, and further developed. Further, we refer to the *attachment-behavioral system,* which implies that the behaviors that may be classed together as attachment behavior come to operate systematically together. Specifically, the behavioral system in question is highly responsive to situational factors. Thus some situations activate the behavioral system at higher levels of intensity than other situations. The intensity of activation of the system may affect not only the intensity with which a specific behavior is shown, but also which specific attachment behaviors are activated—whether smiling or approaching or tightly clinging, for example. Furthermore, the attachment-behavioral system is only one of a number of behavioral systems, and the extent to which it is manifest in behavior is conceived to depend on its intensity of activation relative to the intensity of activation of other behavioral systems that may be either in competition or compatible with it. Thus whereas attachment behaviors may be manifested only intermittently and are closely tied to situational determinants, attachment as a bond is conceived as more or less constant and little affected by situational factors (except perhaps over a very long period of time). The fact that a baby is busily exploring his environment at time A and showing no overt attachment behavior does not mean that he is not attached to his mother at that time, or that he is less attached than at time B when he is alarmed, for example, and wants to be in close physical contact with her.

These definitions and distinctions are not shared by most of those who have approached a study of attachment from a social-learning point of view. They neither distinguish between attachment and attachment behavior nor espouse the construct of a behavioral system. Those who explicitly or implicitly view attachment as a trait (or general motive)—and this includes those for whom the dimension of strength or intensity of attachment has primary salience— consider attachment behaviors as indices of attachment, but then define attachment solely in terms of its indices. Those who hold that infant–mother attachment is neither more nor less than the stimulus-response contingencies implicit in mother–infant interaction explicitly disclaim the need for a construct of attachment in distinction from attachment behavior.

It seems to us self-evident that infants become bonded to attachment figures not only in the human species but also in many other species. It seems to us unnecessary to "validate" that such a phenomenon exists. The problem is to understand how the bonding takes place, how different experiences affect the nature of the bond, and what effect differences in the nature of the bond have upon subsequent development. To be sure, different constructs of attachment may imply different hypotheses about the formation, nature, and effects of the attachment bond, and these are subject to the usual kind of hypothesis-testing procedures. But to say that the notion of attachment—in general, and presumably as a phenomenon rather than as a particular set of hypotheses about its nature—is proven invalid or unnecessary, as Maccoby and Feldman (1972), Rosenthal (1973) and Weinraub, Brooks, and Lewis (1977) have concluded, appears to us as absurd as it would be to deny the existence of some kind of thermal regulatory system in mammals.

Let us restate our view of attachment as distinct from attachment behavior:

> We infer the existence of an attachment from a stable propensity over time to seek proximity and contact with a specific figure, even though attachment behavior may appear only intermittently, or—in the case of major separations—may be absent for long periods. The term "attachment" refers to the propensity, whereas the term "attachment behavior" refers to the class of diverse behaviors which promote proximity and contact, at first without discrimination of figure, but later with increasing specificity in regard to the figure(s) to whom the child is or is becoming attached.
>
> It is further suggested that it is useful to view attachment—as a construct—as an inner organization of behavioral systems which not only controls the "stable propensity" to seek proximity to an attachment figure, but also is responsible for the distinctive quality of the organization of the specific attachment behaviors through which a given individual promotes proximity with a specific attachment figure. Such an hypothesis implies some kind of stable intraorganismic basis for individual differences in the organization of attachment behaviors. Such a relatively stable inner organization must be conceived as interacting with environmental conditions and other "situational" intraorganismic conditions— neurophysiological, hormonal, and receptor processes—to activate, terminate, and direct attachment behavior in any specific situation. It is conceived as a hierarchical organization that permits more or less interchangeable behaviors to be directed by any one of several general plans or strategies that may be specifically tailored to fit the requirements of different situations. A hierarchical organization of this kind suggests internal structure [Ainsworth, 1972, p. 123].

Obviously this kind of hypothesized intraorganismic structure is alien to social-learning-theory formulations—at least to those that have attempted to grapple with the notion of attachment, whether from their own data, other people's data, or without any data at all.

Implicit in the aforementioned view is the notion that there are individual differences in the intraorganismic structure that constitutes attachment— differences attributable to differences in long-term interaction with the attachment figure. It is to such differences that we refer when speaking of differences in the quality of attachment.

To assert the theoretical distinction between attachment behavior and attachment, we have often used the term "attachment relationship" when referring to the bond. Hinde (1976a, 1976b) views a "relationship" between two individuals as an abstraction from a multiplicity of interactions between them. It is anchored in neither of the individuals concerned but is a convenient construct for characterizing the nature of the interactions between them. Ordinarily, an attachment relationship would be a relationship between two individuals who are attached to each other.

It is conceivable, however, that an infant might be attached to his mother but that the mother might not be bonded in a complementary way to her infant— as perhaps in the case of Harlow's (1963) "motherless mothers." It is also conceivable that a mother might be attached to her infant but the infant not bonded to her; indeed this is likely before he has become attached to his mother. Further, an infant may behave with reference to his mother figure in certain ways consonant with the nature of his attachment to her during certain periods when he is not in interaction with her—as, for example, when he is exploring away from her, using her as a secure base, or when he is separated from her but attempting to regain proximity to her. Likewise a mother may behave with reference to her baby in certain ways consonant with the nature of her attachment to him when they are separated.

As a consequence of her relationship to her baby, a mother has an inner representation of him that is not contingent upon his actual presence; and in the course of his development, an infant comes to have an inner representation of his mother. The inner representation that each member of the dyad has of the other is a consequence of the relationship which each has with the other, and these are plainly not identical. Similarly, and underlying the inner representation of the partner, each has built up some kind of intraorganismic structure that we have hypothesized as attachment. Although such a structure can be conceived to be influenced also by the interactions that constitute the relationship, it is obviously different for each partner. On these grounds we hold that the attachment of child to mother is by no means identical to the attachment of mother to child, even though they both share an attachment relationship.

ATTACHMENT IN OLDER PRESCHOOLERS

As we pointed out in Chapter 1, it is a misconception to believe that Bowlby was not concerned with the development of child–mother attachment beyond toddlerhood. To be sure, there had been very little research relevant to the later stages of development of child–mother attachment; thus, his formulations (1969, 1972) of such development were necessarily sketchy and programatic. He acknowledged that proximity-seeking behavior becomes less conspicuous in the child's interaction with his mother as development proceeds. He did not equate this, however, with an attenuation of attachment itself. He emphasized the significance of the develoment of "working models"—inner representations—that the child builds up both of himself and of his attachment figure, and the development of the capacity for making plans, both of which developments begin no later than the second year of life. In the final phase of development, in which a "goal-corrected partnership" is formed and sustained, the partners develop "a much more complex relationship with each other" than is characteristic of a 1-year-old (Bowlby, 1969). In this phase the development of the capacity to take the perspective of another is crucial. As this capacity develops, a child gains insight into his mother's plans, set-goals, and motivations, so that he can form increasingly complex plans that include influencing his mother to fit in with his plan. Indeed Bowlby's notion of "partnership" implies that both partners can negotiate mutual plans that comprehend the set-goals of each.

Obviously a child's cognitive development profoundly changes the specifics of the behaviors that mediate attachment in the older preschooler, as well as in still older children and in adults. Nevertheless, Bowlby (1973) conceived of the attachment of a child to his mother as enduring through a substantial part of life, even though it undoubtedly becomes attenuated, especially in adolescence, and supplemented with other relationships, including a number (a limited number) of other attachments. Furthermore, the fundamentally proximity-promoting nature of attachment behavior does not altogether disappear with increasing sophistication. Bowlby (1973) makes clear that even in infancy, proximity to the mother figure may come to be conceived in terms of her apparent availability—the degree to which she is believed by the child to be accessible to him and responsive to his signals and communications. Increasingly, therefore, proximity becomes less a matter of literal distance and more a matter of symbolic availability. Nevertheless, even in adult life, when the attachment system is activated at a high level of intensity—for example, by severe illness or disaster—the person seeks literal closeness to an attachment figure as an entirely appropriate reaction to severe stress.

To our knowledge, the only body of research that has picked up the threads of Bowlby's discussion of the development of attachment beyond the first year or two of life is that conducted by Marvin and his associates (Marvin, 1972, 1977; Marvin, Greenberg, & Mossler, 1976; Mossler, Marvin, & Greenberg, 1976), discussed in Chapter 10. They have shown that shifts in strange-situation behavior from one age level to another are associated with certain cognitive acquisitions. In particular, they have shown that the ability to take the perspective of another—at least in simple conceptual tasks—generally emerges between the third and fourth birthday. In recent, as-yet-unpublished research, Marvin (personal communication) has been investigating the way in which a child and his mother may negotiate a mutual plan—specifically, one in which the mother's plan (suggested by instructions) is to leave the child alone in a laboratory playroom for a few minutes. He demonstrated that when a mutual plan is negotiated, a 4-year-old shows no separation distress, although if (again according to instructions) the mother does not negotiate in response to the child's attempts to do so, the child is upset. The distress seems more likely to be angry distress, as a result of the mother's arbitrary unresponsiveness to his attempts to communicate his plan to her and to influence her plan, than attributable to mere separation. Furthermore, in the case of dyads who do successfully negotiate a mutual plan, a common compromise is the mother's acceding to the child's request to leave the door open, if only by "just a crack." The implication is that the child does not require his mother's actual presence as long as he feels that she would be accessible to him if he wanted to go to her. All of this is clearly in line with Bowlby's hypothesis about developments in the later preschool years.

As we have already pointed out, the strange situation does not activate attachment behavior at the same high level of intensity in 3- and 4-year-olds as in 1-year-olds. Consequently the patterning of behavior reflected in our classificatory system, dependent as it is on high-intensity activation of the attachment behavioral system (and also upon associated avoidant and resistant behavior), does not occur in older preschoolers in the same way that it does in 1-year-olds. In Chapter 10 we suggested several solutions to this problem. One solution is to use our categorical measures of interactive behavior, as Blehar (1974) did instead of employing our classificatory system—although this implies some loss of the patterning highlighted in classification. Another solution is to modify the classificatory system to make it more applicable to the behavior of the older preschoolers, as Marvin (1972) did. The other possible solutions considered in Chapter 10 involved devising new ways of assessing the attachment of older preschoolers to their attachment figure(s). Clues that might be useful might be found in the results of investigators such as Main, Bell, Connell, and Matas (reported in Chapter 9), who examined individual differences in later behavior of children who had been assessed in the strange situation at the end of the first year. Similarly, Lieberman's study (see Chapter 10) might give leads to variables relating to mother–child interaction at home that might substitute for strange-situation variables in the older preschooler. Marvin's current unpublished work seems likely to yield suggestions for ways in which laboratory assessments might be made more appropriate for the older child.

All of the foregoing implies that the situation-specific behaviors that reflect important qualitative differences in attachment in 1-year-olds may be replaced by a number of equally situation-specific behaviors in older preschoolers. Such a suggestion is akin to the concept of "transformation," proposed by both

Maccoby and Feldman (1972) and Lewis and his associates (Lewis & Ban, 1971; Weinraub, Brooks, & Lewis, 1977); but it demands something less simplistic than their assumption that "proximal" behaviors become transformed into "distal" behaviors in the course of development. Both proximal and distal behaviors are involved in mother–infant interaction throughout the first year of life, and both may be viewed as contributing to the formation and later mediation of the attachment bond. Even though the relative balance between proximal and distal behaviors shifts with increasing age, the distal behaviors remain those that emerge only intermittently and for the most part under conditions of low-level activation of the attachment system, and hence less useful as indices of qualitative differences in attachment, even in the older preschool child. A more important consideration is that the most crucial differences in patterning, even in the 1-year-old child, pertain neither to proximal nor to distal attachment behaviors but to the way in which such behaviors are organized together with key nonattachment behaviors— specifically those that reflect avoidance of or resistance to the attachment figure. Our prediction is that those patterns of behavior in the older preschooler that will be found to link up with earlier strange-situation-based differences in attachment quality are patterns that include negative nonattachment behavior related to avoidance and resistance—and thus to anxiety and anger.

ATTACHMENTS TO FIGURES OTHER THAN THE MOTHER

One of the reasons that the concept of attachment has captured so much of the interest of developmental researchers and clinicians regardless of their initial theoretical starting-points is the implicit hypothesis that the nature of a child's attachment relationship to his mother figure has a profound effect on his subsequent development. (We, as well as Bowlby, emphasize the term "mother figure" to assert our belief that the child's principal caregiver in infancy and early childhood is most likely to become the principal attachment figure—and thus the most important initial influence on subsequent development— whether such a figure be his natural mother, a foster or adoptive mother, a grandmother, a "nanny," or father.) In the beginning stages of research into attachment, it made good sense to focus on attachment to the mother figure, without thereby implying that attachments to other figures were of no consequence, or that other later relationships, whether or not they could be classified as attachments, had little significance in influencing a child's development. It ought to be possible to assert the importance of research into other attachments and other relationships without thereby impugning the value or validitiy of the attachment theory. Thus it seems naive of Willemsen and associates (1974) to have concluded that their finding that the father serves as an attachment figure in the strange situation essentially as the mother does demonstrates the invalidity of attachment theory. It is undeniable that the young child, and indeed also the young infant, develops within the framework of a "social network," as Weinraub, Brooks, and Lewis (1977) have eloquently described. Undoubtedly it is important to trace through the characteristics and effects of relationships other than the child's attachment to his mother figure. It is clearly important to investigate children's relationships with siblings, playmates, teachers, and so on. But this does not mean that attachment theory is of no value.

It seems to us to be of more urgent importance, however, to investigate relationships an infant has with those figures who share the caregiving role with the principal caregiver (usually the mother)—whether these figures include the father, other adults resident in the household, or supplementary or substitute figures such as day-care personnel, long-term "baby sitters," and the like. We need to take advantage of cross-cultural studies and "experiments of opportunity" within our own culture in order to investigate how different patterns of infant care affect the attachments of the infant to those involved in a caregiving role, and how variations on the theme of principal caregiver with supplementary and secondary figures show support and reinforcement for each other, compensatory function, or conflict; and we need to show how at least the more common of the many possible variations affect the development of the child.

Let us pose a few of the questions that readily emerge when one contemplates investigating a child's social network, while still concerning oneself only with his major caregivers. Can a "good" relationship with the father compensate for a conflicted and anxiety-provoking relationship with the mother? Can a few hours of high-quality interaction with the mother compensate for the fact that she leaves the major responsibility for daily infant care to substitute or supplementary figures? If both parents share equally in the care of the infant or young child, does he become equally attached to both, and what influence does this pattern have on his subsequent social development? Does the nature of the attachment a child has to his principal caregiver (mother figure) affect his relationship with other attachment figures, and in what ways? Or is the nature of his relationship with different attachment figures affected only by the nature of his interaction with each figure in isolation from and unaffected by his relationship with other figures? Does a child form significant attachment relationships with day-care personnel, and how do such relationships affect his relationship with his principal attachment figure and indeed his subsequent development? Each of these questions would require very time-consuming and difficult research projects before we begin to know as much about them as we already know about infant–mother attachment, which indeed is all too little.

In short, the fact that ramifications of research into a wide variety of attachments and other relationships have been indeed sparse denies neither the importance of undertaking such research nor the commonsense of beginning with the infant's attachment to his principal caregiver, which, across many cultures and throughout history, implies attachment to his mother.

15

An Interpretation of
Individual Differences

INTRODUCTION

In this chapter we focus chiefly on our own data and on the information about individual differences in infant–mother attachment that they provide; for it is these data that constitute our main case for claiming that our attachment construct can contribute substantially to an understanding of how qualitative differences in attachments arise, how they manifest themselves in behavior, and how they influence subsequent development. The data of particular relevance here are those relating an infant's behavior in the strange situation to: (1) his behavior at home in the fourth and first quarters (Chapter 7); and (2) maternal behavior at home during the same time periods (Chapter 8). We also refer to the work of others, especially to those who relate strange-situation behavior to the behavior of infants and mothers in other situations some months later (Chapter 9). Striking though these data may be in support of our argument that the patterns of strange-situation behavior reflected in the A-B-C classificatory groups are dynamically related to both infant and maternal behavior in other settings both before and after the strange situation, the purely empirical data gain heightened significance within the framework of theory. Let us then combine empirical data and theoretical considerations when presenting our explanations of the hypothesized dynamics of the three major classificatory groups.

In the discussion to follow, we have placed much emphasis on behavior in the strange situation as behavior that is essentially characteristic of the infant. It must be recalled, however, that the design of the strange situation activates attachment behavior at higher intensity than is usually the case in the familiar home environment, and therefore one cannot expect behavior there to be precisely the same as at home.

Our suggestion that the strange situation elicits behavior that is essentially characteristic of the infant should not be taken to imply that there may not be factors either present in the situation or operating immediately before the situation that may influence strange-situation behavior so that it is not characteristic of the child. For example, we omitted two infants from the sample because we later discovered that they were ill, with high fevers—indeed, they showed little or no exploratory behavior in the strange situation. It is conceivable that a baby's strange-situation behavior might be influenced in an "uncharacteristic" direction by uncharacteristic mother–infant interaction on the way to the laboratory, or at home earlier. Where such unusual circumstances are known to the investigator, it would obviously be prudent to discard the data, or interpret it with great caution—or better still to wait until another time to introduce the baby to the strange situation. It is difficult, however, to believe that the significant and complex interrelationships that have emerged in our data between strange-situation behavior and behavior elsewhere could have occurred had temporary factors leading to uncharacteristic behavior in the strange situation played other than a minor role.

Now let us consider the characteristic behavior of the infants classified in each of the three major groups and offer our interpretation of it.

GROUP B

The typical Group-B infant is more positive in his behavior toward his mother than are the infants of the other two classificatory groups. His interaction with his mother is more harmonious, and he is more cooperative and more willing to comply with his mother's requests, both in the last quarter of his first year and later on in the second year. From this we may infer that his affect toward his mother is more positive and less ambivalent and conflicted. This inference is supported by the fact that the infants in the other two groups cry more and specifically show more separation disturbance at home than the Group-B infants—which we interpret to mean that Group-B infants are generally less anxious. It is perhaps particularly noteworthy that they appear to be positive and unconflicted in their response to close bodily contact with the mother, both in the strange situation and at home. The data from our own longitudinal study, as well as data from the studies reported in Chapter 9, support us in our interpretation that Group-B infants are securely attached to their mother figures. Let us interpret behavior in the strange situation in light of these conclusions.

First, the typical Group-B infant uses his mother as a secure base from which to explore an unfamiliar environment, just as at home he spends a large amount of his time in exploratory play. In the very small sample we took of such behavior in Episode 2—together with the fact that this episode provides very strong instigation to exploratory behavior—it is perhaps not surprising that there is very little attachment behavior interspersed with exploratory behavior, whereas at home we can perceive a better-rounded picture of the balance between attachment and exploratory behavior.

Second, we wish to comment further on the fact that at home the typical Group-B baby is not likely to cry when his mother leaves the room. Even when she is out of sight, he nevertheless usually believes she is accessible to him and would be responsive should he seek her out or signal to her. It is our hypothesis that expectations of her accessibility and responsiveness have been built up through his experience of her generally sensitive responsiveness to his signals and communications. Such experience has been repeatedly confirmed by interactions with her in many different contexts—including feeding, face-to-face, close bodily contact, and by her response to his crying—throughout the whole of his first year. By the end of the first year it is probably only when attachment behavior has already been activated to some extent by conditions such as fatigue, hunger, or illness, or by some unaccustomed and somewhat alarming circumstance, that he protests her departure and/or continuing absence. His expectations of his mother's accessibility and responsiveness may carry over to the strange situation so that he may not protest her first departure in Episode 4. Nevertheless it would appear likely that his attachment-behavioral system has been activated to some extent, for his exploratory behavior is less active than in Episode 2; and, as Sroufe and Waters (1977b) have shown, he shows a characteristic acceleration of heart rate on her departure, whether he cries or not. The combination of the unfamiliarity of the situation, the length of his mother's absence, and especially a second and even longer separation in Episodes 6 and 7, tends to invalidate his expectations that his mother is accessible to him when she is out of sight in *this* unfamiliar environment, so that his attachment behavior tends to be activated at high intensity, and he tends to cry or to try to follow his mother (or does both) in Episode 6.

Regardless of whether he protested his mother's departure in one or another separation, his response to her return demonstrates that the attachment-behavior system had indeed been intensely activated by separation, for he tends immediately to seek not only proximity to her but also (especially in the case of the normative Subgroup B$_3$) close bodily contact. He may be sufficiently reassured by her return that he ceases crying as soon as she returns, but if he has been acutely distressed (as is common during the second separation) it may take a few moments for him to stop crying. Nevertheless, it is noteworthy that the typical Group-B infant is quickly soothed by close bodily contact with his mother. The intensity of the activation of his attachment behavior diminishes only gradually, however, as he is held by his mother and in turn clings to her or nestles close to her, for if she tries to put him down prematurely he actively resists release. He seems to need a minute or two of close contact before attachment behavior is terminated and before the instigation to exploration provided by the array of toys (perhaps supported by his mother's efforts to involve him again with the toys) is again relatively strong enough to override the attachment system. That the Group-B baby should both seek contact and be soothed by it could have been expected from his long history of positive experience in the context of close bodily contact with his mother.

Finally, let us consider three effects of a secure attachment to the mother—effects in the sense of assessments of behavior of Group-B babies that occurred either substantially later or at least entirely independent of either the strange-situation classification at the end of the first year or the kinds of mother–infant interaction at home that led us to conclude that Group-B behavior in the strange situation may be interpreted as reflecting secure attachment. First, Group-B babies tend to be more readily "socialized"—that is, more cooperative and willing to comply with mother's commands and requests—than non-B babies (as shown directly by Main & Londerville, 1978, and Matas, 1977, and indirectly by Stayton, Hogan, & Ainsworth, 1971). Stayton and associates have provided an ethological interpretation of this finding—namely, that the baby's attachment behavior is adapted (in an evolutionary sense) to an environment that includes a primary caregiver responsive to his needs, signals and communications. When this feature of the environment of evolutionary adaptedness is approximated in the contemporary situation, the baby responds with a general orientation toward behaving in accordance with the demands of such a figure; he is predisposed to comply with her efforts to control his behavior across a distance through signals and verbal commands. Such a predisposition is viewed as adaptive, insofar as infant response to signals across a distance extends the protective function of the mother figure (primary attachment figure) beyond the early period during which baby and mother, through their complementary attachment behaviors, remain in close proximity to each other.

Second, babies deemed to have a secure attachment to the mother figure are found to be more positively outgoing to and cooperative with relatively unfamiliar adult figures than is true for those deemed to be anxiously attached. Our chief support for this conclusion comes from Main (1973, 1977a), who showed that Group-B infants, more readily than non-B infants, respond positively to a familiarized adult playmate and cooperatively to the examiner who administers the Bayley test.

Third, babies who in the first year have a secure relationship with the mother tend to be more competent than babies whose relationship has been characterized as anxious. They explore more effectively and more positively, and thus they have a headstart in learning about the salient features of the environment (Main, 1973, 1977b). They are more enthusiastic, affectively positive, and persistent, as well as less easily frustrated, in problem-solving tasks (Matas, 1977). They tend to receive significantly higher scores on developmental tests both in the first year and later (Ainsworth & Bell, 1974; Bell, 1978; Main, 1973, 1977b), although to what extent this is attributable to development that has somehow been accelerated by the infant's secure relationship with his mother (including his ability to use his mother as a secure base for exploration) and to what extent it is attributable to the fact that the Group-B infant is more cooperative with the examiner and more likely to show a "game-like spirit" in the test situation (Main, 1973, 1977b) is difficult (and perhaps fruitless) to attempt to disentangle.

In conclusion, we may conclude that Group-B infants have secure attachments to their mothers, and thereby enjoy an advantage in various aspects of social and cognitive development.

GROUP C

We can say less about Group-C babies than about the other groups, if only because they have proved to be the least numerous group in any of the samples so far assembled, whether by ourselves or by other investigators. Nevertheless certain aspects of their experience seem fairly clear. Their mothers are much less responsive to crying and to signals and communication in general than are Group-B mothers. On the other hand, their mothers are not rejecting like Group-A mothers, and in particular they seem to have no aversion to physical contact with their babies, nor do they tend to be as compulsive or as lacking in emotional expression as Group-A mothers. Therefore there is no reason to expect Group-C babies to have the kind of approach-avoidance conflict that we believe to be characteristic of Group-A babies.

Nevertheless there is every reason to believe that Group-C infants are anxious in their attachment to the mother. Both at home and in the strange situation, they cry more than Group-B babies. They manifest more separation anxiety. They do not seem to have confident expectations of the mother's accessibility and responsiveness. Consequently they are unable to use the mother as a secure base from which to explore an unfamiliar situation—at least not as well as infants in Group B; in Episode 2 it seems to be only Group-C infants who are distressed. Furthermore, they are more likely to be distressed and/or to seek proximity to the mother when the stranger is present in Episode 3, as though wariness/fear of the stranger, combined with anxiety about the mother's accessibility and responsiveness, constitute a compound fear situation (Bowlby, 1973). Because they are chronically anxious in relation to the mother, they tend to respond to the mother's departures in the separation episodes with immediate and intense distress; their attachment behavior has a low threshold for high-intensity activation.

Perhaps because their mothers tend to lack the fine sense of timing that is characteristic of Group-B mothers (which is shown in the latter by sensitivity to infant signals in all kinds of contexts), their experience in close bodily contact has not been as consistently positive as that enjoyed by B babies. Consequently, even at home they seem more ambivalent about physical contact than B babies. This ambivalence reflects a kind of conflict that differs from that characteristic of A babies, however. They protest—and presumably protest angrily—if the mother's pick-up is badly timed; but they especially protest if they are not picked up when they want to be, or if they are put down when they still want to be held. This is the kind of angry ambivalence (scored as resistant behavior) that is conspicuous in C babies in the strange situation, and especially in the reunion episodes. They are slower to be soothed than B babies; they are angry when their mothers do not pick them up but rather attempt to play with them; and even when they are picked up, the accumulated frustration of attachment behavior activated by separation at a high level of intensity may lead them to mingle angry resistance with clinging and with other manifestations of contact-maintaining behavior. Thus, on the whole, Group-C babies seem to behave in the strange situation very much as one might expect from the way they behave at home, assuming that one acknowledges that the instigation to both attachment behavior and anger is more intense in the strange situation.

Main (1973, 1977b) has suggested that Group-C infants are handicapped by their anxiety in leaving the mother to explore and learn through their explorations, and hence it is they, more than Group-A infants, who advance more slowly in cognitive development than do securely attached infants. Matas (1977) found that Group-C toddlers were easily frustrated, overreliant on their mothers, and generally incompetent in problem-solving situations. Connell (1974) reported that Group-C infants were so distressed by the novel stimulus object that his habituation experiment had to be terminated.

Group C is a heterogeneous group. We should like to draw attention to the babies of Subgroup C_2, who were very passive. It is difficult to say how much of the difference between Groups C and B in regard to competence, developmental measures, exploration, problem solving, and the like are attributable to this passive subgroup. We suggest that C_2 babies have a poorer prognosis than C_1 babies. Passivity is notoriously resistant to treatment and reversal in later years. The passive-aggressive personality—the criteria for which fit our C_2 babies very well, even in the first year of life—is obviously associated with profound problems in dealing with the issues and challenges of later life. From our point of view the passivity of the C_2 infant seems to be deeply rooted. An infant whose mother almost never responds contingently to his signals must have a profound lack of confidence in his ability to have any effective control of what happens to him.

GROUP A

We have mentioned that the contrast between behavior at home and in the strange situation presents an apparent paradox in the case of Group-A babies. Furthermore, it was long a puzzle to us that Group-A babies in the strange situation were so different from Group-C babies, even though their behavior at home resembled that of C babies in many ways. In particular both cried more, and more frequently showed separation anxiety than did Group-B babies. The paradox lies in the relatively frequent separation distress the Group-A baby shows at home, whereas in the separation episodes of the strange situation he cried little or not at all. The key to understanding Group-A behavior seemed obviously to lie in their avoidance of the mother in those very episodes of the strange situation in which the attachment behavior of other babies was activated at high intensity—in the reunion episodes. It has taken some years, however, to arrive at an interpretation of Group-A behavior that seems to account for all the facts at our disposal and not merely for those two most conspicuous facts. We began (Ainsworth & Bell, 1970) by noting the similarity between avoidance of the mother in the reunion episodes and the "detachment" behavior that has been observed to result from "major" separation experiences—both during the separation itself and upon reunion—and sometimes persisting long after the initial reunion (Heinicke & Westheimer, 1966; Robertson & Bowlby, 1952). We suggested that both mother avoidance in the strange situation and detachment during and after longer separations served a defensive function. Our next clue (Ainsworth, Bell, & Stayton, 1971) was to note that the mothers of Group-A infants were more rejecting than either Group-B or Group-C mothers. The major progress in interpretation of Group-A behavior is due to the work of Main, both through her own research with the infants of Samples 3 and 4 and through intensive additional analyses of our home data in Sample 1 (Main, 1973, 1977a; Blehar, Ainsworth, & Main, 1978). In the interpretation which follows we are deeply indebted to Main and her work.

Mothers of Group-A babies were indeed demonstrated to be rejecting. One major way in which they rejected their infants was to rebuff infant desire for close bodily contact. These mothers themselves tended to find close contact with their babies aversive. Furthermore, Main confirmed the implications of our acceptance-rejection rating scale, in that Group-A mothers tend more frequently to be angry with and irritated by their babies than other mothers; even though they attempt to suppress expression of anger, videotape records make it manifest to the careful observer. It is perhaps because of chronically suppressed anger that Group-A mothers tend to lack mobility in their characteristic facial expression while in interaction with their infants. GroupA mothers are also found to be characteristically rigid and compulsive. This trait is likely to activate anger when the baby's demands interrupt the mother's ongoing activities or when he does not instantly do what she wants him to do. Whether because irritation engenders rough handling or because compulsiveness leads to the use of physical force, the mother tends to give her baby unpleasant experiences in the context of physical contact. Furthermore, the unresponsiveness or overt rebuff a baby experiences from a mother who finds physical contact with him aversive itself constitutes a frustrating, unpleasant experience.

Those babies in Sample 1 who were eventually identified as Group-A babies on the basis of their strange-situation behavior were at the beginning quite capable of responding positively to close bodily contact—as the visitor-observers themselves ascertained by picking up the babies. We assume that they, like other human infants, wanted contact with their mother when the attachment-behavioral system was activated at high intensity. Maternal rebuff itself (Bowlby, 1969) is a condition that activates or increases the intensity of activation of attachment behavior. On the other hand, their unhappy experiences with their mothers in the context of close bodily contact set the stage for the approach–avoidance conflict over close contact with their mothers that seems characteristic of A babies.

In Chapter 7 we detailed the various behaviors that made this conflict manifest to the observer of their behavior at home. Main suggested that another outcome of their experience was that their attachment behavior, even though more frequently aroused than in the case of babies who have experienced little rebuff, tended not to be terminated, for they rarely had the well-rounded experience of being cuddled and soothed by their mothers that is the most effective terminator of intensely activated attachment behavior. Following Bowlby's (1973) proposition that the continuing frustration of attachment behavior experienced in a major separation engenders anger, Main (1977a) argued that Group-A infants, whose attachment behavior is also chronically frustrated, tend to be angry infants. It is difficult for an observer to distinguish the expression of anger from the expression of other feelings and emotions, such as fear or distress, in the case of a young infant. By the fourth quarter of the first year, however, it becomes feasible to do so. A coder working without knowledge of strange-situation classifications yielded data that demonstrated that Group-A babies were indeed more frequently angry than the other infants of Sample 1.

Let us return to a consideration of avoidant behavior in the reunion episodes of the strange situation. The most striking avoidance is steadfast ignoring of the mother, despite her efforts to coax the baby to come to her. It is striking also when the baby begins to approach his mother but then suddenly turns away or moves away from her. Also classed as avoidant behavior, however, are instances in which the baby, having looked at or even greeted his mother, averts his gaze, thus interrupting or discouraging interaction between them.

Gaze aversion in the strange situation is common enough, but it usually occurs in Episode 3, in response to the stranger's entrance and/or approach. Thus, it is not the behavior pattern, gaze aversion, that is unusual per se, but the fact that it occurs with reference to the mother in a context in which the normative response is either to gain contact with her or at least to reestablish interaction with her. Gaze aversion in early infancy has been suggested by Stern (1974) to be a baby's means of modulating his level of arousal when in face-to-face encounters with his mother. Intermittent gaze aversion alternates with interaction, as though the baby had occasionally to look away in order to cope with the presumably pleasant but exciting engagement. Bronson (1972) and Sroufe, Waters, and Matas (1974) have also suggested that gaze aversion, in the context of encounter with strangers, may constitute a coping mechanism. Yet gaze aversion, as well as other modes of avoidant behavior that occur in the 1-year-old in the context of reunion with the mother seems to be of a different order.

Main (1977a) offers a hypothesis that, in our opinion, both accounts for avoidant behavior toward the mother in the strange situation and links this response to the other findings on gaze aversion in human infants. She draws on Chance's (1962) hypothesis that gaze aversion can be interpreted as a "cut-off behavior." Examples of cut-off behavior—averting the eyes, turning the head away or down, displacing or redirecting the attention, and closing the eyes— are identical with behaviors that we have classed as avoidance behavior. Chance observed this kind of behavior in terns, gulls, and other birds (but also in rats) in the context of an approach–avoidance conflict. For example, the male black-headed gull, a highly territorial creature, experiences conflict in courtship because he not only acts so as to attract a female into his territory but also has strong tendencies either to fight with or flee from any conspecific who intrudes on his territory. In the course of the courtship display, after a female has approached, the male shows certain postures that are clearly avoidance— averting the gaze and posturing so as to turn away from the prospective mate. Chance suggests that the sight of the partner might activate the aversive drives of flight or aggression, whereas looking and turning away defuses the situation, so that the male can stay in the proximity of the female rather than either fleeing from her or driving her away, thus leaving the possibility open for further, more constructive interaction when his arousal level has been lowered by the cut-off behavior.[1]

_____

[1]Robert Hinde has drawn to our attention that Tinbergen had an alternative explanation for the turning away of the head in black-headed gulls (Tinbergen, 1959).

This hypothesis seems to be very relevant to an infant's averting his gaze from his mother, and indeed to other forms of avoidant behavior as well. Assuming that the infant, like the black-headed gull, has an approach–avoidance conflict, avoidant behavior tends to reduce the arousal level engendered by the conflict, and yet also to enable the infant to remain in proximity to his mother. To remain in proximity to his mother ensures not only that the biological function of attachment (i.e., protection) is operative but also that the situation is left open to the possibility of subsequent positive interaction.

Our interpretation of the paradoxical behavior shown by Group-A babies in the strange situation focused on the proposition that their attachment behavior was strongly activated both in the separation episodes (even though they tended not to show distress overtly) and in the reunion episodes (even though they avoided their mothers). Support for this proposition comes from Sroufe and Waters (1977b), who found characteristic heart-rate acceleration in both separation and reunion episodes among Group-A babies, as well as among B and C infants. Furthermore, just as the strange situation activates the attachment system at a higher level of intensity than the low-stress conditions normally pertaining at home (or in free-play laboratory sessions), it also activates A babies' approach–avoidance conflict more intensely so that the avoidant outcome is more conspicuous. The tendency for Group-A infants to maintain exploration at a relatively high level across separation and reunion episodes was interpreted in Chapter 7 as a displacement behavior. This interpretation is also supported by Sroufe and Waters, who report absence of the intermittent decelerations of heart rate that normally occur in exploratory activity, as though the displacement exploration lacked the moments of interested attentiveness characteristic of true exploration.

Our emphasis upon conflict relevant to close bodily contact in Group-A babies should not make us lose sight of the fact that they are anxious as well as avoidant. They show more separation distress in little everyday separation situations at home than do Group-B babies, and they cry more in general. Their mothers, like the mothers of Group-C infants, are relatively unresponsive to infant signals and communications throughout many contexts in the course of the first year. Indeed the rigidity and suppressed anger of Group-A mothers would obviously interfere with sensitive responsiveness to infant cues. Consequently, Group-A babies, like Group-C babies, lack confidence in their mothers' accessibility and responsiveness. The anxiety implicit in the Group-A attachment relationship surely must itself make the approach–avoidance conflict more intense than it might otherwise be, for the attachment behavior of an anxious baby tends to be more readily activated and at a more intense level. Furthermore, as Bowlby (1969) pointed out, rebuff itself intensifies attachment behavior.

Nevertheless the avoidant behavior characteristic of the Group-A baby in the strange situation represents a method of coping with a very difficult kind of conflict situation. Avoidance short circuits direct expression of anger to the attachment figure, which might be dangerous, and it also protects the baby from reexperiencing the rebuff that he has come to expect when he seeks close contact with his mother. It thus somewhat lowers his level of anxiety (arousal). It also leads him to turn to the neutral world of things, even though displacement exploratory behavior is devoid of the true interest that is inherent in nonanxious exploration.

What the long-term outcome of mother avoidance in infancy may be is yet to be ascertained. The findings of Connell (1976), Main (1973, 1977b; Main & Londerville, 1978), and Matas (1977) strongly suggest, however, that the Group-A pattern persists into the second year of life, with consequent deficiencies in exploratory behavior and cooperativeness and difficulties with inappropriate aggression and in establishing harmonious interaction with adult figures. Furthermore, Main and Londerville found that they showed continuing tendencies to avoid the mother. To be sure, it is possible that both Group-A and Group-C children may later experience better interaction with their mothers or somehow find other relationships that offer compensatory experiences for a continuing anxious attachment to the mother figure. Even so, it may well be that early experiences of anxiety and conflict in the mother–attachment relationship are difficult to overcome altogether, that the anxiously-attached infant may grow into a child who is very cautious about trusting the accessibility and responsiveness of later attachment figures, and that the mother–avoidant infant may continue to be somewhat detached in his interpersonal relationships, and chary of establishing close interactions. Longitudinal research is desperately needed. In such research, behavior in the strange situation at the end of the first year might well provide an anchor point against which subsequent developments could be judged.

Assertion of the future value of the strange situation in longitudinal research provides us with an occasion for inserting a note of caution about the scoring of avoidant and resistant behavior (especially the former) in the reunion episodes. To the untutored eye, avoidance is not easy to see. The Group-A infant who is active, not distressed, not wary with the stranger, and who does not cling to his mother in the reunion episodes appears to many—including experienced developmental psychologists—as a robust, friendly, independent child. It is only when one is reminded that this is an unusual way for a 1-year-old to behave in separation and reunion episodes in a strange environment and that only infants who have had a characteristic kind of experience of rejection by their mothers show this pattern, that one is inclined to take avoidance seriously. Looking away (gaze aversion) can be distinguished from looking toward something or someone else, even without the benefit of heart-rate monitoring. The baby does not seem to be looking at anything in particular when he averts his gaze, but at the floor or at his hands; and even though he may look toward some specific aspect of the physical environment, such as a toy, he gives no evidence of interest. Similarly, ignoring the mother in the reunion episodes is viewed as avoidance because of the context in which it appears—the mother's return after an absence and usually also her efforts to attract the baby's attention and/or approach. As Marvin (1977) has shown, 3- and 4-year-olds who do not seek proximity to their mothers on reunion nevertheless tend not to ignore her, but rather converse with her, show her what they have been playing with, and the like. At home a baby may be so preoccupied with his play that he notices neither when his mother leaves the room nor when she returns. This cannot be the case with the 1-year-old in the strange situation who registers his mother's departure when she says "Bye, bye!" to him, who may even search for her when she is absent, but who steadfastly refuses to acknowledge her return, except perhaps with an initial neutral look. Furthermore, even postural adjustments that imply turning away may be overlooked if one is not trained to observe avoidance.

At high levels of intensity of activation, resistant behavior is more difficult to overlook. But minor and subtle manifestations of resistance, especially when not accompanied by any overt angry behavior, may pass unnoticed by the inexperienced observer. As with avoidant behavior, the observation of resistant behavior requires training and/or experience.

CONCLUSION

From the beginning our interest in the strange situation was focused on individual differences. As we pointed out in the preface to this volume, the procedure was devised as a standardized laboratory situation in which we could observe behavior of infants about whom we already had much information concerning behavior in the natural environment of the home. Even though the three questions we hoped would be clarified by the strange situation were, in a sense, normative questions (i.e., use of mother as a secure base for exploration, response to separation, and response to a stranger—all in an unfamiliar environment), the major thrust of this aspect of our research has focused on individual differences.

Quite beyond our initial expectations, we submit, the strange situation has proved useful for the identification and exploration of individual differences in the quality of infant–mother attachment. Nevertheless we must emphasize that individual differences in strange-situation behavior would have been well-nigh uninterpretable without extensive data about correlated individual differences in other situations, and especially without the naturalistic data that we collected in regard to Sample 1 at home throughout the first year of life. To be sure, one should be conservative in generalizing from a sample of 23 infants from whom both longitudinal, naturalistic data and strange-situation data were available. The many confirming studies that compare strange-situation behavior with behavior in other situations served sufficiently to overcome our basic conservatism and to prompt this book, in the belief that the total effort herein presented (1) throws important light on the concept of infant–mother attachment as viewed from an evolutionary–ethological standpoint, and (2) offers a procedure, much better validated than others, for assessing individual differences in attachment. Research into early social development has been greatly handicapped by a dearth of valid measures. Furthermore, evaluation of alternative methods of infant care—including evaluation of interventions— has also been handicapped by lack of appropriate and valid measures of outcome. It is our hope that this detailed account of strange-situation behavior and its correlates may be useful in future research, much of which must necessarily be focused on the effect on social development in general (and on attachment in particular) of various alternative modes of infant care, whether occurring naturally or as a result of programs of intervention.

We would be the first to acknowledge that research into the important attachments a person forms in the course of his life span has just begun. It made sense to us to begin at the beginning, and to focus on what is obviously one of the most important attachments—namely, that of an infant to his mother figure or principal caregiver. It is our hope that our work relevant to this early and important attachment will provide a useful background for further investigation of both this and other types of attachment. Let us acknowledge that research into attachment relationships is extremely complex. It is a pity that this complexity and difficulty so long delayed a beginning. Let us hope that we can dare to continue to face these complexities and difficulties, and finally tackle intensive and comprehensive research into one of the most important aspects of human behavior and development.

| # Instructions to the Mother

This is a set of instructions to explain what will happen from the moment you arrive at Room —— in ——. Here we will discuss any questions about the observation of the baby in the strange situation, and leave coats. When we are all ready to proceed, you will be shown the door of the observation room, then taken into the experimental room. You will stay with your baby in the experimental room until the end of Episode 3 (see below). Then you may go into the observation room to watch him/her through a one-way vision mirror.

We would like to stress an important aspect of your role in the strange situation: Try to be as natural in your responsiveness to the baby as you would generally be. Do not actively engage him in play with the toys in the first three episodes until we give you the signal to do so, but feel free to respond to his advances (smiling, approaching, etc.) as you ordinarily would at home. If the baby is distressed at any time while you are in the room, please feel free to react as you normally would in order to make him comfortable again. We want to watch the baby's spontaneous response to the toys and to the strangeness of the situation. For this reason we ask the mother not to intervene and attract her baby's attention. Yet we don't want the baby to feel that his mother is acting strangely.

Thus, yours is a delicate task of reassuring the baby of your support as you would normally do when he seems to need it, without interfering with his exploratory behavior.

EPISODES

Episode 1. Mother, Baby, Experimenter. We will show you into the experimental room with the baby. We want to see how the baby reacts to a new environment from the safety of his mother's arms. You will therefore carry the baby into the room. The experimenter will show you where to put him down and where you are to sit, and then he (she) will leave.

Episode 2.   Mother, Baby (3 minutes).   As soon as the experimenter has left, you are to put the baby down on the floor on the specified spot, facing the toys. You then go to your chair and pretend to read a magazine. You will respond to the baby quietly if he makes overtures to you, or reassure him if he is uneasy or upset, but you are not to try to attract the baby's attention. We want to see the kind of interest the baby has in a new situation. If the baby spontaneously begins to play with the toys or to explore the room, we let him continue to do so without interruption for 3 minutes. If, at the end of 2 minutes, he has not begun to play with the toys, a knock will sound on the wall signaling you to take him over to the toys and to try to arouse his interest in them. Then, after a moment, you will go back to your chair, and we will see what he does for 1 additional minute.

Episode 3.   Stranger, Mother, Baby (3 minutes).   A stranger—a woman—enters, introduces herself briefly, and then goes to her chair, across the room from yours, and sits quietly for 1 minute. Then she will engage you in conversation for 1 minute, and, finally, she will invite the baby's attention for 1 minute. Throughout this, you are to sit quietly in your chair and talk only when the stranger talks with you. The first two knocks on the wall will be cues to the stranger to change her activities. We wish to observe the baby's responses to gradually increased attention from a stranger, with his mother present but not active. When the third knock comes, you are to leave the room as unobtrusively as possible leaving your handbag behind on your chair. Please close the door when you leave.

Episode 4.   Stranger, Baby (3 minutes or less).   You are to come to the observation room to watch the baby through the one-way glass. Meanwhile the stranger remains with the baby. We want to see what the baby's interest is in an unfamiliar room with only a stranger present. Some babies become upset when their mothers leave. Should your baby become too upset, we will terminate the episode. If you feel that the episode should be terminated, just tell us, and you can go back to the experimental room immediately.

Episode 5.   Mother, Baby (3 minutes or more).   Someone will tell you when it is time to begin the episode. You will go to the door of the experimental room and, before opening it, call to the baby loudly enough for him to hear you through the closed door. Pause a moment, then open the door and pause again. We are interested to see how the baby will greet his mother spontaneously after she has been absent. After this pause, greet the baby and make him comfortable for the next episode, finally settling him on the floor, interested in the toys. After 3 minutes, or when the observer judges that the baby is settled enough to be ready for the next episode, he will signal by a knock on the wall. This will give you your cue to leave the baby alone in the room.

Episode 6. *Baby Alone* (3 minutes or less).   After the knock comes, pick a moment when the baby seems cheerfully occupied with the toys, get up, put your handbag on your chair, and go to the door. Pause at the door to say "bye-bye" to the baby, and then leave the room, closing the door behind you. Come again to the observation room to watch him through the one-way glass. We want to see how the baby reacts to your departure and what he will do all by himself in a strange room. He may be quite content, but if he becomes too upset we will terminate the episode.

Episode 7. *Stranger, Baby* (3 minutes or less).   The stranger enters, and we can see how the baby reacts to a stranger, without his mother present and after being alone. If he has been unhappy without his mother, we want to see whether he can be comforted by a stranger. In any case, we want to see whether he will play with her or with the toys in her presence.

Episode 8. *Mother, Baby* (3 minutes).   Someone will tell you when it is time to go back into the experimental room. This time you can go directly in, but after opening the door pause for a moment to see what the baby will do spontaneously when he sees you. Then talk to him for a moment, then pick him up. We will come to the door to tell you when the episode is over. In the meantime do whatever seems the natural thing to do under the circumstances.

Instructions for Coding and Tabulating Frequency of Behaviors

INSTRUCTIONS FOR CODING

General

Coding is undertaken for each 15-second time interval, for each episode separately. The frequency of the behavior is measured in terms of the number of time intervals in which it occurs.

When the account of more than one observer is used, it may be found that what one observer reports at the end of one time interval a second observer may report at the beginning of the next time interval. The rule for coding is to assign the score to the time interval in which it was first reported by one observer.

In general, if a behavior item is reported by one observer but not by another, it is assumed to have occurred and will be coded. The chief discrepancies between reports tend to be in respect to direction of visual regard and facial expression, behaviors that one observer may be able to see but not the other. Sometimes, however, an observer intent on one aspect of the baby's behavior may not see a relevant bit of behavior that another observer picks up, or may see it but not squeeze it into his verbal description. There are occasional discrepancies between reports that cannot be dealt with by this rule of thumb, however. In these instances the coder must exercise judgment about which report to use in his coding. The following rules will be observed in regard to demarcation of the episodes. Episode 2 begins when B has been put down (whether or not the observer has left). Episodes 3 and 7 begin as soon as the stranger enters, and Episodes 5 and 8 begin when the mother actually comes in the door. Episodes 4 and 6 begin when the mother actually goes out the door. Mother crossing the room belongs to Episodes 3 and 5. Episode 8 ends when someone comes in to tell the mother the situation is over. Code until that point. In the case of an incomplete time interval at the beginning or end of an episode, behavior occurring in it will be coded: (1) as part of the coding of the time interval immediately following (or, in the case of the end of the episode, preceding) if the part interval is clearly less than half of a 15-second standard interval; or (2) as a separate interval if the part interval is half or more of a standard 15-second interval.

Preparation of the Coding Sheet

An 11″ × 8½″ page of squared paper will be divided into columns, headed:

1. Episode and time interval
2. Locomotion
3. Body movement*
4. Body posture*
5. Hand movements
6. Visual regard
7. Location
8. Contact (Adult)*
9. Contact (Baby)*
10. Crying
11. Vocalization
12. Oral behavior
13. Smiling
14. Remarks

Each row will be devoted to the coding of behaviors occurring in one time interval. The time intervals will be numbered from the beginning of each episode. The end of each episode will be indicated by a line drawn across the page. The three sections of Episode 3 will also be divided by lines drawn across the page.

The coding symbols and instructions for using them are presented in the following sections. *Note:* It is helpful to refer to the tabulation rules while coding.

---

*Behaviors included under these headings have not yet been used by us in frequency measures. Recent ethological studies of young humans suggest that bodily movements and orientation, as well as hand gestures and facial expression, are noteworthy social behaviors. We therefore did not omit body movement and posture from this set of instructions. As for the contact items, they are useful descriptively, even though they represent some overlap with the system for scoring interactive behavior.

Coding of Locomotion

The mode of locomotion will be indicated as:

W = walk
Cp = creep on hands and knees
Cr = crawl on belly
Hi = hitch; B hitches himself along in a sitting position

The *objective* of the locomotion (if any) will be indicated by an arrow; W → M = walk to mother. The objectives will be indicated as:

M = mother
S = stranger
T = toy
D = door
Ch_M = mother's chair
Ba_M = mother's handbag
M_i = moves to M at M's invitation.
S_i = moves to S at S's invitation.
T_M = moves to toy being manipulated by M.
T_S = moves to toy being manipulated by S.
(E) = moves in an exploratory way, even though not to a specific toy or other physical objective.

Avoidance behavior will also be coded, when B clearly moves away from a person—whether the stranger or the mother in the reunion episodes—not merely happening to move away from the person in the course of approaching a toy. The person avoided will be indicated by an arrow, thus: W S →. In Episode 3 the baby may at the same time avoid the stranger and approach the mother. This will be coded as follows: W S → M.

To prepare for tabulation, we distinguish exploratory locomotion from other locomotion. Exploratory locomotion is locomotion in the course of which a baby crawls, creeps, walks, or hitches about, either to explore the physical environment including the toys, or merely to engage in the activity itself. Included are such items as: Cp → T; Cp (E); Cp → D (in Episodes 2, 3, 5, or 8); Cp → T; or Cp → T_S, provided that the approach seems to be to the toy that the adult is manipulating and not to the adult herself.

All locomotions other than exploratory locomotions will be circled, so that they may subsequently be identified easily and excluded from the tabulations of exploratory locomotion. To be excluded are approach and following behavior (e.g., Cp → M; Cp → S), search behavior in the separation episodes (e.g., Cp → D or Cp → Ch_M), or random locomotion when a baby is acutely distressed.

Occasionally an observer may have failed to describe locomotion, but locomotion may be inferred from the coding of B's location. Thus, if B is said to be in square 5 in one time-interval and in square 7 in another, it may be assumed that there was locomotion, unless, of course, he was moved by M or S. Inferred locomotion will also be noted.

Body Movement

Body movement refers to movement not involving locomotion. Coding of such movements are included for descriptive completeness but, to date, have not been used in statistical comparisons. Suggested coding symbols are:

 St = stands up.
 Sq = squats or stoops.
  L = leans body forward.
  R = reaches with arms, with body leaning forward.
  G = gross motor movement, such as bouncing, rocking, jiggling.
  T = twists.
  K = kicks feet.
 Si = sits down.
 Kn = kneels.
 Th = throws self about, thrashes.
 Cp = gets into a creeping position.
 Rig = becomes rigid, stiffens.
 Pi = pivots.
  F = falls.

For some movements the objective will also be indicated. Thus L_M = leans toward mother.

Coded items that are clearly social in their implications, or are clearly related to separation anxiety, to response to reunion, or that otherwise imply emotional disturbance will be circled in order to draw attention to them. Thus Ⓖ may indicate that B is rocking in distress, or bouncing with delight upon mother's return.

Body Posture

Body posture will be recorded for time intervals in which neither locomotion nor body movement is recorded. Suggested symbols are:

 Si = sitting
 Cp = on hands and knees in a creeping position
  P = prone, lying flat on belly
 Su = supine, lying on back

St = standing
Sq = squatting or stooping
Kn = kneeling
Hu = hunched into a little bundle

Again, coded items that are clearly related to emotional disturbance will be circled. Thus: (Hu) .

Hand Movements

Hand movements with respect to persons or objects will be coded, and those related to persons will be represented by circling the coded symbol. Suggested symbols are:

T = touch, without taking hold of or grasping.
F = fingers; refers to random fingering while attending to something else, rather than to exploratory manipulation.
G = grasps or picks up; refers to the initial grasping and not to holding onto something over a period of time.
FM = fine manipulation, exploring with the fingers, moving parts of an object with the fingers, turning an object over in order to examine it, and so on. Included here also will be exploratory fingering, such as fingering a textured object. We also counted as FM an attempt, successful or otherwise, to place a ball in a hole, a shape in a slot, an object in the toy milk bottle; or an attempt to remove an object from a narrow or tight container; or putting sticks through holes in objects.
GM = gross hand movements, such as patting, squeezing, banging, pushing, pulling, throwing, shaking, and knocking something over. GM does not necessarily imply a large, vigorous movement; a little push would be coded GM. In a few instances dropping may be coded as GM, but only if it is part of a repetitive kind of pick-up-and-drop- or -throw play. Often dropping is mere releasing and should not be coded GM, because it has no exploratory implications.
R = reaching with the hands.
GM_A = an angry push, or angry throwing away, etc.
O = offers toy to a person.
Ta = takes toy from person.
Ge = a gesture with no obvious relationship to a toy or to a person.

The chief coding difficulties are encountered in distinguishing between fine and gross manipulatory movements—that is, between FM and GM. The distinction is difficult to make for 1-year-olds, although it tends to be clear enough with older children. When in doubt, code GM.

It is assumed that T, F, G, FM, GM, and R refer to toys unless otherwise specified. If the object is a person, this should be indicated. Thus:

R_M = reaches toward M.
O_M. = offers toy to M.
T_{aS} = takes toy from S's hand.
F_B = fingers some part of his own body, face, ear, etc.
F_{Cl} = fingers his own clothing.

Unusual objects, such as the doorstop, books, and so on, may be indicated by a jotted note; or if they are clearly part of the whole pattern of exploratory manipulation of the environment, they may be considered equivalent to toys, and no subscript or note added.

Hand movements with a subscript referring to persons will be circled, for these are generally considered social and are not included in the statistical frequency count of exploratory manipulation. Fingering of one's own body or clothing may frequently be considered a tension movement; if this is the case, the item is circled.

Some babies suck and chew toys or otherwise put them to their mouths. When they grasp such an object to take it to or from the mouth, this is not to be coded G, but rather to be considered part of the oral activity and coded in another column.

It may be noted that only uncircled R, G, GM, and FM are included in the statistical count for exploratory manipulation. T and F are excluded. Nevertheless they are retained in the coding for descriptive purposes—they suggest that B is being very tentative or muted in his attempts to explore manually.

Visual Regard

The critical distinction here is whether the visual regard is directed toward a toy or some other aspect of the physical environment in an exploratory sense, or whether it is directed toward a person or some aspect of the physical environment, such as the door or mother's chair during her absence, which may be assumed to be associated with the person.

M = mother, either face or body or both
S = stranger, either face or body or both
Ex = experimenter (chiefly in Episode 1)
T = toy, or the pile of toys collectively
D = door
Ch_M = mother's chair
Ba_M = mother's handbag, left behind when she leaves
W = one-way-mirror windows

   Ca = camera or cameraman
    E = some other aspect of the physical environment
 Det = detached; the baby either is so withdrawn or is crying so hard that he
          may be assumed not to have visual regard, even though his eyes may
          seem fixed on something.

The coding of visual regard sometimes depends on inference. Thus if the baby is moving toward a toy, or manipulating it, it is usually a reasonable inference that he is also looking at it, or if he is approaching a person he is also looking at her. Special subscripts will be used, however, when a person directs the baby's visual regard:

   T_S = toy manipulated, offered, or shown by the stranger
   T_M = toy manipulated, offered, or shown by the mother
   S_T = stranger, while she manipulates, offers, or shows a toy
   M_T = mother, while she manipulates, offers, or shows a toy

The distinctions between T_M and M_M between T_S and S_T are sometimes difficult to make, but they are important. M_T and S_T will be used when the baby seems to be looking both at the adult and at what the adult is doing with a toy, and not merely at the toy to which the adult is trying to attract attention. Subsequently, M_T will be tabulated as visual regard toward the mother and S_T as visual regard toward the stranger. T_M and T_S will not, however, be tabulated as visual exploration, for it is assumed that the visual regard of the toy was induced by the action of the adult and therefore lacks the spontaneity characteristic of visual exploration. (Similarly, induced visual regard directed toward some other feature of the physical environment, as, for example, when the adult distracts an unhappy baby by showing him a poster on the wall, will be given a subscript—E_S—so that it is not later counted as visual exploration.)

If the baby looks at a toy at the instigation of the stranger, therefore, it is coded as T_S in the relevant 15-second time interval; but if the baby continues to look at it in a subsequent time interval, after the stranger has ceased manipulating it, then the coding is T. For example, a baby may look at a ball that the stranger is about to roll (T_S), but then may turn to look at the ball after the stranger has rolled it away (T). Or a baby may look at a toy that his mother offers (T_M), take the toy, and continue to look at it as he holds it himself (T).

If a baby looks both at an adult manipulating a toy and also clearly at the toy that she is manipulating, both S_T or M_T and T_S and T_M may be coded in the same time interval.

Although, as stated, it is often necessary to infer the direction of visual regard from what the observer reports the baby as otherwise doing, inference must not be stretched too far. Thus, for example, it cannot be inferred that a baby is looking at an adult because he is being held by her. The adult may be holding the baby up over her shoulder, or on her lap facing out, but even when the position is not specified, it can usually be assumed that the baby is not looking at the adult who is holding him. Therefore visual regard directed toward M or S when the baby is being held is coded only if the observer had specifically reported that the baby looked up at the adult or that he was held in a face-to-face confrontation.

Location

This coding refers to the location of the baby in the room with reference to the squares marked off on the floor. It is intended to indicate where a baby goes on his own initiative and when out of contact with an adult. The coding for each time interval is by the square in which the baby is during that time interval for example, 7 or 6/7 if he is on the line between 6 and 7, or

$$\begin{array}{c|c} 6 & 7 \\ \hline 10 & 11 \end{array}$$

if he is at the point of intersection of the four squares 6, 7, 10, and 11. Movement from one square to another is indicated by arrows. Thus $8 \rightarrow 11 \rightarrow 14$ indicates that the baby moved from square 8 to square 14 through square 11. Be sure to include all squares through which a baby moved to get from one point to another. If the observer(s) did not include all such squares in their dictation, the path of the baby may be reconstructed assuming that he took a direct line from the square in which he started to the square in which he ended up.

Other locations to be noted in the location column are:

O = in an area of the floor outside the grid of squares
H_M = held by the mother
H_S = held by the stranger
C_M = in contact with the mother, but not being held
C_S = in contact with the stranger, but not being held

If the baby is being held, that is all that it is required to note. It is not necessary to trace the location of the adult who is holding the baby.

Contact Adult

In this column is indicated the adult's action in any time interval in which the adult and the baby are in physical contact. This column is descriptively useful, but is not used for any frequency measures. The following symbols may be used:

P/U = adult picks baby up.

P/D = adults puts baby down after holding him.

  H = adult holds the baby.

  M = adult moves the baby from one location to another without picking him up.

H/O = one adult hands the baby over to another adult.

  C = adult maintains physical contact with the baby—for example, keeping an arm around him without actually picking him up or holding him.

If there is any ambiguity about the identity of the adult, the subscript M or S may be added to the contact symbol.

Contact Baby

In this column indicate the baby's action in any time interval in which he is in physical contact with an adult. It is included for descriptive purposes and is not represented in any frequency measure.

The following symbols may be used:

    H = holds on or clings.

    T = touches—that is, with the hands, without grasping or clinging

    C = contact without holding on for example, the baby steadies himself against the mother's knees, or has his back against her knees

   Cl = clambers, tries to climb up on adult's lap.

Res = resists release by adult, by actively holding on or by turning back to make contact again after being released.

  Pr = protests release by adult by crying.

   P = protest or resists being held by the adult.

Crying

Six degrees of crying are distinguished and recorded in this column:

  C_1 = a hard cry, or screaming, and especially crying in which the baby is crying so hard that he seems quite detached from any interest in his environment.

  C_2 = crying; definite crying rather than fussing, but not as hard a cry as in C_1.

  C_3 = fussing; a more muted and less violent kind of crying.

  C_4 = a single cry (or fuss); this is a definite cry (or fuss) but isolated and not repeated. If there is a sequence of separated cries or fusses, they are coded as C_2 or C_3, not C_4.

C_5 = a cry-face; a facial expression characteristic of crying, without; an accompanying vocal crying.

C_6 = an unhappy noise, without an accompanying cry-face; a vocal protest.

Observers may sometimes report "unhappy noises" when perhaps it would be better to have reported fussing or crying. This is probably because at the time they cannot see the baby's face to notice whether or not there is a cry-face. If there is a single report of an unhappy noise or protest, especially if it is specified that there is no cry-face, code C_6. But if there is a series of unhappy noises, code this as fussing (C_3) or as crying (C_2). It may be noted that C_1, C_2, C_3, and C_4 are tabulated as "real crying," whereas C_5 and C_6 are counted as "minimal crying."

Additional codings that are useful for descriptive purposes are:

L = lulls, diminishes intensity of cry, or stops crying momentarily.

S/C = stops crying or fussing (referring only to C_1, C_2, or C_3); if the S/C occurs in the middle of a time interval, it may be assumed that the baby cried earlier in the interval, and the same cry coding will be carried forward that was coded in the previous interval.

A lull presents some difficulty if it occupies a whole time interval. Then it is important to indicate whether the lull is a mere diminution in intensity; in this it would be better to code a shift—say, from C_2 to C_3 or from C_1 to C_2. In this way the crying behavior for the time interval in question can be scored as "real crying" even though there has been a reduction in intensity. Sometimes, if a baby is really screaming, he may let out one burst and then hold his breath for a while as though merely gathering his strength for the next burst, with his face meanwhile contorted and usually red. If such a silent period should occupy a whole 15-second time interval, the coding of crying must reflect the context of the sequence and not isolated fragments. Thus there is no sense in a sequence of C_4, C_4, and C_4. This is obviously intermittent crying or fussing, and thus should be recorded in successive time intervals as C_2, C_2, and C_2 or as C_3, C_3, and C_3.

For the purposes of the descriptive summary, in which response to separation is of interest, it is significant to note other manifestations of distress than crying. Although some or all of these may be noted in other columns, it is useful to highlight them by repeating the entry in the crying column. For example, note in conjunction with crying such behaviors as random crawling, hunching into an abandoned little bundle, burying the face against the floor, detached visual regard, or eyes closed. Similarly, "tension movements" such as hunching, stretching, rubbing the ear, rubbing the back of the neck, and the like may give the clear impression that they occur as part of an effort not to cry. If so, mention may be made of these in the crying column.

Vocalization

In this column merely enter a check mark for each time interval in which a baby emits a vocalization not codable as a cry. Wherever possible indicate by a subscript whether the vocalization seems clearly directed to M or to S. Thus $\sqrt{}$ indicates a mere vocalization, whereas $\sqrt{}$ M indicates a vocalization directed to the mother. Vocalizations occasionally include laughs; these are infrequent enough not to require a symbol, but may be represented in a written entry. Coughs will also be noted, but will not be included in the subsequent tabulation of vocalizations; it cannot be assumed that coughs are social or communicative, as vocalizations tend to be.

Oral

In this column indicate oral behavior of the sucking, chewing, mouthing, or mouth-movement variety, but neither vocalization nor kissing nor biting. (Vocalization will be recorded in the "vocalization" column, and kissing and biting are considered "interactive" and should be noted in the "remarks" or contact baby column.) Symbols for oral behavior are:

F = chews or sucks finger(s) or thumb.
T = chews or sucks toy, or puts it into his mouth.
P = has pacifier in his mouth.
B = has nipple of bottle in his mouth.
M = mouth movements of a conspicuous sort, without
 having any object in the mouth to chew or suck on.

Do not record as oral putting a finger or toy "to the mouth" or moving it "toward the mouth." The object has to go into the mouth to be counted.

Smile

In this column will be recorded a baby's smiles. In lieu of check marks the following symbols will be used to indicate whether or not a smile was directed toward a person.

M = smiles at the mother.
S = smiles at the stranger.

E = smiles, but not at a person; smiles, perhaps
while playing with a toy or while exploring.

A mere "pleasant face" will not be coded as a smile, but "little smiles" and "half-smiles" may be so coded.

Remarks

Because the coding sheet has a generally descriptive use, as well as being a source of frequency tabulations, the use of the "remarks" column is encouraged. In it can be recorded behaviors or aspects of behavior that are not represented in the coding system, or highlights of behavior that were particularly striking.

INSTRUCTIONS FOR TABULATION

The following behaviors will be tabulated:

1. Exploratory locomotion
2. Exploratory manipulation
   (a) fine manipulation
   (b) gross manipulation
   (c) total manipulation
3. Visual exploration
4. Visual orientation
   (a) to Mother
   (b) to Stranger
5. Change of location
6. Crying
   (a) "Real" crying
   (b) "Minimal" crying
   (c) Total crying
7. Vocalization
8. Oral behavior
9. Smiling
   (a) to Mother
   (b) to Stranger
   (c) All smiling

In this analysis we are concerned only with Episodes 2 through and including 8. Episode 1 is omitted because it is so brief.

It is assumed that each of the episodes consists of 12 time intervals of 15 seconds each. If an episode contains 13 or more time intervals (as is often the case, particularly with Episode 5), or fewer than 12 (as is the case if the episode was curtailed), the frequency measure will be prorated. Thus, for example, if Episode 4 lasted 3 minutes and 15 seconds, (i.e., 13 time intervals) the frequency for the episode would be expressed as 12/13 of the actual frequency. Or if Episode 6 lasted only 2 minutes (i.e., 8 time intervals), the frequency would be expressed as 12/8 of the actual frequency.

To prepare the tabulation sheet allow a double column for each of the behaviors listed above. In the left-hand column state the obtained frequency, and in the right-hand column state the prorated frequency (or repeat the obtained frequency if it does not need to be prorated). To assist in the prorating, you will find it convenient to have a column at the extreme left showing the number of time intervals in each episode.

Episode 3 presents a special problem, for it consists of three segments of 1 minute (4 time intervals) each. When prorating, each segment is to be dealt with separately, assuming each to have four time intervals. Thus, for example, if the third segment lasted 1 minute and 15 seconds, the frequency for that segment would be 4/5 of the obtained frequency. Once each segment has thus been dealt with, the corrected frequencies of the three segments are summed.

The details for tabulation of the behaviors are as follows:

Exploratory Locomotion

This is locomotion in the course of which a baby creeps about (or crawls, walks, or hitches), either to explore the physical environment, including the toys, or merely to perform the activity itself.

Included are:

1. Locomotion to the toys (e.g., $Cp \rightarrow T$), even to one that is being manipulated, offered, or shown by an adult (e.g., $W \rightarrow T_S$).
2. Locomotion to any other aspect of the physical environment (except for the door or the mother's chair in the separation episodes).
3. Locomotion for its own sake—for example, $Cp \rightarrow (E)$.

Excluded are the following:

1. Approach to a person (e.g., $Cp \rightarrow M$, $W \rightarrow S$).
2. Following a person (e.g., $Cp \rightarrow M$).
3. Search behavior in separation episodes (e.g., $W \rightarrow D$, $Cp \rightarrow Ch_M$).
4. Moving away from a person in a way that is interpreted as avoidance (e.g., $Cp\ S \rightarrow$).

5. Random locomotion shown by some babies while acutely distressed. This tabulation is easier if all behaviors to be excluded had been circled in the course of coding them.

Exploratory Manipulation

This refers to hand movements that are exploratory—that is, directed to toys or some aspect of the physical environment with manipulatory or exploratory intent (or, indeed, in play); it is intended to exclude hand movements that are part of social interaction or physical contact, or that are merely expressive of affect or are random.

Included in the FM column is:

FM—fine manipulation of a toy or other object.

Included in the GM column are:

GM—"gross" manipulation of a toy or other object.
  R—reaching with the hands for a toy or some other object, except for the door or doorknob or mother's handbag or chair in the separation episodes.
  G—grasping or picking up a toy or other object.;

The figure in the total column is *not* the sum of the items in the FM and GM columns; it is the total number of time intervals in the episode in which either FM or GM (or R or G) or both occur.

Excluded from the tabulation of exploratory manipulation are:

1. Grasping (G) or reaching (R) for a person or a part of her clothing.
2. T—merely touching an object, even a toy; this is considered too tentative to be exploratory manipulation.
3. F—fingering an object, except when it is clearly a mode of exploring a textured surface. Fingering is often a manifestation of tension and not exploratory.
4. GM_A—implies banging, pushing, or throwing done aggressively, in petulance or anger, and not in exploration.
5. Offering or showing toys to another person, or taking toys offered by another person.
6. Any hand movement directed toward the door, the mother's chair, or mother's handbag in any separation episode.
7. Any hand movement, whether fingering or actual manipulation, that the baby directs toward his own person or clothing.

8. Any sustained holding on to a toy without manipulating it in any way. (Many babies at this age will hold a small toy in one hand for long periods, without looking at it and without manipulating it, even holding on to it while creeping.)
9. Any hand movement, even G or GM, undertaken while crying hard, for this does not seem to be exploratory.
10. Ge—gesture made with the hand, even while holding a toy, when B is not actually manipulating the toy.

Again, it is obvious that tabulation is facilitated if items to be excluded as exploratory manipulation are circled in the course of coding.

Visual Exploration

This refers to behavior in which the baby spontaneously looks at (explores visually) a toy or some other aspect of the physical environment, such as the doorstop, the furniture, or pictures on the wall, or if he looks around the room generally.
  Included are:

  T—the baby looks at a toy spontaneously.
  E—the baby looks at some unspecified aspect of his physical environment (e.g., looks around the room).
  W—the baby looks at the window mirror spontaneously.
  D—the baby looks at the door, except in separation episodes.

  Excluded are:

1. Looking at a person.
2. Looking at the door, the chair, or the mother's handbag in any of the separation episodes.
3. Looking at a toy (T_M or T_S) at the instigation of another person.
4. Looking at the window mirror, the pictures, and the like at the instigation of another person.

Visual Orientation

The interest is in the proportion of time spent in looking at the mother or at the stranger, rather than at the toys or other aspects of the physical environment. The frequency counts are made separately for the mother and for the stranger. A score of 1 is given for each time interval in which the baby looks at the mother, whether or not he has also looked at the stranger, at the toys, or at anything else in the same time block. If he glances twice or more at the mother in the same time block, the score is still 1. A similar procedure is to be followed for tabulating frequency of looking at the stranger. The frequency of looking at the toys or at other aspects of the physical environment is identical with the visual-exploration score that has already been obtained.

Included are:

M—looking at Mother.

S—looking at Stranger.

M_T—looking at Mother while she is manipulating a toy or otherwise trying to attract the baby's attention to it; the baby looks at the adult or the adult–toy configuration and not specifically at the toy.

S_T—looking at the Stranger while she is manipulating a toy; similar to M_T.

Excluded are:

T_M and T_S—looking at a toy being manipulated by the adult, or at the instigation of the adult, to be distinguished from M_T and S_T.

Crying

Three columns are provided for crying in the tabulation sheet:

Real crying includes all crying coded as 1, 2, 3, or 4. A score of 1 will be given for each time interval in which crying 1, 2, 3, or 4 occurs, even though there may also be a lull (L), stopping crying (S/C), or crying coded as 5 or 6 in the same time interval.

Minimal crying includes crying coded as 5 or 6. A score of 1 is given for each time interval in which such crying occurs, provided there is no cry in the same time interval that has been coded 1, 2, 3, or 4.

Total crying includes all crying—1, 2, 3, 4, 5, and 6. It is the sum of the other two frequency figures.

If an episode was curtailed because the baby was unduly distressed, it may be assumed that he would have continued to cry throughout all remaining time intervals had the episode not been curtailed. Therefore, instead of prorating such episodes, the time intervals eliminated by the curtailment will be counted as "real crying." Thus if the baby began to cry after 30 seconds had elapsed and continued until the episode was curtailed at 60 seconds, he would receive a score of 10 for crying in that episode.

Vocalization

Because vocalizations at age 1 tend to be discrete rather than continuous (as crying tends to be), and because they are relatively infrequent (in comparison with looks), absolute frequency of occurrence in each episode may be more useful than the frequency measure based on the 15 second time intervals. In either case, include laughs as vocalizations, but not coughs. Score separately vocalizations, directed to the mother, to the stranger, and total vocalizations, including those not clearly directed toward a person.

Smiling

For the same reasons indicated for vocalization, absolute frequency of occurrence of smiling in each episode may be more useful than the frequency measure based on the 15 second time intervals. Score separately smiles to the mother (M), to the stranger (S), and the total number of smiles, including those not clearly directed toward a person (E).

Oral Behavior

This includes oral behavior that is of an autoerotic, tension-reducing variety. It also includes chewing or biting that might be exploratory. In the case of a 1-year-old, it seems age-inappropriate to explore by oral means, and it seems likely that such behavior has at least an element of the autoerotic and tension reducing in it. We have also included here the rare instances in which the baby sucks on the nipple of a bottle or pacifier that has been provided for him.

Score all time intervals, therefore, in which an F, T, P, B, or M has been recorded.

Scoring System for Interactive Behaviors

PROXIMITY- AND CONTACT-SEEKING BEHAVIOR

This variable deals with the intensity and persistence of the baby's efforts to gain (or to regain) contact with—or, more weakly, proximity to—a person, with the highest scores reserved for behavior in which the baby both takes initiative in achieving contact and is effective in doing so on his own account. If an episode contains several instances of proximity-seeking behavior, the episode will be judged in terms of the instance that qualifies for the highest rating, unless otherwise specified below.

7 *Very Active Effort and Initiative in Achieving Physical Contact.* The baby purposefully approaches the adult, creeping, crawling, or walking. He goes the whole way and actually achieves the contact through his own efforts, by clambering up on or grasping hold of the adult. The cooperation of the adult is not required. Contact is more than momentary; the baby does not turn away to other things within 15 seconds.

Note: In Episodes 5, 7, and 8 this top score cannot be used if the initial approach (even though it otherwise meets the above criteria) is delayed substantially (i.e., more than 30 seconds). If, however, there is an initial approach or signal for contact without substantial delay, followed later by another approach meeting the above criteria, the episode may be coded 7, even though the initial bid for contact does not qualify for this coding.

6 *Active Effort and Initiative in Achieving Physical Contact.* This coding will be used for an approach and/or clamber showing initiative and active effort that nearly, but not quite, fulfills the specifications for a coding of 7.

a. The baby purposefully approaches the adult (i.e., he does not merely happen to approach while pursuing a toy). He goes the whole way and then signals by reaching or equivalent behavior that he wants to be picked up; but he does not clamber up or hold on to make contact entirely on his own initiative. He requires the cooperation of the adult in gaining contact.

b. The baby purposefully approaches the adult, going the whole way, and signals his desire to be picked up, but the adult does not cooperate; the adult does not pick him up or hold him, and contact is thus not achieved—*provided that* the baby make *at least two other* active bids for contact within the episode, whether these are successful or not.

c. In episode 5, 7, or 8 an approach that otherwise would be scored 7, except that it is substantially delayed, is scored 6.

d. The baby at least three times does a full approach with clamber and/or brief contact (held only 5 to 15 seconds)—any one of these instances being too brief to qualify for a coding of 6 or 7.

e. The baby does not begin his approach purposefully, but rather approaches in the course of exploration; finding himself close to the adult, he then completes his approach purposefully, and clambers up or holds on, achieving contact (and holding it for more than 15 seconds) on his own initiative.

5 *Some Active Effort to Achieve Physical Contact.* This score will be given to an active effort to achieve contact that in one way or another does not quite fulfill the specifications of a coding of 6.

a. The baby approaches purposefully and fully but does not end the approach even with a reach or other signal (except perhaps for a cry), but rather is picked up without any signal beyond the approach itself.

b. The baby, being held by a stranger, cannot approach his mother through locomotion, but he does the best he can by actively and strongly straining toward her. This straining implies tension involving the whole body and goes beyond mere lifting of arms or a casual reach.

c. The baby, either because he is at the door already or because he is put down by the stranger close to the mother, is too close to approach, but nevertheless he reaches strongly for the pick-up.

d. In Episode 5, 7, or 8 the baby, having delayed substantially in making an active effort to regain contact, now makes a full approach ending with a signal that he wishes to be picked up (either a reach or a cry), but requires adult cooperation to achieve contact.

e. The baby makes at least three active bids for contact (e.g., an approach, a reach, or a "directed cry") at least one of which is a purposeful reach; he may be scored 5 even though he does not complete contact in any of them, presumably because the adult does not cooperate.

4 *Obvious Desire to Achieve Physical Contact, but With Ineffective Effort or Lack of Initiative OR Active Effort to Gain Proximity Without Persisting Toward Contact.*   This middle score, as the heading suggests, is for babies who obviously desire contact but show relatively little active effort or initiative in gaining it, and for babies who are competent and effective in their approach behavior but who are content with minimal contact or with mere proximity.

a. The baby spontaneously (i.e., before the adult approaches and/or offers her hands or invites him) signals his desire to regain contact by a reach, lean, or "directed cry" as though he expected the adult to pick him up. (A "directed cry" is a signal-like cry—either an isolated cry or a distinct increase of intensity of crying—obviously directed toward the adult; it is to be distinguished from continuous or intermittent crying that expresses distress but does not seem to be emitted as an attempt to communicate to the adult a specific desire to be picked up and to be picked up now.)
b. The baby begins to approach the adult but goes only part of the distance, and either with or without a further signal waits for the adult, who completes the pick-up. (If, however, the baby goes a substantial part of the distance and presumably would have gone the whole way had he not been approached by the adult simultaneously, this will be counted as a full approach and given a higher score.)
c. The baby makes repeated full approaches either without completing contact or with only momentary contact.
d. baby makes a full approach, obviously wanting contact, but the adult does not cooperate and does not pick him up. (See, however, 6b and 5e for specifications of nonreciprocated approaches that may be given higher scores.)
e. The baby makes a full approach that ends in contact (either on the baby's initiative or with the adult's cooperation), but he does so only after the adult has invited him to do so by offering her hands or by otherwise coaxing him to come.

3 *Weak Effort to Achieve Physical Contact OR Moderately Strong Effort to Gain Proximity.*   The baby may display a desire to gain contact but a relatively weak or ineffective effort to implement his desire. Or he may take initiative in approaching the adult in order to interact with her or merely to increase proximity. In the latter case it is quite obvious that the baby does not achieve contact because he does not especially seek it, not because the adult disappoints him by her lack of cooperation.

   a. The baby is distressed, crying, and may be presumed to want contact because he stops crying or at least substantially lulls when he is given contact; but he does not give any specific signal that he wants contact—neither a reach nor an approach nor a "directed cry."

   b. As above the baby is distressed and crying and does reach, lean, or even slightly crawl to indicate his wish for contact—but only after the adult has begun pick-up or has offered her hands, or after a long delay.

   c. The baby makes a spontaneous full approach but neither makes contact nor seems to want to do so. Instead he offers a toy or initiates some other kind of interaction, or he seems content with mere proximity.

   d. The baby makes a spontaneous full approach and either merely touches the adult in an exploratory way or pulls himself into a standing position, giving the clear impression that he is using the adult as he would a chair or other inanimate support and that sustained contact is not the goal. (If, however, the baby remains steadying himself against the adult, he will be assumed to desire contact even though he seems off-hand about it, and will be given a higher score. Category 3d is only for *momentary* contact of this sort.)

   e. The baby spontaneously and deliberately signals his desire for contact with a reach (and with no cry) but, in the face of lack of response from the adult, he does not persist in his bid for contact. (The absence of the cry implies a relatively weak desire for contact.)

   f. The baby, having been invited by the adult to approach across a distance, makes a full approach, which ends neither in contact nor with a signal indicating a wish for contact.

2   *Minimal Effort to Achieve Physical Contact or Proximity.*

   a. The baby begins to approach (in a sort of intention movement) but stops, having gone only a short way, and does not follow up this beginning with any further signals of a desire for contact.

   b. The baby seems to be making a full approach, but changes direction to approach something else, or passes beyond the adult—for example, to go out the door, to the door, or to explore something beyond the adult, without pause for any kind of interaction en route.

   c. After the adult offers her hands, the baby reaches in an almost automatic gesture. The weakness of desire for contact (with the mother) is underlined by the fact that the baby is not even crying when the invitation is given.

1 *No Effort to Achieve Physical Contact or Proximity.* Episodes will be scored 1 whenever the baby is occupied with play and exploration—or with desperate crying—and pays little attention to the adult. In addition, episodes will be scored 1 in which are displayed the following behaviors, which are considered to indicate no effort (and no real desire) to achieve contact proximity.

  a. The baby merely looks, or smiles, or interacts across a distance without any increase of proximity or any signal indicating that contact is desired.
  b. The baby accepts contact, even being picked up, but merely accepts it. He did not indicate his wish for it by a cry, approach, or reach. Even though he had been crying, he shows that he had no particular desire for contact (and this occurs especially with the stranger) by the fact that he neither diminishes his crying nor hugs, clings, nor holds on.
  c. The baby approaches accidentally in the course of exploration or pursuing a rolling toy, and neither makes contact with the adult nor pauses to interact with her when he comes to her.

CONTACT-MAINTAINING BEHAVIOR

This score deals with the degree of activity and persistence in the baby's efforts to maintain contact with the adult once he has gained it, having either approached her to make contact himself or been picked up either with or without having signaled his desire to be picked up. The relevant episodes for interaction with the mother are 2, 3, 5, and 8. The relevant episodes for the stranger are 3, 4, and 7— and, in a few instances, also 8.

Although the baby's behavior is the focus of attention here, it must be viewed within the context of interaction with the adult. Because the adults, as well as the babies, differ in the extent to which they initiate or accept contact, each of the score points has several alternatives, in an attempt to encompass a variety of contingencies.

7 *Very Active and Persistent Effort to Maintain Physical Contact.*

  a. The baby, in the course of contact *lasting over 2 minutes,* shows at least *two* instances of active resistance to release or to cessation of contact— and indeed these efforts are in part responsible for the long period of contact. These efforts include clinging when the adult shifts his position in her arms or attempts to put him down, turning to clutch the adult or to clamber up on her again soon after being put down, or turning to the adult to make closer contact.

b. The adult holds the baby for 2 minutes or more, but does not attempt to release him. The baby, meanwhile, embraces the adult, or sinks in, or reclines against her in a relaxed manner, or otherwise clings to her.

c. The baby initiates contact and remains in contact (e.g., standing holding on to the mother's knee) for over 2 minutes and in addition shows at least two instances of active resistance to cessation of contact.

6 *Active and Fairly Persistent Effort to Maintain Physical Contact.*

a. The baby, in the course of contact lasting between *1 and 2* minutes, shows *at least one* instance of active resistance to release (e.g., by clinging, clambering up, etc.). For the rest of the period of contact, he may be more passive, but even then he shows his desire for contact by sinking in, holding on, or reclining against the adult.

b. The baby, having spontaneously approached the adult, sustains contact for longer than 1 minute, and shows at least *one* active clambering or resisting cessation of contact after the initial behavior that made the contact.

c. The baby, in the course of contact lasting longer than 2 minutes, clings or, if an attempt is made to release him, actively resists it; but when finally put down, he merely cries and makes no active effort to regain contact.

5 *Some Active Effort to Maintain Physical Contact.*

a. The baby, in the course of contact lasting for *less than a minute,* shows *one* marked instance of resistance to release (clinging on attempted release, clambering up after being put down, turning to the adult to make closer contact), which, as it turns out, does result in maintaining contact or at least in delaying the release.

b. Or, he shows *two* instances of active behavior of this sort, neither of which results in more than brief contact.

c. Or, having actively initiated contact by clambering up (or some similarly active behavior), he resists release once even though this may not be a marked instance of resistance.

d. The baby is held by the mother *for more than a minute;* the baby may be crying and/or clinging, but he makes no active effort to resist release or to clamber up again after being put down—although he may perhaps reach a little. The point here is that the baby shows his desire for contact by clinging or by diminishing crying, but the adult's response to his behavior (continued holding) gives him no opportunity to demonstrate more active behavior in maintaining physical contact, at least not until after the contact has been long enough for him to be thoroughly comforted.

e. Or, the baby is held for less than a minute, *clinging markedly,* and protests strongly when put down, even though he may not actively attempt to clamber up or to clutch at the adult in resistance to release.

4 *Obvious Desire to Maintain Physical Contact but Relatively Little Active Effort to Do So.*

a. The baby has been held, perhaps clinging a little, perhaps having diminished his crying when picked up; when put down he decisively protests, giving more than a brief cry.
b. The baby was picked up when he was quite distressed; although he seems not to have been truly comforted by the contact, nevertheless he shows his desire to maintain contact by clinging markedly.
c. The baby, having been picked up when crying, quiets, perhaps with some clinging; after being held for *less than 1 minute*, he is put down; he either makes no protest, or the protest is both considerably delayed and minimal. He may, however, signal briefly by reaching that he would like to maintain contact, but he makes no more effective effort than this to do so.
d. The baby, having been held, is released; he resists release briefly, by attempting to hold on or by clinging briefly, but when this is ineffective he accepts the release without protest and without further effort to maintain contact.

3 *Some Apparent Desire to Maintain Physical Contact but Relatively Little Active Effort to Do So.*

a. The baby initiates contact twice or more during the episode—by approaching and by touching or by clambering up—but each contact is held only briefly and then broken either by the baby himself or by the adult, with no protest or resistance from the baby.
b. The baby initiates contact once during the episode and shows some additional active attachment behavior (beyond that necessary to achieve contact—e.g., clutching, burying the face, reclining against the adult), but does not persist in the contact for more than a few moments, and spontaneously breaks away.
c. The adult initiates the contact, picking the baby up or holding him, with perhaps a signal from the baby (cry or reach); the baby accepts the contact but does not cling; when he is put down he protests briefly with a cry (not merely with an unhappy noise or cry face).
d. The adult initiates the contact, perhaps after a signal from the baby; the contact persists for a minute or more; the baby accepts the contact passively and gives the impression of liking it; but when he is put down he makes no protest.

2 *Physical Contact, but Apparently Little Effort or Desire to Maintain It.*

   a. The baby initiates contact no more than once during the episode, and either breaks it off himself after a few seconds, or, if the adult makes the break, makes no effort to maintain the contact.

   b. The adult initiates contact, and the baby either accepts it briefly and then breaks it or gives a brief, minimal protest (unhappy noise or cry face) when put down.

   c. The adult picks up the baby, who is very distressed; the baby accepts the contact, but, although his crying may diminish, he is not really comforted. When he is put down, he cries and may cry more intensely, but this does not seem so much a definite protest against the cessation of contact as a response to the whole distressing situation. The point is, however, that even though he is very distressed, he seems somewhat less distressed when in contact with the adult than when he is not.

1 *Either No Physical Contact or No Effort to Maintain It.*

   a. The baby is not held or touched.

   b. Or, if picked up, he neither clings nor holds on, and when he is put down he makes no protest; if he is not put down he may still be coded 1 if he seems indifferent to being held. Furthermore, he has taken no initiative in making the contact in the first place.

RESISTANT BEHAVIOR

This variable deals with the intensity and frequency or duration of resistant behavior evoked by the person who comes into contact with or proximity to the baby, or who attempts to initiate interaction or to involve him in play. The mood is angry—pouting, petulance, cranky fussing, angry distress, or full-blown temper tantrums. The relevant behaviors are: pushing away, throwing away, dropping, batting away, hitting, kicking, squirming to be put down, jerking away, stepping angrily, and resistance to being picked up or moved or restrained. More diffuse manifestations are: angry screaming, throwing self about, throwing self down, kicking the floor, pouting, cranky fussing and petulance. These behaviors may alternate with active efforts to achieve or maintain contact with (or proximity to) the person who is being rejected. If both kinds of behavior are marked, the baby's behavior could be scored high in both variables.

One is reminded of the "weaning tantrums" of infant monkeys. The implication is that the baby rejects his mother, being angry with *her* for having left (rejected, abandoned) him. Often enough it is clear that he rejects toys that are offered to him as a redirection of rejection of or anger toward the person who offers them. It seems likely that the rejection of the stranger is either a redirection of anger at the mother or anger at the stranger because she is not the mother. This latter point raises the question of distinguishing "fear" of strangers from this kind of rejection. For the sake of consistency, all instances of resistance to the stranger have been included in this scale, including clear protest at the entrance of the stranger (in Episode 7), or her approach, or her attempt to make contact. Similar protests at the return or approach of the mother are also included here.

7 *Very Intense and Persistent Resistance.* The baby shows *two or more* of the following behaviors in the episode being coded:

   a. Repeated hitting of the person, or other similar directed aggressive behavior;

   b. Strong resistance to being held, shown by pushing away strongly, struggling, or strongly squirming to be put down;

   c. A full-blown temper tantrum, with angry screaming—the baby either being rigid and stiff or throwing himself about, kicking the floor, batting his hands up and down, and the like;

   d. Angry resistance to attempts of the adult to control the baby's posture, location, or action;

   e. Strong and repeated pushing away, throwing down, or hitting at toys offered to him.

6 *Intense and/or Persistent Resistance.* Any *one* of the following behaviors:

   a. Repeated or persistent temper tantrum, with throwing self about, kicking, and/or rigid, stiff, angry screaming;

   b. Very strong and/or persistent struggle against being held;

   c. Definite and repeated rejection of the person, even in the absence of directed aggression or angry screaming;

   d. Repeated, strong rejection of toys—pushing away, throwing down— accompanied by an angry cry or fuss;

   e. A combination of less intense manifestations of resistance, including squirming to be put down, resistance to interference, refusal of contact, rejection of toys, and petulance.

5 *Some Resistance, Either Less Intense, or, if Intense, More Isolated and Less Persistent Than the Above.* Any one of the following:

   a. Repeated rejection of toys (e.g., dropping or throwing down) but with no strong pushing away or batting away. The rejection does not seem as angry as in scores of 6 or 7. At least *three* such behaviors.

b. Persistent resistance to the adult when she seeks interaction—but without the intensity of struggling, pushing away, hitting, and so on of the higher scores. An example would be a fuss or increased intensity of crying whenever the adult approaches, offers a toy, and the like.

c. Resistance to being held by the mother, shown by squirming immediately to be put down, but without the intense struggle implied in the higher scores.

d. Persistent low-intensity pouting or cranky fussing, with at least *one* other manifestation of rejection, such as protesting interference, rejection of a toy, and the like.

4   *Isolated but Definite Instances of Resistance in the Absence of a Pervasive Angry Mood.*   Any one of the following:

a. Refusal of contact with the stranger. One definite, initial refusal, but without any implications of intense struggle.

b. Two refusals of toy, or kicking movements, or resistance to inteference, accompanied by a cry, but without any other manifestations of rejection or angry mood.

c. One strong but isolated behavior, accompanied by a cry—for example, angry stepping when put down, one strong refusal of toy (strong push or batting away), stiff steps when approaching (as though showing bodily resistance), and the like.

d. One manifestation of resistance to being held by the mother, less definite than above for example, a slight jerk or push away in the context of apparent "wanting to be held," or a definite squirm to be put down after accepting contact for at least 15 seconds.

3   *Slight Resistance.*   Any one of the following:

a. Two instances of resistant (or aggressive) behavior that is neither intense nor strong and is not accompanied by crying—for example, little kicks of the feet, dropping toys, and the like.

b. One instance of resistant (or aggressive) behavior if accompanied by a pout or protest, or in itself fairly intense (and yet not covered by higher scoring categories).

c. A marked pout, not prolonged enough to warrant a score of 5 and not accompanied by other manifestations of resistance or aggression.

2   *Very Slight Resistance.*   Any one of the following, with no other manifestations of resistance:

a. One isolated instance of nonintense resistance—for example, a little kick of the legs when being picked up.

b. One brief, slight protest noise when the adult enters, or advances, or picks the baby up.

1 *No Resistance.*   None of the above behaviors. The baby either accepts or is unresponsive to proximity, contact, or interaction offered by the adult— or he may merely avoid it. He may be occupied with other things, or he may be crying and not increase the intensity of his cry when approached by the adult. *Note:* Because babies nearly always resist having their noses wiped, such behavior will not be scored as resistant.

AVOIDANT BEHAVIOR

This variable deals with the intensity, persistence, duration, and promptness of the baby's avoidance of proximity and of interaction even across a distance. The relevant behaviors are: increasing distance between self and the person, whether through locomotion or by leaning away from; turning the back on the person; turning the head away; averting the gaze; avoidance of meeting the person's eyes; hiding the face; or simply ignoring the person. Ignoring the person does not refer, however, to mere exploration of the environment, especially in Episodes 2 and 3. Ignoring or avoiding the person is most marked when she is trying to gain the attention of the baby or to get a response from him. It also may be considered avoidance if the baby ignores the mother's entrance to the room after an absence, whether or not she seeks a response from him, or if he does not respond to the entrance of the stranger or to her attempt to engage him in play or interaction.

This variable deals chiefly with interaction across a distance, whereas the resistance variable is concerned with interaction in contact or in close proximity. The two sets of behaviors are usually easy to distinguish, because resistance is so frequently tinged with anger or aggressive movement, while avoidance seems either to be neutral in tone or perhaps to reflect apprehension. The more neutral the tone of the avoidance, however, the more likely it seems to be defensive in character—a defense that hides feelings, perhaps including those of resentment.

Although in the case of the other variables, behavior in interaction with mother or stranger could be comprehended in the same categories, in this coding it seems necessary to distinguish between mother and stranger.

7 *Very Marked and Persistent Avoidance.*
Of mother: The baby does not greet the mother upon her return in a reunion episode (episode 5 or 8)—neither with a smile nor with a protest. He pays little or no attention to her for an extended period *despite the mother's*

efforts to attract his attention. He ignores her, and may turn his back to her. If his mother nevertheless picks him up, he remains unresponsive to her while she holds him, looking around, seemingly interested in other things.

Of stranger: The baby repeatedly and persistently avoids the stranger, by some kind of strong behavior, either locomotor withdrawal or hiding the face, perhaps combined with looking away. In Episode 3 the baby may go to his mother in his repeated withdrawals from the stranger.

6   *Marked and Persistent Avoidance.*

Of mother: (a) The baby behaves as above, giving the mother no greeting, except perhaps an initial look, and paying little or no attention to her for an extended period; but in this case the mother does not persist in her attempt to gain the baby's attention—she merely greets him and then sits quietly. *Or* (b) the baby greets his mother, perhaps with a smile or a fuss or with a partial approach, and then behaves as above, paying little or no attention to the mother for an extended period, despite the mother's efforts to attract his attention.

Of stranger: This score is reserved for an episode in which the end of the episode comes before it is confirmed that the baby's avoidance would have been repeated and persistent. The baby strongly withdraws from the stranger with behavior and in a context that makes it seem very probable that the avoidance would have been persistent had the episode not ended.

5   *Clear-Cut Avoidance But Less Persistent.*
Of mother:

a. The baby may look, but gives the mother no greeting, then looks away, or turns away and ignores the mother for about 30 seconds, during which time the mother makes no special effort to gain his attention; then he looks again and seems more responsive to her, but he does not seek contact and may even avoid it if it is offered.
b. The baby gives the mother no greeting; the mother strives to gain his attention; after about 15 seconds he gives her his attention but he is fairly unresponsive even then.
c. The baby greets his mother or starts to approach her, but then he either markedly turns away (or looks away) or tries to go past her out the door; he ignores her efforts to gain his attention for an appreciable time, although he may then respond by approaching, reaching, or accepting a toy.

Of stranger: The baby repeatedly and persistently avoids the stranger, but without the intensity of the avoidance implicit in a coding of 7. In Episode 3 the baby may retreat to his mother, but without apparent intense anxiety, and then later show some other clear-cut manifestation of avoidance of the stranger. Regardless of the episode, the baby clearly does not want to have anything to do with the stranger—neither contact nor interaction—but his efforts to avoid her do not have the frantic persistence of those coded 7.

4 *Brief But Clear-Cut Avoidance OR Persistent Low-Keyed Avoidance.*
Of mother:

a. The baby greets his mother or starts to approach her; he then clearly turns away or looks away as in 5c. In this instance, however, the mother goes to her chair and sits, without making any effort to elicit responsiveness in the baby. The baby goes on playing, perhaps with occasional looks and smiles at the mother; both behave (in a reunion episode) much as the average couple in Episode 2. In view of the mother's lack of participation, one can be justified in counting only the initial avoidance behavior (i.e., that following greeting) as avoidance on the baby's part. It is assumed that he is not ignoring his mother and that he would approach her or respond to her if given a cue.
b. The baby at first "snubs" the mother by failing to greet her and either by being slow to look at her or by looking away or both (or perhaps by trying to go out the door); but after this initial avoidance behavior, the baby responds by reaching to the mother's outstretched hands and/or by regaining responsiveness after being picked up.
c. The baby fails to greet his mother and ignores her for a time (15 to 30 seconds) and then takes the initiative in making contact or undertaking interaction, even though the mother has not sought his attention.

Of stranger:

a. The baby shows one clear-cut avoidance or several slight ones, but at least looks at the stranger and at what she is doing for part of the episode, even though there is no positive response to her.
b. The baby persistently avoids meeting the stranger's eyes with his. He may watch her, but as soon as she looks at him he averts his gaze; but there is no stronger instance of avoidance than this.

3 *Slight, Isolated Avoidance Behavior.*
Of mother:

a. The baby is distressed and is slow either in looking at his mother or in responding to her overtures—but then he does, either crying more loudly or reaching or both.
b. The baby is not distressed; he looks up at his mother when she arrives, perhaps greeting her, then looks away briefly; then he is responsive, either interacting with her or exchanging looks and smiles in the course

of play. He does not, however, take the initiative in seeking contact.

Of stranger:
a. In Episode 3 the baby at one point retreats from the stranger to his mother, but without apparent anxiety. He does not approach the stranger, but on the other hand he does not further avoid the stranger's advances in this episode.
b. One isolated but clear-cut instance of avoidance of the stranger, by twisting away, turning away, or moving back a little; but for the rest of the episode the baby accepts the stranger's advances and may be fairly friendly, or, if the episode ends soon, there is no implication that the avoidance will be persistent.

2   *Very Slight Avoidance.*
Of mother: The baby may delay very briefly in responding to his mother's return or may give her a brief snub by looking away, but very soon he takes the initiative in seeking contact or interaction with or proximity to her.

Of stranger: One slight instance of avoidance of the stranger. The baby who is not distressed (because of separation) may look away coyly or turn away momentarily as the stranger approaches, or perhaps he may seem to avoid her eyes for a while. The baby who is distressed by separation may not be responsive to the stranger, but he shows only one slight instance of avoidance—looking away or moving his hands away.

1   *No Avoidance.*
Of mother: The baby responds appropriately to his mother and to her behavior, neither avoiding her overtures nor ignoring her return after an absence. In Episode 2, however, he may be quite preoccupied with exploration while she sits quietly; and in Episode 3, he may be absorbed either with continuing exploratory play or with staring at the stranger.

Of stranger: The baby may be friendly with the stranger. He may be too distressed by his mother's absence to be friendly. He may angrily resist the stranger or the toy she offers. He may continue playing, paying little spontaneous attention to the stranger. But he does not avoid the stranger, and he at least watches her when she tries to interest him in toys.

SEARCH BEHAVIOR DURING
THE SEPARATION EPISODES

This variable deals with the degree of activity and persistence of behavior that may be interpreted as an attempt to search for and to regain the mother during the episodes when she is absent from the room. Of these behaviors the most obviously appropriate, even though necessarily ineffective, is following the mother to the door and trying to open it. The efforts to open it or to get someone to open it include trying to insert the fingers in the crack of the door or under it, trying to reach the knob or looking up at the knob, which is beyond reach, or banging on the door. Also relevant to a desire to regain the mother is merely looking at the door or at the mother's chair or handbag, or going to one of these locations associated with the mother and remaining oriented to it for longer or shorter periods of time. Crying may also be interpreted as behavior that signals the baby's desire for his mother to return; but it is *not* included in the present scoring system, but rather it is dealt with in a separate analysis.

7 *Very Active and Persistent Search Behavior.* The baby goes to the door without substantial delay (within 45 seconds). He either tries to open it, or reaches for the knob, or bangs on the door. *Either* he remains at the door and oriented to it for 30 seconds or more after his initial effort to open it, *or* he returns again to the door after leaving it.

6 *Active and Persistent Search Behavior.* Any one of the following:
a. The baby goes promptly to the door and stays there persistently. He either looks up at the knob or touches the door, but he does not try to open it, reach for the knob, or bang on the door. Even though he may be crying hard, he remains oriented to the door.
b. The baby delays in going to the door (i.e., for over 45 seconds) but then tries to open it or reaches for the knob or bangs on the door; he remains at the door for 30 seconds or more or returns to the door after leaving it (i.e., the same behavior that is scored 7, except for the initial delay).
c. The baby makes an active effort to reach the door but is prevented from actually reaching it or from staying there, either because he is picked up and held by the stranger or because the episode is curtailed. It is assumed that he would have displayed 6a behavior had the intervention not occurred.
d. The baby repeatedly goes to the door and touches it at least once, although he neither tries to open it nor remains near the door for an extended time.

5 *Some Active Search.* Any one of the following:
a. The baby goes to the door across a fair distance (i.e., he is not already within a couple of steps of the door); but, either because of delay or because of absence of active effort to open the door or because he does not remain near the door and oriented to it, his behavior cannot be scored 6 or 7.
b. In Episode 7 the baby is at the door when the stranger enters, and he tries to go out the door and/or helps to open the door.
c. The baby struggles hard to go to the door, but he is so distressed that his

locomotion is too inefficient for him to be able to get to the door.
d. The baby is held by the stranger and therefore cannot go to the door, but nevertheless he strongly and persistently leans or reaches toward the door out of the stranger's arms.

4   *Obvious Desire to Regain the Mother, But the "Search" Behavior is Incomplete or Weak.*
a. The baby displays five or more instances of "weak" search behavior—for example, looking at the door, looking at the mother's chair, or going to the mother's chair or to her handbag.
b. The baby begins to approach the door but goes only part way.
c. The baby is near the door and goes the whole way to the door, but he does not touch the door and he does not remain there for more than a few seconds.
d. The baby goes to the mother's chair in a purposeful way (i.e., he does not merely happen to get there in pursuit of a toy or in the course of exploration); in addition he shows one other instance of weak search behavior.

3   *Some Apparent Desire to Regain the Mother, But the Search Behavior is Weak.*   Any one of the following:
a. The baby displays three or four instances of "weak" search behavior, as defined above.
b. The baby looks at the door and continues doing so for at least 30 seconds or for all of a curtailed episode of less than 30 seconds.
c. The baby goes to the mother's chair in a purposeful way; this is the only instance of search behavior he displays.

2   *Very Slight Effort to Search for the Mother.*   The baby displays only one or two instances of weak search behavior, which includes looking at the door, looking at the mother's chair or handbag, or making a mere intention movement toward the door (e.g., taking one or two steps toward the door when at a distance from it), or going to the mother's chair in such a way that it is doubtful whether the approach was purposeful.

1   *No Search for the Mother.*   Episodes will be scored 1 whenever the baby does not go to or look at the door and does not go to or look at the mother's chair or handbag. He may, however, show any one of the following behaviors that are not identified as search behavior: watching the mother leave and continuing to look at the door for a few seconds after it has closed; in Episode 4 looking at the mother's chair as the first perception of her absence (i.e., the baby has not seen the mother leave the room); looking at the door at the very end of a separation episode, in probable response to hearing a person outside and about to enter. In other words, "search behavior" occurs after the baby perceives his mother's departure or absence and before the mother (or stranger) gives an auditory cue of her impending entrance.

DISTANCE INTERACTION

This variable deals with positive social behaviors—smiling, vocalizing, intent looking, showing of toy, and play—that indicate that a baby is interested in the adult, although he may not be in close proximity to her. The term "distance interaction" is defined to include behaviors that can occur across the room from the adult or in the course of a partial approach to her, but not those that occur immediately preceding or during a full approach.

In the scoring and in defining distance interaction, distinction has been made between mother and stranger in some cases. Interaction that occurs between mother and infant in Episodes 2, 5, and 8 and is instigated by the mother upon instructions to engage or reengage the baby in play is *not* scored as distance interaction, because it is not spontaneous and because it occurs when mother and infant are in close proximity. (Otherwise, contingencies of both maternal and infant behavior have been taken into account in the coding.) On the other hand, the responses to the stranger's systematic approaches in Episode 3 have been coded as distance interaction, for it is of interest to note how readily and enthusiastically the baby accepts and responds to the social overtures of an unfamiliar person. Separate provision has also been made for distance interaction that may occur immediately following reunion with the mother in Episodes 5 and 8.

7 *Very Active and Persistent Distance Interaction.*
a. The baby and the adult establish a reciprocal interaction that lasts for 45 seconds or longer; or they establish briefer reciprocal interactions twice in the course of the episode.
b. The baby offers or shows a toy to the adult two or more times in the course of the episode, although he does not seek proximity to her in order to do so.
c. The baby appears to pause and attend to what the adult is saying for 45 seconds or more; or he does so twice in the course of the episode for briefer periods. This is reported as attending by the observers, and is clearly more than mere occasional looking at the adult when she speaks.

Reunions only. The baby does not make an immediate approach to his mother, but he greets her within 15 seconds by smiling, showing a toy, or vocalizing; and he is responsive to her in the course of the episode. That is, he smiles and vocalizes to her and engages in a reciprocal interaction with her at least once in the course of the episode.

6 *Very Active and Fairly Persistent Distance Interaction.* The baby engages in a reciprocal interaction, briefer than the above. He pushes a toy back and forth to the adult in play, or he takes a toy and gestures to the adult about it. Or he engages in a brief reciprocal vocalization or smiling exchange.

Reunions only. The baby does not make an immediate full approach to his mother, but he greets her within 15 seconds with a smile, a show of a toy, or a vocalization and is responsive to her in the course of the episode. He smiles and vocalizes to her five or more times, or he may offer the mother a toy or otherwise attempt to communicate with her about his environment. However, no reciprocal interaction occurs.

5 *Active Distance Interaction.*
Mother. The baby smiles and vocalizes to his mother four or more times in the course of the episode.

Reunions only. The baby does not make an immediate full approach to his mother but instead greets her within 15 seconds with a smile, a show of a toy, or a vocalization; he makes other distal bids (smiles, vocalizations, showing a toy) three or four other times in the course of the episode.

Stranger. The baby takes a toy directly from the stranger and offers her a toy once in the course of the episode; or he indicates a toy to her by pointing or trying to communicate to her about it.

4 *Moderate Distance Interaction.*
Mother

a. The baby smiles or vocalizes to his mother two or three times in the course of the episode.
b. The baby gestures about a toy or points out something in the room to his mother once in the course of the episode.

Reunions only. The baby does not make an immediate full approach to his mother, but greets her with a smile or a vocalization within 15 seconds, and also smiles or vocalizes to her twice subsequently in the course of the episode.

Stranger

a. The baby accepts more or less readily a toy that the stranger offers, perhaps smiling at her; but he shows no tendency to reciprocate by engaging her in further play.
b. The baby vocalizes and/or smiles to the stranger three times during the episode.

3   *Little Distance Interaction.*
Mother

   a. The baby looks at the mother frequently in the course of his exploration (these are described as more than glances or very brief looks); and he orients to her for more than 15 seconds at least once during the episode, perhaps smiling at her.

   b. The mother initiates an interaction across the distance with the baby by smiling at or vocalizing to the baby, and she receives a smile or two in the course of the episode. But the baby takes no initiative in interactive bids during the episode.

Reunions only

   a. The baby may smile at his mother when she enters initially, and he may be happy to see her; but he does not make an immediate full approach. Either because he later achieves contact or because he glances at his mother, or vocalizes to her only once in the course of the ensuing episode, he does not get a higher score.

   b. The baby greets his mother with a smile upon reunion, but he shows no tendency to seek her proximity. However, the mother picks him up. Because one can infer that he would have made more distal bids had the mother not intervened, the baby receives this score.

Stranger

   a. If the stranger approaches the baby, he may look at her attentively, as well as at the toy that she is offering. However, he does not directly take the toy that she brings, although he may make an "intention movement" toward it. This score is different from a score of 2 because, in this case, the baby is obviously more directly interested in the stranger.

   b. The baby smiles at and/or vocalizes to the stranger twice in the course of the episode.

2   *Very Little Distance Interaction.*
Mother.   The baby glances at the mother four or more times in the course of the episode, and he might vocalize to and/or smile to her once; but he engages in no more active type of distance interaction.

Reunions only.   The baby does not make an immediate full approach. He may look at his mother initially, twisting around briefly to see her, and he may be described as having a pleasant expression on his face. If he is not picked up, he may occasionally look at her (five or fewer times), but he engages in no more active types of behavior.

Stranger

a. The baby may pause and stare at the stranger with obvious curiosity, or he may glance at her frequently (five or more times). But beyond this, he shows no tendency to engage her socially.
b. If the stranger offers the baby a toy, he may focus his attention on it, perhaps making a slight intention movement toward it; or he may pick it up after the stranger has put it down. Hence he is interacting with her indirectly, but he gives her no more direct attention than a few brief glances.

1   *No Distance Interaction.*
Mother and Stranger

a. The baby makes no bids for distance interaction with the adult. He may glance briefly at her (two or three times); or if she attempts to engage his attention, he may look at her at least part of the time. However, he shows no further tendency to interact with her.
b. The baby may be distressed and may seek proximity to and/or contact with the adult. He may look at the adult a few times before approaching, but he seems to want physical closeness. Although he may be highly responsive to the adult while in contact or while standing by her chair, he shows no desire to increase the distance between them.

Stranger

a. The baby is distressed when the stranger approaches. He may accept her or prefer to ignore her. He may look briefly at a toy that she offers, but he is completely unwilling to become involved with it. *Note:* If the baby responds positively to what the stranger is doing for at least part of the time, he receives a higher score than 1.
b. The stranger does not approach the baby. He confines himself to giving her a few brief glances that do not linger on her face and that are not meant to evoke a social response from her; or he gives her one or two more prolonged looks with no interactive tendencies.

Supplementary Statistical Findings

TABLE 30
Percentages per Episode of Infants Displaying
a Given Behavior (Frequency Measures)

Behavior	Episodes						
	2	3	4	5	6	7	8
Exploratory manipulation	94	92	81	96	62	64	82
Exploratory locomotion	89	51	37	67	44	26	40
Visual exploration	100	99	95	98	76	79	98
Crying	12	23	49	53	78	71	53
Oral behavior	43	42	36	47	38	40	54
Smiling	59	66	46	58	5	31	50
Smiling at mother	53	37	—	48	—	—	41
Smiling at stranger	—	57	42	—	—	33	—
Vocalization	80	56	58	71	46	44	60
Vocalization to mother	47	19	—	43	—	—	32
Vocalization to stranger	—	25	23	—	—	25	—
Looking at mother	100	96	—	98	—	—	100
Looking at stranger	—	100	98	—	—	95	—

TABLE 31
Percentages per Episode of Infants Displaying
Interactive Behaviors

Behavior	Episode						
	2	3	4	5	6	7	8
Proximity and contact seeking to mother	34	47	—	72	—	—	87
Contact maintaining to mother	20	26	—	41	—	—	83
Distance interaction with mother	82	55	—	64	—	—	42
Proximity and contact seeking to stranger	—	19	26	—	—	36	—
Contact maintaining to stranger	—	02	16	—	—	33	—
Distance interaction to stranger	—	99	74	—	—	44	—
Search behavior	—	—	70	—	86	62	—

TABLE 32
Means and One-Way ANOVAs for Strange-Situation Variables
That Do Not Distinguish Among Groups A, B, and C

Variable	Epi-sode	Persons Present	Means A	B	C	Total	F (2,102)
Interactive Behaviors with M							
Proximity seeking	2	M, B	1.61	1.99	2.23	1.94	0.63
	3	S, M, B	2.04	2.75	2.85	2.60	1.02
Contact maintaining	2	M, B	1.30	1.70	2.31	1.69	1.69
	3	S, M, B	1.54	1.86	2.77	1.90	2.21
Distance interaction	2	M, B	2.83	3.04	2.65	2.95	0.40
	3	S, M, B	1.50	2.17	1.80	1.98	2.80
	5	M, B	2.65	2.55	1.38	2.43	3.82
	8	M, B	2.35	1.67	1.15	1.76	4.78
Interactive Behaviors with S							
Proximity seeking	3	S, M, B	1.30	1.42	1.31	1.38	0.16
	4	S, B	1.37	1.61	1.77	1.58	0.71
	7	S, B	1.83	1.67	1.92	1.73	0.37
Contact maintaining	4	S, B	1.04	1.45	1.92	1.42	2.74
	7	S, B	1.26	1.94	2.77	1.90	4.40
Avoidance	3	S, M, B	2.09	2.13	2.85	2.21	1.13
	4	S, B	1.48	1.67	1.69	1.63	0.20
	7	S, B	1.43	1.90	2.08	1.82	1.11
Distance interaction	3	S, M, B	3.63	3.42	2.65	3.37	2.78
Search							
	4	S, B	2.39	2.91	2.38	2.73	1.12
	6	B	4.61	4.29	3.69	4.29	0.86
	7	S, B	2.54	2.41	1.54	2.33	1.66
Exploratory Behaviors							
Exploratory locomotion	2	M, B	3.40	3.29	2.25	3.19	1.12
	6	B	2.54	1.51	0.42	1.60	4.15
Exploratory manipulation	2	M, B	8.45	7.07	5.32	7.16	3.78
	6	B	5.77	4.18	1.45	4.19	4.72
"Discrete" Behaviors							
Vocalization to mother	2	M, B	4.43	5.43	5.58	5.23	1.76
	3	S, M, B	3.07	4.30	5.10	4.13	4.21
	5	M, B	5.86	5.95	5.68	5.89	0.07
	8	M, B	5.42	5.34	3.40	5.12	3.98
Smiling at mother	2	M, B	1.15	1.07	1.32	1.12	0.14
	3	S, M,B	0.58	0.82	0.45	0.72	0.62
	5	M, B	1.37	1.20	0.21	1.11	2.72
	8	M, B	1.03	0.88	0.08	0.81	2.50

(continued)

TABLE 32 (continued)

| Variable | Epi-sode | Persons Present | Means | | | | F |
			A	B	C	Total	(2,102)
Looking at mother	2	M, B	0.83	0.91	0.37	0.93	1.31
	3	S, M, B	0.13	0.38	0	0.28	2.73
	5	M, B	0.85	1.00	0.38	0.89	1.23
	8	M, B	1.08	0.70	0.15	0.71	2.17
Oral Behavior	2	M, B	1.57	1.00	0.49	1.06	1.38
	3	S, M, B	1.74	1.17	1.35	1.32	0.58
	4	S, B	2.20	1.20	0.43	1.33	2.38
	5	M, B	2.10	1.14	0.50	1.27	3.01
	6	B	1.15	1.16	0.33	1.05	1.16
	7	S, B	2.23	1.22	0.14	1.31	3.67
	8	M, B	1.34	1.58	1.68	1.54	0.12

TABLE 33
Subgroup Means and Standard Deviations
for Measures of Interactive Behavior With Mother
in Each Relevant Strange-Situation Episode

Subgroup	Episode 2 $\bar{X}$	σ	Episode 3 $\bar{X}$	σ	Episode 5 $\bar{X}$	σ	Episode 8 $\bar{X}$	σ
Proximity and Contact Seeking								
A_1	1.50	1.00	2.00	1.54	1.33	0.65	1.42	0.67
A_2	1.60	1.58	1.60	1.27	2.30	1.64	3.20	1.40
B_1	1.80	1.03	2.25	1.46	2.40	1.71	2.90	1.79
B_2	1.82	1.94	1.82	1.17	2.45	2.02	5.27	1.56
B_3	2.19	1.90	3.11	2.40	4.44	1.90	4.98	1.36
B_4	2.50	3.00	2.75	1.26	4.25	0.50	4.00	0.82
C_1	2.43	2.23	4.86	2.85	3.83	1.94	4.00	1.63
C_2	2.14	2.27	1.43	1.13	3.43	1.27	2.86	1.07
Contact Maintaining								
A_1	1.25	0.62	1.08	0.29	1.08	0.29	1.17	0.58
A_2	1.10	0.32	1.65	1.49	1.00	0	3.05	1.61
B_1	1.30	0.95	1.20	0.63	1.20	0.63	2.20	1.14
B_2	1.73	1.62	1.36	1.21	1.36	0.81	4.50	1.53
B_3	1.77	1.67	2.03	1.76	3.23	2.32	5.73	1.44
B_4	2.75	2.06	2.75	2.06	2.75	2.06	4.50	0.58
C_1	3.00	2.65	4.29	2.56	4.29	1.80	4.29	1.89
C_2	1.86	2.27	1.71	1.89	3.86	1.95	4.57	1.72
Resistance								
A_1	1.00	0	1.00	0	1.08	0.29	1.83	1.64
A_2	1.00	0	1.00	0	1.08	0.29	3.23	1.65
B_1	1.30	0.95	1.00	0	1.20	0.42	1.60	1.08
B_2	1.00	0	1.00	0	1.36	0.67	1.64	0.92
B_3	1.00	0	1.00	0	1.60	1.36	1.53	1.01
B_4	1.00	0	1.00	0	2.25	1.89	2.38	2.43
C_1	2.14	2.27	1.64	1.70	4.43	2.58	4.86	1.46
C_2	1.43	0.79	1.14	0.38	2.29	1.89	3.29	2.29
Avoidance								
A_1					5.79	0.89	5.92	1.38
A_2					4.10	1.45	4.70	1.69
B_1					3.70	1.25	3.40	1.35
B_2					3.55	1.86	1.82	1.25
B_3					1.56	1.14	1.28	0.81
B_4					1.00	0	2.25	1.50
C_1					2.29	1.89	3.57	2.30
C_2					1.86	1.57	2.29	1.60

(continued)

TABLE 33 (continued)

Subgroup	Episode 2		Episode 3		Episode 5		Episode 8	
	$\overline{X}$	σ	$\overline{X}$	σ	$\overline{X}$	σ	$\overline{X}$	σ
Distance Interaction								
A_1	2.58	1.88	1.58	1.02	2.17	0.78	2.20	0.71
A_2	3.20	1.34	1.45	0.69	3.40	1.65	2.65	1.77
B_1	2.95	1.26	2.65	1.49	3.50	2.06	2.35	1.00
B_2	2.55	1.19	2.27	1.01	2.68	1.23	2.45	1.98
B_3	3.17	1.79	2.05	1.41	2.36	1.48	1.37	0.73
B_4	2.75	1.94	1.50	0.58	1.63	1.25	1.00	0
C_1	2.43	1.51	1.14	0.38	1.14	0.38	1.13	0.35
C_2	2.79	1.35	2.36	1.03	1.57	1.13	1.14	0.38

TABLE 34
Subgroup Means and Standard Deviations for Measures
of Interactive Behavior With the Stranger in
Each Relevant Strange-Situation Episode

Subgroup	Episode 3 $\bar{X}$	σ	Episode 4 $\bar{X}$	σ	Episode 7 $\bar{X}$	σ
Proximity and Contact Seeking						
A_1	1.17	0.39	1.55	1.81	1.92	1.51
A_2	1.50	0.97	1.15	0.47	1.80	1.03
B_1	1.60	1.08	1.30	0.95	1.60	0.84
B_2	1.09	0.30	1.91	1.04	2.00	1.61
B_3	1.49	1.24	1.56	0.92	1.60	1.03
B_4	1.00	0	2.00	1.56	1.50	1.00
C_1	1.14	0.38	1.86	1.07	1.71	0.95
C_2	1.00	0	1.57	0.98	2.00	1.29
Contact Maintaining						
A_1	1.00	0	1.08	0.29	1.08	0.29
A_2	1.00	0	1.00	0	1.10	0.32
B_1	1.00	0	1.00	0	1.45	1.01
B_2	1.00	0	1.09	0.30	1.82	1.66
B_3	1.04	0.21	1.53	1.22	2.12	1.64
B_4	1.00	0	2.50	2.38	1.25	0.55
C_1	1.00	0	1.86	1.46	2.86	2.12
C_2	1.00	0	2.00	1.73	2.71	1.98
Resistance						
A_1	1.00	0	1.00	0	1.25	0.87
A_2	1.25	0.87	1.00	0	1.08	0.29
B_1	1.00	0	1.00	0	2.00	1.89
B_2	1.36	1.21	1.18	0.40	2.32	1.52
B_3	1.09	0.29	1.79	1.57	2.60	1.97
B_4	1.75	1.50	1.25	0.50	1.25	0.50
C_1	2.43	1.90	3.86	2.85	5.50	1.38
C_2	2.14	1.95	4.14	2.27	2.86	2.12
Avoidance						
A_1	1.72	1.01	1.08	0.29	1.17	0.58
A_2	1.90	1.20	1.70	1.25	1.80	1.23
B_1	2.20	1.48	1.40	0.97	1.60	1.27
B_2	1.18	0.40	1.28	0.90	2.91	1.97
B_3	2.30	1.72	1.82	1.44	1.76	1.49
B_4	4.25	1.89	2.50	1.73	1.50	0.58
C_1	4.71	2.06	2.29	2.36	2.14	1.68
C_2	1.57	1.51	1.43	1.13	1.86	1.57

(continued)

TABLE 34 *(continued)*

Subgroup	Episode 3		Episode 4		Episode 7	
	$\overline{X}$	σ	$\overline{X}$	σ	$\overline{X}$	σ
Distance Interaction						
A_1	3.63	0.71	4.71	1.60	3.90	2.30
A_2	4.22	1.20	4.18	1.75	3.88	2.18
B_1	3.45	1.40	3.18	1.68	2.17	1.44
B_2	3.43	0.88	3.82	1.59	2.73	1.59
B_3	3.55	1.33	2.89	1.94	1.61	1.30
B_4	2.00	0.50	1.17	0.29	1.00	0
C_1	2.68	1.24	1.86	1.31	1.04	0.09
C_2	2.43	0.94	1.29	0.57	1.00	0

TABLE 35
Subgroup Means and Standard Deviations
for Measures of Search Behavior
in Each Relevant Strange-Situation Episode

Subgroup	Episode 4		Episode 6		Episode 7	
	$\overline{X}$	σ	$\overline{X}$	σ	$\overline{X}$	σ
A_1	2.50	2.07	4.42	2.31	2.71	2.05
A_2	2.40	1.51	4.80	1.81	2.50	1.35
B_1	2.10	1.20	4.20	2.04	3.00	2.16
B_2	3.27	1.79	5.09	1.87	2.54	2.12
B_3	3.16	1.78	4.29	2.01	2.27	1.66
B_4	1.50	0.58	3.00	2.71	2.00	0.82
C_1	2.71	1.38	4.86	1.46	1.14	0.38
C_2	1.86	1.07	2.71	1.80	1.86	1.46

TABLE 36
Subgroup Means and Standard Deviations for Measures of Exploratory Behavior and Crying in Each Strange-Situation Episode

Subgroup	Episode 2		Episode 3		Episode 4		Episode 5		Episode 6		Episode 7		Episode 8	
	$\bar{X}$	σ	$\bar{X}$	σ	$\bar{X}$	σ	$\bar{X}$	σ	$\bar{X}$	σ	$\bar{X}$	σ	$\bar{X}$	σ
Exploratory Locomotion														
A_1	3.73	2.35	2.64	3.11	2.33	2.81	3.32	3.53	2.71	2.40	1.55	1.95	2.03	1.41
A_2	3.24	1.96	2.93	2.87	2.77	2.80	3.36	2.64	2.89	1.91	2.96	2.12	2.27	2.68
B_1	3.26	1.47	1.01	1.27	1.54	2.36	2.51	1.65	2.47	2.63	1.16	1.53	2.05	1.65
B_2	3.54	2.76	1.24	2.10	2.91	2.86	4.74	3.25	2.86	2.67	1.51	1.99	1.03	0.74
B_3	3.34	2.52	1.29	1.44	0.56	1.39	1.24	1.37	0.54	1.33	0.10	0.32	0.55	1.18
B_4	1.38	2.75	0	0	0	0	0	0	0	0	0.20	0.40	0	0
C_1	3.15	3.07	0.40	0.77	0.27	0.46	1.33	1.75	0.50	1.23	0	0	0.40	1.20
C_2	1.17	1.81	0	0	0	0	0.14	0.38	0.34	0.91	0	0	0	0
Exploratory Manipulation														
A_1	8.16	2.80	7.93	1.92	8.29	3.64	8.91	2.06	6.80	3.14	6.80	3.20	5.65	3.16
A_2	9.24	2.60	7.50	3.58	8.13	3.60	8.34	2.11	5.10	4.28	7.60	2.01	6.61	2.15
B_1	8.27	3.09	6.77	2.63	7.58	2.01	8.71	1.55	8.60	2.91	6.68	3.65	7.37	2.41
B_2	7.41	3.77	6.11	2.87	7.55	3.28	8.34	2.22	6.29	4.11	4.96	3.48	4.06	2.20
B_3	6.98	3.03	5.35	2.80	4.04	3.77	5.91	2.93	2.89	3.89	2.41	3.04	2.58	2.98
B_4	2.83	3.20	1.38	1.18	1.45	1.90	4.44	3.81	0.75	1.50	1.00	2.00	1.50	3.00
C_1	6.87	4.05	4.14	3.71	2.39	2.30	4.52	2.37	0	0	0.43	1.13	3.18	4.03
C_2	3.59	3.78	1.89	1.96	1.33	1.87	4.53	2.92	2.27	3.14	0.49	1.29	1.57	3.73

(continued)

TABLE 36 (continued)

Subgroup	Episode 2 $\bar{X}$	σ	Episode 3 $\bar{X}$	σ	Episode 4 $\bar{X}$	σ	Episode 5 $\bar{X}$	σ	Episode 6 $\bar{X}$	σ	Episode 7 $\bar{X}$	σ	Episode 8 $\bar{X}$	σ
Visual Exploration														
A_1	11.08	1.53	9.12	1.88	9.55	2.32	10.12	1.58	9.38	3.64	8.79	2.35	9.84	1.20
A_2	11.55	0.64	9.54	1.52	10.29	2.02	9.97	1.91	9.46	2.73	8.53	2.04	7.53	1.91
B_1	10.87	1.52	9.60	1.21	10.25	1.37	9.54	1.56	9.49	2.51	7.97	3.14	9.94	1.73
B_2	11.39	0.77	8.56	2.14	9.09	3.49	9.84	1.71	10.71	1.00	6.49	3.45	7.63	1.73
B_3	10.92	1.39	7.61	2.17	6.19	3.66	7.13	3.18	5.41	4.90	3.61	3.57	6.57	3.04
B_4	9.88	1.60	5.40	2.87	3.18	2.62	5.57	3.78	3.75	4.50	2.88	2.21	7.55	4.18
C_1	10.04	2.90	6.47	2.90	5.04	3.52	6.61	2.78	2.30	2.69	2.80	3.10	8.78	0.29
C_2	9.13	3.45	4.64	3.30	3.17	2.84	5.41	2.99	3.57	3.77	2.77	2.03	7.04	2.24
Crying														
A_1	0.17	0.58	0.29	1.01	0.33	1.16	0.08	0.26	2.16	3.43	0.68	1.46	0.20	0.41
A_2	0	0	0	0	0	0	1.24	3.49	4.66	4.96	0.54	1.42	0.93	1.18
B_1	0.09	0.29	0	0	0.37	0.90	0.42	0.72	2.67	3.57	1.35	2.33	0.20	0.86
B_2	0	0	1.16	2.44	1.25	3.60	0.15	0.32	3.85	4.10	2.98	2.64	1.91	2.15
B_3	0.20	0.94	0.33	0.94	4.17	4.11	2.31	2.60	8.62	4.69	7.24	4.98	3.08	2.18
B_4	0.75	1.14	3.58	2.66	6.63	3.04	4.35	2.39	12.00	0	9.80	4.40	6.38	2.25
C_1	1.89	3.63	2.70	2.66	7.26	3.95	5.57	3.34	9.26	4.20	9.60	2.60	8.25	3.44
C_2	2.19	3.40	2.23	3.11	7.41	4.57	6.10	3.59	10.29	4.54	8.77	3.58	5.73	3.74

References

Ainsworth, M. D. The effects of maternal deprivation: A review of findings and controversy in the context of research strategy. In *Deprivation of maternal care: A reassessment of its effects*. Public Health Papers, 14. Geneva: World Health Organization, 1962.

Ainsworth, M. D. Patterns of attachment behavior shown by the infant in interaction with his mother. *Merrill-Palmer Quarterly*, 1964, *10*, 51–58.

Ainsworth, M. D. S The development of infant–mother interaction among the Ganda. In B. M. Foss (Ed.), *Determinants of infant behaviour II*. London: Methuen, 1963. (New York: Wiley)

Ainsworth, M. D. S. *Infancy in Uganda: Infant care and the growth of love*. Baltimore: Johns Hopkins University Press, 1967.

Ainsworth, M. D. S. Object relations, dependency and attachment: A theoretical review of the infant–mother relationship. *Child Development*, 1969, *40*, 969–1025.

Ainsworth, M. D. S. Attachment and dependency: A comparison. In J. L. Gewirtz (Ed.), *Attachment and dependency*. Washington, D.C.: V. H. Winston, 1972.

Ainsworth, M. D. S. The development of infant–mother attachment. In B. M. Caldwell & H. N. Ricciuti (Eds.), *Review of child development research* (Vol. 3). Chicago: University of Chicago Press, 1973.

Ainsworth, M. D. S. Infant development and mother–infant interaction among Ganda and American families. In P. H. Leiderman & S. Tulkin (Eds.), *Culture and infancy: Variations on the human experience*. New York: Academic Press, 1977.

Ainsworth, M. D. S., & Bell, S. M. Some contemporary patterns of mother–infant interaction in the feeding situation. In A. Ambrose (Ed.), *Stimulation in early infancy*. London and New York: Academic Press, 1969.

Ainsworth, M. D. S., & Bell, S. M. Attachment, exploration, and separation: Illustrated by the behavior of one-year-olds in a strange situation. *Child Development*, 1970, *41*, 49–67.

Ainsworth, M. D. S., & Bell, S. M. Mother–infant interaction and the development of competence. In K. J. Connolly & J. Bruner (Eds.), *The growth of competence*. London & New York: Academic Press, 1974.

373

Ainsworth, M. D. S., Bell, S. M., & Stayton, D. J. Individual differences in strange situation behavior of one-year-olds. In H. R. Schaffer (Ed.), *The origins of human social relations.* London & New York: Academic Press, 1971.

Ainsworth, M. D. S., Bell, S. M., & Stayton, D. J. Individual differences in the development of some attachment behaviors. *Merrill-Palmer Quarterly,* 1972, *18,* 123–143.

Ainsworth, M. D. S., Bell, S. M., & Stayton, D. J. Infant–mother attachment and social development: "Socialisation" as a product of reciprocal responsiveness to signals. In M. P. M. Richards (Ed.), *The integration of a child into a social world.* London: Cambridge University Press, 1974.

Ainsworth, M. D. S., & Wittig, B. A. Attachment and exploratory behavior of one-year-olds in a strange situation. In B. M. Foss (Ed.), *Determinants of infant behaviour IV.* London: Methuen, 1969.

Anderson, J. W. Attachment behaviour out of doors. In N. Blurton Jones (Ed.), *Ethological studies of child behaviour.* London: Cambridge University Press, 1972.

Arsenian, J. M. Young children in an insecure situation. *Journal of Abnormal and Social Psychology,* 1943, *38,* 225–249.

Baerends, G. P. An evaluation of the conflict hypothesis as an explanatory principle for the evolution of displays. In G. P. Baerends et al. (Eds.), *Essays on function and evolution in behaviour.* London: Oxford University Press, 1975.

Beckwith, L. Relationships between attributes of mothers and their infants' IQ scores. *Child Development,* 1971, *42,* 1083–1097.

Bell, S. M. The development of the concept of the object as related to infant–mother attachment. *Child Development,* 1970, *41,* 291–311.

Bell, S. M. *Cognitive development and mother–child interaction in the first three years of life.* Monograph in preparation, 1978.

Bell, S. M., & Ainsworth, M. D. S. Infant crying and maternal responsiveness. *Child Development,* 1972, *43,* 1171–1190.

Bijou, S. W., & Baer, D. M. *Child Development.* (Vol. 2). New York: Appleton-Century-Crofts, 1965.

Bischof, N. A systems approach toward the functional connections of attachment and fear. *Child Development,* 1975, *46,* 801–817.

Blatz, W. E. *Human security: Some reflections.* Toronto: University of Toronto Press, 1966.

Blehar, M. C. Anxious attachment and defensive reactions associated with day care. *Child Development,* 1974, *45,* 683–692.

Blehar, M. C., Ainsworth, M. D. S., & Main, M. *Mother–infant interaction relevant to close bodily contact: A longitudinal study.* Monograph in preparation, 1978.

Blehar, M. C., Lieberman, A. F., & Ainsworth, M. D. S. Early face-to-face interaction and its relation to later infant–mother attachment. *Child Development,* 1977, *48,* 182–194.

Block, J. Advancing the psychology of personality: Paradigmatic shift or improving the quality of research? In D. Magnusson & N. S. Endler (Eds.), *Psychology at the crossroads: Current issues in interactional psychology.* Hillsdale, N.J.: Lawrence Erlbaum Associates, 1977.

Blurton Jones, N. Categories of child–child interaction. In N. Blurton Jones (Ed.), *Ethological studies of child behaviour.* London: Cambridge University Press, 1972.

Blurton Jones, N., & Leach, G. M. Behaviour of children and their mothers at separation and greeting. In N. Blurton Jones (Ed.), *Ethological studies of child behaviour.* London: Cambridge University Press, 1972.

Bowlby, J. Some pathological processes set in train by early mother–child separation. *Journal of Mental Science,* 1953, *99,* 265–272.

Bowlby, J. The nature of a child's tie to his mother. *International Journal of Psychoanalysis,* 1958, *39,* 350–373.

Bowlby, J. *Attachment and loss* (Vol. 1). *Attachment.* New York: Basic Books, 1969. (London: Hogarth)

Bowlby, J. *Attachment and loss* (Vol. 1). *Separation: Anxiety and anger.* New York: Basic Books, 1973. (London: Hogarth)

Brannigan, C. R., & Humphries, D. A. Human non-verbal behaviour, a means of communication. In N. Blurton Jones (Ed.), *Ethological studies of child behaviour.* London: Cambridge University Press, 1972.

Brazelton, T. B., Koslowski, B., & Main, M. The origins of reciprocity: The early mother–infant interaction. In M. Lewis & L. A. Rosenblum (Eds.), *The effect of the infant on its caregiver.* New York: Wiley, 1974.

Bretherton, I. Making friends with one-year-olds: An experimental study of infant–stranger interaction. *Merrill-Palmer Quarterly,* 1978, *24,* 29–51.

Bretherton, I., & Ainsworth, M. D. S. Responses of one-year-olds to a stranger in a strange situation. In M. Lewis & L. A. Rosenblum (Eds.), *The origins of fear.* New York: Wiley, 1974.

Brody, S., & Axelrad, S. *Anxiety and ego formation in infancy.* New York: International Universities Press, 1970.

Brookhart, J., & Hock, E. The effects of experimental context and experiental background on infants' behavior toward their mothers and a stranger. *Child Development,* 1976, *47,* 333–340.

Bronson, G. W. Infants' reactions to unfamiliar persons and novel objects. *Monographs of the Society for Research in Child Development,* 1972, *37*(Serial No. 148).

Brooks, J., & Lewis, M. The effects of time on attachment as measured in a free-play situation. *Child Development,* 1974, *45,* 311–316.

Cairns, R. Attachment and dependency: A psychobiological and social-learning synthesis. In J. L. Gewirtz (Ed.), *Attachment and dependency.* Washington, D.C.: V. H. Winston, 1972.

Caldwell, B. M., Wright, C., Honig, A., & Tannenbaum, J. Infant day care and attachment. *American Journal of Orthopsychiatry,* 1970, *40,* 397–412.

Carr, S. J., Dabbs, J. M., & Carr, T. S. Mother–infant attachment: The importance of the mother's visual field. *Child Development,* 1975, *46,* 331–338.

Chance, M. R. A. An interpretation of some agonistic postures: The role of "cut-off" acts and postures. *Symposium of the Zoological Society of London,* 1962, *8,* 71–89.

Chomsky, N. *Aspects of the theory of syntax.* Cambridge, Mass. M.I.T. Press, 1965.

Cicchetti, D., & Sroufe, L. A. The relationship between affective and cognitive development in Down's syndrome infants. *Child Development,* 1976, *47,* 920–929.

Coates, B., Anderson, E. P., & Hartup, W. W. Interrelations in the attachment behavior of human infants. *Developmental Psychology,* 1972, *6,* 218–230. (a)

Coates, B., Anderson, E. P., & Hartup, W. W. The stability of attachment behaviors in the human infant. *Developmental Psychology,* 1972, *6,* 231–237. (b)

Cohen, J. A coefficient of agreement for nominal scales. *Educational and Psychological Measurement,* 1960, *60,* 37–46.

Cohen, L. J. The operational definition of human attachment. *Psychological Bulletin,* 1974, *81,* 207–217.

Cohen, L. J., & Campos, J. J. Father, mother, and stranger as elicitors of attachment behavior in infancy. *Developmental Psychology,* 1974, *10,* 146–154.

Cohler, B., Weiss, J., & Grunebaum, H. *Manual for the maternal attitude scale.* Unpublished manuscript, University of Chicago, 1974.

Connell, D. B. *Individual differences in infant attachment related to habituation to a redundant stimulus.* Unpublished master's thesis, Syracuse University, 1974.

Connell, D. B. *Individual differences in attachment: An investigation into stability, implications, and relationships to structure of early language development.* Unpublished doctoral dissertation, Syracuse University, 1976.

Connell, D. B., & Rosenberg, S. E. *Classification of individual differences in strange-situation behavior: A pattern recognition approach.* Unpublished manuscript. Syracuse University, 1974.

Cooley, W. W., & Lohnes, P. R. *Multivariate data analysis.* New York: Wiley, 1971.

Cox, F. N., & Campbell, D. Young children in a new situation with and without their mothers. *Child Development,* 1968, *39,* 123–131.

Cronbach, L. J., & Meehl, P. E. Construct validity in psychological tests. *Psychological Bulletin,* 1955, *52,* 281–302.

Darlington, R. B. Multiple regression in psychological research and practice. *Psychological Bulletin,* 1968, *69,* 161–182.

Feldman, S. S., & Ingham, M. E. Attachment behavior: A validation study in two age groups. *Child Development,* 1975, *46,* 319–330.

Fleener, D. E. *Experimental production of infant–maternal attachment behavior.* Paper presented at the annual meeting of the American Psychological Association, Montreal, August 1973.

Fleener, D. E., & Cairns, R. Attachment behaviors in human infants: Discriminative vocalizations on maternal separations. *Developmental Psychology,* 1970, *2,* 215–223.

Fliess, J. L., Cohen, J., & Everitt, B. S. Large sample standard error of KAPPA and weighted KAPPA. *Psychological Bulletin,* 1969, *72,* 323–327.

Gewirtz, J. L. A learning analysis of the effects of normal stimulation, privation, and deprivation on the acquisition of social motivation and attachment. In B. M. Foss (Ed.), *Determinants of infant behaviour I.* New York: Wiley, 1961. (London: Methuen)

Gewirtz, J. L. Mechanisms of social learning: Some roles of stimulation and behavior in early human development. In D. A. Goslin (Ed.), *Handbook of socialization theory and research.* Chicago: Rand McNally, 1969.

Gewirtz, J. L. Attachment, dependence, and a distinction in terms of stimulus control. In J. L. Gewirtz (Ed.), *Attachment and dependency.* Washington, D.C.: V. H. Winston, 1972. (a)

Gewirtz, J. L. On the selection and use of attachment and dependence indices. In J. L. Gewirtz (Ed.), *Attachment and dependency.* Washington, D.C.: V. H. Winston, 1972. (b)

Goldfarb, W. Effects of early institutional care on adolescent personality. *Journal of Experimental Education,* 1943, *12,* 106–129.

Harlow, H. F. The development of affectional patterns in infant monkeys. In B. M. Foss (Ed.), *Determinants of infant behaviour I.* New York: Wiley, 1961. (London: Methuen)

Harlow, H. F. The maternal affectional system. In B. M. Foss (Ed.), *Determinants of infant behaviour II.* New York: Wiley, 1963. (London: Methuen)

Hebb, D. O. On the nature of fear. *Psychological Review,* 1946, *53,* 250–275.

Heinicke, C., & Westheimer, I. *Brief separations.* New York: International Universities Press, 1966.

Hinde, R. A. *Biological bases of human social behavior.* New York: McGraw-Hill, 1974.

Hinde, R. A. Interactions, relationships and social structure. *Man,* 1976, *11,* 1–17. (a)

Hinde, R. A. On describing relationships. *Journal of Child Psychology and Psychiatry,* 1976, *17,* 1–19. (b)

Hock, E. *Alternative approaches to child rearing and their effects on the mother–infant relationship.* Final Report to the Office of Child Development, Washington, D.C.: 1976.

Hock, E., Coady, S., & Cordero, L. *Patterns of attachment to mother of one-year-old infants: A comparative study of full-term infants and prematurely born infants who were hospitalized throughout the neonatal period.* Paper presented at the biennial meeting of the Society for Research in Child Development, Philadelphia, March 1973.

Klaus, M. H., & Kennell, J. H. *Maternal–infant bonding: The impact of early separation or loss on family development.* St. Louis: Mosby, 1976.

Konner, M. J. Aspects of the developmental ethology of a foraging people. In N. Blurton Jones (Ed.), *Ethological studies of child behaviour.* London: Cambridge University Press, 1972.

Kotelchuck, M. *The nature of a child's tie to his father.* Unpublished doctoral dissertation, Harvard University, 1972.

Kotelchuck, M., Zelazo, P., Kagan, J., & Spelke, E. Infant reaction to parental separations when left with familiar and unfamiliar adults. *Journal of Genetic Psychology*, 1975, *126*, 255–262.

Kuhn, T. S. *The structure of scientific revolutions*. Chicago: University of Chicago Press, 1962.

Lamb, M. E. Effects of stress and cohort on mother–and father–infant interaction. *Developmental Psychology*, 1976, *12*, 435–443. (a)

Lamb, M. E. Interactions between eight-month-old children and their fathers and mothers. In M. E. Lamb (Ed.), *The role of the father in child development*. New York: Wiley, 1976. (b)

Lamb, M. E. Twelve-month-olds and their parents: Interaction in a laboratory playroom. *Developmental Psychology*, 1976, *12*, 237–244. (c)

Lamb, M. E. Father–infant and mother–infant interaction in the first year of life. *Child Development*, 1977, *48*, 167–181. (a)

Lamb, M. E. The development of mother–infant and father–infant attachments in the second year of life. *Developmental Psychology*, 1977, *13*, 637–648. (b)

Lamb, M. E. The development of parental preferences in the first two years of life. *Sex Roles*, 1977, *3*, 495–497. (c)

Lamb, M. E. *Qualitative aspects of mother- and father-infant attachments*. Manuscript in preparation, 1978.

Lenneberg, E. H. *Biological foundations of language*. New York: Wiley, 1967.

Lewis, M., & Ban, P. *Stability of attachment behavior: A transformational analysis*. Paper presented at the biennial meeting of the Society for Research in Child Development, Minneapolis, March 1971.

Lewis, M., Goldberg, S., & Campbell, H. A developmental study of information processing within the first three years of life: Response decrement to a redundant signal. *Monographs of the Society for Research in Child Development*, 1969, *34*(Serial No. 133).

Lieberman, A. F. Preschoolers' competence with a peer: Influence of attachment and social experience. *Child Development*, 1977, *48*, 1277–1287.

Londerville, S. *Socialization in toddlers*. Paper presented at the biennial meeting of the Society for Research in Child Development, New Orleans, March 1977.

Maccoby, E. E., & Feldman, S. S. Mother-attachment and stranger-reactions in the third year of life. *Monographs of the Society for Research in Child Development*, 1972, *37*(Serial No. 146).

Maccoby, E. E., & Jacklin, C. N. Stress, activity, proximity seeking: Sex differences in the year-old child. *Child Development*, 1973, *44*, 34–42.

Maccoby, E. E., & Masters, J. C. Attachment and dependency. In P. H. Mussen (Ed.), *Carmichael's manual of child psychology* (Vol. 2). New York: Wiley, 1970.

Main, M. *Exploration, play and level of cognitive functioning as related to child-mother attachment*. Unpublished doctoral dissertation, Johns Hopkins University, 1973.

Main, M. Analysis of a peculiar form of reunion behavior seen in some daycare children: Its history and sequelae in children who are home-reared. In R. Webb (Ed.), *Social development in daycare*. Baltimore: John Hopkins University Press, 1977. (a)

Main, M. Sicherheit und Wissen. In K. E. Grossman (Ed.), *Entwicklung der Lernfähigkeit in der sozialen Umwelt*. München: Kinder Verlag, 1977. (b)

Main, M., & Londerville, S. B. *Compliance and aggression in toddlerhood: Precursors and correlates*. Paper in preparation, 1978.

Marvin, R. S. *Attachment and cooperative behavior in two-, three-, and four-year olds*. Unpublished doctoral dissertation, University of Chicago, 1972.

Marvin, R. S., An ethological-cognitive model for the attenuation of mother–child attachment behavior. In T. M. Alloway, L. Krames, & P. Pliner (Eds.), *Advances in the study of communication and affect* (Vol. 3). *The development of social attachments*. New York: Plenum, 1977.

Marvin, R. S., Greenberg, M. T., & Mossler, D. G. The early development of conceptual perspective taking: Distinguishing among multiple perspectives. *Child Development,* 1976, *47,* 511–514.

Masters, J., & Wellman, H. Human infant attachment: A procedural critique. *Psychological Bulletin,* 1974, *81,* 218–237.

Matas, L. *Consequences of the quality of infant–mother attachment for the adaptation of two-year-olds.* Paper presented in the symposium on "The organization of early development and the problem of continuity in adaptation" at the biennial meeting of the Society for Research in Child Development, New Orleans, March 1977.

Matas, L., Ahrend, R. A., & Sroufe, L. A. Continuity of adaptation in the second year: The relationship between quality of attachment and later competence. *Child Development,* 1978, *49,* 547–556.

McGrew, W. *An ethological study of children's behavior.* New York: Academic Press, 1972.

Miller, G. A., Galanter, E., & Pribram, K. H. *Plans and the structure of behavior.* New York: Holt, Rinehart & Winston, 1960.

Moore, T. Children of full-time and part-time mothers. *International Journal of Social Psychiatry,* 1964, *2,* 1–10.

Moore, T. Stress in normal childhood. *Human Relations,* 1969, *22,* 235–250.

Morgan, G. A., & Ricciuti, H. N. Infants' responses to strangers during the first year. In B. M. Foss (Ed.), *Determinants of infant behaviour* IV. London: Methuen, 1969.

Mossler, D. G., Marvin, R. S., & Greenberg, M. T. The early development of conceptual perspective taking in 2- to 6-year-old children. *Developmental Psychology,* 1976, *12,* 85–86.

Nie, N. H., Hull, C. H., Jenkins, J. G., Steinbrenner, K., & Bent, D. H. *Statistical package for the social sciences* (2nd ed.). New York: McGraw-Hill, 1975.

Omark, D. R., & Marvin, R. S. *Problems with observational methodology.* Manuscript in preparation, 1978.

Pentz, T. *Facilitation of language acquisition: the role of the mother.* Unpublished doctoral dissertation, Johns Hopkins University, 1975.

Piaget, J. *The language and thought of the child.* New York: Harcourt, Brace, 1926 (Originally published, 1924.)

Piaget, J. *The origins of intelligence in children* (2nd ed.). New York: International Universities Press, 1952. (Originally published, 1936.)

Piaget, J. *The construction of reality in the child.* New York: Basic Books, 1954. (Originally published, 1937.)

Provence, S., & Lipton, R. C. *Infants in institutions.* New York: International Universities Press, 1962.

Rheingold, H. L. The effect of a strange environment on the behavior of infants. In B. M. Foss (Ed.), *Determinants of infants behaviour IV.* London: Methuen, 1969.

Rheingold, H. L., & Eckerman, C. O. The infant separates himself from his mother. *Science,* 1970, *168,* 78–83.

Rheingold, H. L., & Eckerman, C. O. Fear of the stranger: A critical examination. In H. W. Reese (Ed.), *Advances in child development and behavior* (Vol. 8). New York: Academic Press, 1973.

Ricciuti, H. N. Fear and the development of social attachments in the first year of life. In M. Lewis & L. A. Rosenblum (Eds.), *The origins of fear.* New York: Wiley, 1974.

Robertson, J., & Bowlby, J. Responses of young children to separation from their mothers. *Courrier du Centre International de l'Enfance,* 1952, *2,* 131–142.

Robertson, J., & Robertson, J. Young children in brief separation: A fresh look. *Psychoanalytic Study of the Child,* 1971, *26,* 264–315.

Rosenberg, S. E. Individual differences in infant attachment: Relationships to mother, infant and interaction system variables (Doctoral dissertation, Bowling Green state University,

1975). *Dissertation Abstracts International,* 1975, *36,* 1930B. (University Microfilms No. 75-22, 954)

Rosenthal, M. K. The generalization of dependency behavior from mother to stranger. *Journal of Child Psychology and Psychiatry,* 1967, *8,* 117–134.

Rosenthal, M. K. Attachment and mother–infant interaction: Some research impassés and a suggested change in orientation. *Journal of Child Psychology and Psychiatry,* 1973, *14,* 201–207.

Ross, G., Kagan, J., Zelazo, P., & Kotelchuck, M. Separation protest in infants in home and laboratory. *Developmental Psychology,* 1975, *11,* 256–257.

Saint-Pierre, J. *Étude des différences entre la recherche active de la personne humaine et celle de l'objet inanimé.* Unpublished master's thesis, University of Montreal, 1962.

Salter, M. D. An evaluation of adjustment based on the concept of security. *University of Toronto Studies, Child Development Series* (No. 18). Toronto: University of Toronto Press, 1940.

Sander, L. W. Adaptive relationships in early mother–child interaction. *Journal of the American Academy of Child Psychiatry,* 1964, *3,* 231–264.

Schaffer, H. R., & Callender, W. M. Psychological effects of hospitalization in infancy. *Pediatrics,* 1959, *24,* 528–539.

Schaffer, H. R., & Emerson, P. E. The development of social attachments in infancy. *Monographs of the Society for Research in Child Development,* 1964, *29*(Serial No. 94).

Schaffer, H. R., & Parry, M. H. Perceptual-motor behavior in infancy as a function of age and stimulus familiarity. *British Journal of Psychology,* 1969, *60,* 1–9.

Schaffer, H. R., & Parry, M. H. Effects of stimulus movement on infants' wariness of unfamiliar objects. *Developmental Psychology,* 1972, *7,* 87.

Serafica, F. C., & Cicchetti, D. Down's syndrome children in a strange situation: Attachment and exploration behaviors. *Merrill-Palmer Quarterly,* 1976, *22,* 137–150.

Spelke, E., Zelazo, P .R., Kagan, J., & Kotelchuck, M. Father interaction and separation protest. *Developmental Psychology,* 1973, *9,* 89–90.

Spitz, R. A. *The first year of life.* New York: International Universities Press, 1965.

Sroufe, L. A., & Waters, E. Attachment as an organizational construct. *Child Development,* 1977, *48,* 1184–1199. (a)

Sroufe, L. A., & Waters, E. Heartrate as a convergent measure in clinical and developmental research. *Merrill-Palmer Quarterly,* 1977, *23,* 3–28. (b)

Sroufe, L. A., Waters, E., & Matas, L. Contextual determinants of infant affective response. In M. Lewis & L. A. Rosenblum (Eds.), *The origins of fear.* New York: Wiley, 1974.

Stayton, D. J., & Ainsworth, M. D. S. Individual differences in infant responses to brief, everyday separations as related to other infant and maternal behaviors. *Developmental Psychology,* 1973, *9,* 226–235.

Stayton, D. J., Ainsworth, M. D. S., & Main, M. B. The development of separation behavior in the first year of life. Protest, following, and greeting. *Developmental Psychology,* 1973, *9,* 213–225.

Stayton, D. J., Hogan, R., & Ainsworth, M. D. S. Infant obedience and maternal behavior: The origins of socialization reconsidered. *Child Development,* 1971, *42,* 1057–1069.

Stern, D. N. A micro-analysis of mother–infant interaction: Behavior regulating social contact between a mother and her 3½-month-old twins. *Journal of the American Academy of Child Psychiatry,* 1971, *10,* 501–517.

Stern, D. N. Mother and infant at play: The dyadic interaction involving facial, vocal, and gaze behaviors. In M. Lewis & L. A. Rosenblum (Eds.), *The effect of the infant on its caregiver.* New York: Wiley, 1974.

Tatsuoka, M. M. *Discriminant analysis: The study of group differences.* Champaign, Ill.: Institute for Personality and Ability Testing, 1970.

Tatsuoka, M. M. *Multivariate analysis: Techniques for educational and psychological research.* New York: Wiley, 1971.

Tatsuoka, M. M., & Tiedeman, D. V. Discriminant analysis. *Review of Educational Research,* 1954, *25,* 402–420.

Tinbergen, N. Comparative studies of the behaviour of gulls (Laridae): A progress report. *Behaviour,* 1959, *15,* 1–70.

Tolan, W. J. *Maternal facial expression as related to the child-mother attachment.* Unpublished senior thesis, University of California, Berkeley, 1975.

Tolan, W. J., & Tomasini, L. *Mothers of "secure" versus "insecure" babies differ themselves nine months later.* Paper presented at the biennial meeting of the Society for Research in Child Development, New Orleans, March 1977.

Tomasini, L. *Maternal behavior during a play session at 21 months as related to infant security of attachment at 12 months, and toddler affective and social development at 20.5 and 21 months.* Unpublished senior thesis, University of California, Berkeley, 1975.

Tracy, R. L., Lamb, M. E., & Ainsworth, M. D. S. Infant approach to behavior as related to attachment. *Child Development,* 1976, *47,* 571–578.

Waters, E. The reliability and stability of individual differences in infant-mother attachment. *Child Development,* 1978, *49,* 483–494.

Waters, E., Matas, L., & Sroufe, L. A. Infants' reactions to an approaching stranger: Description, validation and functional significance of wariness. *Child Development,* 1975, *46,* 348–356.

Weinraub, M., Brooks, J., & Lewis, M. The social network: A reconsideration of the concept of attachment. *Human Development,* 1977, *20,* 31–47.

Willemsen, E., Flaherty, D., Heaton, C., & Ritchey, G. Attachment behavior of one-year-olds as a function of mother vs. father, sex of child, session and toys. *Genetic Psychology Monographs,* 1974, *90,* 305–324.

Wolff, P. H. The natural history of crying and other vocalizations in infancy. In B. M. Foss, *Determinants of infant behaviour* IV. London: Methuen, 1969.

Yarrow, L. J. The development of focused relationships during infancy. In J. Hellmuth (Ed.), *Exceptional infant* (Vol. 1). Seattle: Special Child Publications, 1967.

INDEXES

Author Index

Italics denote pages that contain complete bibliographical information.

Subject Index